# HIDDEN TREASURES REVEALED

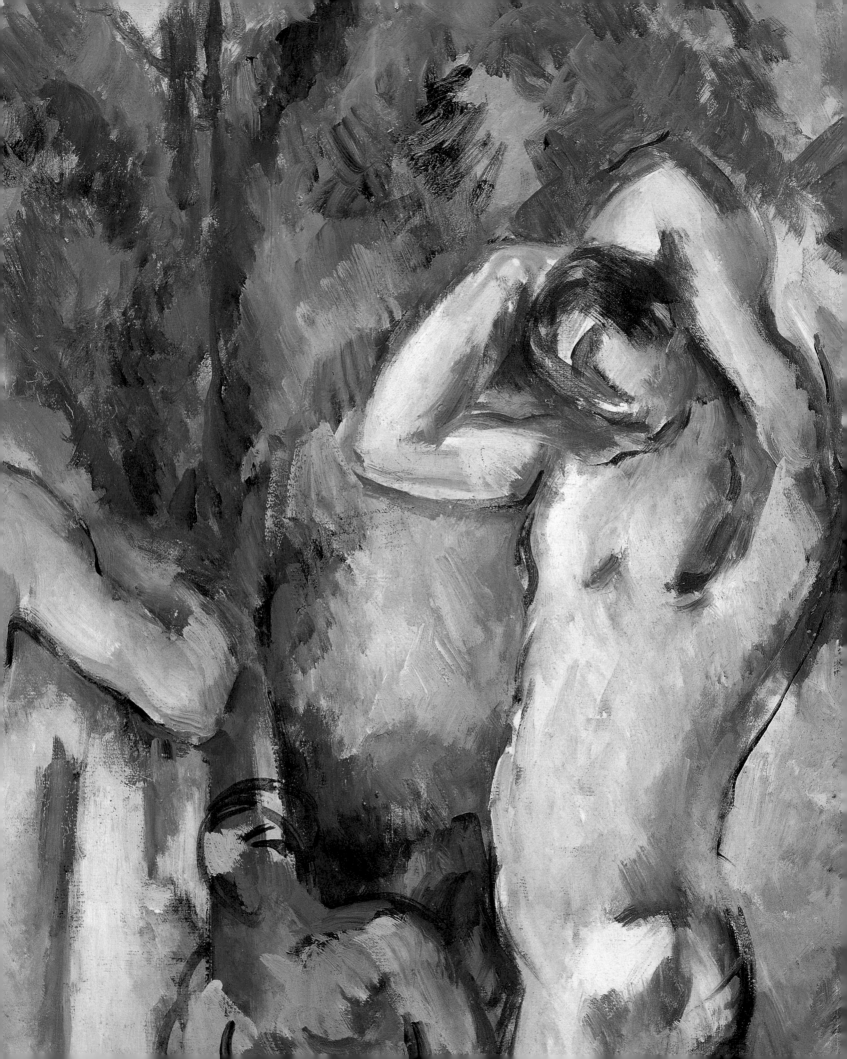

# HIDDEN TREASURES REVEALED

Impressionist Masterpieces and Other Important
French Paintings Preserved by
The State Hermitage Museum, St. Petersburg

*Albert Kostenevich*

The Ministry of Culture of the Russian Federation
The State Hermitage Museum, St. Petersburg
*in association with*
Harry N. Abrams, Inc., Publishers

*Editor:* JAMES LEGGIO

*Editorial Coordinator:* ELLEN ROSEFSKY COHEN

*Designers:* MIKO McGINTY, SAMUEL N. ANTUPIT

*Documentary Photo Research:* BARBARA LYONS

*Research:* JANE NIEHAUS

*Color Photography:* VLADIMIR TEREBENIN,
LEONID KHEIFETS

Translated from the Russian by Elena Kolesnikova and
Catherine A. Fitzpatrick of The Russian Connection
Unlimited and Stas Rabinovich of STAS International

Library of Congress Catalog Card Number: 94–73477
ISBN 0–8109–3432–9

Published in 1995 by Harry N. Abrams, Incorporated,
New York
A Times Mirror Company

*Printed and bound in Italy*

FRONTISPIECE: Paul Cézanne, *Bathers* (detail of plate 51)
PAGE 8: Pierre-Auguste Renoir, *Portrait of a Woman*
(detail of plate 21)
PAGE 288: Édouard Manet, *Portrait of Mademoiselle
Isabelle Lemonnier* (detail of plate 13)

# CONTENTS

# FOREWORD

Russia is organizing a series of exhibitions of the art objects removed from Germany at the end of World War II. Showing these works, which were excluded for decades from the international art community, demonstrates the goodwill with which Russia is pursuing the difficult search for the proper solution to the problem of "relocated" art.

The State Hermitage Museum is now exhibiting masterpieces of French painting of the nineteenth and twentieth centuries, works once in German private collections. The present exhibition catalogue boasts many famous names, such as Paul Cézanne, Gustave Courbet, Edgar Degas, Pierre-Auguste Renoir, Paul Gauguin, Vincent van Gogh, and Claude Monet, among others. Many of these paintings have never been publicly exhibited before, even in prewar times. Art historians and art lovers in general will discover much that is new to them about some of the world's most revered painters and encounter new facets of their talent.

I welcome all those who will be coming to the exhibition. I have no doubt that this occasion will advance the cause of worldwide culture—establishing a sense of mutual trust and helping us all to address our disagreements through constructive dialogue (however lengthy the dialogue may be), rather than through confrontation.

Dr. Yevgeny Sidorov
*Minister of Culture*
*Russian Federation*

# PREFACE

## Bringing What Was Hidden into the Light

In presenting this exhibition, the State Hermitage Museum brings before the public seventy-four paintings that almost no one has seen before. The works were in private collections in prewar Germany, and only a few were lent to public exhibitions in that period. During World War II, the pictures were hidden away; after the war, they were moved to the Soviet Union, like many other cultural objects at the time. A considerable number of those objects were returned to Germany in the 1950s.

The paintings we are exhibiting today are part of what has been kept in closed storage on the premises of the Hermitage. The museum was charged with providing safe conditions for these works of art, and this it has done. The pictures have been preserved in much the same way as the Hermitage collections themselves, although they have not been exhibited or made available for study.

The radical changes in Russia in recent years, its transition from a policy of confrontation to one of openness, and its movement toward the resolution of long-standing problems, created the present possibility for the Hermitage, in cooperation with the Ministry of Culture, to exhibit artworks from its closed storage.

The future of these works of art is for lawyers, politicians, and diplomats to decide. The role of the museum is to show to the people of the world and of our country what was hidden from them for many years—while we waited for the peace treaty that was never signed. This is a complex, emotionally charged issue. We believe that a public exhibition of the objects now under intensive discussion will help us all find an honorable solution, one that our descendants will approve.

Such developments do not mean, however, that we are about to forget Nazi Germany's invasion of our country. The Nazis' deliberate, relentless policy not only of robbing and pillaging, but of undertaking the total cultural extermination of the nation, forever deprived our people of major monuments of their heritage—from the frescoes of Novgorod to the palaces around St. Petersburg.

Nonetheless, this exhibition is not being held to make a point in an argument, but is rather an event in the life of the arts. It is a fulfillment of our duty to preserve, study, and exhibit works of art. History, in its unpredictable way, has in this instance conducted a unique experiment: dozens of masterpieces—by such great artists as Paul Cézanne, Edgar Degas, Claude Monet, Camille Pissarro, Pierre-Auguste Renoir, Paul Gauguin, Vincent van Gogh, Henri de Toulouse-Lautrec, and many others—happened to be out of reach of the public, as well as of specialists, during a time when a new critical evaluation of the Impressionists and Post-Impressionists was being formed. The paintings now returned to the public will add to, and considerably alter, our understanding of these great masters.

Moreover, the sequestering of the paintings for decades has to a large extent allowed them to retain their original appearance, with no need for the kind of overly energetic restoration that can alter a work. These paintings come before us looking surprisingly fresh, sometimes with an unexpected color scheme. Viewers will make many astonishing discoveries for themselves.

This exhibition will bring back not only the paintings, but also the names of the remarkable collectors who sought out and cherished these works, and whose collections were monuments to their love of art. In this respect, the exhibition is not unlike those devoted to particular collectors in recent years at many of the world's major art museums, including the Hermitage.

Today, the Hermitage and its guests share in the unique sense of discovery that, by the unpredictable will of fortune, awaits us in this historic exhibition.

Dr. Mikhail Piotrovsky
*Director*
*The State Hermitage Museum, St. Petersburg*

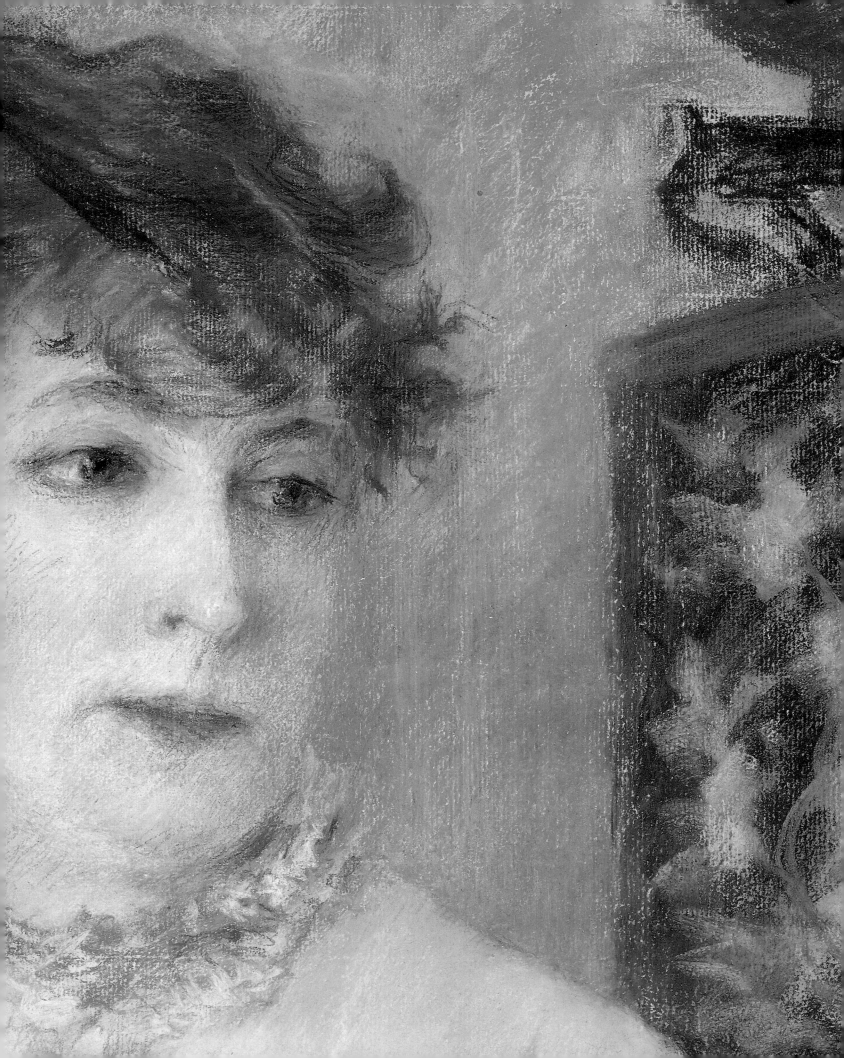

# INTRODUCTION

The pictures in this book, now on public exhibition at the State Hermitage Museum, have a most unusual history. Of the seventy-four works, only two have ever been published in color before, while a large number of them have never been published at all. They were created not yesterday but a hundred years ago (a few of them a little later), yet they are virtually unknown, not only to the public but to the most conscientious scholars—a fact all the more remarkable since these are works of outstanding artistic quality, by artists everyone knows.

The sudden appearance of masterworks no one has seen before, though some people will have heard of certain of them, must generate mixed feelings. The beauty of these works cannot forestall the inevitable questions: Are the "new" paintings genuine? If so, why have they remained hidden until now? What place will they come to occupy within a general understanding of art history, and within the oeuvre of each painter?

Anyone who endeavors to exhibit objects that are not yet established in museum practice is obliged first of all to prove their authenticity. In this case, however, the matter is often complicated by the absence of many historical documents. The pictures, arriving from a defeated Germany in 1945, or later, were, of course, accompanied by appropriate instructions from the authorities, but not by the kind of documented proof of their prior history that former owners might have possessed. Even if anyone attempted to look for such proof at the time, it seems highly unlikely that their efforts would have met with the least success, with Europe lying in ruins. At the end of the hostilities, works of art were turning up in many different, un-expected places, often in unsafe conditions. Private collections and museum objects that had found their way into specially prepared bunkers were the best pro-tected. In this regard, the natural wish of collectors to

save their paintings had made them turn to museums for help. Guns were still firing when Soviet troops began to discover these bunkers. Those who tried to sort out the contents faced great difficulties. The iden-tities of the pictures and the painters who made them could be determined only by lists of a most general nature or old inscriptions and labels on stretchers, aided, of course, by the stylistic analysis that museum work-ers used to puzzle out the titles and the artists' names.

Of the works of art from German collections stored at the Hermitage since the end of World War II, and still kept here, possibly the greatest attention will be paid to the group of French paintings created during the hundred years between 1827 and 1927, a glorious period extending from the earliest work reproduced in this book, *Rocks* by Camille Corot, to the latest, *Ballerina* by Henri Matisse. We decided to exhibit this group first. It is relatively small and is being shown practically in full. A few works were excluded because, despite respectable origins and the famous names associated with them, there remained some slight residual doubt as to their authenticity.

A great deal of effort went into preparing the cata-logue entries in this volume, as we searched for any and all publications and documents, past or present, in which these pictures might have been cited. The refer-ence sections of the catalogue—usually of interest only to specialists, and listing provenance, exhibitions, and bibliographical references—in this instance have a special meaning. Wherever possible, we have traced a picture's journey through collections, auctions, and exhibitions, though, as a rule, the relevant events occurred such a long time ago that the facts we most want to know have mostly been forgotten.

Fortunately, however, some of the paintings were at earlier times included in major catalogues raisonnés, such as the indispensable volume by J.-B. de la Faille devoted to Vincent van Gogh, or the catalogue of Paul Cézanne's work compiled by Lionello Venturi, or the Camille Pissarro catalogue published by Venturi with the artist's son Ludovic-Rodolphe Pissarro. All the pictures by van Gogh, Cézanne, and Pissarro in the present book from the collections of Otto Krebs and Bernhard Koehler were included in those three catalogues.

It is a different story with an artist such as Paul Gauguin. Out of the four Gauguin pictures included here, only one is mentioned in the respected catalogue by Georges Wildenstein. The other three are absolutely unknown, even to specialists. There is no doubt as to the signature or, more important, the quality of each of the three paintings; still, to be on the safe side, corroborating evidence is required. Such evidence can sometimes arise when analysis of a picture leads to links with other works by the artist, in particular to those that share similar details. Although not all research of this kind will yield convincing results, in some instances we were truly lucky—as when we discovered the relationship between Gauguin's masterpiece *Piti teina* (plate 57) and certain drawings from his Tahitian sketchbook that turned out to be preparatory studies for it. Later, we found that this completely forgotten painting had indeed been mentioned in the catalogue of a small exhibition of Gauguin's pictures—held a century ago, in 1895, to raise funds for the artist's second trip to Oceania, from which he was not destined to return.

Sometimes, though, the most intensive search for evidence of authenticity proved fruitless. For instance, neither of the two works by Camille Corot (plates 2, 3) is cited in the catalogue by Alfred Robaut, still the principal reference on the artist. The delicate problem here is that few other artists' paintings have been forged as often as Corot's. Consequently, any painting not mentioned by Robaut immediately comes under suspicion and is subjected to the third degree, so to speak. In such cases, laboratory analysis can be of some assistance by helping to determine that the paints are of the period when Corot worked and that the signature was done at the same time as the painting and not later. The most telling arguments, however, are those derived from studying all the individual features of the painting as they cohere into a single entity, whether they are stylistic or compositional features,

particularities of brushstroke, or color scheme—everything that allows the professional to make a positive identification. It must be kept in mind that works similar to the two Corots in this exhibition, and also not listed in the Robaut catalogue, do appear from time to time at museum exhibitions and auctions and, provided their quality is reasonably convincing, are incorporated into the artist's body of work. To make a definitive judgment about the authenticity of a painting in cases like those, a certain period of time must pass, for which this exhibition is the starting point.

Undoubtedly, it is the impressive Impressionist and Post-Impressionist paintings shown here that will arouse the most interest. Perhaps no other period in the history of art has been so thoroughly researched as this one, and it might seem almost impossible, nowadays, to exhibit such a large group of very important and yet essentially unknown pictures. All the corners of the world have by now been scoured for works by Monet, Pissarro, Degas, Gauguin, van Gogh, and the rest. It is possible that the paintings exhibited today at the Hermitage are the last as yet undiscovered islands on the map of the Impressionist era.

———————————

We know, of course, that most of these works have never been publicly exhibited before. Yet even those that were shown left little or no trace of their passage, if only because exhibition catalogues in the late nineteenth and early twentieth centuries did not as a rule carry illustrations or indicate materials or dimensions. There are, in fact, several interconnected reasons why some masterpieces remain unknown to the public, some arising from the limits of exhibition documentation, others from the practices of dealers. At the turn of the century, the success of the Impressionists and their successors in gaining recognition depended not only (and, at times, not so much) on the artists' efforts as on the dealers', with their special ways of getting the public's attention. Dealers were interested in getting good prices, too, and sometimes this tended to keep certain works in the shadows. A clever dealer, having gotten his hands (and cheaply) on a masterpiece that the public has not yet learned to appreciate, can hold on to it, even hide it away, hoping for a more favorable market in the future. Ambroise Vollard, for example, kept beautiful paintings in storage in his Paris gallery for years, even decades, patiently waiting until enough interest developed in the artist's work to warrant a higher price. In this his instincts were uncanny.

Eventually, when paintings went from a dealer such as Vollard to a collector like the German industrialist Otto Krebs, they still did not achieve fame, but remained within the relative obscurity of a private collection. Unlike the prominent Russian collector of the previous generation, Sergei Shchukin, Krebs did not collect art "for my country and the nation," as Shchukin used to say, but for his personal pleasure. He did not participate in the struggle between artistic styles or promote the avant-garde in any way. He simply bought what he liked, hanging the pictures in his isolated mansion in little-known Holzdorf, a village near Weimar.

Even so, among these "unknown" masterpieces are several paintings that were indeed known to art historians, though the images were vague, going back to old photographs of poor quality. Recent reproductions of those photographs, still further removed from the originals, are even less adequate, but they do remind us that the paintings themselves were too important to lose sight of, even in bland reproductions. In their captions, those halftones were accompanied by the inevitable sighs of regret, "Lost during World War II," "Whereabouts unknown," or "Presumed destroyed in 1945."

Here we return to what is, of course, the main reason for the general obscurity surrounding the pictures published in this book: they have spent the half century since the war in Special Storage at the Hermitage.

Let us go back fifty years to the end of World War II, the most terrible armed conflict in human history. The year 1945 saw not only the end of the war but also the beginning of the next historical period, the postwar era, which has lasted until these past few years. The most important aspect of that era was the confrontation between the East and West, the polarization of nations along ideological lines. The fate of the works of art relocated to the Soviet Union at the end of World War II was in many ways subject to the fault line that divided nations like a geographic principle. What happens to a group of paintings, even masterpieces, may be only a small epiphenomenon compared to the vast losses suffered by humankind during that time of global antagonism. But for those who are not indifferent to the values of European culture—who see a kind of salvation in the reconciliation between nations—for such people, the opportunity at last to see these long-imprisoned pictures is a very moving event. It is capable of provoking feelings not unlike those experienced by the relatives of an inmate released from jail after many years of incarceration.

The title of the English edition of this book, *Hidden Treasures Revealed,* captures something of this complicated state of affairs: the hope that a solution to an old problem will be revealed, along with the paintings themselves, and a concern for the future of cultural treasures. We believe that art lovers will finally be able freely to enjoy these paintings by so many great artists, of which previous generations have been deprived. Together, the exhibition and this book constitute the first and perhaps most important step toward the solution of this long-standing problem.

———————

It is not for me to go into the legal issues involved here. For such matters, there is the Restitution Commission formed by both German and Russian museum authorities. Professional legal talent can be expected to have its say. There are also governments and parliaments to be heard from. But one way or another, the subject has been broached. At this juncture, we would do well to recall some historical issues sometimes overlooked, or deliberately ignored, by journalists hunting for sensational copy.

In newspapers these days, both American and European, the paintings relocated to the Soviet Union from Germany in 1945 are often called "stolen," and are sometimes even said to have been "smuggled out," which is quite ridiculous if one considers the historical circumstances in which this relocation was conducted. Secretly storing the objects for so many years at the Hermitage has indeed inspired many such epithets, but they reflect what is, after all, a recent point of view, and not the only one at that. Half a century ago, views were otherwise. In 1945, the different armies of the Allies acted in rather similar fashion on the "art front." Each had special teams, headed by art specialists, charged with gathering works of art. Acting not only on the orders given them, but also according to

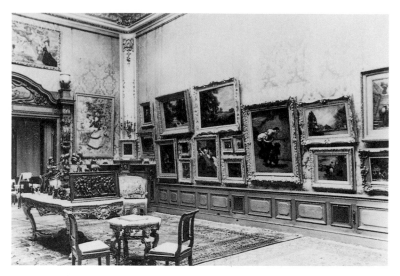

*Residence of Otto Gerstenberg, Berlin, before World War II. Left: Renoir's* In the Garden (*plate 24*). *Center of right wall: Daumier's* The Burden (*plate 4*)

their own sense of justice, members of those teams did not always stop to reflect upon the nature of national institutions or the rights of private citizens in the defeated country. They were in a hurry to collect valuable art objects, which, under those conditions, only meant saving them. In the context of the impending Cold War, the Allies could not resist indulging in a kind of competition, each trying to acquire works before the others did. Several years passed before the American side returned rare collections (now in the Gemäldegalerie of the Dahlem Museum) to West Berlin. In 1955, the Soviet government made a reciprocal move, not without its propaganda effect, returning to its "own" East Germany the Dresden Gemäldegalerie paintings stored until then at the Pushkin State Museum of Fine Arts, Moscow. A little later, some works of art from Berlin museums (including the famous Pergamon altar) and paintings from Leipzig and elsewhere, stored until that time at the Hermitage, were returned to the German Democratic Republic.

Of course, there was a signal difference between the American and the Soviet ways of handling these art treasures. American officials, when taking custody of museum objects, generally did not remove them from Germany, while Soviet representatives sent to the East everything they considered important. This was not just a matter of strict orders from Moscow; such actions seemed completely appropriate in the minds of

the Soviet military on reaching the German capital. The whole nation, having suffered unspeakable losses as a result of the Nazi invasion, felt the same way. Germany, they thought, ought to pay for the irreparable damage it had done, and the paintings were considered rightful acquisitions. Soviet officials hardly stopped to think that it was the Nazi leaders, not art museums or private collectors, who were responsible for the acts of the Hitler regime. The first to attack, Germany was seen as doubly guilty. Officials felt that since the Soviet Union had lost a great many art treasures, even whole collections, as a result of Nazi aggression, reparations were in order.

Very few of those who were professionally engaged at the time in collecting artistic spoils are still living. Most of those who survive are still convinced—as are many others in Russia—that our country should not have returned what it has, and that it should not return what is left.

What *is* left? In addition to works of art from private collections, there are a few works from museums in what became West Germany after the war and which, having been transferred, during the hostilities, to what would become East Germany, fell into the hands of the Soviet army. It would not have made sense to give them to the GDR at the time when other objects were returned, since that would have created discomfort in East Germany itself. And the then prevalent ideology prevented the Soviet Union from returning them to their rightful owners.

Thus, Moscow and Leningrad kept the works taken from the Kunsthalle, Bremen. Three years ago, the Hermitage organized an exhibition of drawings from that museum. They had found their way to Russia by a number of routes. A part of the famous collection was sent to storage in the Hermitage. The other, more valuable part, discovered accidentally by soldiers, was stolen. Fortunately, Captain Victor Baldin, who had been an architecture student before the war, learned of this. He did not need to be told who Dürer or van Gogh were, and as far as he could, he gathered the priceless drawings from individual soldiers. But how many like Baldin were there? In a long and cruel war, there were people who could not suppress the desire to turn a profit as soon as the shooting stopped, or even before. This temptation could as easily intoxicate a soldier from Texas as a colonel from Kiev. The role that the members of the official search teams played in saving art objects—first of all, from their own compatriots in uniform—cannot be overestimated.

How did the paintings shown in this exhibition come to the Hermitage? One must not look for devious plans here. Art objects were coming in from different places, in railroad cars. It was impossible to sort them out methodically. They were being sent to the Hermitage, and to the Pushkin State Museum of Fine Arts, haphazardly, without advance planning, simply because it was known that trained professionals could be found there, and because those museums could provide proper storage conditions, at a time when Russia itself faced a long period of rehabilitation and rebuilding. The problem posed by these objects was addressed more specifically only where certain very large and important collections were concerned, the fate of which it was necessary to determine in advance. The initial idea was, presumably, to add the holdings of the Dresden Gemäldegalerie to the Moscow museum and create thereby one of the largest concentrations of artworks in the world. The collection of antiquities known as "Schliemann's gold," from Berlin, was also stored there. It is soon to be shown to the public.

All the artworks coming from Germany were considered to be the rightful property of the museums that received them. There are still visitors to the Hermitage old enough to remember a time when, alongside famil-iar Hermitage objects, there might appear unexpected antique statues, or a work by Goya, from Berlin. But such sightings were brief. As soon as Western newspapers printed a photograph of a very rare visit, in those Iron Curtain years, by an American delegation to the Hermitage, posing with Greek sculptures, there was the smell of scandal in the air, since one could glimpse a work from the Pergamon Museum, Berlin, among the other objects. Measures were quickly taken: the careless museum guide was fired (though soon reinstated) and works were sent to storage, where they remained until it was decided to return them to the German Democratic Republic.

Works were returned, but others, mostly those from private collections, were still kept in storage. An anomaly in the present group is Claude Monet's *The Garden* (plate 38) from the Kunsthalle, Bremen. This one picture not from a private collection is included in this exhibition, first, because it would be difficult to imagine another occasion like this and, second, because it looks so well in the context of these major paintings by French artists.

---

The existence of these paintings has always been cloaked in mystery, but many rumors circulated about them, tempting people to try somehow to see the hidden pictures. I was lucky enough to get inside Special Storage thirty years ago, when I was a graduate student studying western European art. This was a blatant violation of the regime's directives, and the woman in charge of the storage at the time, who let me make these forbidden visits, would have been severely reprimanded if anyone in the inner circle had broken the vow of silence.

As time went by, the prohibitions became even stricter, so that the very idea of one day acknowledging Degas's *Place de la Concorde* (plate 16) or van Gogh's *Morning* (plate 61) seemed like a pipe dream. But come to think of it, who at that time could have ever imagined the disintegration of the Soviet Union? Only after the dramatic changes of recent years, which are still unfolding in our country, transforming the agencies that used to control and monitor every field of culture, did the opportunity arise to show these hidden paintings to the public.

Intensive preparations for the exhibition have been under way for the last year, involving the efforts of many members of the Hermitage staff, from selecting frames (most of the old ones have been lost) and conducting laboratory tests to undertaking architectural and design work and providing research support for the project.

One cannot but praise the conservation work, which was done with exceptional caution and great ingenuity. Old surface dirt was removed from the paintings so that the colors could shine with their original brightness. In only one instance was serious intervention deemed necessary: layers of yellowed varnish mixed with dirt had to be removed from Gustave Courbet's *Reclining Woman* (plate 6). When this procedure was successfully completed, it became obvious why the painting was so greatly admired in the late nineteenth century. In general, one of the most striking features of the exhibition is the excellent condition of the paintings. We did not have to do any of the kind of aggressive cleaning that is widely discussed today by artists, curators, and conservators around the world. Unfortunately, one can sometimes see, even in leading galleries, paintings ruined by inept "restoration," even if, generally speaking, that kind of thing has not been done by museums. It is very sad to see such works, their paints gone dull under yellow varnish or washed out by too vigorous cleaning, or their brushstrokes flattened.

Many pictures in this exhibition are remarkable for their astonishingly fine condition. They will lead us to revise our understanding of several of the painters. For example, I have seen many Renoirs, but none of them possess such clarity of color as his *Portrait of a Woman* (plate 21). It has not aged at all: as soon as it was finished, it was put behind glass, ideally enveloped, and from the beginning was kept in moderate light or in shadow; for the last half century, it has been stored under the same unchanging temperature and humidity conditions, with practically no light, and was not moved. This picture could well be considered a prime specimen of original painting features. There cannot be many such paintings in the world, but there are several of them here: Henri de Toulouse-Lautrec's *Woman with an Umbrella* (plate 63), Georges Seurat's *View of Fort Samson* (plate 53), Paul Cézanne's *Jas de Bouffan, the Pool*

(plate 46), and Renoir's *In the Garden* (plate 24).

These "hidden treasures" are remarkable not only for their artistic qualities but also for their historical interest. Many pictures draw us to them because they are associated with the names of important dealers and famous collectors, or because they were shown at those landmark exhibitions at which the future of new art was decided. For example, Pissarro's *Town Park in Pontoise* (plate 41) was shown at the first Impressionist exhibition, a fact now virtually forgotten; Monet's *The Grand Quai at Havre* (plate 36) was shown at the third such exhibition, and Seurat's *View of Fort Samson* at the eighth and last Impressionist exhibition. Toulouse-Lautrec's *Woman with an Umbrella* was shown at the seventh exhibition of Les Vingt, the Brussels group. Honoré Daumier's *The Burden* (plate 4) and Cézanne's *Jas de Bouffan, the Pool* were shown at the Paris World's Fair in 1900. Daumier had died long before, but his manner of painting had not yet received general recognition. For Cézanne, who was still active, such an exhibition was an important opportunity to bring before the public the new artistic principles he was seeking to establish. Some other episodes in the lives of these paintings may at first glance seem less significant, but we do gain a better sense of the arts during this brilliant era by knowing that Courbet's *Reclining Woman* was included in the Hoschedé sale of 1875, or that Édouard Manet's *Girl in a Wing Collar* (plate 12) was in the posthumous sale of paintings from the artist's studio.

Then, too, it is illuminating to know which collectors possessed these works at one time or another. The best example of this is probably Manet's *Portrait of Mademoiselle Isabelle Lemonnier* (plate 13), whose owners included Count Armand Doria, Auguste Pellerin, and Baron Marczell de Nemes—people whose taste was ahead of their time, and who could pride themselves on their familiarity with the new painting. Or, to take another example, Cézanne's *Self-Portrait* (plate 49) first belonged to Camille Pissarro, then to the famous writer Octave Mirbeau, who supported the Impressionists. Another picture by Cézanne, *Still Life with Apples* (plate 50), went from the Ambroise Vollard gallery to the author and critic Gustave Geffroy. Van Gogh's *Morning* (plate 61) went from the artist's sister-in-law Johanna van Gogh-Bonger to the famous German collector Karl-Ernst

Osthaus, founder of the Museum Folkwang in Hagen. Another masterpiece by van Gogh, *Landscape with House and Ploughman* (plate 60), belonged to Doctor Paul Gachet, who played an important role in the life of the painter and was a remarkable figure in France's artistic scene in the latter part of the century. Matisse's *Ballerina* (plate 74) was (though not for long) a jewel in the collection of Samuel Courtauld, founder of the Courtauld Institute in London.

A further consideration enhancing the interest of the paintings exhibited today at the Hermitage is the fact that most of them passed through the galleries of the leading art dealers, who tied their hopes to the art of the Impressionists and their successors, and who played an important part in promoting the new art: Paul Durand-Ruel, Georges Petit, Ambroise Vollard, the Bernheim-Jeune firm, and Paul Cassirer. Is it possible to imagine the European artistic scene in the late nineteenth and early twentieth centuries without those names? It is hard to say which way avant-garde art would have gone without their support for Monet, Pissarro, Renoir, and other painters, who were considered clumsy illiterates by the official masters of the Salon.

––––––––––

A few words should be said about the collectors who were responsible for bringing to Germany the paintings comprising this exhibition. Otto Krebs, who owned most of these paintings, should be mentioned first. His collection, with the exception of a few things that were lost (fortunately, not major works), is in the Hermitage today. We know very little about Krebs himself. He was born in Wiesbaden in 1873, and his full name was Josef Karl Paul Otto Krebs. He died in 1941, leaving his money to a medical institution involved in cancer research that is still active today in the city of Manheim, the Stiftung für Krebs- und Scharlach-forschung. (Incidentally, the German word *Krebs* means "cancer" or "crab," as in the sign of the Zodiac.)

After finishing his university training, Krebs proved a very good businessman. Starting as the manager of the Strebel factory that produced steam boilers, he increased production considerably. At his estate in the village of Holzdorf, he began collecting a wide variety of things, from old furniture to modern paintings. He

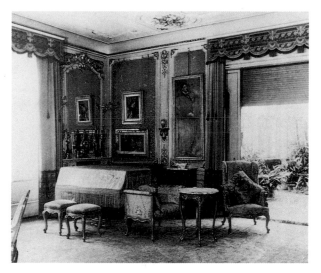

*Residence of Otto Gerstenberg, Berlin, before World War II. Center: Renoir's* Man on a Stair *(plate 19)*

was enthusiastic about Romantic art, but his collection was rather modest in that area. The late nineteenth and early twentieth centuries were quite another matter. In the 1920s, as his factory prospered, Krebs, through German intermediaries, bought various paintings of the Impressionist era, from two excellent portraits by Manet and the very unusual *Portrait of a Woman* by Renoir to Pissarro landscapes.

The core of the collection was a very impressive group of paintings by Cézanne, van Gogh, and Gauguin. Somewhat like Albert C. Barnes of Philadelphia in his inclinations, Krebs often showed better judgment than the famous American collector: he did not buy in such large quantity, so none of his Cézannes is less than excellent. Five beautiful canvases reflect the full scope of the artist's work—still life, portrait, figure composition, landscape—and each can safely be called a masterwork. The same can be said about the van Goghs and the Gauguins. Again, the works are all very different from each other. Otto Krebs wanted a comprehensive representation of each artist's work, and also to reflect particular facets of his talent.

Both early still lifes by Gauguin are highly resolved works, and at the same time it is hard to find works with which to compare them. *Bouquet* (plate 56), with its flaming berries, painted from nature, already anticipates, in its dramatic manner, his later, more symbolic pictures. The painting most characteristic of Gauguin is *Taperaa mahana* (plate 58). It has everything one expects from the Tahitian period: narrative of the life of the islanders, juicy colors, and a lively rhythm that controls both the characters and nature. All these the picture possesses in the highest degree. Still, the best Gauguin in the Krebs collection is perhaps *Piti teina* (plate 57), a painting that combines monumental solemnity with a delicacy and charm characteristic of childhood, while avoiding altogether the sentimentality that spoils most portraits of children.

Krebs was drawn to van Gogh no less than to Cézanne or Gauguin. In this he made one, perfectly understandable mistake, purchasing *Plate with Buns,* which, even in the 1920s, J.-B. de la Faille, the authority on van Gogh's work, accepted as genuine and included in his catalogue (it was stricken from the second edition). The four others are not only genuine van Goghs but can be placed among his most important creations. When building his collection, Krebs concentrated on the artist's French years. *Plate with Buns* was supposed to represent the Arles period as well as the subject of still life. The other paintings were from the two succeeding periods, representing major van Gogh subjects: the portrait, the figure composition, and the landscape. It is especially to be noted that Krebs managed to obtain two such superb examples of van Gogh's landscapes as *Landscape with House and Ploughman* (plate 60) and *The White House at Night* (plate 62).

When we stop to consider that, along with lovely though less important Vuillards, Marquets, and Derains, Krebs owned undisputed masterpieces by Toulouse-Lautrec, Rouault, and Picasso, we cannot but admit that the best in French painting of the turn of the century was very prominently represented in his collection. In keeping abreast of his time, the German collector bought Matisse's *Ballerina* of about 1927 (plate 74) only three or four years after it was painted. The picture marked the end of his collecting. It seems that he relinquished such activities in the 1930s: to be known as a champion of modernist art did not sit well with the image of a successful businessman in the Germany of that time.

Another collector, in Krebs's class, was Bernhard Koehler (1849, Ellierode–1927, Berlin). Koehler was an industrialist closely connected with the Blaue Reiter artists. His niece Elisabeth married August Macke,

and it was Koehler who put up the money for Macke's first trip to Paris in 1907. Through Macke, Koehler got in touch with Franz Marc and began to give him a monthly stipend. He substantially supported the *Blaue Reiter Almanach* as well as the Erste Deutsche Herbstsalon in Berlin, and he was also a benefactor of Macke's trip to Tunis. In 1908, together with Macke and his wife, he traveled to Paris, where they visited the galleries of Ambroise Vollard (there meeting Degas), Bernheim-Jeune, and Durand-Ruel. At that time, Koehler bought paintings by Courbet, Manet, Pissarro, and Monet.

Koehler's collection was wide-ranging, including pictures by Macke, Marc (particularly important is *Blue Horse* by the latter, now in the Lenbachhaus, Munich), Kandinsky, Delaunay, Renoir, Gauguin, and van Gogh. Pride of place belonged to Cézanne.

Koehler is said to have gone with Marc to Vollard's to select his Cézannes. Among them we can note *Mont Sainte-Victoire* (plate 52), one of the great achievements of the artist, a work breathtaking in its transparency, clarity, and fine color, its convincing construction combining finesse with monumentality. Much the same can be said of another masterpiece belonging to Koehler: Seurat's *View of Fort Samson* (plate 53), with its sophisticated simplicity and rare serenity.

The interest in the art collectors of the first half of the twentieth century evident all over the world today will eventually help us to find out more about two now almost forgotten names, Alice Meyer and Friedrich Siemens. Though collectors of a lesser order, they are still worthy of note. Siemens came from a well-known family of German industrialists. He had no ambition to build a collection on the scale of Krebs's, but he was deeply involved with art and used to be a habitué of the Cassirer gallery in Berlin in the 1920s, the most important art gallery in the German capital at the time. Siemens was especially attracted to the Impressionists, and it seems only right that such a fine Degas composition as *Interior with Two Figures* (plate 14) came into his hands. After the unsuccessful attempt on Hitler's life on July 20, 1944, Siemens's brother-in-law, Count Yorck von Wartenburg, who was involved in the conspiracy, was executed, and the entire family's possessions were to be confiscated. Siemens made desperate attempts

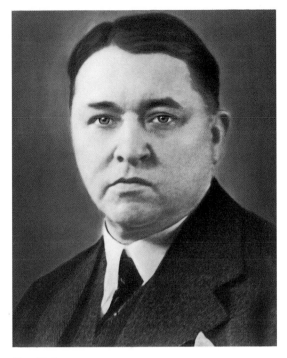

*Otto Krebs*

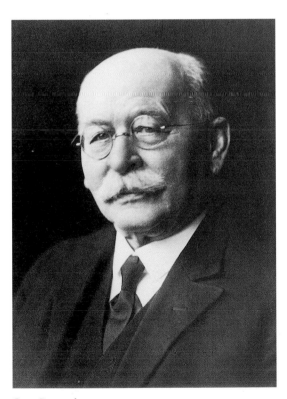

*Otto Gerstenberg*

to save his pictures and persuaded a friend, the director of the Pergamon Museum, to hide them in the museum's basement. A year later, the pictures, along with the Pergamon altar sculptures, were shipped to the Hermitage.

Probably the best known among German collectors of the early twentieth century was Otto Gerstenberg (1848–1935). In his youth, he had studied mathematics and philosophy. At the age of twenty-five, he joined the Railroad Insurance Society in Berlin, which two years later became the Victoria public insurance company. As early as 1877, Gerstenberg was made Executive Director, and eleven years later First Director, of the company. For several decades he was very influential in business circles.

Gerstenberg became a collector in his forties. In the 1890s he concentrated on Old Master drawings and on Japanese prints. In 1922 and 1923, for financial reasons, he had to part with this collection, which was so huge that no single buyer could purchase all of it at once. The collection was sold piecemeal in Switzerland and scattered all over the globe. The prints and drawings that used to belong to Gerstenberg, which bear a small Victoria insignia, are highly regarded by specialists.

In 1904–5, in the Grunewald district of Berlin, the successful capitalist had built himself a townhouse soon boasting several Constable landscapes and a Joshua Reynolds portrait; at the turn of the century, English painting was becoming fashionable on the Continent. Soon these works were joined by several El Grecos and Goyas and also by works of Salomon van Ruysdael, Meindert Hobbema, Jan van Goyen, Jan Steen, and Adriaen van Ostade. He seems not to have been deeply attached to his Dutch paintings, since they went the way of his drawings. His great passion became the French school of painting, from the Romantic era to the Impressionists. Delacroix, Corot, Daumier, Courbet, Daubigny, Manet, Degas, Monet, Renoir—these are the artists about whom he was most enthusiastic.

In the early years of the century, he became close to Max Liebermann, sharing his passion for the French Impressionists. In 1911, Liebermann made the collector's portrait and then, seven years later, during a time of turmoil, did his best so that Gerstenberg could keep his villa, to house his paintings.

Gerstenberg owned the world's finest collection of Daumiers. It included practically all the lithographs, a number of sculptures and drawings, and an excellent selection of paintings. It was a natural transition from Daumier to Toulouse-Lautrec; a few paintings and drawings by Lautrec were purchased in the first decade of the century. Gerstenberg was particularly attached to Manet's work, having bought seven of his paintings by 1913. His eye did not miss any of the major artists of the Impressionist era. Two Renoir pastels and five paintings, among which were such key works as the decorative canvases made for the Charpentiers (plates 19, 20) and the painting *In the Garden* (plate 24); two Sisley landscapes; two Degas pastels—all these prompted Gerstenberg's contemporaries to speak of him as an

extraordinary connoisseur of Impressionist painting. Purchasing Degas's *Place de la Concorde* in 1911 for the then very tidy sum of 120,000 francs further enhanced the reputation of his collection.

After Gerstenberg died, his pictures went to his daughter, Frau Margarete Scharf. During the war, from 1943, the greater part of his collection was stored in the Nationalgalerie in Berlin. The rest, put in storage at the Victoria firm before the war, was burned during an air raid, and such important paintings as *The Awakening* by Courbet were lost. What was stored in the museum bunker survived and was later shipped to the Soviet Union—now to be seen, along with so many once hidden masterpieces, in this extraordinary exhibition at the Hermitage.

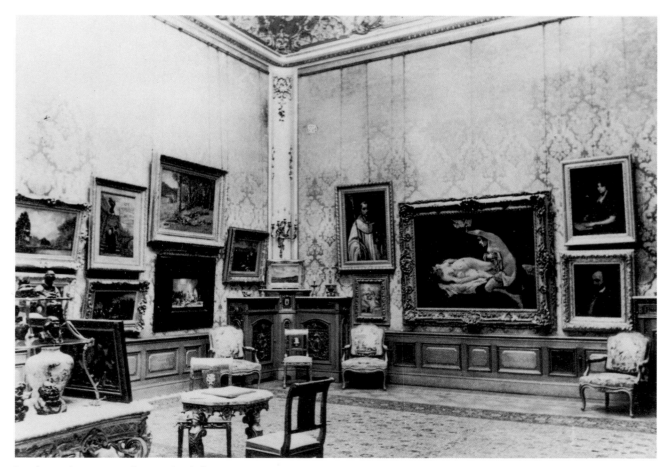

*Residence of Otto Gerstenberg, Berlin, before World War II. Center of right wall: Courbet's* The Awakening *of 1864 (destroyed; Fernier no. 371)*

# CATALOGUE

In each plate caption, the relevant German collection as of 1945 is indicated, as well as the provisional identification number subsequently assigned at the State Hermitage Museum, St. Petersburg. Whenever possible, further information on provenance, along with a list of exhibitions, bibliographical references, and catalogue raisonné citations, is given following the commentary on the work. Bibliographical references for supplementary works appear within the body of the text. Inscriptions are noted. Dimensions are given first in inches, then in centimeters; height precedes width.

# EUGÈNE DELACROIX

## FLOWERS

Still life is not a subject generally characteristic of Romantic painting. Eugène Delacroix first turned to it in 1826, in *Still Life with Lobsters* (Musée du Louvre, Paris), a commissioned work that he sent to the Salon the following year. It can be supposed that its commissioning predetermined the motif of the picture, which is a *nature morte* in the literal sense of the term. Ten years later, Delacroix began painting flowers and thereafter repeatedly came back to still life.

The subject of the present painting is reminiscent of the well-known Louvre watercolor *Bouquet of Flowers,* usually dated 1848, which once belonged to Paul Cézanne and inspired him to create his own version in 1902–4 (The Pushkin State Museum of Fine Arts, Moscow). One should also recall the group of canvases with flowers generally considered to have been painted in the late 1840s and early 1850s, which had little in common with previous renderings of floral still lifes in France. Particularly striking in this group is *Study of Asters and Balsamine* from the Kunsthaus, Zurich, a canvas of almost the same dimensions and analogous in composition to the present work, so that the two might even be said to form a kind of diptych.

It is possible that another of this group, *Peonies* (fig. 1; Nasjonalgalleriet, Oslo), tentatively dated to about 1846 (see P. Georgel and R. Bortoletto, *Eugène Delacroix* [Paris, 1975], no. 531), was actually painted even earlier. In that work, a new compositional rhythm can already be discerned; the vertical stalks, a change from the previous filling of space with profuse foliage, give the picture far more definition.

Some years ago, Lee Johnson revised the dating of the group of flower paintings to about 1833. In that year, Delacroix painted *Vase of Flowers* (National Gallery of Scotland, Edinburgh; Johnson no. 492), which belonged to Frédéric Villot, who wrote: "This brilliant study has been done at M. V[illot]'s in Champrosay. Its success immediately led Delacroix to begin several flower pictures" (see L. Johnson, *The Paintings of Eugène Delacroix: A Critical Catalogue* [Oxford, 1986], vol. 3, p. 258). Accordingly, Johnson tentatively dated the Zurich picture as well as the closely related *Study of Dahlias* (Wildenstein & Co., New York; Johnson nos. 495, 496) to the year 1833. It is perhaps more convincing, however, to specify *after* 1833.

The original format of this painting has been altered: when the canvas was transferred to a new stretcher, the turned borders were straightened and areas of loss at the edges of the picture were restored with putty and repainted. Apparently, pieces of the old stretcher were used in making the new one. On the lower strip of wood an old wax seal with the letters ED has been preserved.

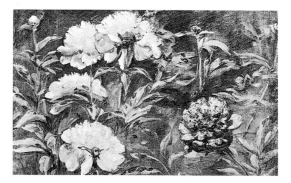

*Fig. 1. Eugène Delacroix.* Peonies. *after 1833. Nasjonalgalleriet, Oslo*

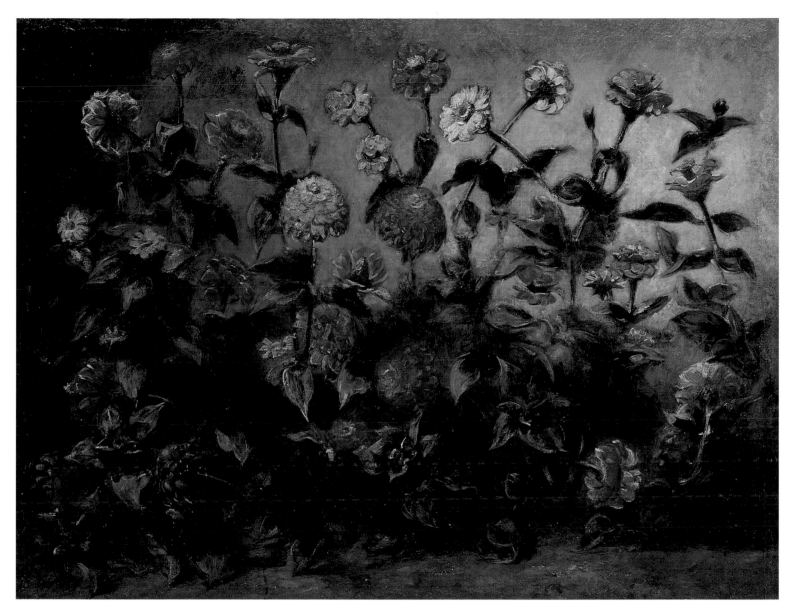

Eugène Delacroix (1798, Charenton-St.-Maurice–1863, Paris)
1. FLOWERS
*Les Fleurs.* after 1833
Oil on canvas, 27 ¼ × 36 ½" (69.3 × 92.5 cm)
No. 3K 924. Former collection unknown

# JEAN-BAPTISTE-CAMILLE COROT

## Rocks

Although the motif of large rocks is not often encountered in Corot's work, it attracted the artist from his earliest years. Even at that time the Romantic cult of nature found a sincere devotee in him. Corot began making paintings of rocks in the mid-1820s, in renderings of the forest of Fontainebleau. Traveling to Italy soon afterward, the young artist was entranced with the rocks of Etruria, the austere region of Cività Castellana and Castel Sant'Elia.

Corot spent the summer of 1828 in and around Naples, making excursions to its outskirts, climbing Mt. Vesuvius, and spending time on the islands of Capri and Ischia. Alfred Robaut, the artist's biographer, in an account of the trip to Naples noted that "he marked his traveling route sometimes with a drawing, sometimes with a painting" (A. Robaut, *L'Oeuvre de Corot: Catalogue raisonné et illustré* [Paris, 1905], vol. 1, p. 47). It can be supposed that *Rocks*, an unusual landscape for Corot without any direct analogues in his other paintings, was made at just this time. On the whole, seashores rarely evoked in the artist a wish to paint them. In fact, this painting does not give the impression of a study from nature and could have been made later. It is known that Corot sent an unidentified painting called *View of Ischia* to the Salon of 1837.

The red caps of the men at the opening of the grotto, a characteristic item of dress for Neapolitan fishermen, help link this painting to Naples, and the peculiarities of the landscape place it even more precisely. It may be the shores of Ischia that are depicted here, a volcanic island where Greek colonists settled in the eighth century B.C., or another area near Naples. The ancient appearance of the majestic coast—where architecture, unable to compete with nature, is molded to the incline, almost merging with it—attracted the artist in the same way as the ancient ruins of Rome and the remote, unspoiled areas of the Roman Campagna. The painting lacks the freshness of many of Corot's landscapes of that time, perhaps because of the artist's wish to preserve the particularity of the site more accurately: the general color scheme of *Rocks* is defined by the natural grayish-yellow color of the island's stone.

An old pencil inscription on the stretcher, "Baron von der Heydt," proves that the painting once belonged to this famous collector, the founder of the Von der Heydt-Museum in Wuppertal. However, the last location of the painting in Germany remains unknown.

PROVENANCE: Galerie Matthiesen, Berlin; Baron von der Heydt, Berlin.

EXHIBITIONS: Paris (the customs label on the reverse side reads, "Douane—expositions. Paris," although the exhibition in which it was shown is unknown).

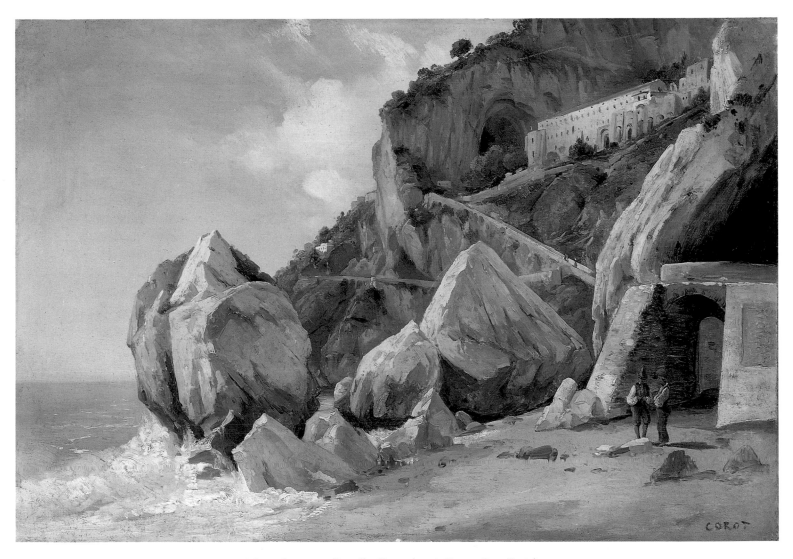

Jean-Baptiste-Camille Corot (1796, Paris–1875, Paris)
## 2 . ROCKS
*Les Rochers.* c. 1828
Oil on canvas, 15¼ × 22½" (39 × 57.2 cm)
Signed lower right: "Corot"
No. 3K 232. Formerly collection Baron von der Heydt, Berlin (?)

# JEAN-BAPTISTE-CAMILLE COROT

## Landscape with a Boy in a White Shirt

A preference for sweeping panoramas emerges very early with Corot, by the mid-1820s, in the landscapes of Rome and its environs: *Lake Albano and Castel Gandolfo* of 1826–28 (The Metropolitan Museum of Art, New York) and *The Roman Campagna with the Tiber* of 1826–28 (private collection; Robaut no. 103). This type of composition followed the French eighteenth-century tradition wherein a very wide vista was effortlessly combined with an intimacy of feeling typical of the Rococo. In particular, it may recall such paintings as Louis-Gabriel Moreau the Elder's *View of the Château de Vincennes from Montreuil* of about 1770 (Musée du Louvre, Paris) or the landscapes of P. H. de Valenciennes.

In these small, sunny panoramas, Corot found something directly in contrast to the mysterious, remote forest places that a significant portion of his painting is devoted to. During trips around France,

from time to time he was attracted by the soft, captivating contours of the river valleys, similar to those that he recorded in such paintings as *Rouen: Panorama of the Valley of the Seine* of 1855–60 (Robaut no. 994) and *Panoramic Landscape* (Robaut no. 878), fairly close in composition and technique to the present painting, *Landscape with a Boy in a White Shirt.* A remarkable feature of this and similar landscapes is the artist's closeness to nature, the intimacy of feeling, so notable in the so-called lyrical landscapes, painted in the studio, but which can be seen also in works painted from nature. Incidentally, although this painting depicts a specific view (quite possibly on the outskirts of Ville d'Avray), most likely it was painted not outdoors, but in the studio. Support for such a hypothesis may be the use of a method learned in the lyrical landscapes—enlivening an environment restrained in color with some small, bright spot (here, the boy's shirt).

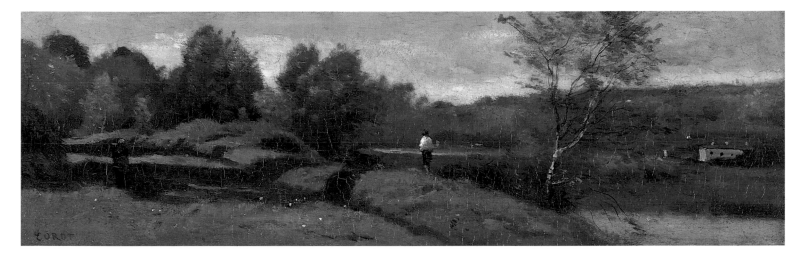

Jean-Baptiste-Camille Corot

3. LANDSCAPE WITH A BOY IN A WHITE SHIRT

*Paysage avec un garçon à chemise blanche.* c. 1855–60

Oil on canvas, 6¾ × 20¼" (17 × 52 cm)

Signed lower left: "Corot"

No. 3K 114. Formerly collection Alice Meyer, Berlin

# HONORÉ DAUMIER

## THE BURDEN (THE LAUNDRESS)

In the late 1840s, Honoré Daumier's interests were clearly shifting to painting, although he continued to produce numerous lithographs. The paintings differ from his printed works not only in their medium but also in their subject matter. Although the thematic range of his printed works is wide, among Daumier's thousands of lithographs it is impossible to find anything like *The Burden* and the entire cycle of *The Laundress*. Here, the irony of Daumier's graphic work is absent and he is a Romantic, in sympathy with his subject. At the same time, however, it is possible to see an interchange between his two kinds of work, but only by means of their contrasting treatment of related subjects.

For example, on September 19, 1859, in the periodical *Le Charivari* a composition appeared under the title *Aux bains de mer* (fig. 1), showing a bourgeois family at the beach, shielding themselves from the fierce wind and rain with parasols. The caption reads: "And here they call this a gust of wind—but no light has broken through for two whole hours . . . I don't dare open my mouth; I'm sure this rain is terribly salty!"

In *The Burden*, which might also well be called "The Gust of Wind," a woman strains against the elements. The picture is executed with a truly Romantic tension, to which are equally subordinate both this woman, who sees nothing of joy in her life, and the landscape, where the severe outline of the houses reiterates the desperate movements of the figure.

Such a dramatic interpretation of a subject of this kind had no precedent in European painting. In French art of the eighteenth century (Jean-Baptiste Chardin, Jean-Honoré Fragonard, and others), such subjects were colored in lyrical, tranquil tones and did not admit the drama that defined Daumier's picture. While living on the Île Saint-Louis in Paris, Daumier

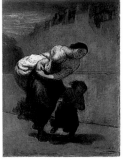

regularly walked along the riverbanks, where he saw not only strolling couples or people of the middle class taking their constitutionals, but those for whom the Seine meant monotonous, heavy labor. Here, as in several other paintings depicting laundresses, the scene takes place at the Quai d'Anjou, along the northern side of the Île Saint-Louis.

In itself, the motif of labor is secondary for the artist. The main thing for him is the drama of life, which he reveals not so much through the subject as through the movement of the painting's masses and the contrasts of light and shadow. That is why he omits anecdotal detail and avoids the finished quality that the public of his day expected in paintings.

The earliest mention of this work is from 1852, when Charles Baudelaire, together with the publisher Poulet-Malassi, visited Daumier at his studio. In describing the visit, Poulet-Malassi noted that, besides many lithographs and an unfinished painting on an easel, there were several canvases leaning against the wall in the room. He called them sketches (*ébauches*) and picked out among them a picture that particularly impressed him. The painting showed a laundress tugging a little girl along the quai while fighting a strong wind.

In all likelihood, the elaboration of this subject in painting was preceded by the small terra-cotta statue (35 centimeters high) now in the Walters Art Gallery, Baltimore (fig. 2). Such creative methods were peculiar to Daumier. Compared with paintings, the development process in sculpture was more concrete; the angle and turn of the figure of the laundress, the overall nature of movement, was defined there.

That this subject was of exceptional importance for Daumier can be seen from the fact that he executed at least ten versions of it. The abundance of replicas illustrates that Daumier highly valued his compositional discovery. Seven works are variations on *The Burden;* another three show the laundress with a child on the upper part of a stairway (see fig. 5). Also belonging to this group is the painting *The Laundresses,* a scene with two women on the steps to the Seine.

These works not only display Daumier's social sympathies, they embody a profound personal symbolism. Here, an expressive metaphor of a hard life is at work. "Few single themes," wrote Karl-Eric Maison, "so consistently occupied Daumier in his painting as that of a woman burdened with a heavy bundle of laundry, dragging her child along the walls of the quais or ascending or descending the steps leading to the Seine. Over a period of more than ten years he repeated the theme . . . varying it fundamentally three times" (K.-E. Maison, *Honoré Daumier: Catalogue Raisonné of the Paintings, Watercolors, and Drawings* [London, Greenwich, Conn., and Paris, 1968], p. 72).

In Maison's opinion, the first version of the composition was a little painting on wood of 1850–52 (fig. 3; Jäggli-Hahnloser collection, Winterthur; Maison no. I–37). It was likely preceded by pencil drawings. Maison says: "The first time the idea for this composition was put to paper was presumably in the unpretentious little crayon study D 228, where it is twice tried out within a space of less than 16 cm. Another study (D 229) seems much later, others have undoubtedly been lost. A larger charcoal drawing in a Californian collection is too badly worked over by a later hand to be taken into consideration" (ibid., p. 73).

The drawings identified as D 228 (Hohl collection, Basel) and D 229 (whereabouts unknown) by Maison date from an even earlier small painting, from about 1847, *On a Bridge at Night* (fig. 4; The Phillips Collection, Washington, D.C.; Maison no. I–9). In the painting from the Phillips Collection, the situation of loneliness is already established, Romantically heightened by the time and place of the action, although there is not yet that powerful dynamic peculiar to the subsequent variations of *The Burden.*

The drawings noted above do not possess this energy either. In them, the laundress and the child are seen from behind, a perspective rejected by the artist as insufficiently expressive when he went from paper to wood and canvas supports.

As for the painting, as both Maison and Bruce Laughton believe, the large canvas belonging to Otto

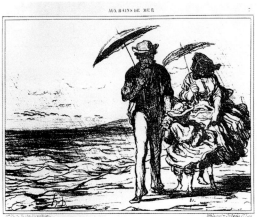

*Fig. 1. Honoré Daumier.* Aux bains de mer. *Published in* Le Charivari, *September 19, 1859, p. 7*

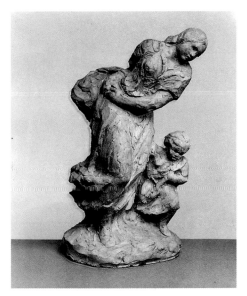

*Fig. 2. Honoré Daumier.* The Burden. *1849–50. The Walters Art Gallery, Baltimore*

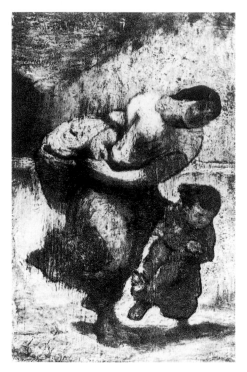

*Fig. 3. Honoré Daumier. The Burden. 1850–52. Collection Jäggli-Hahnloser, Winterthur*

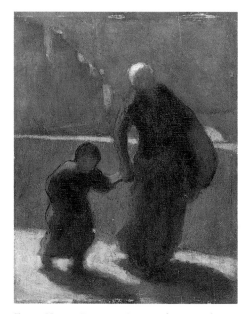

*Fig. 4. Honoré Daumier. On a Bridge at Night. c. 1847. The Phillips Collection, Washington, D.C.*

Gerstenberg followed the small painting from the Jäggli-Hahnloser collection. Incidentally, in the Gerstenberg collection there was one more painting devoted to laundresses, *The Laundresses from the Quai d'Anjou*.

Though Maison in fact stated that the chronology of the entire group remains problematic, recent researchers of Daumier's work still adhere to the order Maison established. In keeping with this order, after the Gerstenberg large *Burden* comes the painting from the Národni Galeri, Prague (Maison no. I–43). Two later versions are placed in 1855–56: Art Gallery and Museum, Glasgow, Maison no. I–85; and the Howard collection, London, Maison no. I–86. The end of the 1850s is considered the period when two further versions were done: the largest canvas (147 by 95 centimeters, 1858–60, Gutzwiller collection, Paris; Maison no. I–121), which once belonged to Arsène Alexandre, and a gouache (Musée des Beaux-Arts, Dijon; Maison no. II–13), which has been so ruined by restorers that its authenticity is in question.

According to B. Laughton, it was the Gerstenberg *Burden* that Poulet-Malassi saw in 1852. It was very well known in the early twentieth century. Arsène Alexandre, who owned it at the time (just as he owned the version that appeared at the 1993 Sotheby's sale and which brought a record appraisal), particularly valued the work that later became Gerstenberg's property. It was this work that he sent to the Paris World's Fair of 1900 and to the major Daumier retrospective the following year. At that time, it was still considered unfinished by many experts; later, at the Berlin Sezession of 1911, it was viewed as finished. The question of the completeness of his paintings gave the artist no peace. On February 5, 1849, Delacroix wrote in his diary (citing Baudelaire, who had visited him) that Daumier always found it hard to finish a painting. The instinct of a great artist told Daumier that the quality of completeness, as the society of his day understood it, only spoiled the work, and no matter how bitter the lack of recognition of his paintings by the public and the experts, Daumier could not succumb to the temptations of success.

PROVENANCE: Arsène Alexandre, Paris; Allard de Cholet, Paris; Allard de Cholet sale, Paris, June 7, 1910 (purchased by Otto Gerstenberg for 16,940 francs); Otto Gerstenberg, Berlin; Margarete Scharf, Berlin.

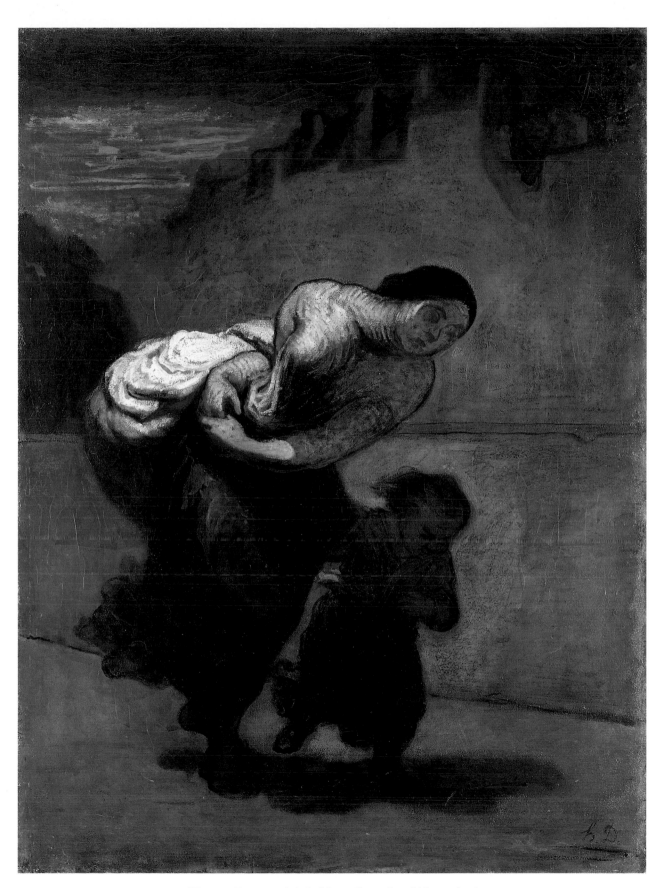

Honoré Daumier (1808, Marseilles–1879, Valmondois)
## 4. THE BURDEN (THE LAUNDRESS)
*Le Fardeau (La Blanchisseuse).* c. 1850–53
Oil on canvas, 51⅛ × 38⅝" (130 × 98 cm). Signed lower right: "h.D"
No. 3K 1500. Formerly collection Gerstenberg/Scharf, Berlin

EXHIBITIONS: 1900, Paris, "Exposition internationale universelle," no. 90; 1901, Paris, "Honoré Daumier: Exposition rétrospective," École des Beaux-Arts, no. 1; 1911, Berlin, Sezession, no. 44.

LITERATURE: *Catalogue de la vente Arsène Alexandre* (Paris, 1903), no. 15; *Catalogue de la vente A[llard] de C[holet]* (Paris, 1910), no. 19; *Bulletin d'art*, June 6, 1910, p. 180; *Kunst und Künstler*, vol. 9, no. 10 (June 1911), p. 489 (reprod.); E. Klossowsky, *Honoré Daumier* (Munich, 1923), p. 227, pl. 94; E. Fuchs, *Der Maler Daumier* (Munich, 1927), p. 72; N. Kalitina, *Honoré Daumier* (Moscow, 1955) (in Russian), pp. 120–21; K.-E. Maison, "Daumier's Painted Replicas," *Gazette des beaux-arts*, vol. 57, nos. 1108, 1109 (May–June 1961), pp. 369–77, fig.1; K.-E. Maison, *Honoré Daumier: Catalogue Raisonné of the Paintings, Watercolors and Drawings* (London, Greenwich, Conn., and Paris, 1968), I–42; *L'Opera completa di Daumier*, Introduction by L. Barzini, Catalogue by G. Mandel (Milan, 1971), no. 46; *Tout l'Oeuvre peint de Daumier*, Introduction by P. Georgel, Catalogue by G. Mandel (Paris, 1972), no. 46 (dated 1851); B. Laughton, "Honoré Daumier: *Le Fardeau*," in *Impressionist and Modern Paintings, Drawings, and Sculpture: Part I* (Sotheby's, London, June 22, 1993), pp. 14–19.

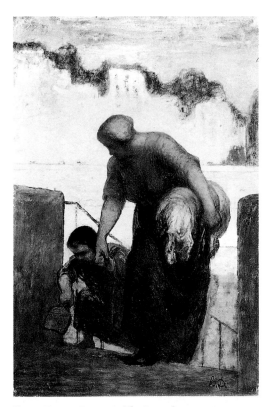

*Fig. 5. Honoré Daumier.* The Laundress. *c. 1863. Musée d'Orsay, Paris*

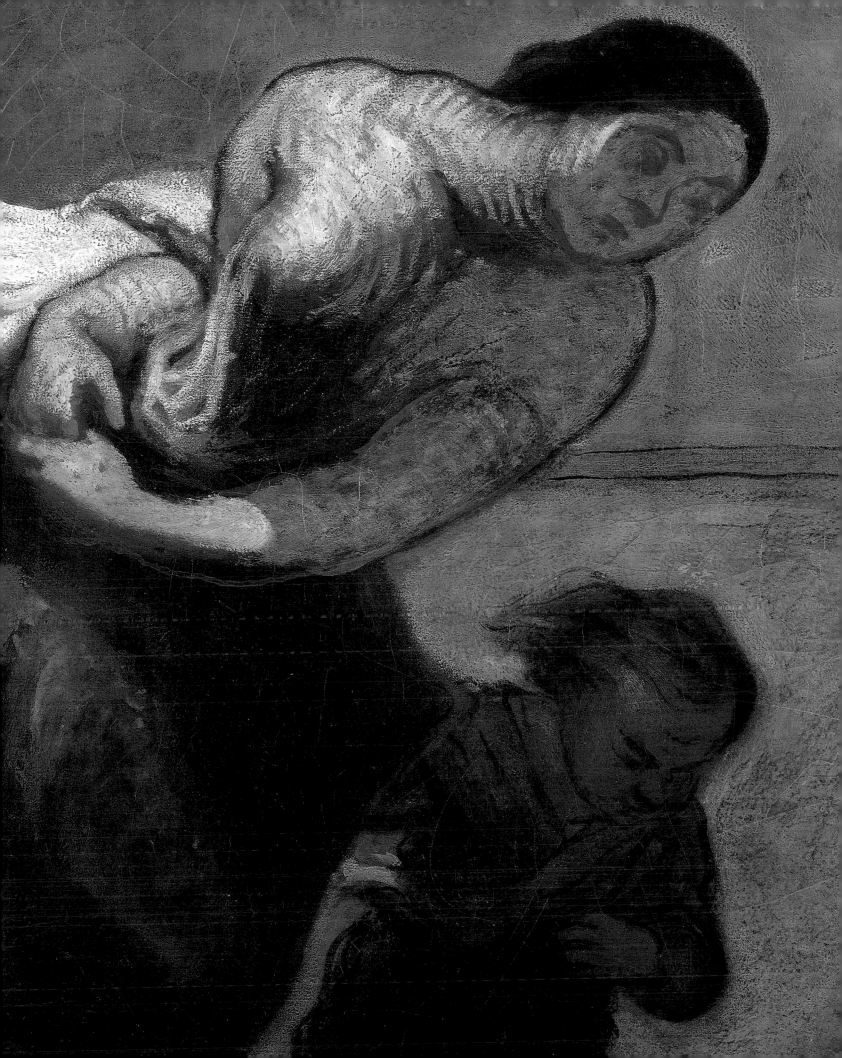

# GUSTAVE COURBET

## STILL LIFE OF FLOWERS

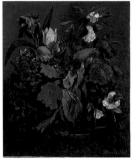

This still life was painted in the spring of 1863, most likely in Saintes. At that time Courbet completed ten paintings showing flowers, having finished seven the preceding summer—more than during any other period, and comprising a significant portion of his production of that time. Up until this trip to the Saintonge region in the west of France, his entire oeuvre had contained only three floral still lifes.

Courbet spent ten months in Saintonge. He traveled there accompanied by his friend the art critic Jules-Antoine Castagnary, a native of Saintes. Somewhat earlier, Castagnary had introduced him to the philanthropist and budding writer Étienne Baudry, whom he persuaded to purchase several of Courbet's canvases, including *The Young Ladies on the Banks of the Seine* of 1856–57 (Musée du Petit Palais, Paris). Baudry invited the artist to visit him in May 1862 at his Château de Rochemont, near Saintes. There, an entire group of still lifes with flowers was done. Some of Courbet's commentators connect this group with one of Courbet's preoccupations at the time. In particular, Charles Léger explained the appearance of the flower paintings as Courbet's effort to win favor with a certain woman. The artist himself wrote to his friend Léon Isabay about his arrival in Saintes: "Perhaps it was love that brought me to this country; in any case, I've finished lots of paintings" (R. Bonniot, *Gustave Courbet en Saintonge* [Paris, 1973], p. 1).

Bonniot tried to explain in detail this continued work in a genre unexpected for Courbet, toward which it might seem he would have no inclination. He noted that in Rochemont, with its marvelous gardens at every step, Courbet would have seen many rare, beautiful flowers, and sooner or later this should have moved him to paint floral still lifes.

According to Bonniot, Courbet painted the earliest of them not for a woman, but for a male friend. Indeed, at first they could have been intended for Baudry. But the atmosphere in which Courbet lived at the time was festive; he was an honored guest at various celebrations in Saintonge and was surrounded by attentive females. Courbet loved to demonstrate his art, and his flower compositions could easily garner him success in the society of Saintes.

In addition, an attempt to paint several beautiful real objects *à la flamande* can be seen here, following the example of the Dutch and Flemish masters of the seventeenth century, whose pictures Courbet copied even before his arrival in Paris, in the early 1840s, and had later studied in Belgium and Holland in 1846–47, and again in Antwerp in 1861. Like his predecessors, he tried not only to depict the most attractive and decorative forms of flora but to imbue them with deep symbolic meaning. In the exhibition catalogue in Saintes in 1862, Courbet wrote about his *Poppies* of that year (Fernier no. 304): "Death conquers desire, and poppies put to sleep the cares of life." About another still life he said: "The rose petals fall because of life's cares" (Bonniot, p. 83).

In March 1863, Courbet moved into Saintes itself. He was occupied chiefly with painting the portraits of Madame Laure Borreau and her daughter, and settled in a place not far from the Borreaus' home. Malicious gossips claimed that this was done only to be closer to Madame Borreau; the famous painter from the capital was too prominent a figure to escape the curiosity of the townspeople. The rumor that the lady of the house had become his lover ("sa dernière conquête") apparently had some basis.

Once again he began to paint flowers, even more enthusiastically than in Rochemont. It is plausible that the making of flower paintings was to some extent connected to his romance with Madame Borreau, the owner of the fabric store and lady's confectionery in Saintes. *The Woman in the Black Hat: Portrait of Madame L. (Laure Borreau)* of 1863 (fig. 1; The Cleveland Museum of Art; Fernier no. 358), one of Courbet's most fascinating portraits, shows this fashionably dressed mature woman, not unlike women described by Honoré de Balzac as "of a certain age," with a bouquet of flowers in her hand—perhaps from the artist himself. Another portrait of Madame Borreau (Fernier no. 359) was shown at the Salon in 1863 and provoked some critical attacks at the time; it is noteworthy that the picture remained in the artist's possession until his death.

Regardless of his feelings toward Madame Borreau, Courbet saw his flower paintings from a pragmatic point of view as well as an artistic one. "Since I sent the paintings to the exhibition," he wrote Léon Isabay, "I have made four more pictures with flowers. I'm making money with my flowers!" (P. Courthion, *Courbet raconté par lui-même et par ses amis* [Geneva, 1950], vol. 2, p. 31). Undoubtedly, this still life was among the pictures Courbet meant.

Of the works painted in Saintes, the closest to the present painting is *Peonies (Still Life with Flowers)* (fig. 2; Fernier no. 363), which has the same dimensions and also depicts flowers in earthen pots. It is known that the latter painting was done in Saintes, where, as Fernier supposes, the "flowers in two rustic pots" were also painted.

At no previous time was Courbet's art noted for such divergent subjects. It was in Saintes that he painted the famous *Return from the Conference*, a very large, satirical work ridiculing drunken rural clergymen, a canvas later destroyed by a pro-clerical collector who bought it especially for that purpose. The anti-Church paintings and the still lifes with flowers marked the extremes in Courbet's art at one of the critical moments of his creative career.

*Peonies* and the present *Still Life of Flowers* unquestionably served as an impetus for several still lifes with flowers soon painted, following Courbet's example, by young artists who a decade later united into the group called the Impressionists. In the first place should be noted Claude Monet's *Spring Flowers* of 1864 (The Cleveland Museum of Art) and Pierre-

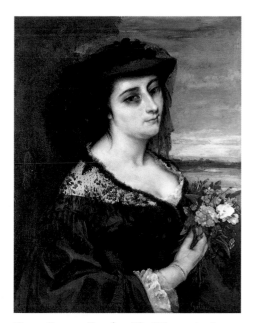

*Fig. 1. Gustave Courbet*. The Woman in the Black Hat: Portrait of Madame L. (Laure Borreau). *1863. The Cleveland Museum of Art. Leonard C. Hanna, Jr., Fund*

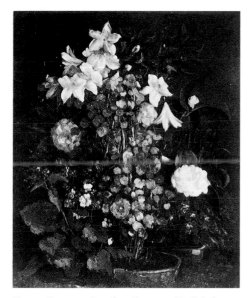

*Fig. 2. Gustave Courbet*. Peonies (Still Life with Flowers). *1862. Private collection*

Auguste Renoir's *Potted Plants (The Greenhouse)* of 1864 (Sammlung Oskar Reinhart, Winterthur), and also Eugène Boudin's *Hollyhocks* of about 1864 as well as the *Flowerpots* (fig. 3) painted sometime later by Frédéric Bazille (both Mrs. John Hay Whitney collection; see J. Rewald, *The History of Impressionism* [New York, 1987], pp. 112–13).

PROVENANCE: Madame Constance Queneaux, Paris; estate sale of Madame Constance Queneaux, Hôtel Drouot, Paris, June 11, 12, 1908; R. Hémard, Paris; Galerie Georges Petit, Paris; Hartz, Holland; Otto Krebs, Holzdorf.

EXHIBITIONS: Paris, Galerie Georges Petit, no. 2; Mannheim, no. 2.

LITERATURE: J. Meier-Graefe, *Courbet* (Munich, 1921), p. 99; Ch. Léger, *Courbet* (Paris, 1929), p. 96; R. Bonniot, *Gustave Courbet en Saintonge* (Paris, 1972), p. 280; R. Fernier, *Gustave Courbet: Catalogue raisonné de l'oeuvre peint* (Lausanne and Paris, 1977), no. 360.

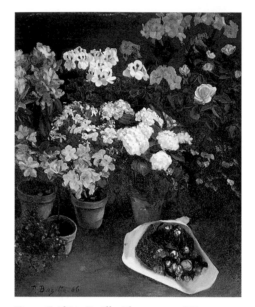

*Fig. 3. Frédéric Bazille. Flowerpots. 1866.
Collection Mrs. John Hay Whitney, New York*

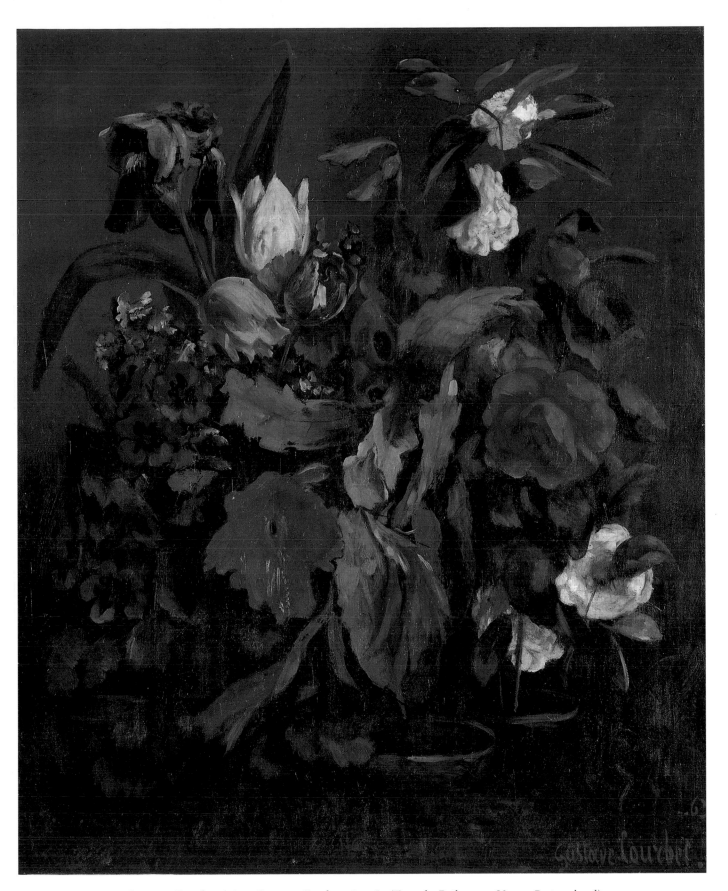

Gustave Courbet (1819, Ornans, Doubs–1877, La Tour-de-Peilz, near Vevey, Switzerland)
## 5. STILL LIFE OF FLOWERS
*Nature morte de fleurs (Camélias, tulipes, iris et autres fleurs jaillissant de deux pots rustiques).* 1863
Oil on canvas, 25⅝ × 21" (65 × 53.5 cm). Signed and dated lower right: ". . . 63 Gustave Courbet"
No. 3KP 505. Formerly collection Otto Krebs, Holzdorf

# GUSTAVE COURBET

## RECLINING WOMAN

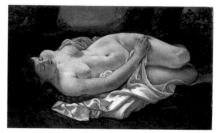

The subject of the painting dates to Courbet's early works, made twenty years previously: *The Hammock* of 1844 (Sammlung Oskar Reinhart, Winterthur) and *Nude Woman Sleeping at a Spring* of 1845 (The Detroit Institute of Arts), and the replica painted the same year, now in the Sammlung Oskar Reinhart. To these paintings should be added *Study of a Sleeping Woman* of 1845 (Otani Memorial Museum of Art, Nishinomiya; Fernier no. 56), depicting a sleeping, half-nude woman at the edge of the forest: here, the conception of the present *Reclining Woman* is essentially already formulated.

In Courbet's portrayal of the nude female body, two opposing tendencies emerged quite early: whether to display the body following the aesthetic ideals of Parisian society of the time or, on the contrary, to show it with heightened realism, as in *Bathers* of 1853 (Musée Fabre, Montpellier), a painting that provoked Napoléon III to strike it with a riding whip in the Salon, prompting the Empress to ask, "Is that too a Percheron?" Later, in *Sleeping Blonde* of 1857 (Fernier no. 226), with the figure's heavy buttocks and impressive stomach, the motif of the paintings of 1845 would seem to be revisited in the spirit of the 1853 *Bathers*. However, the next year Courbet painted a new, large composition, *Bathers* of 1858 (Musée des Beaux-Arts, Nantes; Fernier no. 229), in which nothing provocative remains: the poses are entirely conventional, and the realism is softened to such an extent that it is quite possible to recognize a degree of idealization. Yet painting such a large picture was risky. Its distinguishing feature, moreover, was an allusion to lesbian love, which occupied the artist's imagination and was from time to time reflected, although in a veiled form, in his paintings, especially in the mid-1860s.

It was this eroticism, evident in the forms of the sleeping, nude woman, that became more tangible. Courbet himself understood this. For fear of scandal, he did not dare to show *Reclining Nude* of 1862 (private collection) at the 1863 Saintes exhibition, a work for which a certain Françoise, a young local woman, posed for him in Rochemont. At the same time, the theme of female nudity, in which he strove to follow the Old Masters, almost always held for him a symbolic or allegorical meaning. No wonder that a nude model occupies the most prominent place in the center, next to the painter himself, in his programmatic *The Painter's Studio* of 1855 (Musée d'Orsay, Paris), which Courbet called a "real allegory." Courbet wrote to Champfleury that this figure in *Studio* embodied truth (P. Courthion, ed., *Courbet raconté par lui-même et par ses amis* [Geneva, 1948], vol. 1, p. 47).

The fact that the subject of the female nude was pursued by Courbet with particular devotion in the years 1864–65 can be explained not only by personal considerations (it is perhaps no accident that the confirmed bachelor was at that moment inclined toward marriage as never before), but also by the general situation that had developed in French painting. In the 1863 Salon, the most enthusiastic acclaim was won by Alexandre Cabanel's decorously voluptuous *Birth of Venus* (Musée d'Orsay, Paris), immediately acquired by Napoléon III. The main attraction of another show, the exhibition of the *refusés*, which was just as much the talk of the town as the official Salon, was Édouard Manet's *Le Déjeuner sur l'herbe,* perceived by the public and official circles as a scandalous encroachment on the foundations of art and morality. Courbet, who himself was counting on a succès de scandale, for the sake of which he had prepared the enormous *Return from the Conference,* was deprived of such an opportunity, since that painting was rejected not only by the official Salon but by the Salon des Refusés as well. His portrait of Madame Borreau shown in the 1863 Salon had only a moderate success, not to be compared with the accolades received by Cabanel or the stir around Manet's *Déjeuner.*

Courbet's next undertaking was calculated if not to cause scandal, then at least to gain increased attention from Parisian society: he decided to paint an allegory ridiculing the Romantic poets, including Alphonse Lamartine, Théophile Gautier, and Charles Baudelaire, who were to be shown gathered in a sacred ravine and drinking poisoned water. The chief subject of *The Spring of Hippocrene* was to be a beautiful, naked nymph reclining on mossy rocks and spitting into the spring. Courbet's sister accidentally knocked over the unfinished painting and ripped the canvas, saving him from implementing this unfortunate idea. After inviting a model from Paris to Ornans to pose for the picture, the artist decided to continue working with her on a simpler composition with nude figures.

Courbet may have known that Manet was preparing a large painting with a nude model, a contemporary Venus, for the 1864 Salon (though *Olympia* would not be shown until the following year). He had been jealous of Manet before. Courbet's new major work, *Venus and Psyche* of 1864 (Fernier no. 370), with life-size figures, could be viewed as a challenge to both Cabanel

and Manet, to be made more effective by the evocation of a mythological context. The true challenge lay in the class of subjects that Courbet tried to play upon: he depicted Venus looking angrily at the sleeping Psyche. But the painting was not accepted at the Salon of 1864—not for artistic reasons (as the holder of medals from previous Salons, Courbet had the right to avoid the jury), but for "ethical" ones. The painting was considered immoral. The mythological reference did not dissuade those who saw in the picture a veiled lesbian motif. Courbet could imagine that Venus's jealous gaze at Psyche symbolized the hypocrisy of the age (his biographer, Georges Riat, reiterated this opinion in *Gustave Courbet, peintre* [Paris, 1906], p. 212), but few agreed.

That same year Courbet painted another version, subsequently somewhat altered at the request of the collector who acquired it: a parrot appeared on Venus's arm, which obviated a mythological context and prompted the new name *The Awakening* (illustrated in the Introduction, p. 18; Fernier no. 371). The appearance of this detail—which anticipated the famous *Woman with a Parrot* (fig. 2; The Metropolitan Museum of Art, New York), a painting that appeared two years later and rapidly became a success—surprised several admirers of the artist, but the fact that he himself easily agreed to this request suggests that he found it quite natural. The erotic subtext of the painting is indeed in complete agreement with this seemingly unexpected addition (in this regard, see the chapter "Courbet's

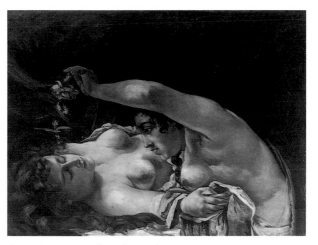

*Fig. 1. Gustave Courbet.* The Awakening. *1866. Kunstmuseum, Bern*

Femininity" in M. Fried, *Courbet's Realism* [Chicago and London, 1990], pp. 189–222 and, on the parrot as a sexual symbol, p. 205).

Not satisfied with the two versions of *Venus and Psyche*, Courbet painted one more, a smaller replica, which was also named *The Awakening*, in 1866 (fig. 1; Kunstmuseum, Bern; Fernier no. 533). In addition, there is a sketch of this two-figured composition, *Red-Haired Woman Sleeping* (Fernier no. 373). It, too, can be seen as a work leading to *Reclining Woman*.

Like his rivals, whether Cabanel or Manet, Courbet had a classical source of inspiration when he began work on *Venus and Psyche*. This was Simon Vouet's painting of the same subject in the Musée des Beaux-Arts, Lyons. But just as for them, the point was not to use a traditional subject, but to provide a contemporary understanding of the purpose of painting and how painting reflected the status of women in society at that time.

With these considerations in mind, when creating a group of nudes in 1866, Courbet faced a dilemma: should the model be shown against the background of nature, suggesting the mythological, or in an interior, suggesting the realistic? It seems that the idea of the interior attracted him more, but as a tactic in his struggle for recognition in the Salon, the depiction of a nude woman under an open sky, personifying a nymph or some other mythological creature, would more easily accomplish his purpose. Almost simultaneously appeared *Sleeping Nymph* of 1866 (fig. 3; Sammlung Oskar Reinhart,Winterthur; Fernier no. 534) and *Sleeping Girl* of 1866 (Museum Mesdag, The Hague). The differences in the way the figure is presented are minimal, but in the first instance the scene takes place in a forest with a spouting spring, while in the second a couch and bed curtain are shown. Apparently, both of these paintings immediately preceded *Reclining Woman* and served essentially as studies for it.

Courbet hoped to attain a critical success at the 1866 Salon and to a certain extent achieved it. He placed his hopes on *The Deer Sanctuary* (Musée d'Orsay, Paris) and *Woman with a Parrot*. Riat writes: "In March 1866, they . . . were almost finished, according to the testimony of Count d'Ideville, who had admired them in Courbet's studio, when the latter, standing with a smoking pipe in front of the nude model, a beautiful red-haired girl, lying on a sofa with

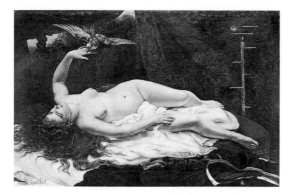

Fig. 2. *Gustave Courbet.* Woman with a Parrot. *1866. The Metropolitan Museum of Art, New York. The H. O. Havemeyer Collection. Bequest of Mrs. H. O. Havemeyer*

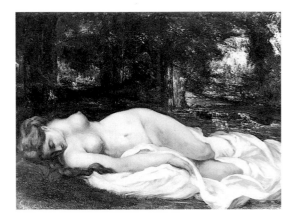

Fig. 3. *Gustave Courbet.* Sleeping Nymph. *1866. Sammlung Oskar Reinhart, Am Römerholz, Winterthur*

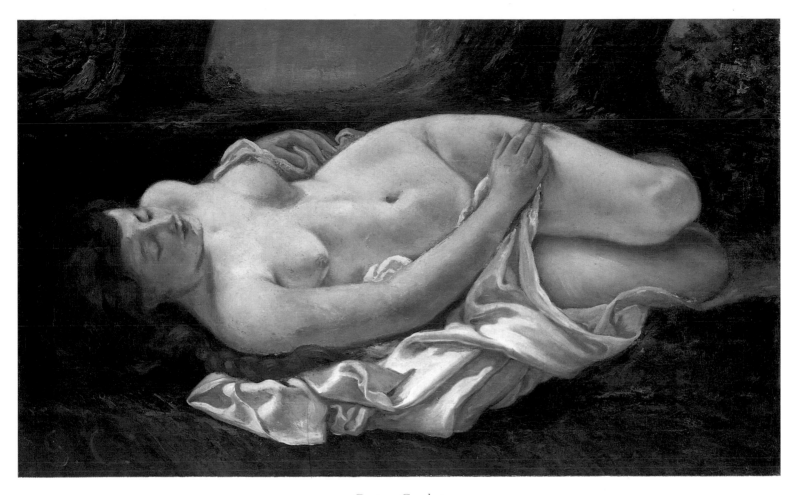

Gustave Courbet

## 6. RECLINING WOMAN

*Femme couchée.* c. 1865–66
Oil on canvas, 30¼ × 50⅜" (77 × 128 cm)
Signed lower left: "G.C."
No. 3K 1394. Formerly collection Bernhard Koehler, Berlin

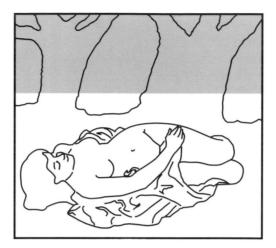

*Fig. 4. Diagram of* Reclining Woman (*plate 6*) *showing area later removed*

a brilliant-colored macaw, suddenly shouted, as [Courbet] applied the finishing touches: 'If they are not happy this year, then they'll be in a difficult position. They will have two pictures, exactly the kind that they are supposed to like, a landscape and a nude—at least, if they don't see a secret society of deer here, who have gathered in the forest to proclaim a Republic.' 'They,' as the visitor translated, were the Academy, the *Ingristes*, the jury, the government, and so on" (Riat, *Gustave Courbet, peintre*, p. 234).

Riat considered *Reclining Woman* the original idea behind *Woman with a Parrot*. "There, at the edge of the forest," he wrote, "presented on a white drape, lying on her back with her hair undone, is a nude girl with a slender and graceful figure" (ibid.). In contrast, Fernier saw the picture as only a later version of the Metropolitan one. Neither view is persuasive. *Reclining Woman*, strictly speaking, could not be considered the original idea for the famous New York painting; it was only one of the links in the chain, although a very important one. Yet it should not be seen as merely a version either, since it clearly preceded *Woman with a Parrot*, reflecting the artist's hesitation as to whether he should act in the spirit of realism or follow tradition as he understood it. We know that, in the final analysis, Courbet chose the former, even if his realism in that case made some concession to academic convention. But first he painted a beautiful nude in a natural setting, weighing the chances, as it were, of a "nymph" in a possible future dispute with the heads of

the Salon and the Academy.

The background of *Reclining Woman*—or, to be more precise, what remains of it (see fig. 4), mostly the lower part of a huge tree trunk—suggests a link with *The Oak at Flagey, Known as the Oak of Vercingétorix* of 1864 (fig. 5; Murauchi Art Museum, Tokyo; Fernier no. 417), a landscape painted from nature, in Flagey, but at the same time imbued with symbolic meaning. The oak was sacred to the Druids, for example, and, in a different context, was associated with Jupiter in classical mythology. Also, it is believed that the oak trees represented in Courbet's early pictures carried a personal association; the oak tree at Flagey, where the artist's family had an estate, was thought at that time to have been the very tree near which Caesar's army defeated Vercingétorix, the leader of the Gauls.

Concerning the figure's place in the natural setting, it can be noted that the sensuality of the reclining woman is expressed not only in the contours of her body but also in the color of her hair. Courbet was particularly attracted to redheads; in this instance, by echoing the color of the woman's hair in the golden-red foliage of the background, he sought to unify the landscape—nature—with the nymph, its most beautiful embodiment. Moreover, the dark landscape provides a finely contrasting setting for her very light flesh.

Yet even though, coloristically, the background is painted in the Old Master tradition, it was worked with the palette knife, not a brush, which the Old

Masters had never done. Energetic, impetuous work with the palette knife anticipates future experiments of an expressionistic kind. The landscape was completely repainted at a late stage of execution, the point when the artist took up the palette knife. In some places, he reworked the figure as well; under infrared light, one can see where the face and knees of the model were repainted. Perhaps after *Venus and Psyche* and *The Awakening,* compositions with two figures, Courbet was uncertain about the single figure of *Reclining Woman,* and hesitated in particular about the final disposition of the legs. There had been no such problem in the preceding two pictures, since in each case the figure to the right concealed the lower legs of the reclining one.

Courbet never tried to place this painting, unlike *Woman with a Parrot,* before the public, but it can be supposed that if he had, *Reclining Woman* would have been received with disdain and would have suffered reproach on grounds of taste. Its way of understanding the nude ran counter to the strict academic standards set for the subject. In the context of the aesthetics of that time, its erotic overtones would not have made such a painting attractive either for a large part of the public or for the pillars of art criticism.

In all likelihood, *Reclining Woman* was painted at the very beginning of 1866. It may have been preceded by some sketches, since originally Courbet had conceived a composition of large dimensions. The format of the painting was changed twice. First, it was trimmed on each side and restretched, so that part of the remaining picture surface was turned back at the edges. However, Courbet did not stop at that. He then cut down the vertical bars of the stretcher by between 25 and 30 centimeters and stretched the canvas over this shortened frame. What had been the central horizontal bar remained intact and now became the upper bar. From its position one can calculate that the original stretcher was about 105 centimeters high. A considerable portion of the landscape in the upper part of the background has thus disappeared (see fig. 4). This is regrettable, since the placid figure depicted by the artist was deprived of much of her natural surroundings. In compensation, however, cutting down the landscape emphasized the figure, giving the composition a sculptural effect.

Conservation work conducted at the Hermitage has freed the painting from a considerable amount of dirt and darkened varnish.

PROVENANCE: Ernest Hoschedé, Paris; Hoschedé sale, Hôtel Drouot, Paris, April 20, 1875; Charles Pillet, Paris; Galerie Durand-Ruel, Paris, no. 30; Hecht, Paris; Hecht sale; Galerie Bernheim-Jeune, Paris; Galerie Gustave Knauer, Berlin; 1908, Bernhard Koehler, Berlin.

EXHIBITIONS: 1930, Berlin, "Ausstellung Gustave Courbet," Galerie Wertheim, no. 23 (reprod.); 1935–36, Zurich, "Gustave Courbet," Kunsthaus, no. 90.

LITERATURE: Le Hir, *Journal des amateurs,* 1875, pp. 115–16; *Gazette des beaux-arts,* 17, p. 526 (engraving of the painting by Waltner); R. Muther, *The History of Modern Painting* (New York, 1896), vol. 2, p. 528; G. Riat, *Gustave Courbet, peintre* (Paris, 1906), pp. 220 (reprod.), 234; G. de Chirico, *Gustave Courbet* (1925) (reprod.); R. Fernier, *Gustave Courbet: Catalogue raisonné de l'oeuvre peint* (Lausanne and Paris, 1977), no. 527; *L'Opera completa di Gustave Courbet: Presentazione e apparati critici e filologici di Pierre Courthion* (Milan, 1985), no. 519.

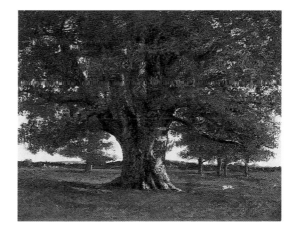

*Fig. 5. Gustave Courbet.* The Oak at Flagey, Known as the Oak of Vercingétorix. *1864. Murauchi Art Museum, Tokyo*

# HENRI FANTIN-LATOUR

## FLOWERS

The early years of Fantin-Latour's career were devoted to portraits, self-portraits, and imaginary compositions. But after he attempted to show at the Salon in 1859 and was rejected, he decided to paint still lifes to earn a living. These still lifes, however, did not win favor either. It is known that around 1860 Fantin made copies at the Louvre. The Louvre archives do not indicate exactly which works he copied, but some scholars suppose that they may have included one of Jean-Baptiste Chardin's still lifes. *Flowers,* though, is not at all reminiscent of the Louvre studies. On the contrary, it is composed in opposition to the traditional bouquet painting. The picture is noteworthy for the fact that earlier than perhaps any painting in French art, it depicts sunflowers, which two decades later would attract Claude Monet and, even later, Vincent van Gogh, who made them the signature subject of his art, and Paul Gauguin.

Fantin-Latour's still lifes attracted the attention of a number of the leading Parisian painters as early as 1863. They made a deep impression on James Abbott McNeill Whistler, who helped Fantin obtain several commissions in London. Whistler believed that Fantin could achieve success in the sale of his paintings there. Following Whistler's advice, in February 1864, when Fantin traveled to London, he brought eight paintings with him, among them six still lifes. It can be surmised that one of them was *Flowers*, since at an early date it was in a London collection.

PROVENANCE: Buckler, London; Buckler sale, London, March 1906 (105 guineas); Galerie Matthiesen, Berlin; Otto Krebs, Holzdorf.

EXHIBITIONS: 1906, Paris, "Exposition de l'oeuvre de Fantin-Latour au Palais de l'École Nationale des Beaux-Arts," Quai Malaquais, no. 75 (?).

LITERATURE: *Catalogue de l'oeuvre complet de Fantin-Latour: Établi et rédigé par Madame Fantin-Latour* (Paris, 1911), no. 149.

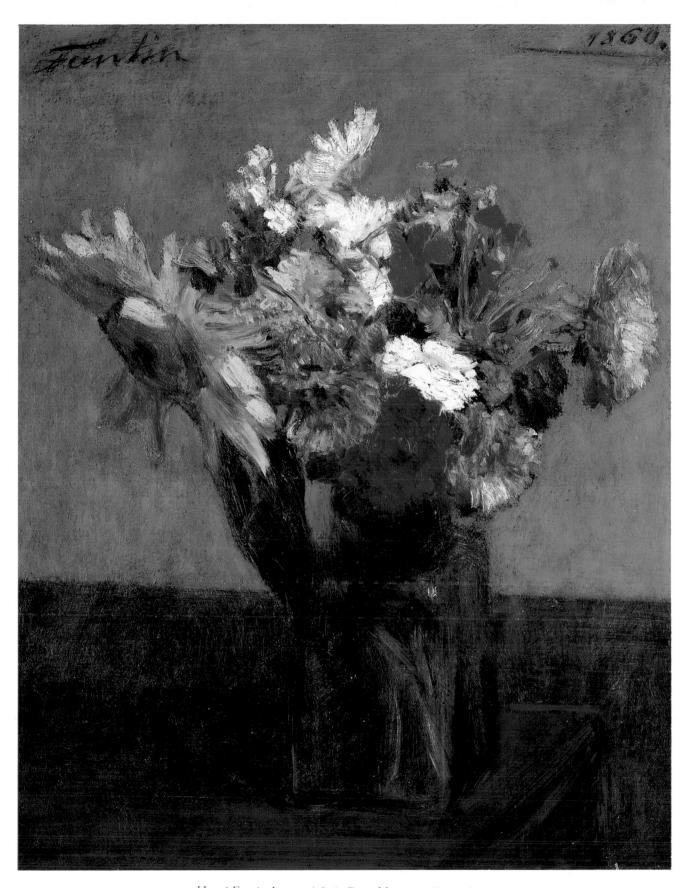

Henri Fantin-Latour (1836, Grenoble–1904, Buré, Orne)
## 7. FLOWERS
*Fleurs.* 1860
Oil on canvas, 16 × 12⅝" (40.5 × 32 cm)
Signed upper left: "Fantin." Dated upper right: "1860"
No. 3KP 557. Formerly collection Otto Krebs, Holzdorf

# HENRI FANTIN-LATOUR

## PEONIES IN A VASE

The dating of this still life is problematic. Fantin painted peonies and other flowers during various periods of his career. He used comparable compositional techniques in particular in his early works, such as *Flowers* of 1864 (Victoria and Albert Museum, London) and *Flower Bouquet* of 1864 (Elmer H. Bobst collection, New York).

Later, too, Fantin often arranged his flower still lifes in a quite similar fashion. For example, there is *Bouquet of Peonies and Iris* of 1884 (fig. 1; private collection), where the flowers are in a similar globe-shaped vase. In the catalogue of Fantin-Latour's painting compiled by his widow, two *Peonies* paintings are listed: no. 784 (1876) and no. 1554 (1894). Some scholars believe that no. 784 is the painting now in the Montreal Museum of Fine Arts (fig. 2). The present painting is probably not no. 1554, since the year 1894 is not very plausible for stylistic reasons. In all likelihood, *Peonies in a Vase* was not recorded in Madame Fantin-Latour's 1911 catalogue.

The state of the painting's conservation also makes dating difficult. The top layers of paint have been subjected to excessive cleaning, apparently before the work's acquisition by Otto Krebs. Taking into account the painting's condition and its stylistic features, an earlier dating, around 1864, seems preferable.

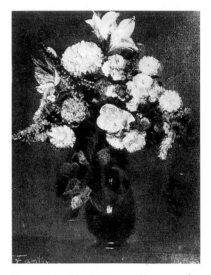

*Fig. 1. Henri Fantin-Latour. Bouquet of Peonies and Iris. 1884. Private collection*

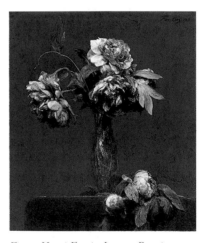

*Fig. 2. Henri Fantin-Latour. Peonies. 1876. The Montreal Museum of Fine Arts. Bequest of Oliver Hosmer*

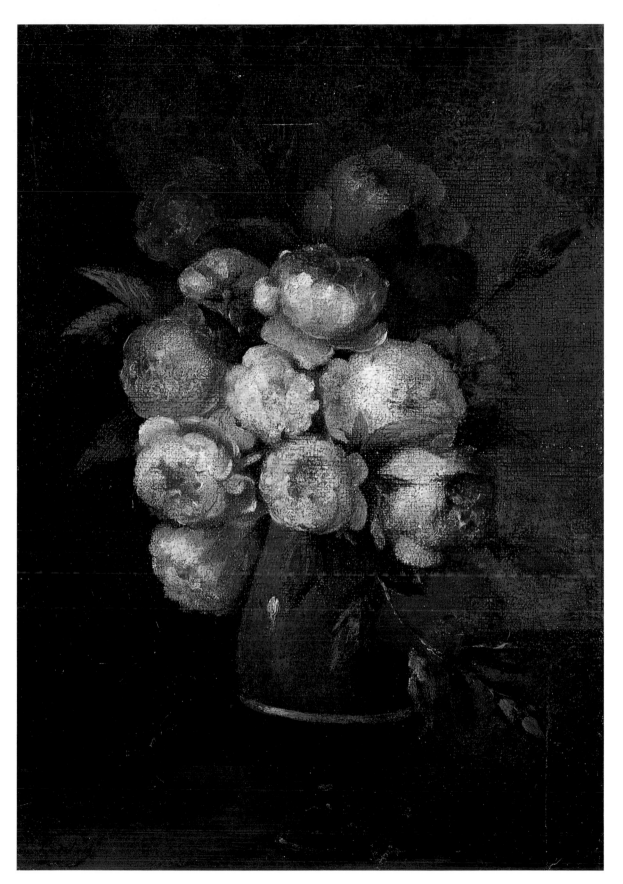

Henri Fantin-Latour
8. PEONIES IN A VASE
*Bouquet de pivoines.* c. 1864
Oil on canvas, 18¾ × 13¼" (46.6 × 33.5 cm). Signed lower left: "Fantin"
No. 3KP 553. Formerly collection Otto Krebs, Holzdorf

# HENRI FANTIN-LATOUR

## LEMON, APPLES, AND TULIPS
## (TULIPS AND FRUIT)

Flowers in a bud vase frequently appear in the paintings of Fantin-Latour. In the portraits, this detail became a special and precious decoration in a tonally restrained composition. And the bud vase became a reliable supporting device when, instead of a bouquet, the artist wanted to paint one or a few flowers. In those modest, plain still lifes, Fantin achieved great things with simple means.

The bud vase establishes the central vertical line in *Lemon, Apples, and Tulips* and seems to govern the entire structure. Several centuries earlier, the open blossom on its stem had led to the idea of the wineglass. The tulips in this painting, the natural embodiment of almost the same configuration, crown the entire composition and create an elegant formal echo: living forms are juxtaposed with the man-made objects that look like them. At the same time, the tulips contrast with the lemon and apples—the delicate arabesques of the flowers with the simpler masses of the fruit. The fruit on the plate in front of the bud vase balance the composition, delineating the foreground, although one can speak of planes in this case only with great caution, since the depth of space is marked here

with the delicacy of Jean-Baptiste Chardin's still lifes.

The tradition of the seventeenth-century Dutch still life, continued and perfected in the next century by Chardin and other French painters, found an extraordinarily gifted heir in Fantin-Latour. The objects in this painting are placed in such a way as to highlight their beauty by means of comparison and contrast: for example, the transparent is placed next to the opaque, glass next to metal. In this regard, the golden yellow lemon is shown to fine advantage on a silver dish. Such well-considered and deeply felt contrasts give the painting its special harmony, without being at all obtrusive.

PROVENANCE: Tavernier, Paris; Galerie Bernheim-Jeune, Paris; T[avernier] collection sale, Hôtel Drouot, April 15, 1907 (5,800 francs); Lindel, Paris; Otto Krebs, Holzdorf.

EXHIBITIONS: 1906, Paris, École des Beaux-Arts, "Exposition de l'oeuvre de Fantin-Latour au Palais de l'École Nationale des Beaux-Arts," Quai Malaquais, no. 113.

LITERATURE: *Catalogue des tableaux, aquarelles, pastels et dessins . . . composant la collection de M.T.* (Hôtel Drouot, Paris, 1907), no. 13 (reprod.); *Catalogue de l'oeuvre complet de Fantin-Latour: Établi et rédigé par Madame Fantin-Latour* (Paris, 1911), no. 280.

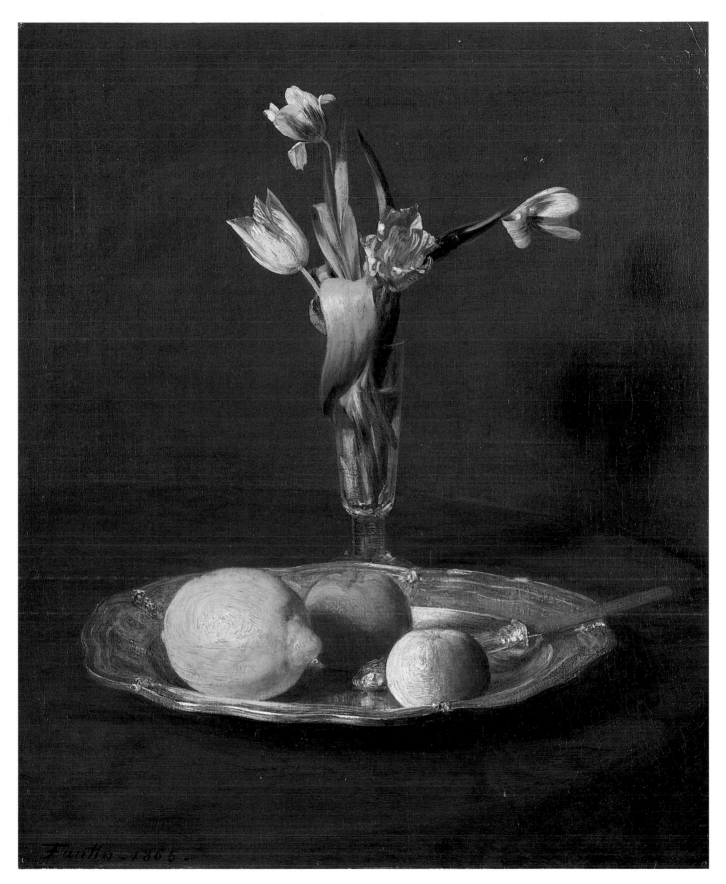

Henri Fantin-Latour
9. LEMON, APPLES, AND TULIPS (TULIPS AND FRUIT)
*Citron, pommes et tulipes (Tulipes et fruits).* 1865
Oil on canvas, 18¾ × 15⅜" (47.7 × 39 cm). Signed and dated lower left: "Fantin 1865"
No. 3KP 550. Formerly collection Otto Krebs, Holzdorf

# HENRI FANTIN-LATOUR

## STILL LIFE: FLOWERS, DISH WITH FRUIT, AND CARAFE

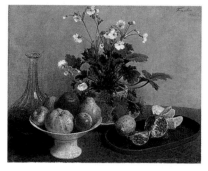

Fantin-Latour's failure with the allegorical painting *The Toast,* sent to the 1865 Salon, prompted him to depart for a time from allegorical and symbolic compositions and concentrate instead on concrete, real subjects, and on a more attentive study of nature, particularly in still lifes. "There I am more sure of myself," he wrote to his friend the dealer and collector Edwards in July of that year (D. Druick and M. Hoog, *Fantin-Latour* [Paris, 1982], p. 115).

In several of the still lifes dating to the mid-1860s, the study of flowers, fruit, and various everyday objects reaches a higher level. These include canvases of similar dimensions painted in the summer and fall of 1865: along with the present *Still Life: Flowers, Dish with Fruit, and Carafe* were such paintings as *Chinese Asters and Fruit* (Carter collection; Fantin-Latour no. 277), *Chrysanthemums and Fruit* (Museum of Fine Arts, Boston), and *Still Life* (private collection, Paris; Fantin-Latour exhibition [Paris, Ottawa, and San Francisco, 1982–83], no. 34). The last is particularly interesting since it is close in composition and the same white fruit dish appears in it. The fruit dish was employed by Fantin later as well, notably in *Wedding Still Life* of 1869 (fig. 1; Musée de Grenoble), Fantin's wedding gift to Victoria Dubourg, and in *Corner of the Table* of 1873 (The Art Institute of Chicago).

The name *Corner of the Table*—chosen by the artist for the Chicago painting, and also for the famous group portrait with Paul Verlaine and Arthur Rimbaud sitting at the corner of a table—seems appropriate for the 1865 still lifes. Fantin favored the table corner in his arrangements, hoping thereby to avoid the appearance of calculation and making the configuration of the corner the basis for the setting. In the works of this group, endeavoring to include more objects than before, he shows an obvious preference for horizontal formats, which provided greater freedom in the resolution of new spatial problems. In such a format, the converging lines of the corner played an important role, helping to organize the composition of flowers, fruit, or plates.

Fantin-Latour did not want to imbue his still-life objects with a significance beyond the painting, with some sort of symbolism; in this he differed from Courbet, who advocated realism but often inclined toward allegory in still life (see plate 5). If it is appropriate in this case to speak of symbols in Fantin's paintings, they are only such in the most general sense—expressions of sensual pleasure as embodied by familiar objects, such as flowers, wine carafes, and fruit. It was at this same time, in the mid-1860s, that Fantin loved to expose the insides of fruits, especially pomegranates and oranges, tempting the viewer with their lush juiciness. This is true in particular with *Flowers and Fruit* of 1866 (fig. 2; The Toledo Museum of Art, Ohio), yet another multi-object pyramidal composition, where, incidentally, the same lacquered platter, most likely Japanese, is included.

The abundance in the still lifes painted around 1865, in comparison with the earlier and later ones, indirectly reflects Fantin's biographical circumstances. At this time his life became much fuller, as he came into broader contact with people in the arts. He was friendly with Édouard Manet, was becoming acquainted with Claude Monet and Frédéric Bazille, and was often at the salon of Paul Meurice and his wife, where he met Manet and Félix Bracquemond and the critics Jules Champfleury and Philippe Burty. His paintings suggest his satisfaction with this life, as the creative

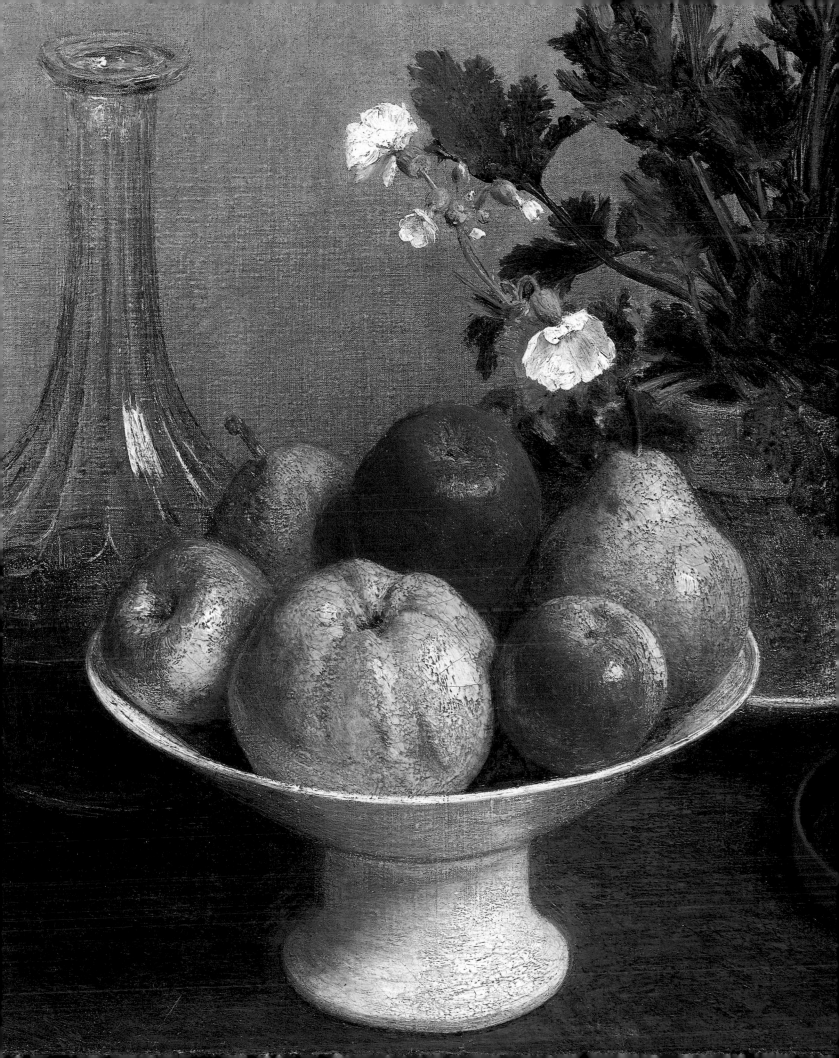

ideas resolved in his pictures become more and more complex.

PROVENANCE: Charles Pacquement, Paris; Galerie Matthiesen, Berlin; Otto Krebs, Holzdorf.

EXHIBITIONS: 1906, Paris, "Exposition de l'oeuvre de Fantin-Latour au Palais de l'École Nationale des Beaux-Arts," Quai Malaquis, no. 72 (as "*Fleurs et fruits: Pommes, grenades et oranges sur un plateau de laque*, etc., appartient à M. Ch. Pacquement"); 1927, Berlin, Galerie Matthiesen, "Das Stilleben in der deutschen und französischen Malerei von 1850 bis zur Gegenwart."

LITERATURE: *Catalogue de l'oeuvre complet de Fantin-Latour: Établi et rédigé par Madame Fantin-Latour* (Paris, 1911), no. 278; B. Werner, "Stilleben von 1850–1926 zur Ausstellung in der Galerie Matthiesen, Berlin," *Die Kunst*, vol. 55 (October 1926–September 1927), pp. 310–11 (reprod.).

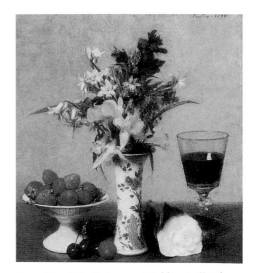

*Fig. 1. Henri Fantin-Latour.* Wedding Still Life. *1869. Musée de Grenoble*

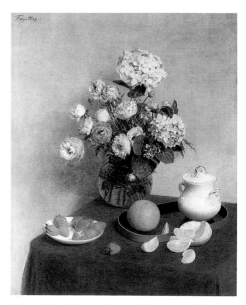

*Fig. 2. Henri Fantin-Latour.* Flowers and Fruit. *1866. The Toledo Museum of Art, Ohio. Purchased with funds from the Libbey Endowment. Gift of Edward Drummond Libbey*

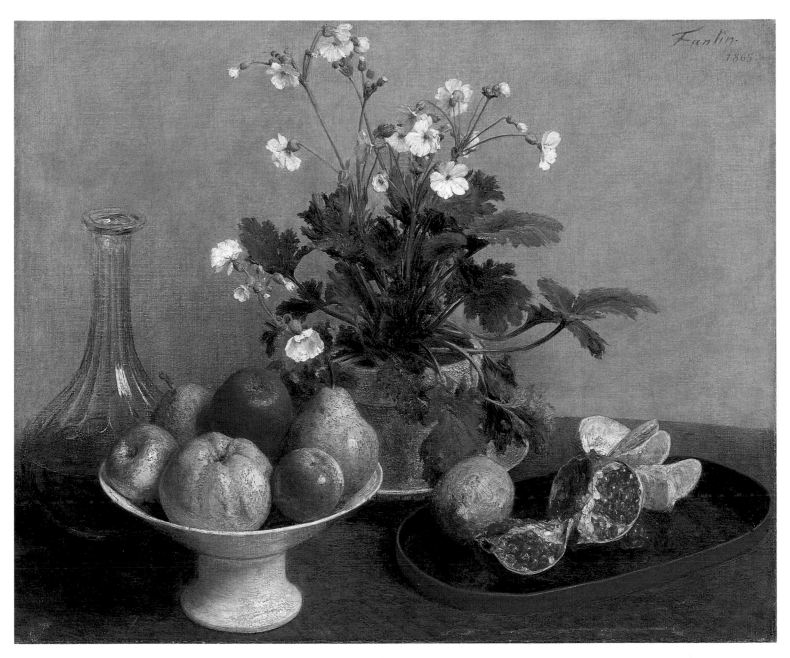

Henri Fantin-Latour
10. STILL LIFE: FLOWERS, DISH WITH FRUIT, AND CARAFE
*Nature morte: Fleurs, compotier et carafe*. 1865
Oil on canvas, 21⅝ × 28" (55 × 68.5 cm). Signed and dated upper right: "Fantin 1865"
No. 3KP 520. Formerly collection Otto Krebs, Holzdorf

# HENRI FANTIN-LATOUR

## PETUNIAS

There is another still life with this same title, also dated 1881 and very similar in composition, but larger, measuring 38 by 58 centimeters (fig. 1; The Detroit Institute of Arts); see *Flowers by Fantin-Latour* (Acquavella Galleries, New York, 1966), no. 19, and F. Gibson, *The Art of Henri Fantin-Latour: His Life and Work* (London, 1920), pl. 33. Both books refer to the 1911 complete catalogue of Fantin-Latour's paintings, where the still life *Petunias* is listed as no. 1033. But since that catalogue does not indicate either the provenance or the dimensions of the work, either of these two paintings may claim this number.

LITERATURE: *Catalogue de l'oeuvre complet de Fantin-Latour: Établi et rédigé par Madame Fantin-Latour* (Paris, 1911), no. 1033 (?).

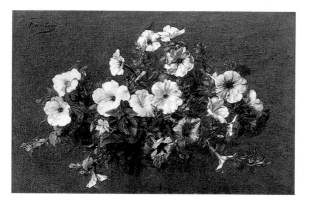

*Fig. 1. Henri Fantin-Latour. Petunias. 1881. The Detroit Institute of Arts. Bequest of Ruth Nugent Head, in memory of her mother, Anna E. Kresge, and her husband, Henry W. Nugent Head*

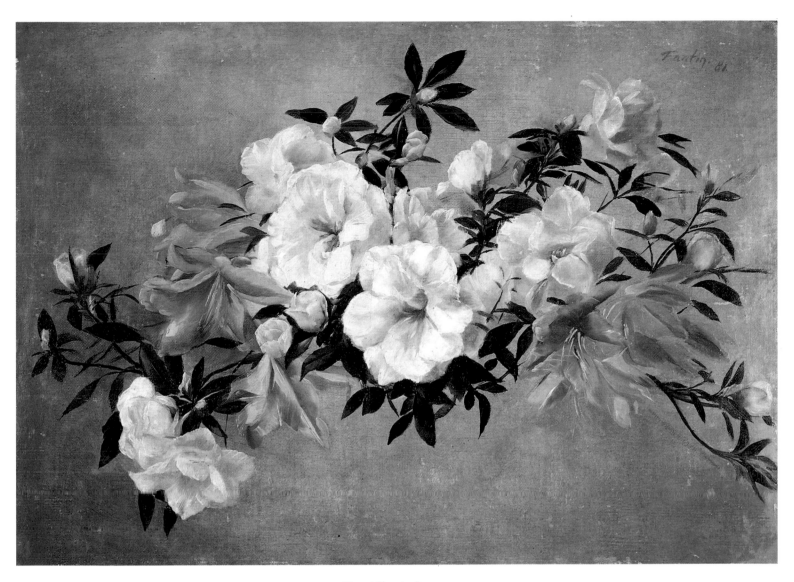

Henri Fantin-Latour
## 11. PETUNIAS
*Pétunias.* 1881
Oil on canvas, mounted on cardboard, 11⅝ × 16⅝" (29.6 × 42.4 cm)
Signed and dated upper right: "Fantin 81"
No. 3KP 556. Formerly collection Otto Krebs, Holzdorf

# ÉDOUARD MANET

## GIRL IN A WING COLLAR

Manet's first attempt to work in the medium of pastel was early in his career, in 1856, and was followed by an almost twenty-year hiatus. In 1873–74, with a new, although to be sure episodic, use of this medium, he immediately made himself known as a master, and in the late 1870s pastel became Manet's favorite medium. It seemed most appropriate for women's portraits. By that time in Manet's studio on the rue d'Amsterdam there were quite a few admirers, chiefly ladies of the demimonde or those attracted not only by the virtuoso manner of the artist but by his clever talk.

In an article in *Le Figaro* on February 5, 1884, on the first day of the Manet estate sale, when *Girl in a Wing Collar* was being offered, P. Edel wrote of the series of pastels that it represented a virtual parade of Parisian women, who, in the opinion of the critic Jules Claretie, were notable for their unusual freshness and liveliness. E. Bazire, one of Manet's first biographers, in a book published at the same time (E. Bazire, *Manet* [Paris, 1884]), aptly noted (clearly following the artist's ideas) that pastel should not suffer from "anemia"— that Manet knew how to find within it a full range of colors, not rejecting it because he found the nuances difficult, but striving to give life to the figures he depicted.

The identity of the girl in a wing collar remains unknown. No matter how summarily the dress was painted, Manet, being a man of the world, treated new trends in fashion with due attention. For him and his friends, fashion was one of the leading characteristics of the time, and Manet insisted on reflecting it in painting. Apparently, the subject was not a model but one of the visitors to the studio, who commissioned her portrait from Manet. It can be supposed that the picture, which shows her *en face* (Rouart/Wildenstein date it to 1880), did not satisfy her, and Manet then executed another pastel portrait of the subject with the same dimensions, this time in profile (fig. 1; private collection, Paris; Rouart/Wildenstein, vol. 2, no. 44). The second was signed by the artist, and most likely went to the woman who commissioned it, whereas the first remained in the studio and four years later was included in the estate sale of Manet's works.

The picture itself is very fragile and has a number of small losses, which were almost impossible to avoid because, instead of cardboard or paper support, the artist chose prefabricated primed canvas, unsatisfactory for pastel.

PROVENANCE: Manet sale, Hôtel Drouot, Paris, 1884; Léon Hennique, Paris; Otto Krebs, Holzdorf.

LITERATURE: *Catalogue de la vente Édouard Manet* (Paris, Hôtel Drouot, February 4–5, 1884), no. 112; T. Duret, *Histoire d'Édouard Manet et de son oeuvre* (Paris, 1902), no. 48; E. Moreau-Nélaton, *Manet raconté par lui-même* (Paris, 1926), no. 413; A. Tabarant, *Manet* (Paris, 1931), no. 22; P. Jamot and G. Wildenstein, *Manet: Catalogue critique* (Paris, 1932), no. 440; A. Tabarant, *Manet et ses oeuvres* (Paris, 1947), p. 368, no. 479; M. Bodelsen, "Early Impressionist Sales, 1874–1894," *The Burlington Magazine*, vol. 110, no. 783 (June 1968), pp. 341–43; *L'Opera completa di Édouard Manet*, Introduction by D. Rouart, Catalogue by S. Oriente (Milan, 1970), no. 292b; D. Rouart and G. Wildenstein, *Édouard Manet: Catalogue raisonné* (Lausanne, 1975), vol. 2, no. 45.

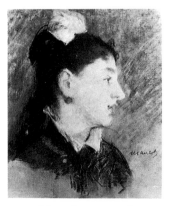

*Fig. 1. Édouard Manet.* Girl in a Wing Collar, in Profile. *1880. Private collection, Paris*

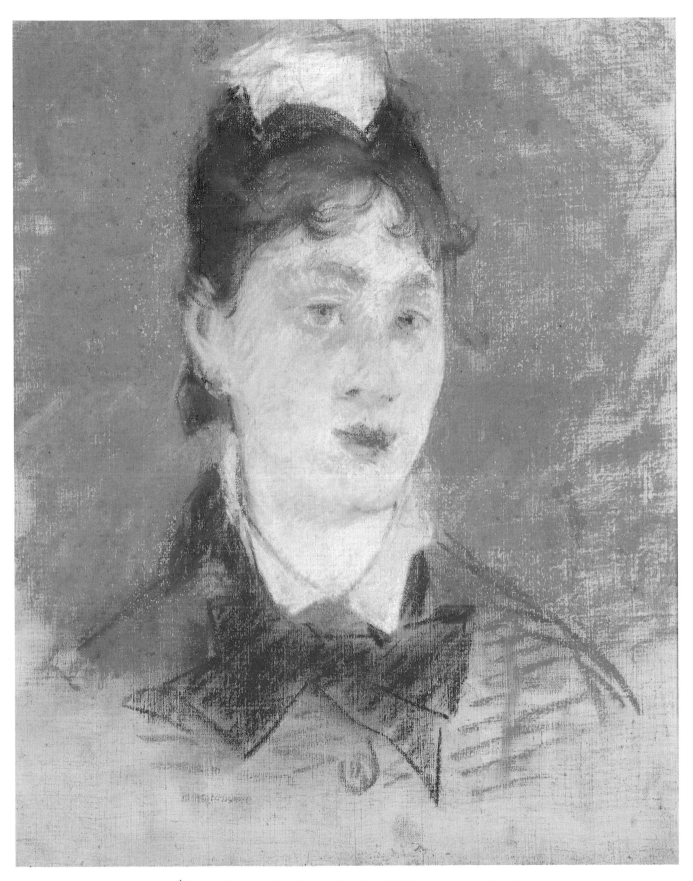

Édouard Manet (1832, Paris–1883, Rueil-Malmaison, near Paris)
## 12. GIRL IN A WING COLLAR
*Jeune Fille au col cassé, de face.* c. 1879–80
Pastel on canvas, 18¼ × 15⅛" (46.5 × 38.5 cm)
No. GR 155-101. Formerly collection Otto Krebs, Holzdorf

# ÉDOUARD MANET

## PORTRAIT OF MADEMOISELLE ISABELLE LEMONNIER

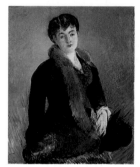

Isabelle Lemonnier was one of the models whom Édouard Manet painted most often; the number of portraits painted of her is second only to those of Berthe Morisot. Six of her portraits in oil and pastel are known, and also several watercolors. Almost all are notable for their effortlessness and rapid execution. Each time presented in a new gown, Isabelle was hardly likely to have posed for long. An exception of sorts, perhaps, is this work, one of the two largest in the entire series. It is obvious that the head was radically redone. The paint was scraped off and applied anew, perhaps more than once. Although it is known that Manet asked Mademoiselle Lemonnier to give him some photographs for work on the portraits, each of the paintings was undoubtedly done from life, and very quickly: the artist always hastened to render an impression from the model while it was fresh.

Isabelle Lemonnier was the daughter of a prominent jeweler from the Place Vendôme. Consequently, from the outset she was predestined to occupy a place in Parisian society, especially since her elder sister had married the publisher Georges Charpentier, and the Charpentiers' salon in the 1870s was prominent in the French capital's literary and artistic life (see the commentaries on plates 19 and 20). The Charpentiers actively supported the Impressionists, especially Pierre-Auguste Renoir. Manet came to the salon a number of times and was accepted there; in one of his letters to Isabelle he asks her to send greetings to her sister and the publisher.

Georges Charpentier had influence over the publication of the illustrated weekly *La Vie moderne*, headed by Émile Bergerat. In the gallery adjoining the office of this journal, exhibitions were organized to support the Impressionists. The first was devoted to Manet. It opened on May 8, 1880, and the artist showed his latest works. According to Manet's biographer Étienne Moreau-Nélaton, a portrait of Isabelle Lemonnier ("une certaine demoiselle Lemonnier") was in the exhibition (E. Moreau-Nélaton, *Manet raconté par lui-même* [Paris, 1926], vol. 2, p. 68). Moreau-Nélaton claimed that this was a portrait in pastels. The portraits in oils most likely were not shown during the artist's lifetime.

In the memoirs of Manet's friend Antonin Proust for 1878, when the World's Fair was held in Paris, there is a story of how Frederick Leighton, the president of the Royal Academy of Arts in London, visited Manet's studio; later they were joined by Arsène Ussey, publisher of the journal *L'Artiste* and an inspector of the Department of Fine Arts:

> Arsène Ussey, coming into the studio, asked:
> "Whose large portrait is that in oil?"
> "That is the portrait of Mademoiselle Lemonnier."
> "In your place, Manet, I would not touch this anymore."
> "In that regard I must say that for me it is extremely important that the sittings are not interrupted. When I take up something, I am most afraid that the model will disappoint me, that I will not be able to conduct such a number of sittings and under the conditions that I need. The model comes, poses, and then disappears, saying, 'Well, now he can finish without me!' But that's not the case; it is impossible to finish alone; it has to be finished that same day. But usually you have to begin again, and then it stretches to many days."
> (A. Proust, *Édouard Manet: Souvenirs* [Paris, 1913])

If we are to believe Proust that this episode really did take place in 1878, the temptation arises to relate his comment to this portrait from the Krebs collection, first because it is large, and second because the artist was forced here to repaint the face. It is more likely, however, that the Krebs portrait was painted later, and that the reference in Antonin Proust's memoirs is to a work of similar dimensions with the same name, which could have been painted at that time (*Portrait of Mademoiselle Isabelle Lemonnier*, Rouart/Wildenstein no. 304).

There is, however, no documented confirmation of exactly when this painting was done. Rouart and Wildenstein, in their catalogue of Manet's works, have dated all the portraits of Isabelle Lemonnier to 1879, which cannot always be granted. Thus, the organizers of the largest exhibition of Manet's work, which took place in Paris and New York in 1983, in their very impressive catalogue gave the painting period for *Portrait of Isabelle Lemonnier with a Muff* (fig. 1; Dallas Museum of Fine Art) as 1879–82 (F. Cachin and Ch. Moffett, *Manet* [Galeries Nationales du Grand Palais, Paris; The Metropolitan Museum of Art, New York, 1983], no. 190). Moreau-Nélaton dated that painting to 1880. Meanwhile, it is quite possible that the Dallas portrait was executed at approximately the same time as the present work. In both cases the model is shown with the same fur coat. Knowing what great importance this young woman attributed to clothes, it is hard to imagine that she came to the artist wearing the same outfit for very long. The fur coat provides some grounds for narrowing the dating of both portraits to the winter of 1879–80.

Rouart and Wildenstein, in publishing the portraits of Isabelle Lemonnier in their catalogue (no. 299–304), noted that the works had been given different dates in other publications. They themselves, however, did not try to establish a sequence in assigning all the pictures to 1879: no. 299, *The Girl with the White Kerchief* (fig. 2; Ny Carlsberg Glyptotek, Copenhagen); no. 300, *Woman with a Gold Pin* (private collection, United States); no. 301, *Portrait of Isabelle Lemonnier* (formerly collection Otto Krebs); no. 302, *Isabelle Lemonnier with a Muff* (Dallas Museum of Art); no. 303, *Mademoiselle Isabelle Lemonnier Seated* (William Coxe Wright collection, St. Davids, Pennsylvania); no. 304, *Portrait of Mademoiselle Isabelle Lemonnier* (private collection, Switzerland; formerly collection Berthe Morisot). It can be surmised that the last two portraits listed are the earliest in the series, which

was completed by the portrait of the girl in the fur coat. They were painted in the studio at 77, rue d'Amsterdam, where Manet worked in April 1879.

Aside from the smallest painting, *Mademoiselle Isabelle Lemonnier Seated* (no. 303), all the rest were conceived in more or less standard portrait formats. In them, the figure is shown sitting, frontally, sometimes with a slight turn, framed to below the waist. The clothing is rendered quickly throughout and quite summarily, with the expectation that it would not be repainted later. The face was another matter. The artist's efforts were concentrated there, and not on the figure, in an effort to capture each new nuance of expression, so that taken together this group of paintings forms a kind of series.

Manet was a man easily captivated. There was no question that he very much liked Isabelle Lemonnier. However, their relations did not have, nor could they have, any true depth. Isabelle was flattered, in a way, that she was making an impression on an artist much talked about in society, but of course she did not wish any more than some quite innocent and fashionable signs of attention. Manet, too, could hardly have expected more: there was the great difference in their ages, his prominent place in society, the code of manners to which he adhered, and, most important, his illness.

He was already seriously ill at the time of the exhibition at the gallery of *La Vie moderne*. At his doctor's advice, he began hydrotherapy treatment, for which he settled in Bellevue, not far from Paris. Manet was grateful to Mademoiselle Lemonnier that she allowed him to write to her: "Since you have permitted it, I will write often." Twenty-one notes from the artist have been preserved. They form a rare collection, published many years later (*Édouard Manet: Letters with Aquarelles* [New York, 1944]).

Wrote Moreau-Nélaton: "During his stay in Bellevue, his thoughts were endlessly carried away by her, entrusted to brief notes, decorated with tiny watercolors, or supplemented with some elegant delicacies: there would be either a flower, or a fruit, or a portrait of Zizi, the cat, whom everybody at home loved, or a portrait of the young woman herself, the sketch of an idea of how she led resort life in Luc-sur-Mer, one time in a beach dress, another in a diving suit. The tone of these notes is the tone of a conversation spoken in joking ease" (E. Moreau-Nélaton, *Manet raconté par lui-même* [Paris, 1926], vol. 2, p. 70).

These letters do not constitute a correspondence; the notes all went in one direction. Manet used them as a means to keep from falling into depression. He joked because it gave him courage. He could even allow himself some simple impromptu lyrics: "For Isabelle, / This yellow plum. / Who is most beautiful? / It's Isabelle [À Isabelle, / Cette mirabelle. / Et la plus belle, / C'est Isabelle]." Sometimes between Manet's lines something more can be glimpsed. "I won't write to you anymore—you don't answer me at all. . . . Either you're very busy or you're very bad. But I don't have the heart to be angry at you."

By comparison with the drawings in the letters, the portraits in oil are more deliberately conceived, and though they may have been painted in a more or less relaxed manner, there is no lightheartedness in them. Effortlessness came less frequently to Manet now, and in the portrait from the Krebs collection one can sense how keenly Manet desired to achieve it, destroying what was just painted and starting anew at the next sitting. "The sittings to which my grandmother submitted in order to please Manet, who was then quite ill," wrote Isabelle Lemonnier's grandson, Michel Robida, "were extremely exhausting. 'Manet could not draw,' she would tell us with her accustomed verve; 'he was forever starting my portraits over again. Before my eyes he destroyed I don't know how many sketches. I am certain that he would have given them to me if I had asked. But I already had so many portraits' " (M. Robida, *Le Salon Charpentier et les impressionistes* [Paris, 1958], p. 119; cited from the exhibition catalogue *Manet* [Paris and New York, 1983], no. 190).

PROVENANCE: Comte Armand Doria, Paris; 1910, Auguste Pellerin, Paris; Galerie Durand-Ruel, Paris; Galerie Bernheim-Jeune, Paris; 1913, Fakroeus; Baron Marczell de Nemes, Budapest; Knoedler Gallery, New York; Otto Krebs, Holzdorf.

EXHIBITIONS: 1916, Paris, "Exposition de la collection Pellerin," Galerie Bernheim-Jeune, no. 14; 1926, New York, Knoedler Gallery; 1926, Amsterdam, "Exposition rétrospective d'art français," no. 68; 1928, Berlin, "Ausstellung Édouard Manet: Gemälde, Pastelle, Aquarelle, Zeichnungen," Galerie Matthiesen, no. 46.

LITERATURE: *Catalogue de la vente Doria* (Paris, May 1899), no. 189 (as *Femme à l'épingle d'or*); T. Duret, *Histoire d'Édouard Manet et de son oeuvre* (Paris, 1902), no. 236, p. 252 (reprod.); E. Waldmann, "Édouard Manet in der Sammlung Pellerin," *Kunst und Künstler*, vol. 8, no. 8 (May 1910), pp. 387–88; E. Moreau-Nélaton, *Manet raconté par lui-même* (Paris, 1926), no. 277; J. Guiffrey, *Lettres illus-*

trées d'Édouard Manet (Paris, 1929), pl. 2; A. Tabarant, *Manet* (Paris, 1931), no. 311; P. Colin, *Édouard Manet* (Paris, 1932), pl. 74 (as *Isabelle Lemonnier tenant son chapeau*); P. Jamot and G. Wildenstein, *Manet: Catalogue critique* (Paris, 1932), no. 373; G. Jedlicka, *Édouard Manet* (Erlenbach and Zurich, 1941), pp. 304–7; *Édouard Manet: Letters with Aquarelles* (New York, 1944); A. Tabarant, *Manet et ses oeuvres* (Paris, 1947), pp. 362–63; M. Robida, *Le Salon Charpentier et les impressionistes* (Paris, 1958), p. 118, pl. 18; *L'Opera completa di Édouard Manet*, Introduction by D. Rouart, Catalogue by S. Oriente (Milan, 1970), no. 282; D. Rouart and G. Wildenstein, *Édouard Manet: Catalogue raisonné* (Lausanne, 1975), vol. 1, no. 301; E. Darragon, *Manet* (Paris, 1989), pp. 227, 318, 337–39, 374; E. Darragon, *Manet* (Paris, 1991), p. 330; O. Friedrich, *Olympia: Paris in the Age of Manet* (New York, 1992), pp. 283–84.

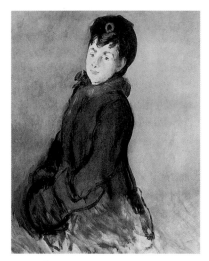

*Fig. 1. Édouard Manet.* Portrait of Isabelle Lemonnier with a Muff. *1879–80. Dallas Museum of Art. Gift of Mr. and Mrs. Algur Meadows and the Meadows Foundation, Incorporated*

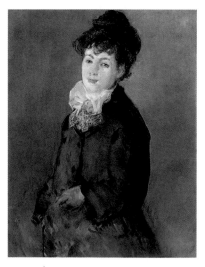

*Fig. 2. Édouard Manet.* The Girl with the White Kerchief. *1879. Ny Carlsberg Glyptotek, Copenhagen*

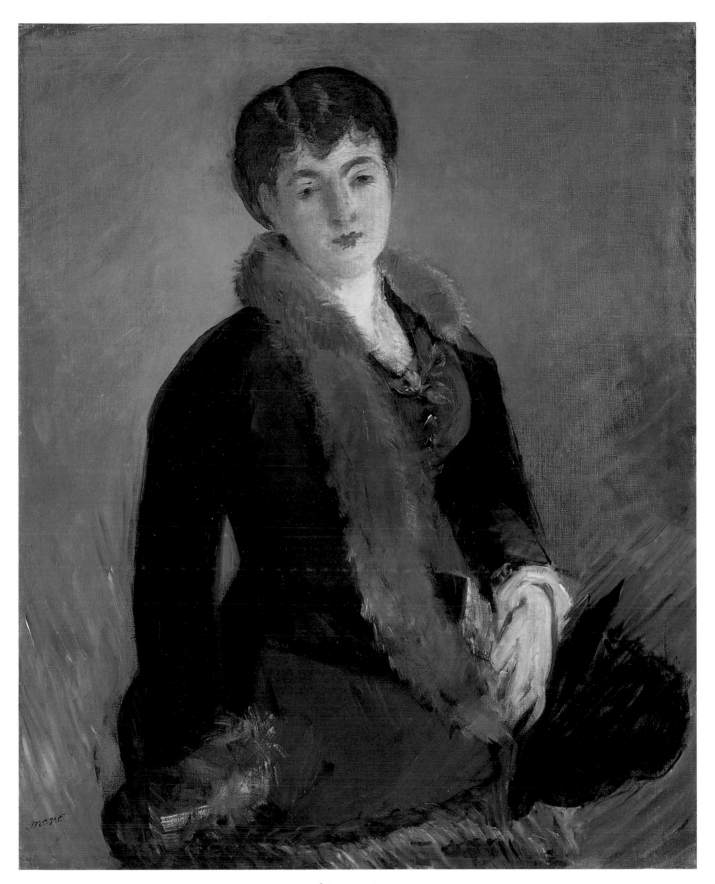

Édouard Manet
## 13. PORTRAIT OF MADEMOISELLE ISABELLE LEMONNIER
*Portrait de Mademoiselle Isabelle Lemonnier.* c. 1879–80
Oil on canvas, 40 × 32" (101.8 × 81.5 cm). Signed lower left: "Manet"
No. 3KP 230. Formerly collection Otto Krebs, Holzdorf

# HILAIRE · GERMAIN · EDGAR DEGAS

## INTERIOR WITH TWO FIGURES

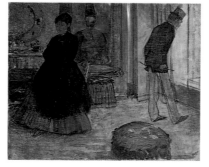

Paul-André Lemoisne, the author of the catalogue raisonné of Degas's work, called this painting *Portraits (Madame Ducros)* and dated it to 1857–59. He based this dating on information received from Miss Musson of New Orleans (the Mussons were relatives of Degas, Herman Musson being his uncle on his mother's side) and also from Degas's granddaughter, Mrs. Millaudon. The Millaudons and the Ducroses, who had married into each other's families, were friends and neighbors of the Mussons in New Orleans.

In 1857–58, Madame Ducros and her son, daughter, and son-in-law, and also the Millaudons with their daughters, went on a trip to Europe, first to Paris and then to Rome, where Degas met with them and made several portraits. Lemoisne, who considers the present painting a portrait, supposed that the figure on the right was Monsieur Ducros or his son, and referred to a letter from Auguste de Gas to the artist, congratulating his son on the portrait studies of Angèle and Gabrielle, the Millaudon daughters, but saying he was "unhappy with the three other portraits of Monsieur and Madame Ducros" (P.-A. Lemoisne, *Degas et son oeuvre* [Paris, 1946], vol. 2, p. 18). If we are to agree with Lemoisne, *Interior with Two Figures* must be acknowledged as virtually the artist's first attempt at a double portrait. In his exhaustive catalogue, Lemoisne cites two works related to *Interior with Two Figures*: a study for a painting he gave the exact same title, *Portraits (Madame Ducros),* with the figures only sketched in (formerly Aubry collection, Paris, present whereabouts unknown; Lemoisne no. 42); and a study of the figure at the left in *Standing Woman in a Black Cape (Madame Ducros)* (Rouart collection, Paris; Lemoisne no. 43).

Lemoisne's opinion was challenged by Jean Sutherland Boggs and James Byrnes. Byrnes dated *Interior with Two Figures* a decade later, to about 1867–69, and supposed that the man and woman in the painting were Madame Millaudon and her husband, shown in a millinery; madame perhaps came to select a hat for her daughter Angèle's wedding, while her bored husband looks out the window. Consequently, the drawing of Madame Ducros seated (Thaw collection, New York) undoubtedly preceded the painting Byrnes considers, albeit with some doubt, to be of Madame Millaudon, and requires redating from 1857 to 1867–69. In any case, the question he has raised must now be taken into account, since first of all, it is known that Degas did paint Madame Millaudon, and secondly, the round-faced lady in *Interior with Two Figures* does look like her.

The evidence for revising the old Lemoisne dating was several drawings from Degas's album preserved in the Bibliothèque Nationale, Paris, later published by Theodore Reff (*The Notebooks of Edgar Degas* [New York, 2nd ed., 1985]). Degas used the album in Paris and Normandy in 1867–74, and it contains preliminary drawings of the female (fig. 3; Reff, notebook no. 22, p. 117) and male (fig. 1; Reff, notebook no. 22, p. 119) figures in the painting, and also a study of the entire composition (fig. 2; Reff, notebook no. 23, p. 34). Reff dates the latter to 1867–74.

Boggs considers that the painting was done no earlier than 1869 and claims that both the style and the costumes in the preliminary drawings presuppose the later date. A perceptive researcher into Degas's portraiture, Boggs does not see this painting as a portrait: "Neither this painting, nor *The Rape,* which also indirectly relates to the theme of marriage, can be considered portraits" (J. S. Boggs, *Portraits by Degas* [Berkeley and Los Angeles, 1962], p. 91). Although in *Interior with Two Figures,* Degas stopped half way, without reaching the degree of realization of the subject or the overall finished quality of *The Rape,* a painting of about 1868–69 (fig. 4; Philadelphia Museum of Art), which the artist himself also called *Interior,* it is nonetheless reasonable to see some similarity between these two works. It is now considered certain by many scholars that in painting *The Rape,* Degas was reacting to Émile Zola's novel *Thérèse Raquin* of 1867. It is quite possible that in this case, too, he could have proceeded from some literary basis. Both pictures may have been conceived precisely as interiors. In the present picture, from the Siemens collection, by the way, the figure of the man was added later. In the same Degas sketchbook (number 22) where we find study drawings for the picture, there is also a drawings of the empty interior for *The Rape.*

Upon close examination of the painting, Byrnes's idea of a millinery becomes unlikely, not least because there are no hats or hatboxes anywhere in sight. Rather, this is a boudoir in a wealthy household. To the left, there is a fireplace with a very effectively depicted fire. Above it there is an oval mirror, fashionable in the late 1860s. This is not at all the type of mirror used by milliners. Between the man and the woman there is a large portrait in a heavy gilded frame—not a mirror, as was mistakenly believed by commentators who could see the painting only in mediocre photographs. The portrait is surely there for a reason, but what that reason may be is impossible to say. The person depicted in the portrait looks somewhat mysterious in his tall hat. And there is another inexplicable thing about the interior—the door next to the window, which opens onto a narrow corridor. Such details are unnecessary in a portrait, but can acquire meaning in a painting of another kind.

The composition of *Interior with Two Figures* is quite laconic, not to say enigmatic. The darkest spots in the painting—the lady's cape and the gentleman's coat—immediately draw our attention to the characters. Their costumes are unusual for an interior: the man is wearing a top hat and has a cane in his hand; the woman has her cape. The couple is dressed for a walk or a visit, but for some reason they are lingering inside, or perhaps they have just arrived. What has

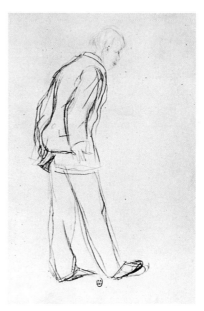

*Fig. 1. Hilaire-Germain-Edgar Degas. Study for* Interior with Two Figures. *c. 1869. Bibliothèque Nationale, Paris*

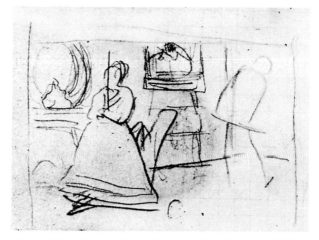

*Fig. 2. Hilaire-Germain-Edgar Degas. Study for* Interior with Two Figures. *c. 1869. Bibliothèque Nationale, Paris*

produced this uncomfortable silence, as the spouses look away from each other? The fact that the scene takes place in a boudoir makes it all the more dramatic and psychologically complex.

Other elements of the interior seem full of meaning: the fire is easily read as an emblem of passion, while the empty window at which the man is staring can be taken as a sign of his blank indifference. The male figure gave the artist a good deal of trouble; it is clear that this area of the picture was scraped down and repainted. The canvas looks somewhat unfinished, but the fact of Degas's signature indicates that he did not intend to add anything further to what he had already said.

The hidden conflict of *Interior with Two Figures* is most likely related to the artist's understanding of the problematics of sex. His attitude toward women was far from simple: often sarcastic and arrogant, at the same time he was no misogynist; he liked women's company, yet remained a bachelor his whole life. In painting *Interior with Two Figures* and *The Rape,* he depicted the fundamental relations between the sexes without any romantic illusions. In these two interiors, the figures do not communicate and are moved apart from each other. Their isolation is a sign of alienation—casual in one case, dramatic in the other.

PROVENANCE: Georges Viau, Paris; Friedrich Siemens, Berlin.

LITERATURE: P.-A. Lemoisne, *Degas et son oeuvre* (Paris, 1946), no. 41 (as *Portraits [Madame Ducros]*); J. S. Boggs, "Degas Notebooks at the Bibliothèque Nationale, III, Groupe C, 1863–1886," *The Burlington Magazine*, vol. 100, no. 664 (July 1958), pp. 243, 244; J. S. Boggs, *Portraits by Degas* (Berkeley and Los Angeles, 1962), pp. 91, 116–17; J. Rewald, J. B. Byrnes, and J. S. Boggs, *Edgar Degas: His Family and Friends in New Orleans* (New Orleans, 1965), p. 68; *L'Opera completa di Degas*, Introduction by F. Russoli, Catalogue by F. Minervino (Milan, 1970), no. 126 (as *The Ducros Spouses*, 1857–59); E. de Keyser, *Degas: Réalité et métaphore* (Louvain-la-Neuve, 1981), p. 54; T. Reff, *The Notebooks of Edgar Degas* (New York, 2nd ed., 1985), pp. 34, 117, 119.

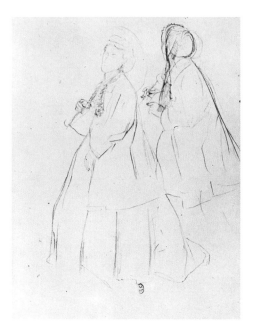

Fig. 3. Hilaire-Germain-Edgar Degas. Study for Interior with Two Figures. *c. 1869. Bibliothèque Nationale, Paris*

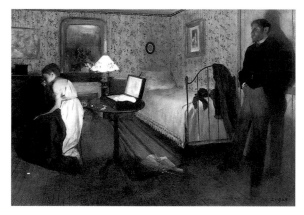

Fig. 4. Hilaire-Germain-Edgar Degas. Interior (The Rape). *c. 1868–69. Philadelphia Museum of Art. The Henry P. McIlhenny Collection in memory of Frances P. McIlhenny*

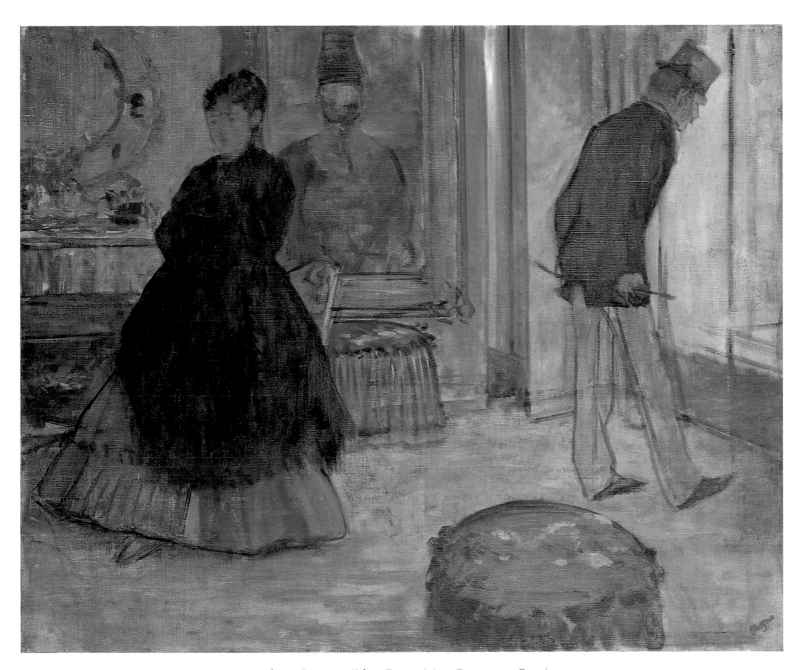

Hilaire-Germain-Edgar Degas (1834, Paris–1917, Paris)
## 14. INTERIOR WITH TWO FIGURES
*Intérieur avec deux personnages.* c. 1869
Oil on canvas. 23¼ × 28¾" (59.5 × 73.2 cm)
Signed lower right: "Degas"
No. 3K 1400. Formerly collection Friedrich Siemens, Berlin

# HILAIRE · GERMAIN · EDGAR DEGAS

## THE DANCER

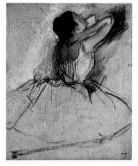

Paul-André Lemoisne considered this study the embodiment of the original idea for the figure of the dancer sitting on the piano in *The Dance Class* of 1874 (fig. 3; Musée d'Orsay, Paris; Lemoisne no. 341). This is not a convincing supposition, however; although the head and torso of the Musée d'Orsay dancer are turned as they are in this study, the positions of the arms are quite different. There is much better reason to link the study with *The Rehearsal of the Ballet on Stage* of about 1874 (two versions hang in the Metropolitan Museum of Art in New York, one in *peinture à l'essence* and the other in pastel; see fig. 1), where the central figure in the foreground is depicted with precisely this gesture. In *The Dance Class*, the ballerina is seated and reaches behind to her shoulder strap from below, rather than from above as in *The Dancer* and *The Rehearsal of the Ballet on Stage*.

Of the two New York versions of *The Rehearsal of the Ballet on Stage*, the pastel from the Havemeyer collection (Lemoisne no. 498) is closer to the present *Dancer*. The authors of the catalogue of the most recent major Degas exhibition (J. S. Boggs, D. W. Druick, H. Loyrette, M. Pantazzi, and G. Tinterow, *Degas* [Galeries Nationales du Grand Palais, Paris; National Gallery of Canada, Ottawa; The Metropolitan Museum of Art, New York, 1988–89]) tentatively dated both New York versions of *The Rehearsal of the Ballet on Stage* to 1874. These were undoubtedly preceded by a painting in oil of the same name, from 1874 (fig. 2; Musée d'Orsay, Paris), but with figures depicted somewhat differently, which was shown at the first exhibition of the Impressionists. It remains unclear when exactly the New York variations were done. The present study from the Krebs collection perhaps occupies an interim position between the *Rehearsal* painting and the two variations. In all three

*Rehearsal* works the dancer is at the lower center in a white tutu, with her elbows out and forward; in the pastel she throws forward one leg, while in the Musée d'Orsay painting, she is sitting on a bench. In the Krebs collection study there is a degree of dynamism beyond what is necessary to depict a resting ballerina, but which informs the compositional structure of the pastel.

The gesture in *The Dancer* was of interest to Degas; he preserved it, with modifications, in several drawings, including in pages from the Cabinet des Dessins at the Louvre (at a recent Degas retrospective they were dated to 1873). It is astonishing that with essentially the same movement, Degas could express such different feelings, whether the ballerina's fatigue (yawning, thrusting her hands behind her head), or the fastidious adjustment of her costume or hairdo, or the urgent motion of the dance itself. The rich potential of such transformations was significant, tempting Degas to keep returning to them.

Like few other paintings, *The Dancer* compels one to turn to the famous entry in Edmond de Goncourt's diary for February 13, 1874:

*Yesterday I spent my afternoon in the atelier of a strange painter named Degas. After many attempts, experiments, and thrusts in every direction, he has fallen in love with modern subjects and has set his heart on laundry girls and danseuses.*

*I cannot find his choice bad, I who in* Manette Salomon *sang the praises of these two professions as furnishing a modern artist with the most pictorial models of the women of today. Indeed, pink flesh in white linen and a milky fog of muslin makes the most charming pretext for pale, tender colors. Degas showed me his laundry girls while speaking their language* and explaining in technical terms the leaning on the iron, the circular movement, etc. . . . Then it was the turn of the ballerinas. We were in their greenroom, with the legs of a danseuse descending a little staircase outlined fantastically against the light from a window, with the bright splash of red on a tartan in the midst of all the ballooning white clouds, and with a ridiculous ballet master serving as a rascally foil; and there before me, caught from reality, was the graceful twisting of the movements and gestures of those little mon-

key girls. The painter presents his pictures to you while from time to time adding to his commentary the mimicry of—to use a danseuse's language—a choreographic développement or an arabesque; and it is really very amusing to see him, with his arms rounded, mix the aesthetic of a dance professor with that of a painter while talking about the delicate muddiness of Velázquez and the silhouetting talent of Mantegna. (translated in R. McMullen, *Degas: His Life, Times, and Work* [London, 1985], pp. 241–42)

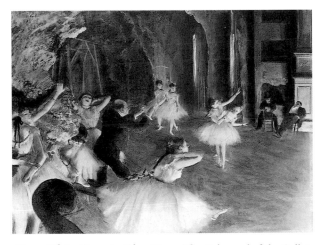

*Fig. 1. Hilaire-Germain-Edgar Degas.* The Rehearsal of the Ballet on Stage. *c. 1874. The Metropolitan Museum of Art, New York. The H. O. Havemeyer Collection. Bequest of Mrs. H. O. Havemeyer*

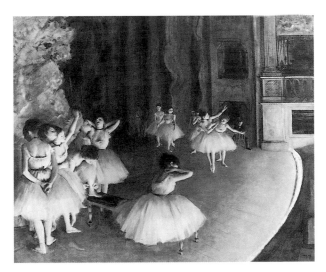

*Fig. 2. Hilaire-Germain-Edgar Degas.* The Rehearsal of the Ballet on Stage. *1874. Musée d'Orsay, Paris*

Goncourt came away from his visit to Degas's studio with mixed feelings. On the one hand, he admitted that he had never met an artist who better captured the spirit of modern life. On the other hand, seeing him as a neurotic, he expressed doubt that Degas would manage to create anything "whole," saying, "He seems to have a very restless mind." Most likely, "whole" meant different things to the writer and the painter. At any rate, Degas, who had already sufficiently tested his powers to create finished works according to the classical recipes, did not conceive of integrity outside the flow of life, with its ceaseless movement and transformations, an idea that connected him to the Impressionists.

PROVENANCE: Atelier de Degas; Nunes et Fiquet, Paris; Otto Krebs, Holzdorf.

LITERATURE: *Catalogue des tableaux, pastels et dessins par Edgar Degas et provenant de son atelier dont la 3e vente aux enchères publiques, après décès de l'artiste, aura lieu à Paris, Galerie Georges Petit, 7, 8 et 9 avril 1919* (Paris, 1919), no. 25 (reprod.); P.-A. Lemoisne, *Degas et son oeuvre* (Paris, 1946), vol. 1, no. 342; *L'Opera completa di Degas*, Introduction by F. Russoli, Catalogue by F. Minervino (Milan, 1970), no. 480 (incorrectly identified as the first idea for *The Dance Class*).

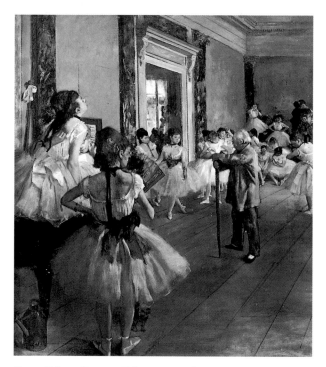

*Fig. 3. Hilaire-Germain-Edgar Degas.* The Dance Class. *1874. Musée d'Orsay, Paris*

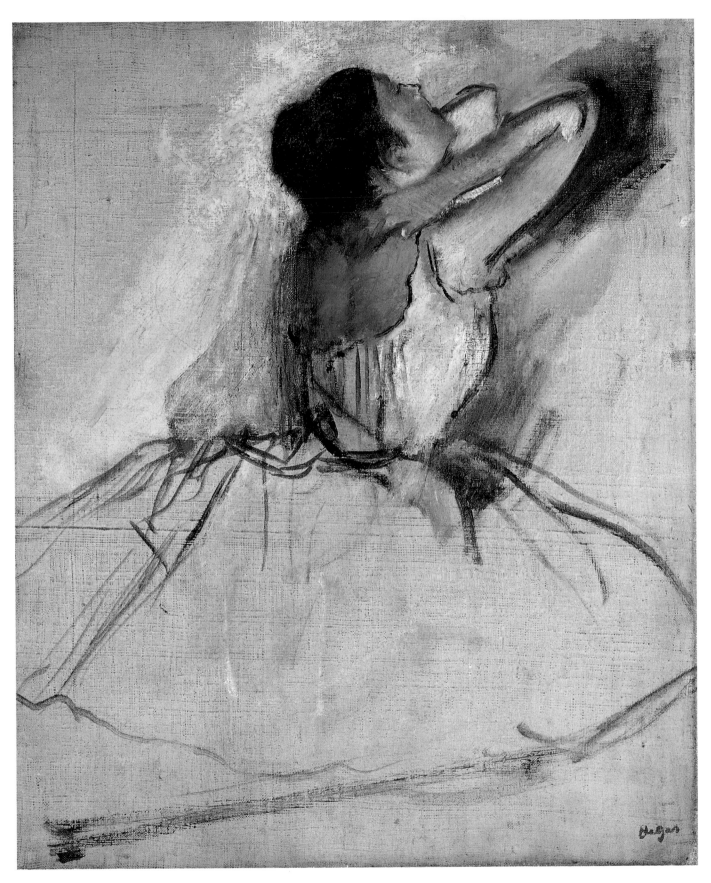

Hilaire-Germain-Edgar Degas
## 15. THE DANCER
*Danseuse.* c. 1874
Oil on canvas, 16 × 12⅞" (40.5 × 32.7 cm). Signed lower right: "Degas"
Stamped on the reverse: "Jerome Otto" No. 3KP 556. Formerly collection Otto Krebs, Holzdorf

# HILAIRE·GERMAIN·EDGAR DEGAS

## PLACE DE LA CONCORDE (VISCOUNT LEPIC AND HIS DAUGHTERS CROSSING THE PLACE DE LA CONCORDE)

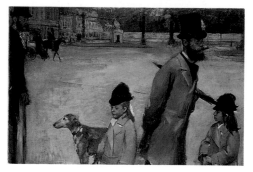

It does not seem at all an accident that this painting is known under two titles. On the one hand, it is a portrait of Viscount Lepic and his two daughters, one of the most unusual portraits in all of Degas's works; on the other hand, it is a scene of Parisian life in which the cityscape plays too active a role to serve merely as background. There is a study drawing showing the buildings in the background, on the rue de Rivoli, adjacent to the Place de la Concorde (fig. 1; T. Reff, *The Notebooks of Edgar Degas* [New York, 2nd ed., 1985], vol. 2, notebook no. 26, p. 96). Along with Lepic, his daughters, and chance passersby, the Place de la Concorde, too, seems to become a protagonist. Much of the canvas is devoted to its open expanse, which, unlike the Place in later times, is very quiet and almost empty, giving the painting a mood unexpected for a portrait. A painting such as this is created not so much to reproduce a particular subject as to render intuitive, private moments. Although it is not clear what Degas himself called his painting, there is reason to believe that it was *Place de la Concorde*, the title used by the Galerie Durand-Ruel (the gallery's label is on the back of the painting, printed "Place de la Concorde").

The chief figure in the painting is Ludovic-Napoléon Lepic (1839–1889), an artist whose work was subsequently forgotten. An aristocrat, grandson of Napoléon's general, and son of a Bonapartist general, he was not interested in a military career, preferring the arts—painting and sculpture, but most of all engraving. He entered the École des Beaux-Arts, studying first with Alexandre Cabanel and then Charles Gleyre during the same time that the future Impressionists—Claude Monet, Pierre-Auguste Renoir, Alfred Sisley, and Frédéric Bazille—appeared.

Soon after joining Gleyre's studio, Bazille wrote to his family that his best friends were Monet and Viscount Lepic. Apparently, Lepic's circle of acquaintances was wide; unlike his new friends from the École des Beaux-Arts, he already knew Degas by that time.

It was none other than Degas who persuaded Lepic to take part in the first exhibition of the Impressionists, who had constituted themselves as the so-called Société Anonyme, in 1874. Lepic contributed four watercolor landscapes and the engravings *Caesar* and *Jupiter* with the subtitle *Portrait of a Dog* (Lepic was an ardent dog lover, as one might suspect from *Place de la Concorde*). Of course, next to Monet, Degas, and Renoir, Lepic remained unnoticed, especially because the public hastening to the show, held in the photographer Nadar's studio, wanted to see something scandalous. Lepic was represented at the second exhibition of the Impressionists by thirty-six entries: watercolors from Italy and Normandy, engravings imbued with Dutch impressions, and a dozen or two paintings and sketches, the vast majority of which were once again landscapes.

Later, when the Impressionists decided to show no longer at the Salon, Lepic ended his cooperation with them. The style of his painting wavered between Impressionism and the realism of the preceding generation, though not without some Romantic elements. The leaders of the Impressionist movement had varying opinions of Lepic and his art. In a letter to Camille Pissarro in 1881, Gustave Caillebotte wrote that Lepic had no talent (see J. Rewald, *The History of Impressionism* [New York, 1980], p. 448). However, the letter was burdened with polemics concerning the dispute with Degas and his supporters over the sixth exhi-

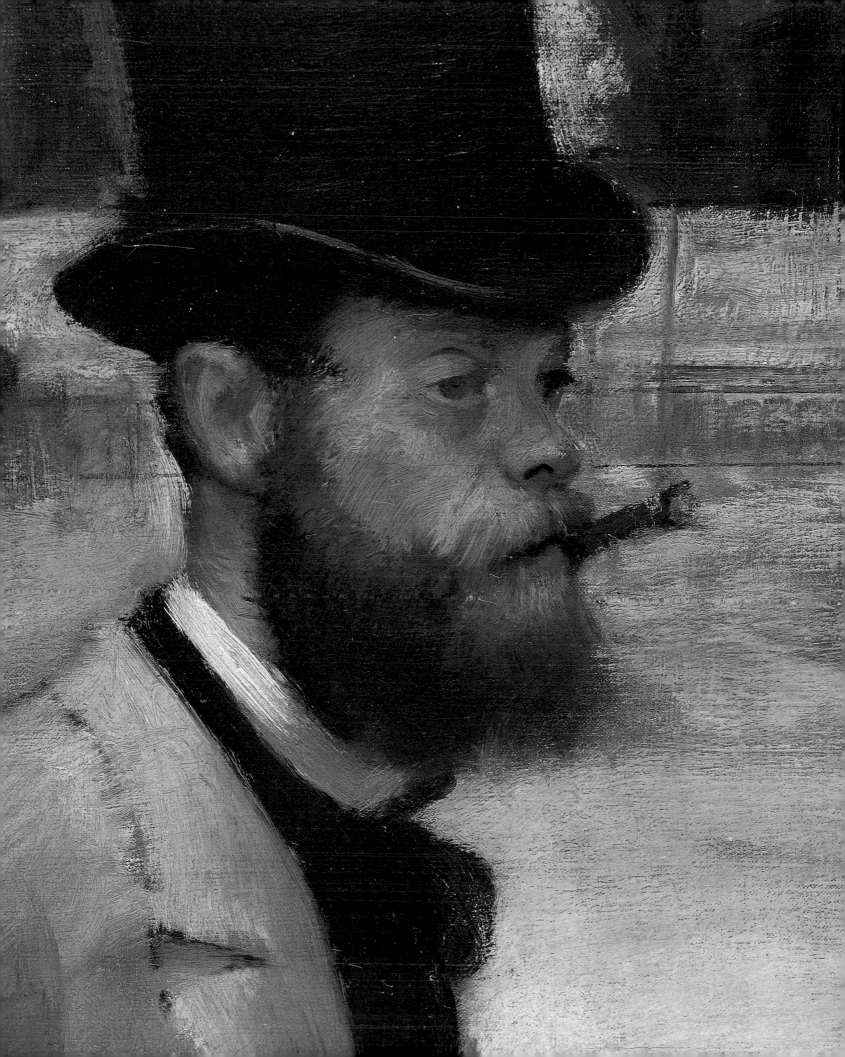

bition of the Impressionists and cannot be considered objective.

Be that as it may, Lepic did have his connoisseurs, even in the leading circles. His works were given an exhibition at the premises of *La Vie moderne,* the weekly published with the sponsorship of Georges Charpentier. And Degas valued Lepic's engravings highly. In 1874, shortly before painting *Place de la Concorde,* he worked with Lepic to make his first monotype, a picture of the famous choreographer Jules Perrot of the Opéra during a rehearsal (both artists loved the ballet). Both names—Degas and Lepic—are signed on the work, an extremely rare occurrence. Degas learned the fine points of the technique of monotype from his friend, and this alone would be enough to prevent the name of Lepic from vanishing completely from the history of art. He experimented a great deal in engraving and invented a special technique called *eau-forte-mobile*. On the whole, the Viscount's artistic interests were notable for their great diversity. In 1872, he founded in Aix-les-Bains, in Savoie, a museum subsequently called the Musée Faure, and became its first curator. Such meritorious efforts earned for Lepic the red ribbon of the Légion d'Honneur that is so clearly visible in this painting.

Lepic had become acquainted very early with Degas and also with his brothers. They went horseback riding together, and it is believed to be Lepic whom Degas painted in *Gentleman's Race* (Musée d'Orsay, Paris). The picture is dated 1862, but was repainted over twenty years later, though it is very difficult to determine its true date. Degas also portrayed Lepic in his second version of *The Ballet from "Robert le Diable"* of 1876 (fig. 2; Victoria and Albert Museum, London; Lemoisne no. 391), where he is shown sitting in the second row, whether napping or engrossed in the music we cannot tell—though in either case he clearly is not following the lively dancing on stage. The artist is being ironic in having a ballet lover react in this way to the famous scene from Giacomo Meyerbeer's opera, in which the ghosts of a convent of nuns rise from their graves. The unusual portrait of Lepic in *The Ballet from "Robert le Diable"* is to that extent comparable to his portrayal in *Place de la Concorde,* though there the irony is more muted.

In *Place de la Concorde,* Viscount Lepic is presented as the father in a family group. He first figured in

this capacity when shown in the Zurich portrait called *Ludovic Lepic and His Daughters* of about 1871 (fig. 3; Stiftung E. G. Bührle, Zurich; Lemoisne no. 272). The two daughters—Eylau (named in honor of the famous battle of 1807 near Eylau) and Janine—were born in 1868 and 1869, respectively. In the Zurich painting, where Degas's interest seems drawn more to Eylau (the three-year-old girl has a very intelligent expression and the bearing of a little woman), Lepic himself is given the somewhat ridiculous role of puppeteer, and his daughters, two pretty little puppets. In *Place de la Concorde* everything is different. Both girls have become entirely independent; the scene creates the impression that they and their father have little to do with each other.

Besides the Zurich *Ludovic Lepic and His Daughters,* there are two more paintings by Degas preserving the figure of his friend. Soon after *Place de la Concorde* came a double portrait with their common friend Desboutin the engraver, *Desboutin and Lepic* of about 1876 (Musée des Beaux-Arts, Nice), and a year before the death of the Viscount, there is a pastel, *Ludovic Lepic with His Dog* of about 1888 (fig. 6; formerly collection Georges Viau, Paris; Lemoisne no. 950). As befitting a true aristocrat, Viscount Lepic was passionate about thoroughbred horses and pedigreed dogs; when Mary Cassatt wanted a dog, Degas asked Lepic to help her.

Along with the Lepic family, another figure is present in the foreground of *Place de la Concorde.* Very little is said about him in the abundant literature on Degas's works, except that this figure is cropped at the picture's edge with all the boldness of which the artist was capable; Degas had mastered the fragmentation found in Japanese woodcuts, but which was unusual for European art. This passerby is cast in a supporting role: by lagging behind, he is supposed to balance the figures on the right side of the composition and accentuate their movement. It is rarely noticed, however, that this figure is no less individualized than Viscount Lepic himself, and is no less a portrait. We do not know the circumstances behind the genesis of this painting nor the earlier one in the Bührle collection, though it is known that the Zurich painting at one time belonged to Lepic. Whether painted at the subject's request or on Degas's initiative, it was in any event conceived as a portrait,

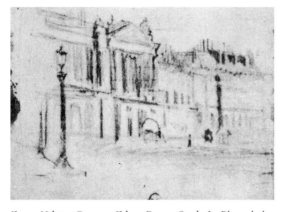

Fig. 1. Hilaire-German-Edgar Degas. Study for Place de la
Concorde. Notebook no. 26. Bibliothèque Nationale, Paris

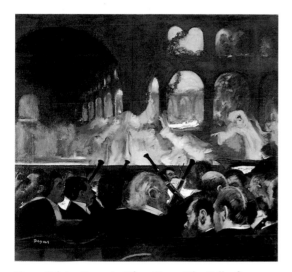

Fig. 2. Hilaire-Germain-Edgar Degas. The Ballet from
"Robert le Diable." 1876. The Board of Trustees of the
Victoria and Albert Museum, London

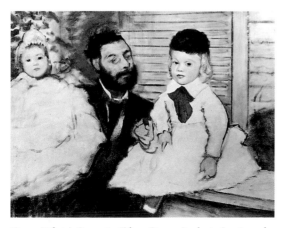

Fig. 3. Hilaire-Germain-Edgar Degas. Ludovic Lepic and
His Daughters. c. 1871. Stiftung E. G. Bührle, Zurich

with all that is particular to that genre.

Place de la Concorde never belonged to Lepic, and
it can safely be said that it was not intended for him. It
remained in the possession of Degas, who for some
reason did not want to exhibit it, and then was sold to
Durand-Ruel. Not meant to be a portrait of Lepic for
Lepic, the work was undertaken as one of the scenes
of contemporary Paris on which in the mid-1870s were
concentrated the best energies of the Impressionists,
and which to a significant extent had been anticipated
by Édouard Manet, as in The Balcony of 1868–69
(Musée d'Orsay, Paris) or The Railroad of 1872–73
(National Gallery of Art, Washington, D.C.).
Caillebotte and Renoir, too, were developing in the
same direction. Like Degas, they crossed the bound-
aries between genres easily. The portraitlike nature of
their Parisian figure compositions gives their canvases
a quality of immediacy, instilling the lively feeling that
an artist has when he paints those close to him.
Caillebotte's Young Man at His Window of 1875 (private collection, Paris; M. Berhaut, Caillebotte:
Catalogue raisonné de l'oeuvre [Paris, 1976], no. 25)
depicts his brother; his Pont de l'Europe of 1876
(Musée du Petit Palais, Geneva; Berhaut no. 44) is a
portrait of the artist. For Ball at Moulin de la Galette of
1876 (Musée d'Orsay, Paris), Renoir posed his friends,
but in these and similar instances the paintings were
not perceived only as portraits.

In this context it seems clear that the person on the
left in Place de la Concorde is as much a portrait as is
the image of Lepic himself, or Renoir's figures in Ball
at Moulin de la Galette. But who is he? The playwright
and novelist Ludovic Halévy (1834–1908) is a likely
candidate. The resemblance to other representations
of him is significant enough to warrant further investigation. Degas had a rather close friendship in the
1870s with Halévy, and both frequently attended the
Opéra. Halévy took part in writing the libretti for
Jacques Offenbach's operettas La Belle Hélène, La Vie
parisienne, La Grande-Duchesse de Gérolstein, and La
Périchole. Degas drew Halévy—along with another
theater lover, Albert Boulanger-Cavé, director of the
censor's office—backstage at the Paris Opéra. Degas
showed this 1879 pastel under the characteristic title
Portrait of Friends Backstage (fig. 4; Musée d'Orsay,
Paris) at the fourth exhibition of the Impressionists.
The portrayal of Halévy in the monotype Ludovic

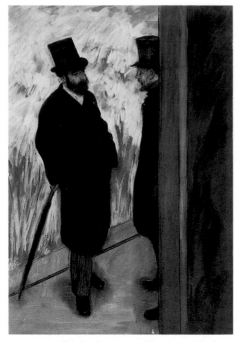

*Fig. 4. Hilaire-Germain-Edgar Degas.* Portrait of Friends Backstage (Ludovic Halévy and Albert Boulanger-Cavé). *1879. Musée d'Orsay, Paris*

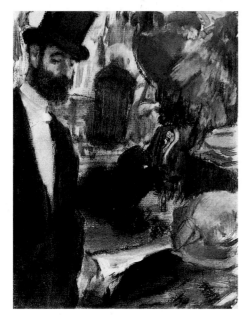

*Fig. 5. Hilaire-Germain-Edgar Degas.* Ludovic Halévy Finds Madame Cardinal in the Dressing Room *(illustration for Ludovic Halévy,* La Famille Cardinal*). 1876–77. Staatsgalerie, Stuttgart*

*Halévy Finds Madame Cardinal in the Dressing Room* of 1876–77 (fig. 5; Staatsgalerie, Stuttgart) bears a particular similarity to the figure in *Place de la Concorde*.

Lepic and his family are crossing the Place de la Concorde, coming from the rue de Rivoli, with the Tuileries behind a stone wall. Faintly visible in the corner of the gardens is the statue of Strasbourg by Pradier, one of the eight stone sculptures erected in the square in honor of the principal cities of France. Several rapid black brushstrokes on gray signify the mourning banners for Alsace, lost to Germany after the Franco-Prussian War. Kirk Varnedoe, who had seen this painting only in reproduction, must be given credit for recognizing these banners from a photograph, which he was able to do, perhaps, because the historical fact of such mourning was well known to him. T. J. Clark then picked up on his observation (from lectures): "History . . . lurks behind the Viscount Lepic's top hat, for example, in Degas's *Place de la Concorde,* where the statue of Strasbourg stands all smothered in wreaths and flowers, the place where Paris mourned Alsace, so recently lost to the Hun" (T. J. Clark, *The Painting of Modern Life: Paris in the Art of Manet and His Followers* [Princeton, 1984], p. 75).

The painting displays movement, in several different directions at once, but the purpose of the movement is not shown. For example, in the background a carriage is moving to the left, about to disappear the next moment, while just next to it, a horseman is riding toward the right: at first glance, the horse and carriage seem to be harnessed together, and only after a second look do we realize that they are moving in opposite directions. Similarly, the figures in the foreground move in contrary directions. It is not essential to know whether the Viscount is taking his daughters somewhere in particular or whether he is simply out on his usual constitutional; he strolls along unhurriedly, with a kind of easy carelessness, typically clutching his umbrella under his arm and not taking his cigar out of his mouth. His frock coat fits him impeccably. Each detail corresponds precisely to the image of a *flâneur,* not in the later sense of an "idler," but in the specific meaning current in the 1860s and 1870s, a characteristic image quite important both for French art of those years and for the life of the Parisian circle to which not only Lepic but Degas himself belonged, as did Manet.

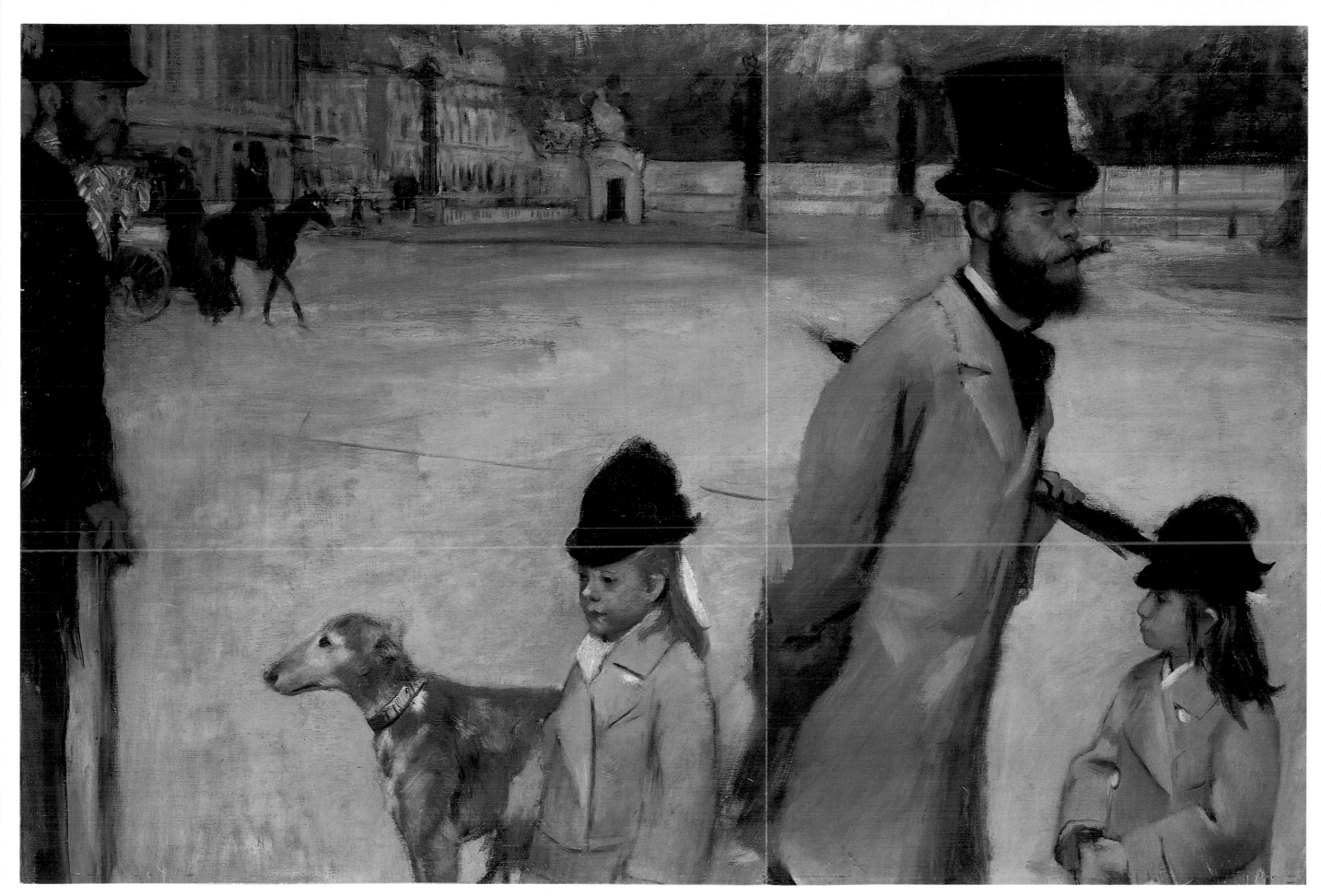

Hilaire-Germain-
Edgar Degas
16. PLACE DE LA
CONCORDE
(VISCOUNT
LEPIC AND HIS
DAUGHTERS
CROSSING THE
PLACE DE LA
CONCORDE)
*Place de la Concorde
(Vicomte Lepic et ses filles
traversant la Place de la
Concorde)*. 1875. Oil on
canvas, 30⅞ × 46¼″
(78.4 × 117.5 cm).
No. 3K 1399. Formerly
collection Gerstenberg/
Scharf, Berlin

Manet looks like a *flâneur* in the famous portrait by Henri Fantin-Latour of 1867 (The Art Institute of Chicago), showing him in a top hat with gloves, a cane in hand, as if he had just set off for a stroll. Caillebotte in particular painted *flâneurs* who could properly be compared with the main figure in *Place de la Concorde,* in two versions of *The Pont de l'Europe* of 1876–77 (Musée du Petit Palais, Geneva, and Kimbell Art Museum, Fort Worth) and in *Street: A Rainy Day in Paris* of 1877 (The Art Institute of Chicago). Of course, the *flâneur* as Caillebotte and Degas painted him was the latest incarnation of the dandyism professed by Charles Baudelaire. It is hard to say whether Viscount Lepic subscribed to this fully or only to a certain extent. Degas's own attitude toward dandyism was ambiguous, to say the least.

This ambiguity, and underlying it a more profound understanding of human nature, is expressed in the composition of *Place de la Concorde* through the roles assigned to the figures. It has long been noted that there is a clash between the different directions in which the father and daughters are moving. Attempts have been made to explain this paradoxical state of affairs, virtually unheard of in portraiture. The simplest explanation is that the children are fidgeting. Eugénie de Keyser finds an element of lightheartedness in this: "There is a certain humor in *Place de la Concorde,* when you see Ludovic Lepic, accompanied by his two daughters, who seem to be going a completely different way, in the wide, open space that all three are lost in" (E. de Keyser, *Degas: Réalité et métaphore* [Louvain-la-Neuve, 1981], p. 54). Robert Herbert sees the children as a means of emphasizing the studied indifference of the *flâneur.* "We do not know what has drawn their curiosity—an omission that Degas teases us with—but by looking to the left, they augment Lepic's detachment. The dog seconds their role, and its pedigreed look makes it a fit companion (Lepic was a dog breeder). The man on the left who stares at this group supplies another contrast to Lepic. He lacks Lepic's more formal coat, and he stands there as a mere *badaud,* an onlooker who is easily distracted by what comes within his notice" (R. L. Herbert, *Impressionism: Art, Leisure, and Parisian Society* [New Haven and London, 1988], p. 35). Herbert concludes from this that no one so emphasizes the essence of the *flâneur* as the onlooker, because a true *flâneur* (here he

is referring to Victor Fournel, a writer of the mid-nineteenth century) is a person who always controls himself, who preserves complete self-possession, observing and reflecting instead of taking part.

Even before Herbert, Denys Sutton touched on this problem, emphasizing with regard to *Place de la Concorde* that Degas himself was a *flâneur:* "[Degas] said to Sickert: 'I don't like fiacres, myself. One doesn't see anybody. That's why I love the omnibus. One can look at people. We are made for looking at each other, after all'" (D. Sutton, *Edgar Degas: Life and Work* [New York, 1986], p. 211). Degas's remark once again demonstrates his interest in people per se, in contemporary Parisians. He did not deal with the signs of the new Paris, such as the powerful iron framework of the Pont de l'Europe or the architectural vistas carved by Baron Haussmann—the things that concerned Caillebotte. *Place de la Concorde* is his sole depiction of Parisian architecture, though not much can be said about this architecture: it was needed only to outline the borders of the square. The *flâneur* observer that was Degas, and Lepic, needed a constant supply of fresh impressions, and a space he could move through to absorb these impressions. That helps explain the unusual spaciousness of *Place de la Concorde.*

A number of recent commentators see the particular expansiveness of the painting as the result of the influence of photography, which was rapidly advancing in those years. For Roy McMullen, *Place de la Concorde* is "a street scene that resembles the stereoscopic snapshots of Paris popular in the 1870s" (R. McMullen, *Degas: His Life, Times, and Work* [Boston, 1984], p. 302). Wilhelm Schmid also sees the achievements of photography at work in the picture, citing for comparison a photograph of the time (c. 1875) showing a crosswalk with pedestrians where the overall compositional effect is obviously related to Degas (W. Schmid, *Wege zu Edgar Degas* [Munich, 1988], pp. 304–6).

Degas, of course, could not help but be interested in photography. Later, he acquired a camera and used it himself. However, we ought not to overestimate the influence of the new technical device on his painting. The whole history of photography shows that it did not overtake painting but followed behind it. The discoveries of photography were not immediately seized upon in Degas's work, but were rather interpreted under another aspect, combining with other, more powerful sources of artistic influence.

In this regard, Jean Sutherland Boggs provides a curious characterization of the figures in *Place de la Concorde*: "The Lepics are just as isolated from the square as we are; it is as if Degas cut their figures out and pasted them on to a separate background, as in a photomontage" (J. S. Boggs, *Portraits by Degas* [Berkeley and Los Angeles, 1962], p. 47). In part these remarks may reflect knowing the painting only in photographic reproduction, since in reproductions the disjunction between the figures and the background is starker. Even so, the effect itself is there, just as Boggs describes it, though its source is not in photography (nor does Boggs actually claim it to be).

Kirk Varnedoe was absolutely right when he warned against exaggeration in such a delicate problem as the use of photographs by Degas: "The advent of true snapshot photography came later, a crucial decade or so after Degas's innovations. The availability of cameras and processing systems simple enough to put photography into the hands of masses of amateurs is a phenomenon of the late 1880s (marked especially by the appearance of the first Kodak in 1888). The *Place de la Concorde* was painted in 1875. No matter how convincingly the picture suggests to us that there is something 'photographic' about it, and no matter how thoroughly we search through archives of stereoscopic views (I have spent many a long hour doing just that), there are no photographs from this date that look like this painting in any serious way" (K. Varnedoe, *A Fine Disregard: What Makes Modern Art Modern* [New York, 1990], p. 49).

In searching for the genesis of the effect of disjunction, it is worth recalling the early Renaissance masters, whose painting Degas studied everywhere, in the Louvre as well as on his Italian travels. As early as 1867, he wrote this significant entry in his notebook: "Ah! Giotto, let me see Paris, and you, Paris, let me see Giotto!" (see T. Reff, *The Notebooks of Edgar Degas* [New York, 2nd ed., 1985], notebook no. 22, Bibliothèque Nationale, Carnet 8, p. 5). *Place de la Concorde* provides perhaps the best example of Paris seen with the help of Giotto. Of course, this is not a question of some direct borrowing, but rather of a way of seeing that generates a particular compositional two-dimensionality: essentially, a friezelike placement of the

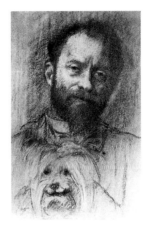

Fig. 6. *Hilaire-Germain-Edgar Degas.* Ludovic Lepic with His Dog. *c. 1888. Formerly collection Georges Viau, Paris*

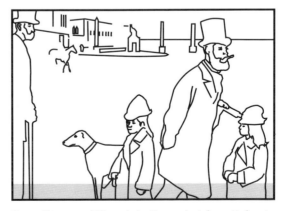

Fig. 7. *Diagram of* Place de la Concorde (*plate 16*) *showing area later removed*

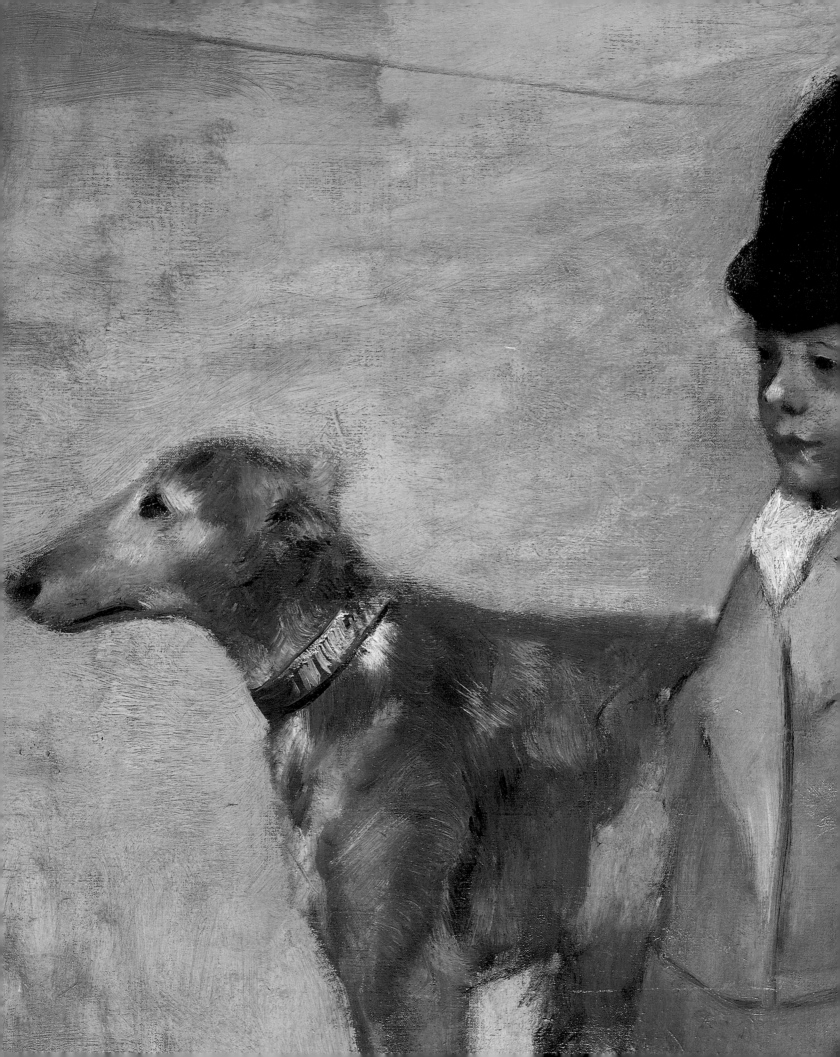

figures in the foreground against a space of limited depth, which becomes their background.

To investigate the special nature of the construction of *Place de la Concorde*, it is worth noting a detail such as the carriage in the upper left of the canvas. It is quite far from the group in the foreground, yet this detail has an important dynamic function: its movement and direction repeat those of Lepic. At the same time, its presence is not without some ambiguity; at first glance, the onlooker's ascot may be perceived as part of the carriage; the bright yellow of the carriage and the light color of the scarf easily blend, since by the logic of pictorial construction it was exactly in this place that a brighter color accent needed to appear. Cézanne also employed such elisions, of course, in his own unique way, while also making use of hints from the Old Masters.

An X-ray analysis of the painting clearly reveals energetic attention to every detail, the search for form with the brush. And under infrared light, it can be seen that the painting underwent some revision. In particular, changes in the contours of the dog and in Eylau's silhouette are revealed, and it is clear that her clothing has been repainted. Originally, the lines of her coat were not vertical, as they later became, but rather diagonal, perhaps explained by a different positioning of the figure. Apparently, at first the girl was only just beginning the process of turning; in the final version she is already moving in an opposite direction, attracted by something that remains a mystery, out of sight.

The format of the painting also was somewhat altered. A strip of the canvas 6 or 7 centimeters wide was folded behind the stretcher all along the lower edge, after the lower edge of the canvas had already been trimmed, probably removing the signature (see fig. 7). This was done by the artist himself, most likely when the painting went to the Galerie Durand-Ruel, and obviously a while after the work was completed, perhaps even several years after, since the painting was well dried before being restretched.

PROVENANCE: Galerie Durand-Ruel, Paris; Otto Gerstenberg, Berlin (purchased from Durand-Ruel in December 1911 for 120,000 francs); Margarete Scharf, Berlin.

EXHIBITIONS: 1912, Frankfurt, Kunstverein.

LITERATURE: M. Liebermann, *Degas* (Berlin, 1899), p. 20 (reprod.); S. Mauclair, *Revue de l'art*, 1903, p. 383; P.-A. Lemoisne, *Degas* (Paris, 1912), p. 56 (reprod.); *Kunst und Künstler*, vol. 11, no. 1 (October 1912), p. 60 (reprod.); P. Jamot, *Gazette des beaux-arts*, vol. 14, sér. 4, no. 695 (April–June 1918), p. 137 (reprod.); P. Lafond, *Degas* (Paris, 1922), vol. 1, p. 119; J. Meier-Graefe, *Degas* (New York, 1923), pl. 19; G. Grappe, *Degas* (Paris, 1936), p. 22; W. Uhde, *Les Impressionistes* (Vienna, 1937), p. 32; G. Rivière, *M. Degas, bourgeois de Paris* (Paris, 1938), p. 143; P. Jamot, *Degas* (Paris and Geneva, 1939), pl. 33; H. Graber, *Edgar Degas* (Basel, 1942), p. 101; M. Rebatet, *Degas* (Paris, 1944), no. 33; P.-A. Lemoisne, *Degas et son oeuvre* (Paris, 1946), vol. 2, no. 368; J. Rewald, *Edgar Degas* (Mulhouse, 1946), no. 33; J. Rewald, *The History of Impressionism* (New York, 1946), p. 264; J. Rewald, *Istoria impressionizma [The History of Impressionism]* (Leningrad and Moscow, 1959), pp. 208, 209 (reprod.); J. S. Boggs, *Portraits by Degas* (Berkeley and Los Angeles, 1962), pp. 46–47, 88; P. Valéry, *Degas: Danse, Dessin* (Paris, 1965), p. 120; *L'Opera completa di Degas,* Introduction by F. Russoli, Catalogue by F. Minervino (Milan, 1970), no. 391; E. Degas, *Pis'ma, Vospominaniya sovremennikov [Letters, Memoirs of Contemporaries]* (Moscow, 1971), no. 18 (reprod.); S. Monneret, *L'Impressionisme et son époque* (Paris, 1978), vol. 1, p. 329; P. Cabanne, *Degas* (Munich, 1978), no. 50; E. de Keyser, *Degas: Réalité et métaphore* (Louvain-la-Neuve, 1981), p. 54; R. McMullen, *Degas: His Life, Times, and Work* (Boston, 1984), p. 302; T. J. Clark, *The Painting of Modern Life: Paris in the Art of Manet and His Followers* (Princeton, 1984), p. 75 (reprod.); N. N. Kaltina, *Franzuskiy portret XIX veka [The French Portrait in the Nineteenth Century]* (Leningrad, 1985), p. 162; T. Reff, *The Notebooks of Edgar Degas: A Catalogue of the Thirty-eight Notebooks in the Bibliothèque Nationale and Other Collections* (New York, rev. ed., 1985), vol. 1, p.124, vol. 2, notebook no. 26, p. 96; D. Sutton, *Edgar Degas: Life and Work* (New York, 1986), pp. 211, 213; E. Lipton, *Looking into Degas: Uneasy Images of Women and Modern Life* (Berkeley and Los Angeles, 1987), pp. 11–13; W. Schmid, *Wege zu Edgar Degas* (Munich, 1988), pp. 304–6; R. L. Herbert, *Impressionism: Art, Leisure, and Parisian Society* (New Haven and London, 1988), p. 35 (color reprod.); J. Milner, *The Studios of Paris: The Capital of Art in the Late Nineteenth Century* (New Haven and London, 1988), pp. 112–13; R. Gordon and A. Forge, *Degas* (New York, 1988), p. 137; K. Varnedoe, *A Fine Disregard: What Makes Modern Art Modern* (New York, 1990), pp. 27, 30 (color reprod.), 43, 49, 52, 53, 80, 85, 88, 108–9, 122; *The Passionate Eye: Impressionist and Other Master Paintings from the Collection of Emil G. Bührle, Zurich* (Zurich and Munich, 1990), no. 32; V. Perutz, *Édouard Manet* (Lewisburg, 1993), p. 177; P. H. Feist, *Impressionist Art, 1860–1920,* vol. 1: *Impressionism in France* (Hamburg, 1993), p. 169.

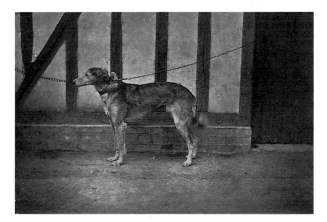

*Fig. 8. Albreckt, Viscount Lepic's Borzoi. Photograph by L. Sauvager. n.d. Private collection*

# HILAIRE·GERMAIN·EDGAR DEGAS

## SEATED DANCER

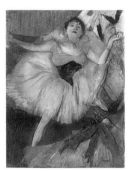

This model is shown in similar poses in the charcoal drawing *Resting Dancer* (Lemoisne no. 822) and in the painting *The Dance Class* (fig. 3; Sterling and Francine Clark Art Institute, Williamstown, Massachusetts; Lemoisne no. 820), for which this pastel apparently served as a study. Lemoisne dated both works to 1885; however, more recent researchers believe that the two were painted about five years earlier.

The narrow, attenuated versions of *Dance Class* upon which Degas worked in the late 1870s show part of a rehearsal hall where several corps-de-ballet dancers are performing their exercises while one or two of them rest. Such was the painting of about 1879 (now in the Mellon collection, Upperville, Virginia) shown at the Impressionists' exhibition in 1880 (the establishment of this fact was what made it possible to correct Lemoisne's dating for the whole group of works). Most likely, the Williamstown canvas was painted after it, about 1880. *Seated Dancer* could have served to prepare the little ballerina at the right; her legs are in exactly the same position, but her arms are lowered. In the Williamstown *Dance Class,* this dancer, deliberately juxtaposed with the whole row of figures, balances the other ballerinas' movements.

The charcoal *Resting Dancer* can be considered a variation of the motif elaborated in *Seated Dancer* of about 1880 (fig. 1; Philadelphia Museum of Art; Lemoisne no. 659), also known under the title *A Coryphée Resting*, where the figure is depicted not frontally, but in a three-quarters view (although it is a different model). There is a theory that the second title was meant to be ironic (see J. S. Boggs, *Drawings by Degas* [City Art Museum of Saint Louis, 1966], p. 160). Although the word *coryphée* does not mean "star," the velvet ribbon around the dancer's neck could still have served as a permissible accessory on stage. Beginning dancers of the corps de ballet might not have been permitted such an ornament, but most likely a *coryphée*—that is, a dancer of the corps de ballet who appeared in the first line and who performed certain small solos—could have indulged herself with such a frill.

In the pastel *Entrance of the Masked Dancers* of 1879 (fig. 4; Sterling and Francine Clark Art Institute, Williamstown, Massachusetts), the seated figure of the present pastel from the Krebs collection is shown straightening her neck ribbon. *Entrance of the Masked Dancers* once again proves that the ballerina shown in the two pastels was not an invented personage, but an actual artiste of the Paris Opéra, since she is painted in a portraitlike manner here: a broad, flat face, widely spaced, small eyes, and a low forehead. It can even be surmised that Degas asked her to be his model when he worked on this painting.

The pose of the seated dancer is unaffected and at ease. Though perhaps not elegant, she is completely natural, which for Degas was more important. Such poses date from *The Bellelli Family* of 1858–59 (Musée d'Orsay, Paris), where the young girl in the center is seated carelessly, almost willfully, not at all the customary pose for commissioned portraits. The youngest daughter may have been allowed such small liberties (see fig. 2). The later variations of this pose in which the dancers appear are notable, of course, for their great relaxation.

In Degas's paintings, any position of the body, even the most unusual, takes on the form of impeccable drawing. Through a complex creative process, the model, miraculously preserving all her naturalness, is transformed into pure color and line.

When Degas said that "a dancer is only an excuse

for a drawing" (see G. Moore, "Memories of Degas," *The Burlington Magazine,* January–February 1918), he was defending himself from the superficial judgments of his art by people who wanted to see him only as a painter of ballerinas, and was deliberately portraying his situation in a somewhat simplified form. Degas, like no other artist, understood and knew how to show in his paintings and pastels everything particular to the dancer's profession. His phenomenal powers of observation and his candor prevented him from ever over-elaborating his figures. By conventional standards, the seated dancer, with her flat face, awkward figure, and short neck, is hard to describe as beautiful. However, this pastel, as a unique combination of splashes of color, is indeed beautiful. The drawing displays true mastery, while the balance of compositional elements is sustained by crossing diagonals. The diagonal marked by the dancer's right leg and the contour of her bodice is the more accentuated one; the direction of the other diagonal is indicated by the movement of the right hand. In the Williamstown painting, the hand is lowered, and its lines, extended in the contours of the leg, are obstructed by a vertical. Clearly, despite all the connections with that painting, *Seated Dancer* cannot be considered a study for it. It is an entirely independent work with another dynamic of drawing all its own.

PROVENANCE: Galerie Étienne Bignou, Paris; Galerie Bernheim-Jeune, Paris; Otto Krebs, Holzdorf.

LITERATURE: P.-A. Lemoisne, *Degas et son oeuvre* (Paris, 1946), vol. 3, no. 800.

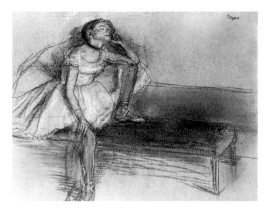

Fig. 1. *Hilaire-Germain-Edgar Degas.* Seated Dancer (A Coryphée Resting). *c. 1880. Philadelphia Museum of Art. John G. Johnson Collection*

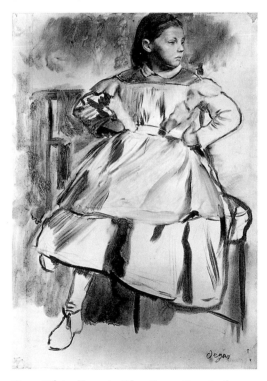

Fig. 2. *Hilaire-Germain-Edgar Degas.* Portrait of Giulia Bellelli. *1858–59. Dumbarton Oaks Research Library and Collection, Washington, D.C.*

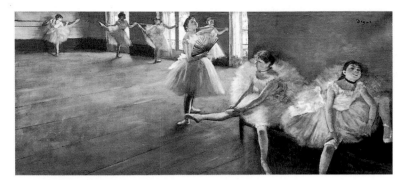

*Fig. 3. Hilaire-Germain-Edgar Degas.* The Dance Class. *c. 1880. Sterling and Francine Clark Art Institute, Williamstown, Massachusetts*

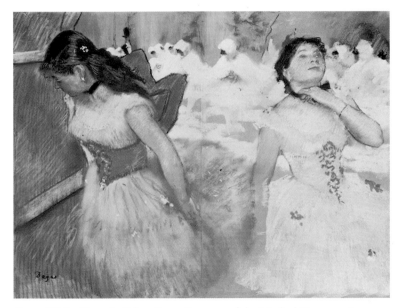

*Fig. 4. Hilaire-Germain-Edgar Degas.* Entrance of the Masked Dancers. *1879. Sterling and Francine Clark Art Institute, Williamstown, Massachusetts*

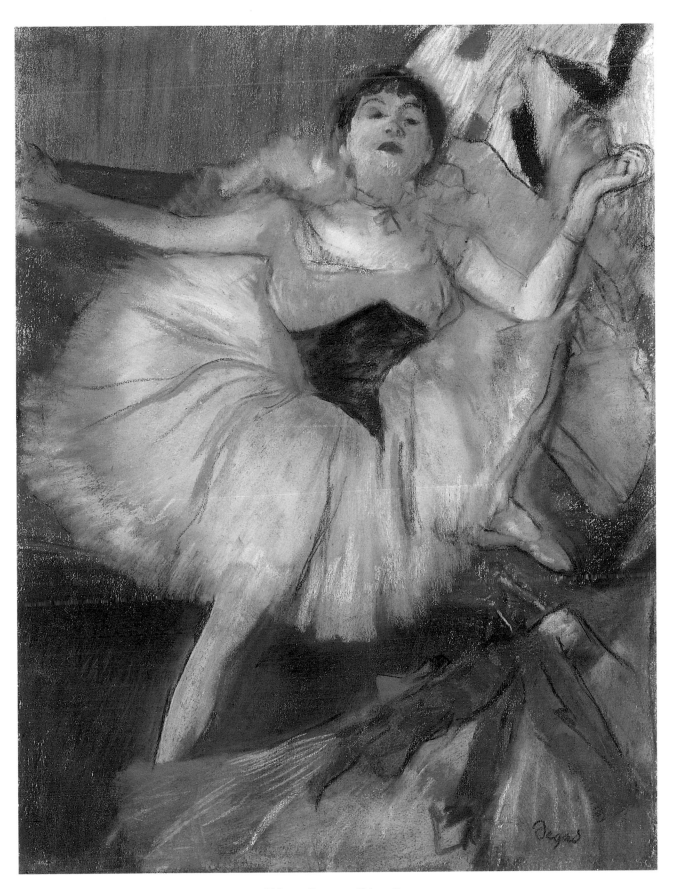

Hilaire-Germain-Edgar Degas
## 17. SEATED DANCER
*Danseuse assise.* c. 1879–80
Charcoal and pastel on paper mounted on pasteboard, 25 × 19⅛" (63.5 × 48.7 cm)
Signed lower right: "Degas". No. GR 155-99. Formerly collection Otto Krebs, Holzdorf

# HILAIRE-GERMAIN-EDGAR DEGAS

## TWO DANCERS

In the second half of the 1890s, Degas painted many dancers caught at the moment just before they go on stage. Usually they are straightening something—a shoulder strap, earring, or coiffure—a gesture which precisely captures their nervous anticipation. Backstage scenes and fleeting episodes in the wings always fascinated him, even more than the brilliance of the stage itself. In later years, he lost interest in the actual performance of the prima ballerina; although he painted more ballerinas than ever, now they were often doing the most ordinary things, or simply getting ready to flit out onto the stage. This subject was even less momentous than that of the rehearsal, but, unlike the ballet performance itself, it still elicited from him the desire to take up his brush or pastels.

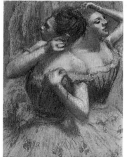

One of the finest compositions of the late 1890s depicting ballerinas backstage is *Three Dancers in Blue* of about 1898 (The Pushkin State Museum of Fine Arts, Moscow). At about the same time, Degas worked on a large painting entitled *Four Dancers* from 1895–1900 (National Gallery of Art, Washington, D.C.). There are several variants of both compositions, such as a pastel with four figures called *Dancers* of about 1898 (Charles Durand-Ruel collection, Paris), where we encounter the same foreshortened ballerina straightening her hair as in the present *Two Dancers* (Degas often showed just two figures). Such variations pursue different goals; not only the number of figures but the medium, color, and drawing change, and each time, new, forceful lines are discovered in the composition. Since Degas's art was markedly formalized, the subject had little intrinsic meaning and was needed only to enable the latest symphony of colors to play. The colors themselves were growing more vigorous and vivid.

Frequently, Degas showed a pair of dancers with one woman fixing an earring and the other adjusting her hair. The very triviality of the motif, constantly repeated, guaranteed absolute concentration on color and form. The movements of the figures vary, but each time are subordinate to pictorial structure. In the present *Two Dancers,* the composition is endowed with both stability and motion. The principle of the pyramid is employed to give stability. A pyramid is formed in the lower part of the picture by the skirts of the dancers. In the upper part there is another pyramid; arms, raised or lowered, together with the head create its outline.

This pastel, unknown to Lemoisne, was probably preceded by several related compositions that Lemoisne dated to 1897 (Lemoisne nos. 1296, 1296 bis, 1298). The first of them (fig. 1; Nationalmuseum, Stockholm) is notable for its spaciousness. The figures are shown from the knees up and there is more background visible. In the last of the three, *Dancers Adjusting Their Coiffures* (fig. 2), the composition is framed as in *Two Dancers*. The latter work is stylistically close to the compositions of 1898–99, in particular to the pastel *Dancers* of about 1899 in the Hermitage, which shows a woman with a raised hand (a woman depicted separately in *Bust of Dancer and Study of an Arm* [Lemoisne no. 1360]).

Degas may have used photographs in working on the pastel. The figure at the right is reminiscent of a photograph known as *Dancer from the Corps de Ballet* of about 1896 (Bibliothèque Nationale, Paris). Since the negative was sent to the Bibliothèque Nationale after the artist's death by his brother René along with various materials that had been in Degas's possession, it seems plausible that the artist used it himself, given his known fascination with photography in those years.

PROVENANCE: Gustave Pellet, Paris; Otto Krebs, Holzdorf.

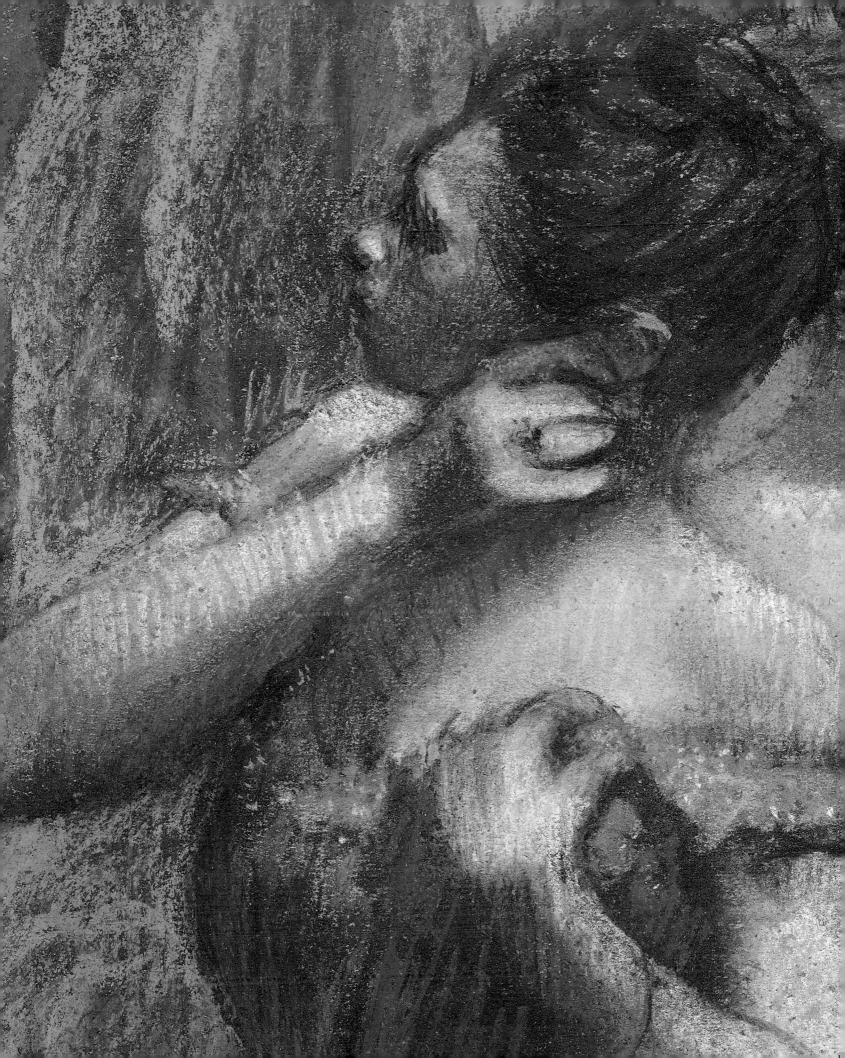

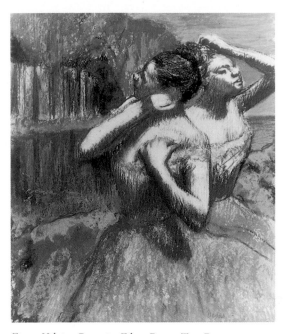

*Fig. 1. Hilaire-Germain-Edgar Degas.* Two Dancers.
*c. 1897. Nationalmuseum, Stockholm. Gift of the Society
of Friends of the Museum*

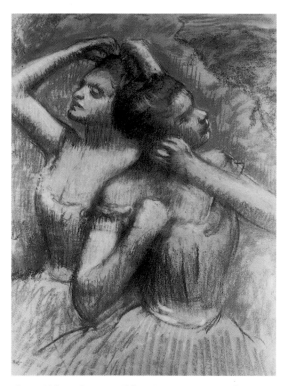

*Fig. 2. Hilaire-Germain-Edgar Degas.* Dancers Adjusting
Their Coiffures. *c. 1897. Private collection, Paris*

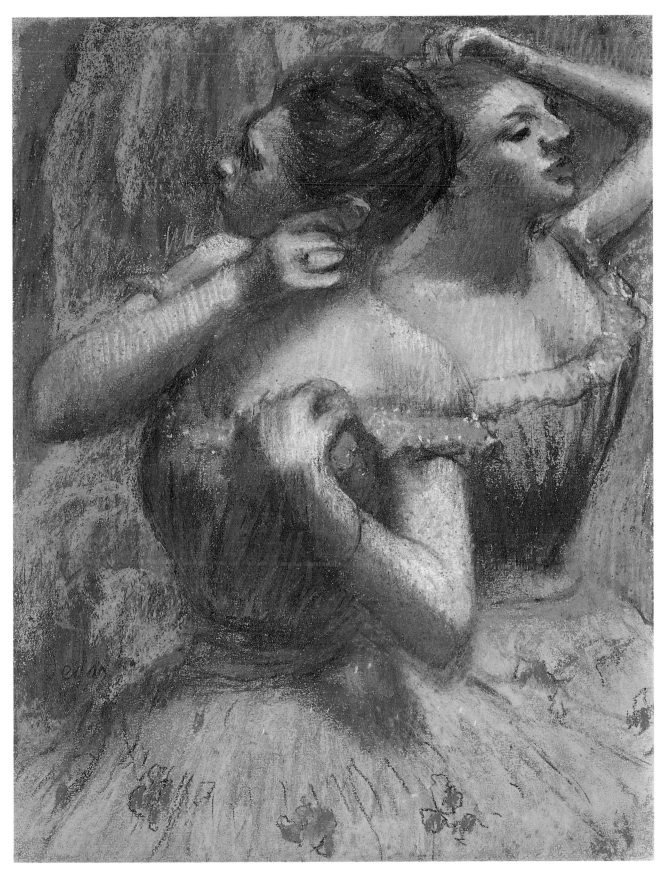

Hilaire-Germain-Edgar Degas
### 18. TWO DANCERS
*Deux Danseuses.* c. 1898–99
Charcoal and pastel on paper, 18¾ × 14¼" (47.8 × 36.2 cm). Signed lower left: "Degas"
No. GR 155-100. Formerly collection Otto Krebs, Holzdorf

# PIERRE-AUGUSTE RENOIR

## Man on a Stair

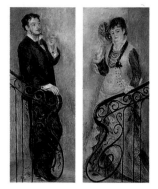

Along with its companion, *Woman on a Stair* (plate 20), this painting served as part of the decoration for the great staircase of Georges Charpentier's mansion at 11, rue de Grenelle, Paris (demolished in 1962), and was sold in 1907, after his death. Decorative projects were not unheard of for the Impressionists, and included, for example, Claude Monet's contemporaneous canvases of 1876 (The State Hermitage Museum, St. Petersburg) painted for Ernest Hoschedé's country house in Montgeron and showing the garden and pond next to the house.

Georges Charpentier (1846–1905), the son of Gervais Charpentier, a famous publisher of the Romantic writers Victor Hugo, Alfred de Musset, and Honoré de Balzac, inherited his father's business in 1871 and began publishing the works of Gustave Flaubert, Edmond de Goncourt, and the writers of the naturalist school—Émile Zola in particular—which brought him great success. In 1872, he married Marguerite Lemonnier, the eldest daughter of the former court jeweler Gabrielle Lemonnier. Three years later, they moved into the house on the rue de Grenelle, which, thanks to Madame Charpentier, became a gathering place for the artistic elite of Paris. The Charpentiers' salon was frequented by the best writers—Flaubert, Théodore de Banville, Goncourt, Zola, Alphonse Daudet, Joris-Karl Huysmans—the composers Emmanuel Chabrier, Camille Saint-Saëns, Jules Massenet, the actors Mounet-Sully, Coquelin Cadet, and Jeanne Samary (who particularly attracted Renoir), and the cabaret singers Aristide Bruant and Yvette Guilbert, whose fame was just beginning. Artists came as well, and not only Édouard Manet and some of the Impressionists, but the successful Salon painters Charles Carolus-Duran and Jean-Jacques

Henner. When one considers in addition the politicians who came, including Georges Clémenceau, Jules Ferry, Henri Rochefort, and Léon-Michel Gambetta (whom Renoir especially noted), it becomes clear that important connections could be made there. In fact, the Charpentiers' salon rather quickly acquired a great deal of influence.

Furthermore, Marguerite Charpentier had a gift for bringing opposites together, so that at her *jours fixes* ("at-home days"), artists of opposing camps would meet, and politicians of the left wing could see such idols of the aristocracy as the Duchesse d'Uzès and the Duchesse de Rohan or Robert de Montesquieu. Without the Charpentiers, Renoir probably would not have made the acquaintance of such people. In the latter half of the 1870s, he came to the salon quite often, and received a number of portrait commissions as a result.

Georges Charpentier, who in his youth had wanted to be an artist, had a passion for painting, which his wife shared. In early 1875, he saw and admired Renoir's *Fisherman with Rod* at a dealer's and soon learned that it would be for sale at an auction that the Impressionists had organized for March 24. It was a very difficult time for the artists, and the sale did nothing to help extricate them from their financial straits. The auction was conducted in an atmosphere of open hostility, and it required considerable determination—in the face of the public's attempts to obstruct the proceedings, howling at each bid—to acquire anything at all. After obtaining *Fisherman with Rod,* Charpentier wanted to meet the artist, an opportunity sent to Renoir as if by fate.

Photographs of the interior of the Charpentier residence unfortunately do not survive. Something of it can be imagined from the arabesque iron grillwork of the stair depicted in both paintings (which are almost certainly faithful renderings of the rue de Grenelle stairway), giving a sense of unhurried elegance. The idea behind Renoir's stairway paintings was presumably to show the master and mistress of the house descending the stairs to greet their guests. The artist did not set himself the task of executing exact portraits, however, which apparently were not even demanded of him (as would seem to be the case also with the depiction of the lady with the fishing rod in Monet's *Pond at Montgeron,* who with some reason is thought to be the mistress of the estate, Alice Hoschedé, though the almost featureless figure can hardly be considered a portrait). A comparison of a photograph of Georges Charpentier (fig. 2) with *Man on a Stair* reveals a significant resemblance, yet it was not Charpentier who posed for the painting, but Edmond Renoir, the artist's younger brother, who looked like him (see fig. 3). The Charpentiers appear to have provided their photographs to Renoir for the paintings (see B. E. White, *Renoir: His Life, Art, and Letters* [New York, 1984], pp. 62–64).

It is difficult to say precisely where the two paintings were executed. In the case of other works commissioned by the Charpentiers, portraits of family members, Renoir painted in their home. Decorations could have been painted just as well in Renoir's Montmartre studio on the rue Saint-Georges.

F. Daulte believes that Renoir's two stairway paintings were preceded by a portrait of the couple's daughter, Georgette Charpentier, dated by the artist himself to 1876, although Daulte cites no documentary evidence. Nonetheless, it may be that Renoir's artistic relationship with the Charpentier family actually began with the stairway pictures.

Apparently the idea of creating a composition with the stairway came from the Charpentiers. At that time, stairway motifs were gaining currency. At the 1874 Salon the public's attention was drawn to Jean-Léon Gérôme's *L'Éminence grise* (fig. 1; Museum of Fine Arts, Boston), where the action, involving Cardinal Richelieu's confidant, Father Joseph, is played out on a grand staircase. That same year, James Tissot sent to the Royal Academy exhibition *London Visitors* (Toledo Museum of Art, Ohio), again a scene on a stairway, but this time a contemporary one (on these paintings, see

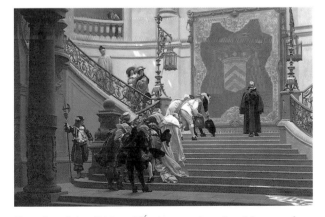

*Fig. 1. Jean-Léon Gérôme. L'Éminence grise. 1873. Museum of Fine Arts, Boston. Bequest of Susan Cornelia Warren*

R. Rosenblum and H. W. Janson, *Nineteenth-Century Art* [New York, 1984], pp. 338, 339, 355–57). The stair motif made available simple yet quite dynamic rhythms, which is why such artists as Gérôme or Tissot, perhaps more sensitive than other Salon masters to new trends, used them. In executing his decorative panels, Renoir entered in some sense into competition with the leading figures of official art.

At some point, both of these paintings were fairly heavily covered with varnish, which has yellowed with age, complicating an appraisal of their remarkable qualities as paintings.

PROVENANCE: Georges Charpentier, Paris; Galerie Druet, Paris; Otto Gerstenberg, Berlin; Margarete Scharf, Berlin.

EXHIBITIONS: 1910, Venice, IX Esposizione Internazionale, no. 9.

LITERATURE: A. Vollard, *Pierre-Auguste Renoir: Les Peintures, pastels et dessins* (Paris, 1918), vol. 1, p. 93, no. 394; J. Meier-Graefe, *Renoir* (Leipzig, 1929), p. 83, no. 79 (reprod.); M. Robida, *Le Salon Charpentier et les impressionistes* (Paris, 1918), p. 67; F. Fosca, *Renoir: His Life and Work* (London, 1961), p. 39; B. E. White, "Renoir's Trip to Italy," *The Art Bulletin*, vol. 51, no. 4 (December 1969), pp. 336, 337; F. Daulte, *Auguste Renoir: Catalogue raisonné de l'oeuvre peint* (Lausanne, 1971), no. 218; *L'Opera completa di Renoir* (Milan, 1972), no. 258; B. E. White, *Renoir: His Life, Art, and Letters* (New York, 1984), pp. 63, 64; J. Rewald, "Auguste Renoir and His Brother," in J. Rewald, *Studies in Impressionism* (New York, 1985), p. 14; S. Monneret, *Renoir* (New York, 1989), p. 152.

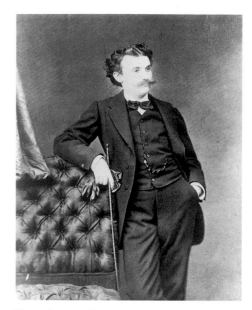

*Fig. 2. Georges Charpentier. c. 1876*

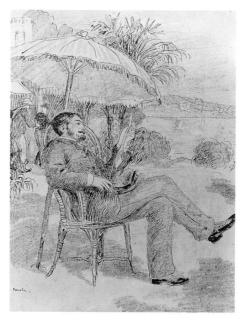

*Fig. 3. Pierre-Auguste Renoir.* Portrait of Edmond Renoir at Menton. *1881. Private collection, New York*

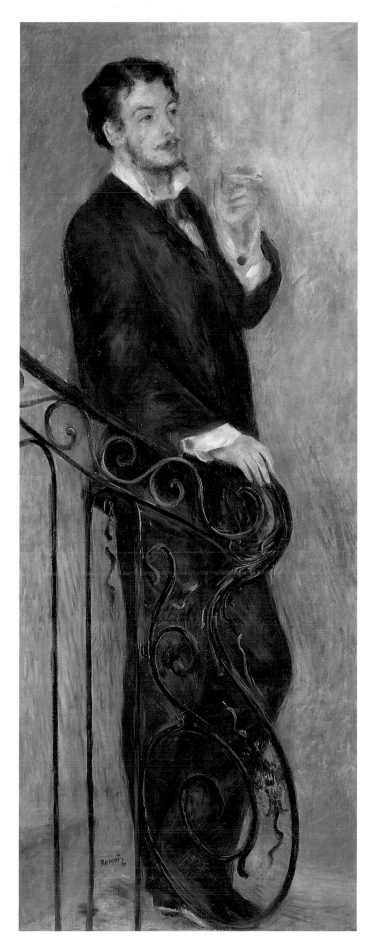

Pierre-Auguste Renoir
(1841, Limoges–1919,
Cagnes-sur-Mer)
19. MAN ON A STAIR
*L'Homme sur un escalier.* c. 1876
Oil on canvas, 65⅞ × 25¾"
(167.5 × 65.3 cm)
Signed lower right: "Renoir"
Pencil notation on stretcher:
"Renoir/Charpentier"
No. 3K 1575
Formerly collection
Gerstenberg/Scharf, Berlin

# PIERRE-AUGUSTE RENOIR

## WOMAN ON A STAIR

Just as the figure in *Man on a Stair* (plate 19) resembles Georges Charpentier, so the companion figure in *Woman on a Stair* is like the publisher's wife, Marguerite. Madame Charpentier had little in common with her younger sister, Isabelle Lemonnier, painted by Édouard Manet (see plate 13). A short woman inclined to plumpness, Madame Charpentier knew how to be charming, but comported herself with a dignity sometimes bordering on arrogance.

Even without knowing the comments of her contemporaries, these features of her character are quite evident in another portrait painted by Renoir a little later, about 1877 (Musée d'Orsay, Paris). The childhood and adolescence of Marguerite Charpentier coincided with the era of the Second Empire and were surrounded with luxury. Thanks to her father, jeweler to Napoléon III (he made the crown for Empress Eugénie, now in the Louvre), she was familiar with the court and the aristocracy. "Your court painter," Renoir called himself in letters to her. Always concerned about the reputation of her salon, Madame Charpentier saw it as the select "court" of the Paris artistic and intellectual circles. She found it agreeable when people called her "Marie-Antoinette," whom she dressed up as at costume balls (though malicious gossips added, Marie-Antoinette "cut off at the bottom"). For the sake of fairness, it must be noted that Marguerite Charpentier was a highly intelligent, educated woman who exerted a great deal of influence on her husband's publishing business and consequently on the literary life of the day.

Madame Charpentier may not have considered her quasi-portrait, *Woman on a Stair*, a great success, although she continued to value Renoir's talent very highly. Most likely to satisfy the hostess of the brilliant

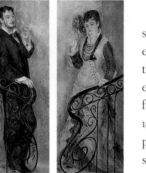

salon, Renoir in his subsequent portrayals either did not accentuate her figure (as in the portrait from the Musée d'Orsay) or else found a flattering pose, as in the famous *Portrait of Madame Charpentier with Her Children* of 1878 (The Metropolitan Museum of Art, New York), where she is seated in such a way that her voluminous black dress quite conceals her true proportions. The latter portrait launched Renoir's fame. The painting is fresh and masterly, and its combination of diverse details turned out to be attractive to a wide audience. The success of that unusual and charming group portrait galvanized Madame Charpentier, who was able to use her influence to have the canvas exhibited in the 1879 Salon in the most advantageous manner.

Renoir was quite at home at the Charpentiers'. He not only painted portraits of madame and her children but performed other small favors for the family, for example decorating their dinner menus with color drawings. A surviving letter from Renoir to Madame Charpentier is written casually, even jestingly, testifying to their closeness.

An intriguing detail in *Woman on a Stair* is the Japanese fan. A love of Japanese art was one of the elements that drew Madame Charpentier to the Impressionists. A chamber in her house called the Japanese Room was chosen as the background for the Metropolitan Museum portrait (this backdrop is perhaps the most remarkable thing about the portrait). Renoir had used the Japanese fan before as a detail in *Still Life with Bouquet* of 1871 (The Museum of Fine Arts, Houston). The fan plays an important role in *Woman on a Stair*. Echoed in the outlines of the female figure and the design of the banisters, it helps to link all the elements together organically. In this

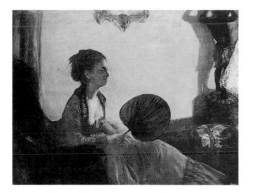

Fig. 1. Hilaire-Germain-Edgar Degas. Portrait of Madame Camus. 1870. National Gallery of Art, Washington, D.C. Chester Dale Collection

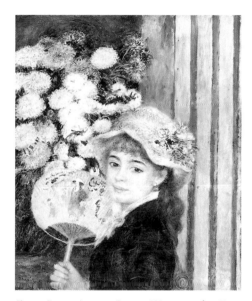

Fig. 2. Pierre-Auguste Renoir. Woman with a Fan. 1881. Sterling and Francine Clark Art Institute, Williamstown, Massachusetts

case, Renoir may have borrowed a device used in a Degas painting executed in 1870 and shown in the same year at the Salon, *Portrait of Madame Camus* (fig. 1; National Gallery of Art, Washington, D.C.), where the Japanese fan is an important expressive feature. Later, in *Woman with a Fan* of 1881 (fig. 2; Sterling and Francine Clark Art Institute, Williamstown, Massachusetts), Renoir once again included a Japanese fan, employing a method already proven in *Woman on a Stair*. The fan served as the symbol of japonisme. No wonder that in his *Japanese Woman* of 1875 (Museum of Fine Arts, Boston), Claude Monet depicted so many of them.

It is believed that, as with *Man on a Stair,* Renoir was here playing a double game; while portraying Madame Charpentier, he painted the figure not from her (see fig. 3), but from another Marguerite, the model Marguerite Legrand, better known as Margot. Although information is scant and contradictory, from the comments of those who knew her it appears that she was often unreliable, when an artist was waiting for her to pose, and was not noted for fine taste. However, Margot's rare vitality could not have left Renoir indifferent. It is believed that she is depicted in one of his most joyous works, *Ball at Moulin de la Galette* of 1876 (Musée d'Orsay, Paris), painted almost simultaneously with *Woman on a Stair*. There, she is dancing passionately with a lanky partner, a Cuban artist, whom Renoir himself had brought together with her.

Margot was Renoir's chief model from 1875 to 1879. There are at least a dozen portrayals, such as *Young Girl with a Cat* of about 1875–76 (National Gallery of Art, Washington, D.C.) and the portrait from 1878 (fig. 4; Musée d'Orsay, Paris) that Renoir gave to Doctor Paul Gachet immediately after Margot's untimely death. François Daulte proposes that in fact another model, Nini Lopez, posed for *Young Girl with a Cat*. The two models did indeed look alike, and either could have served as an example of the "Renoir type." Margot posed for one of Renoir's most important paintings, *The Cup of Chocolate* of 1878 (Edsel and Eleanor Ford House, Grosse Pointe Shores, Michigan; Daulte no. 272), which he sent to the Salon that year, without success.

All the portrayals of Margot identified by Daulte (Daulte nos. 234, 235, 237, 238, 272, 274, 276, 321, 322) are dissimilar to the figure in *Ball at Moulin de la Galette*. However, *Ball at Moulin de la Galette* is not a group portrait, but an invented composition, though one infused with real impressions of Renoir's friends. The dancing girl in that painting is an image compiled from various features, as happened with *Woman on a Stair*. A faithful depiction of Margot, the Musée d'Orsay portrait that belonged to Gachet, represents one of the most charming images in Renoir's entire oeuvre.

It seems that Renoir and Margot formed relations that went beyond those of artist and model. Margot was undoubtedly Renoir's mistress. In January 1879, when she suddenly fell seriously ill, Renoir did everything possible to save her. He appealed to Doctor Gachet to begin paying house calls on her immediately. The visits soon stopped, however. Renoir did not know that Gachet had been in a train accident and feverishly sent him one letter after another ("I've been doing nothing but waiting for you for the whole day"). He turned to Doctor de Bellio, a collector and friend of the Impressionists. Neither doctor could help. Margot was in a fever (according to some versions, typhoid; according to others, smallpox) and died the following month. Renoir paid her funeral expenses.

*Woman on a Stair* thus became a memorial of the relations the artist had with two women who played different but equally important roles in his life.

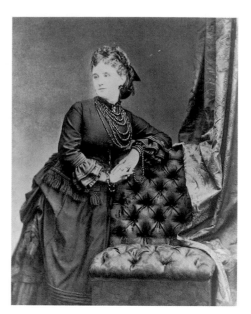

Fig. 3. *Marguerite Charpentier. c. 1876*

PROVENANCE: Georges Charpentier, Paris; Galerie Druet, Paris; Otto Gerstenberg, Berlin; Margarete Scharf, Berlin.

EXHIBITIONS: 1882, Paris, "Septième Exposition des artistes indépendants," no. 160 (*as Femme à l'éventail*); 1910, Venice, IX Esposizione Internazionale, no. 10; 1938, Amsterdam, "Hondert Jaar Fransche Kunst," Municipal Museum, no. 206.

LITERATURE: A. Vollard, *Pierre-Auguste Renoir* (Paris, 1918), vol. 1, p. 93, no. 374 (reprod.); A. André, *Renoir* (Paris, 1923), pl. 3; G. Besson, *Auguste Renoir* (Paris, 1929), no. 2 (as *Femme à l'éventail*, dated 1875); J. Meier-Graefe, *Renoir* (Leipzig, 1929), p. 83, no. 79; A. André, "Renoir et ses modèles," *Le Point*, March 1936, II, p. 27; M. Robida, *Le Salon Charpentier et les impressionistes* (Paris, 1958), p. 67; F. Fosca, *Renoir: His Life and Work* (London, 1961), p. 39; B. E. White, "Renoir's Trip to Italy," *The Art Bulletin*, vol. 51, no. 4 (1969), pp. 336–37; F. Daulte, *Auguste Renoir: Catalogue raisonné de l'oeuvre peint* (Lausanne, 1971), no. 219; *L'Opera completa di Renoir* (Milan, 1972), no. 259; B. E. White, *Renoir: His Life, Art, and Letters* (New York, 1984), pp. 63, 64; S. Monneret, *Renoir* (New York, 1989), p. 152.

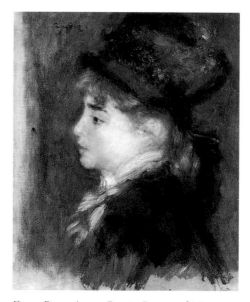

Fig. 4. *Pierre-August Renoir*. Portrait of Margot. 1878. *Musée d'Orsay, Paris*

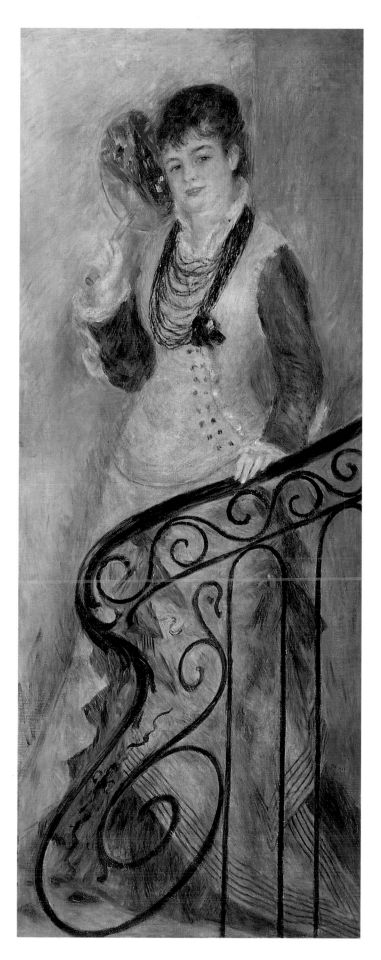

Pierre-Auguste Renoir
## 20. WOMAN ON A STAIR
*Femme sur un escalier.* c. 1876
Oil on canvas, 65⅞ × 25¾"
(167.5 × 65.3 cm)
Signed lower right: "Renoir"
No. 3K 1573
Formerly collection
Gerstenberg/Scharf, Berlin

# PIERRE-AUGUSTE RENOIR

## PORTRAIT OF A WOMAN

It is not known who posed for this picture, but clearly it was a commissioned portrait; the woman's face, her posture, the decorative details of the background all suggest as much. Moreover, the painting was executed in a manner likely to impress the person who commissioned it, and it is even possible that she prompted the choice of medium. Pastel attracted Renoir not least because it was valued by his favorite eighteenth-century masters, though he himself employed it relatively rarely. Thus, he sent fifteen paintings and only one pastel to the public sale in May 1877 he organized along with Gustave Caillebotte, Camille Pissarro, and Alfred Sisley. The failure of the sale was the main reason for his decision to concentrate on portraiture. Since Renoir's most likely source of portrait commissions remained the salon of Madame Charpentier, it is possible that *Portrait of a Woman* depicts one of the ladies who visited the rue de Grenelle.

At that time Renoir's paintings were not selling, and in order to make ends meet, he very much needed commissions. However, discounting the paintings of models and friends, such as Margot Legrand and Jeanne Samary, which brought no income, only a small number of women's portraits in 1877 can be acknowledged as commissioned. In fact, there is no noticeable difference between the two kinds of portrayals. In Renoir's commissioned paintings, even if he took the model's wishes into consideration, he never changed his signature style. The effortless arabesques in the background of *Portrait of a Woman,* reaching near abstraction, remind us that for him, it was the purely pictorial problems that remained fundamental in works of any type.

Joris-Karl Huysmans considered 1877 to be an important landmark in the work of Renoir, notable for "works that were more essential, more resolved in color, and with a surer feeling of modernity" (Huysmans, *L'Art moderne* [Paris, 1911], p. 289). At that time Huysmans was trying to bring to the public's attention the outstanding pictorial qualities of Renoir's pastel portraits. "One would have to be exceptionally dull to think that Chardin's pastels are inferior to his oil paintings. But if we turn to modern art, are not the portraits in colored chalks at one time exhibited by M. Renoir a thousand times more attractive, individual, affective, than all these flat portraits of the official halls?" (J.-K. Huysmans, "L'Exposition des indépendants en 1881," ibid., p. 274).

PROVENANCE: Charles Pacquement, Paris; Otto Krebs, Holzdorf.

EXHIBITIONS: 1924, Paris, "Première Exposition de collectionneurs au profit de la Société des Amis du Luxembourg," no. 223; Barcelona, no. 1565.

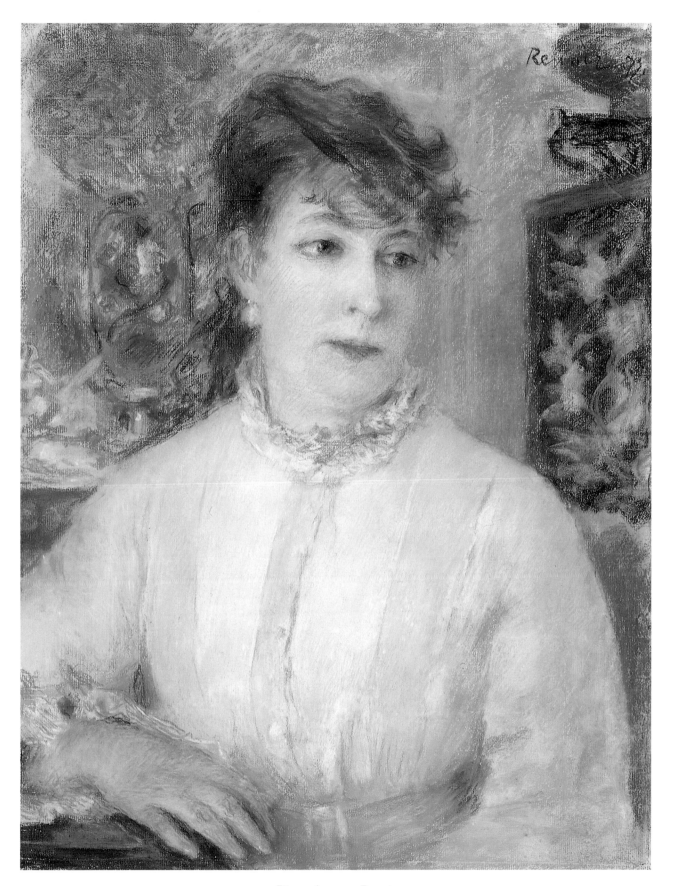

Pierre-Auguste Renoir
## 21. PORTRAIT OF A WOMAN
*Portrait de femme.* 1877
Pastel on bond paper mounted on paperboard, 25⅝ × 19¼" (65 × 48.8 cm)
Signed and dated upper right: "Renoir 77." No. GR 155-95. Formerly collection Otto Krebs, Holzdorf

# PIERRE-AUGUSTE RENOIR

## ROSES AND JASMINE IN A DELFT VASE

In the work of Renoir, acknowledged as a master of figural composition, still life always played a secondary role, though at times a very important one; it was connected with the establishment of a style in the mid-1860s as well as with its alteration toward the beginning of the 1880s. If in the early still lifes realistic moods are strong and the influence of Gustave Courbet is felt, in the 1870s and 1880s Renoir strove for a more decorative quality, with beautiful objects of everyday life. Expensive pottery or porcelain vases take the place of simple rustic flowerpots filled with earth. In the present painting, Renoir took obvious pleasure in juxtaposing the real flowers with the drawn ones on the Delft vase.

By the early 1880s, the time of this painting, Renoir's relations with collectors had changed somewhat. Some of the collectors who had only recently become interested in the painting of the Impressionists went broke, like Hoschedé; others simply stopped buying paintings. Yet at the same time, Paul Durand-Ruel, whose financial situation was improving, began to support Claude Monet, Camille Pissarro, and Renoir on a more regular basis. It is partially due to his influence that Renoir, like Monet, began to paint more still lifes in this period than before. The still lifes, the dealer tried to persuade the artists, found buyers more easily.

An earlier, similar composition is found in the painting *Roses in a Vase* of 1876 (Anderson, *Renoir* [Wildenstein Galleries, New York, 1969], no. 20).

PROVENANCE: Heilbuth, Copenhagen; Moderne Galerie Heinrich Thannhauser, Munich; Otto Krebs, Holzdorf.

LITERATURE: J. Thiis, *Renoir: Den franske kvinnans malare* (Stockholm, 1944), p. 65 (reprod.).

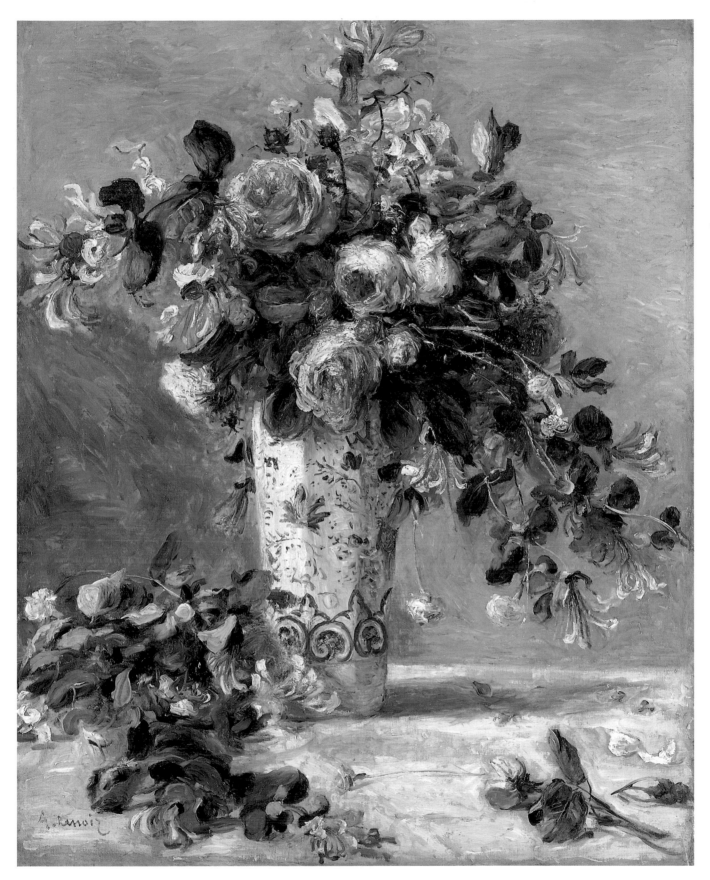

Pierre-Auguste Renoir

## 22. ROSES AND JASMINE IN A DELFT VASE

*Les Roses et jasmin dans le vase de Delft.* c. 1880–81

Oil on canvas, 32 × 25⅝" (81.5 × 65 cm). Signed lower left: "A. Renoir"

No. 3KP 524. Formerly collection Otto Krebs, Holzdorf

# PIERRE-AUGUSTE RENOIR

## Low Tide at Yport

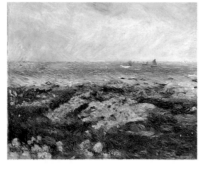

In the summer of 1883, Renoir worked on the Normandy coast, moving from Havre to Dieppe, Étretat, and Tréport. On the recommendation of his friend Dachery, who was also a friend of Alfred Nunès, Renoir went to see Nunès at Yport, located next to Fécamp. A cousin of Camille Pissarro and also a native of the island of St. Thomas, Nunès was the mayor of Yport, a small resort and fishing town on the coast of La Manche in the Havre district. Renoir stayed with Nunès, painting on commission a pair of large portraits of his children, Alina and Robert. The portrait of Robert, also called *Sailor Boy,* of 1883 (fig. 1; The Barnes Foundation, Merion, Pennsylvania), shows the younger Nunès strolling on the beach at low tide in search of seashells. The landscape background takes up a good deal of the painting. The sea is placid in tender morning light—the complete opposite of the mood in *Low Tide at Yport.* No other Renoir seascapes of Yport are known. The reason why the stay in Yport did not become more productive is explained in a letter from Renoir to Paul Bérard, dated August 21, 1883, describing the home of the convivial Nunès: "There are a few too many parties, that's the weak point . . . for at their place you spend a whole day at the table" (B. E. White, *Renoir: His Life, Art, and Letters* [New York, 1984], p. 133).

Unlike the two commissioned canvases, which are peaceful if not idyllic in spirit, Renoir apparently painted *Low Tide at Yport* for himself, and it is executed in a completely different vein, with a Romantic tonality usually not associated with Renoir. The sailboats in the agitated sea evoke the fisherman's life, full of dangers. And although Renoir tried to avoid any kind of literary or illustrative quality, the echo in this painting of an extremely popular novel of the day by Victor Hugo, *Laborers of the Sea,* is perhaps not accidental. Renoir worshiped Hugo. His first work shown at the Salon, *La Esmeralda* of 1863 (no longer extant), was executed on the subject of Hugo's *Notre-Dame de Paris.* And it can be noted that immediately after Yport, Renoir set off for the island of Jersey. "But the goal is Guernsey," Renoir wrote Bérard, "and despite the magnificent sights that unfold before our dazzled eyes, we are waiting impatiently for the boat that is to take us to see the rock on which the great poet [Victor Hugo] groaned for eighteen years" (White, ibid., p. 133).

In Renoir's work, where pure landscapes are encountered relatively rarely, this painting occupies a special place.

PROVENANCE: Galerie Bernheim-Jeune, Paris; Otto Krebs, Holzdorf.

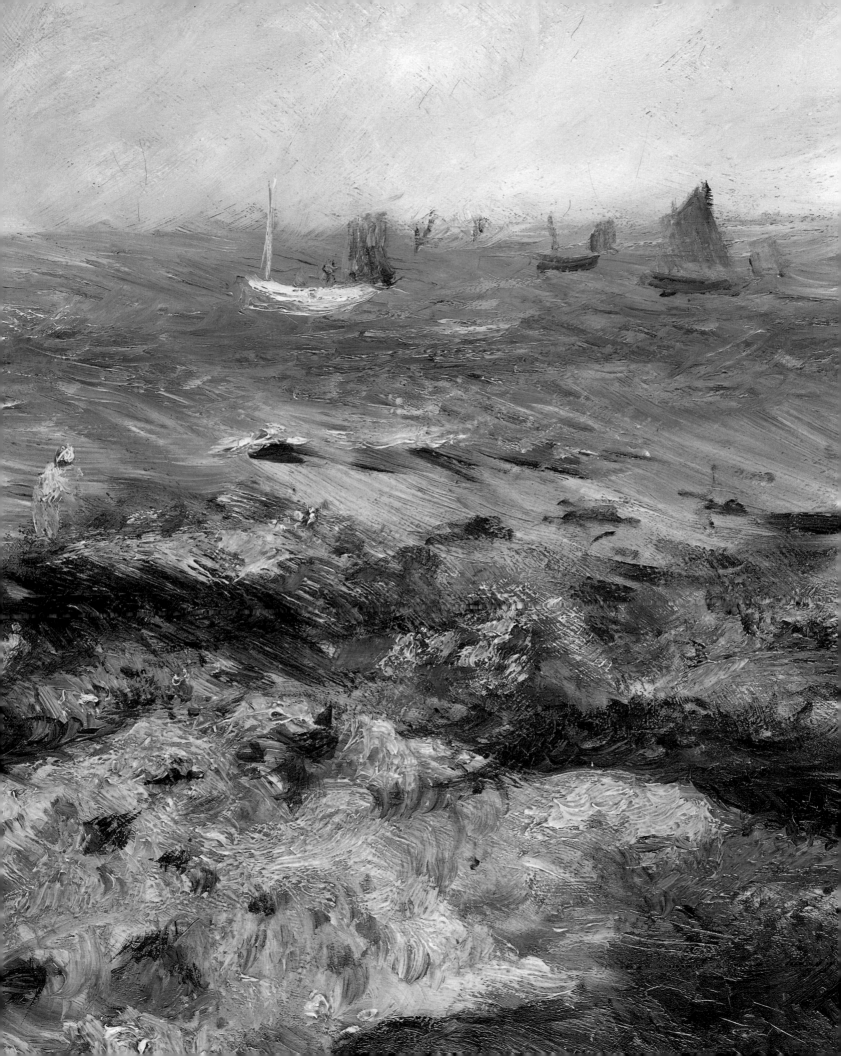

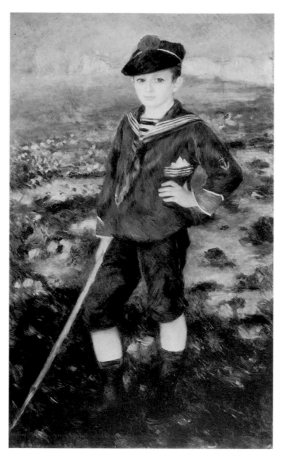

*Fig. 1. Pierre-Auguste Renoir.* Portrait of Robert Nunès on an Yport Beach (Sailor Boy). *1883. The Barnes Foundation, Merion, Pennsylvania. © The Barnes Foundation*

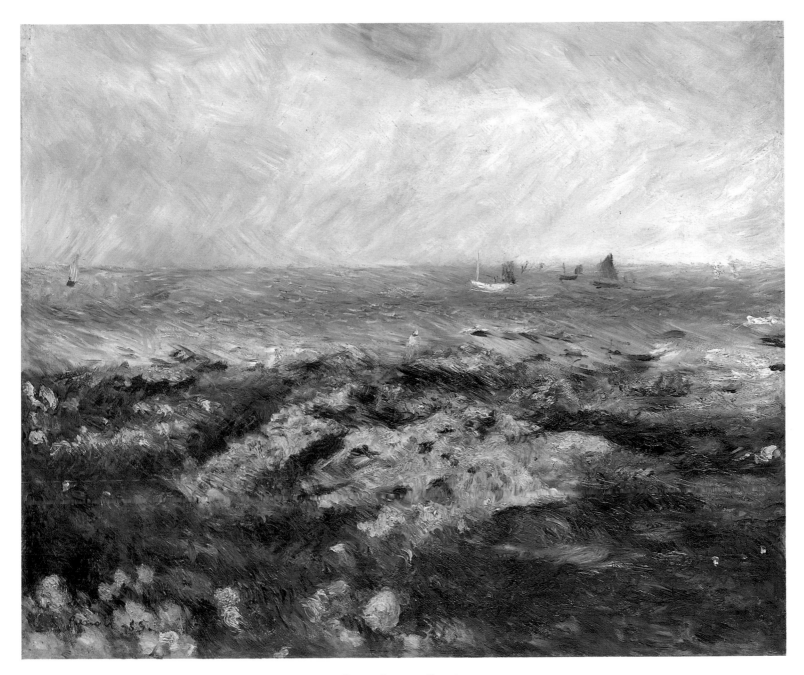

Pierre-Auguste Renoir

## 23. LOW TIDE AT YPORT

*Marée basse à Yport.* 1883

Oil on canvas, 21½ × 25¾" (54.5 × 65.3 cm). Signed and dated lower left: "Renoir 83"

No. 3KP 516. Formerly collection Otto Krebs, Holzdorf

# PIERRE-AUGUSTE RENOIR

## IN THE GARDEN

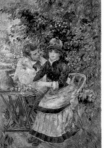

The story behind this painting is unusual. Although one of Renoir's more significant works, it was never exhibited and remained virtually unknown to the public. Barbara White, the leading contemporary critic of his art, writes: "*In the Garden,* a large but intimate canvas completed in 1885, is the last painting in which he depicts the love of a modern man for a modern woman in a rural setting, as *The Umbrellas* and the dance panels were the last contemporary courtship paintings in an urban setting" (B. E. White, *Renoir: His Life, Art, and Letters* [New York, 1984], p. 151).

It should be added that *In the Garden* is not only Renoir's last but perhaps his most unusual composition on the theme of love. Previously in paintings concerned with flirtation or ceremonial courtship, he wished to have the viewer sense the mutual attraction of the man and the woman, yet even so, like all the Impressionists, he avoided any hint of an anecdotal theme. In this case, however, in his largest canvas on the theme of love, Renoir almost succumbed to the temptation to create a topical work, although such a claim does not mean that he fell into the sin of anecdotage. He chose a theme that for any other painter of his day might have invited pseudo-Romantic declamation, or even sentimental tastelessness, but somehow he avoided these dangers.

The scene depicted here is not a typical romantic situation. Something greater than a conventional profession of love, the incident in the painting is conceived as a turning point in the lives of Renoir's subjects. The expectant look of the young man, his entire demeanor, leaves no doubt as to his intentions: he is asking for the hand and heart of the young woman. A detail such as the flowers lying on the little table reveals the prelude to the decisive conversation.

The fixed gaze of the girl reflects not so much her agitation as her transport, into the future, into another life. The seriousness of the young couple's intentions is suggested by the cross worn by the girl, an unusual detail for Renoir, who was not religious, and one not found in any other work of his. It is not presented as some kind of decoration (Renoir generally disliked painting women's ornaments); made fairly prominent, it is placed in the center of the composition, and focuses its meaning.

The appearance of such an unusual painting seems related to events in the life of Renoir himself. The birth of his first son, Pierre, on March 21, 1885, signified the true beginning of family life, which in Renoir's work was expressed by the completion of a group of compositions on the theme of love. This cycle was opened by a painting generally known by the imprecise title *The Sisleys,* of 1868 (Wallraf-Richartz-Museum, Cologne). Now that it has been established that it is not Sisley's wife who is depicted, but Renoir's regular model of those years, Lise Tréhot, the title *The Fiancés* has been suggested for this work. *The Fiancés* in fact is not a portrait but a genre composition of contemporary life in precisely conveyed details.

However, this quite realistically executed genre painting, like the subsequent pictures of couples, has its own subtext. Lise was Renoir's faithful companion for several years. In these love scenes, albeit always chaste ones, of a woman with whom he was involved, or wanted to be, Renoir painted a stand-in for himself. Interestingly, the male partner in these pairs was one of his friends, who was also an artist. In *The Lovers* of about 1875 (fig. 1; Národni Galeri, Prague), one of Renoir's most lyrical works, next to the actress Henriette Henriot, his favorite model of 1875–76, is the painter Franc-Lamy. Later, in two versions of *The*

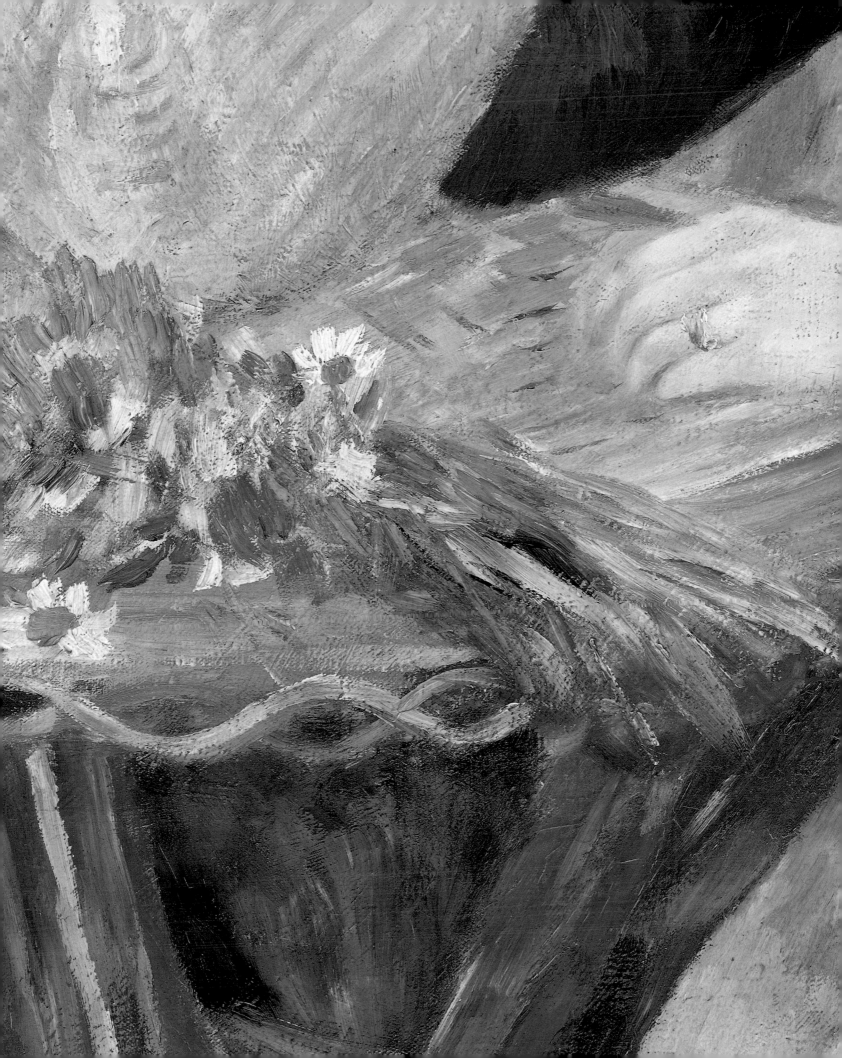

Conversation—Causerie of 1879 (Nationalmuseum, Stockholm; Daulte no. 321) and Conversation of 1879 (Daulte no. 322)—Margot's partner is the painter Frédéric Cordey.

Finally, the subject of the painting In the Garden is yet another artist, Henri Laurent. Twenty-one years old, Laurent was much younger than Renoir. By putting him together in the garden composition with Aline Charigot, Renoir's young girlfriend and later his wife, who was twenty-six years old at the time (he himself was forty-four), Renoir seemingly set himself the goal of depicting an ideal pair, since the ages of the model lovers were proximate.

But Aline here differs quite a bit from her other portrayals of the time. Even in the significantly earlier paintings, such as Portrait of Madame Renoir of 1881 (Daulte no. 366), or The Luncheon of the Boating Party of 1881 (The Phillips Collection, Washington, D.C.), where she is shown in the foreground playing with a dog, Aline Charigot does not seem so young, and the features of her face are less precise. Moreover, in Portrait of Madame Renoir (Philadelphia Museum of Art) and Motherhood (fig. 2; Daulte no. 485), canvases also from the year 1885, Renoir did not flatter his spouse, depicting her as rather plump and round-faced. It is believed that Aline Charigot posed for the artist in both these works. However, if this is indisputably true regarding the latter two works, the story behind In the Garden is evidently more complicated. The contrast is so great that one might suggest the figure of the woman has been painted not from life but from memory. In fact, Renoir quite possibly could have invited some beautiful young woman to pose, which would have been easy to do in Chatou, where the composition was executed. It was in Chatou, where the baths and the famous restaurant Le Père Fournaise were to be found (the terrace of this restaurant was depicted in The Luncheon of the Boating Party), that Aline became his model, their relations soon going further than had been the case with other sitters. At any rate, the artist took her with him the following year to Italy, although secretly. In 1885, they were virtually husband and wife, even though the marriage was not officially registered until five years later. Possibly nothing so visibly demonstrates the happiness of this union as the painting In the Garden.

A small study for this painting exists (fig. 3; private

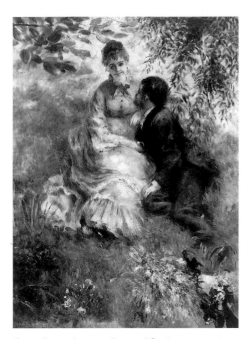

Fig. 1. Pierre-Auguste Renoir. The Lovers. c. 1875. Národni Galeri, Prague

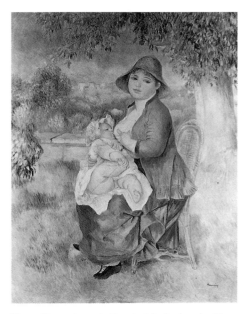

Fig. 2. Pierre-Auguste Renoir. Motherhood. 1885. Private collection, Tokyo

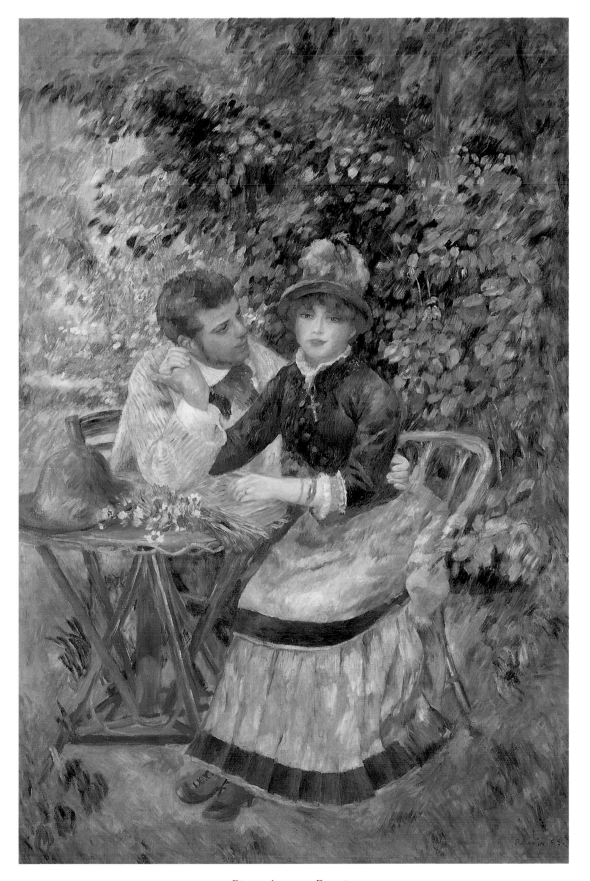

Pierre-Auguste Renoir

24. IN THE GARDEN

*Dans le jardin.* 1885

Oil on canvas, 66⅞ × 44¼" (170.5 × 112.5 cm). Signed and dated lower right: "Renoir 85"

No. 3K 1393. Formerly collection Gerstenberg/Scharf, Berlin

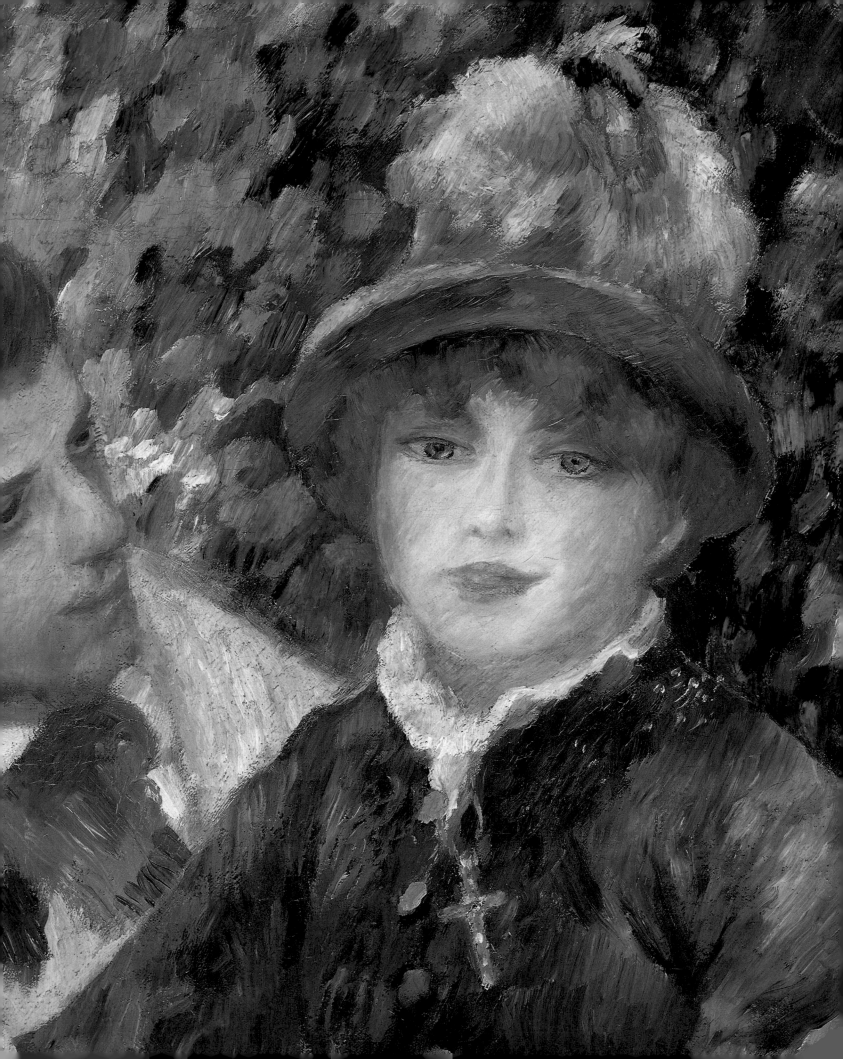

collection, Paris; Daulte no. 482) where only the heads of the figures are drawn, in mirror image to the present canvas. The man is about to kiss the woman. The work of a master of Rococo, François Boucher or Jean-Honoré Fragonard, whom he admired, could have suggested such a turn of subject to Renoir, but later such a thought may have seemed immodest to him. He never painted kisses. The relationship of the lovers in his paintings is limited to conversation, reading together, dancing, or some gesture of trust.

Daulte dated this study to 1885; Ambroise Vollard, who first published it under the title *The Lovers* (*Les Amoureux*) (A. Vollard, *L'Atelier de Renoir* [Paris, 1931], vol. 1, p. 130, no. 516), believed that it was executed in 1880, which is probably untenable. The same source shows a drawing entitled *Esquisse,* which could be considered one of the first ideas for the large composition. It shows a little table in a garden with an indistinct figure, a child to the right of the garden table, and in the upper area, the head of a young woman—an idealized depiction of Aline.

The same setting of the painting *In the Garden* can be found in the right-hand portion of a composition of the same name, *In the Garden* (*Under the Trees at Moulin de la Galette*) of 1875 (fig. 4; The Pushkin State Museum of Fine Arts, Moscow), an extremely characteristic and captivating embodiment of early Impressionism. The painter who ten years later returned to this motif was a master who had experienced disappointment with Impressionist methods and had tried, following the Renaissance masters, to cultivate line drawing. That was when he came to the so-called *aigre* style. Echoes of this style are quite noticeable in the 1885 painting in the faces of the figures, in the outlines of the lips, eyes, and brows. Along with this, linearity is emphasized by the "new" Impressionism, elements of thick, succulent strokes, designed to accentuate the almost porcelain refinement of the subject of the painting.

The painting was executed in at least two stages. After it was finished and the edges pasted with paper for mounting in a frame, Renoir once again applied paint to it, so that the strokes of this last stage of the work cover in some places the protective paper on the edges.

PROVENANCE: Galerie Durand-Ruel, Paris (acquired by Durand-Ruel from Renoir on December 7, 1901, for 10,000 francs); 1911, Otto Gerstenberg, Berlin (acquired from Durand-Ruel on December 8, 1911, for 50,000 francs); Margarete Scharf, Berlin.

LITERATURE: J. Meier-Graefe, *Auguste Renoir* (Munich, 1911) (reprod.); G. Rivière, *Renoir et ses amis* (Paris, 1921), p. 113 (reprod.); J. Meier-Graefe, *Renoir* (Leipzig, 1929), p. 238; G. Grappe, "Renoir," *L'Art vivant,* July 1933, p. 284; F. Daulte, "Renoir, son oeuvre regardé sous l'angle d'un album de famille," *Connaissance des arts,* 153 (November 1964), p. 76, pl. 7; F. Daulte, *Auguste Renoir: Catalogue raisonné de l'oeuvre peint* (Lausanne, 1971), no. 483; B. E. White, *Renoir: His Life, Art, and Letters* (New York, 1984), pp. 147, 151.

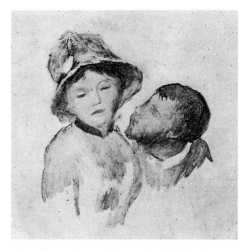

Fig. 3. *Pierre-Auguste Renoir.* Study for In the Garden. *c. 1885. Private collection, Paris*

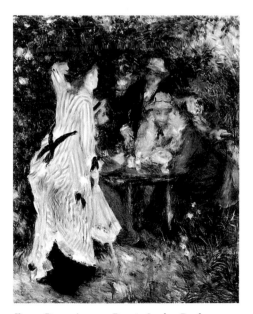

Fig. 4. *Pierre-Auguste Renoir.* In the Garden (Under the Trees at Moulin de la Galette). *1875. The Pushkin State Museum of Fine Arts, Moscow*

# PIERRE-AUGUSTE RENOIR

## Woman Arranging Her Hair

A woman brushing, straightening, or setting her hair is one of the themes running through all of Renoir's work, and usually the figure is shown seminude. The earliest version of this motif is the Barnes Foundation painting from 1873–75, known under various titles: *The Torso, Before the Bath, Toilette, Buste de femme*. In *Woman Arranging Her Hair,* Renoir preserved all the fundamentals of the earlier composition: the format, the figure above the waist, the position of the raised hands. It can be considered that she is also depicted in the two pictures called *Bather* and in *Nude among the Greenery* (Daulte nos. 519, 520, 524). The chief difference between the painting from the Barnes Foundation and *Woman Arranging Her Hair* results from the changes that occurred in Renoir's art with the end of the Impressionist movement. In the earlier canvas, subject to the rules of realism, each detail is motivated by the overall situation; a woman set against an unmade bed is undressing, perhaps preparing to take a bath. Her nightdress is lowered, entirely revealing the upper part of her body.

The later painting reveals rather the "museum" interests of the artist. The way in which the nightdress is painted here, leaving only one breast naked, is an allusion to the Amazons. Museum impressions perceptibly invade Renoir's art in the second half of the 1880s. The background is abstract, unburdened by any elaborative details. More attention is paid to the drawing, quite classic, which is reminiscent of the recent fascination with Jean-Auguste-Dominique Ingres. One of the works that would have led Renoir to a painting such as *Woman Arranging Her Hair* must have been Ingres's *Vénus Anadyomene* of 1848 (Musée de Condé, Chantilly).

The Bathers of 1887 (Philadelphia Museum of Art) was the principal work of the time, a canvas in which the neoclassical tendencies of Renoir's work are more clearly seen. Not only stylistically but in the use of the motif, *Woman Arranging Her Hair* can be linked to the Philadelphia painting. In 1886–87, during the final stage of the work on *The Bathers*, a number of further studies were executed. In two (B. E. White, *Renoir: His Life, Art, and Letters* [New York, 1984], p. 170), among several nude and semidressed bathers, a seated, seminude woman arranges her hair (see fig. 1); although she is viewed from a different angle, her gesture coincides with that of the *Woman Arranging Her Hair.*

Ten years later Renoir once again made use of the compositional scheme of this painting, in *Sleeping Girl* of 1897 (Sammlung Oskar Reinhart, Winterthur).

PROVENANCE: Galerie Durand-Ruel, Paris; Bernhard Koehler, Berlin.

LITERATURE: G. Rivière, *Renoir et ses amis* (Paris, 1921), p. 84 (reprod.); M. Florisoone, *Renoir* (Paris, 1938), no. 139.

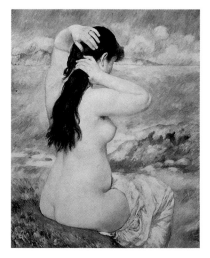

Fig. 1. *Pierre-Auguste Renoir.* Bather Arranging Her Hair. *1885. The Sterling and Francine Clark Art Institute, Williamstown, Massachusetts*

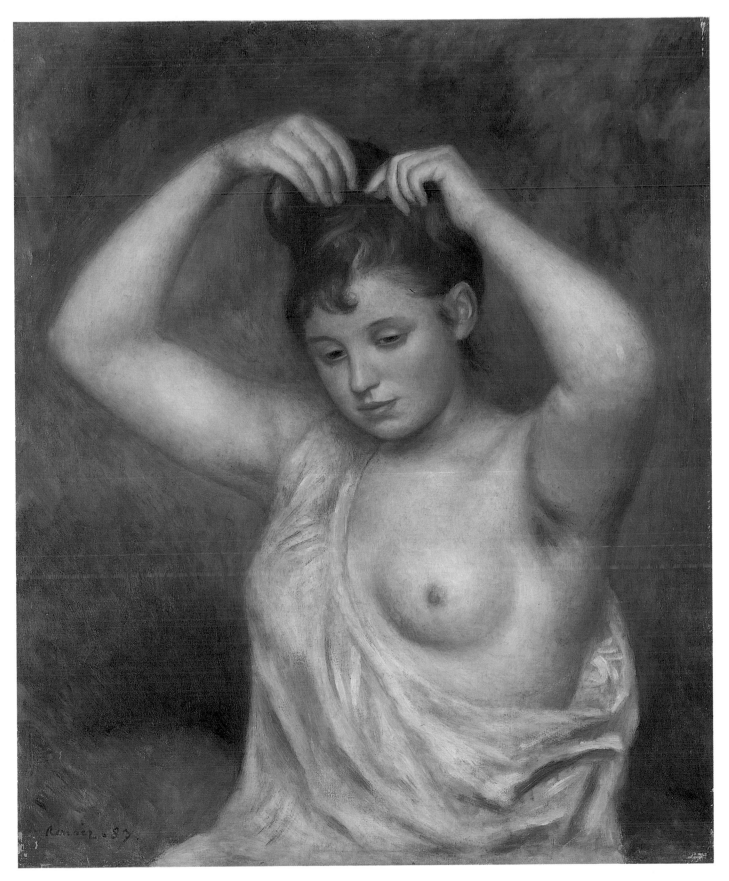

Pierre-Auguste Renoir

## 25. WOMAN ARRANGING HER HAIR

*Femme se coiffant.* 1887

Oil on canvas, 25 ¼ × 21 ¼" (65.3 × 54 cm). Signed and dated lower left: "Renoir 87"

No. 3K 507. Formerly collection Bernhard Koehler, Berlin

# PIERRE-AUGUSTE RENOIR

## YOUNG GIRLS AT THE PIANO

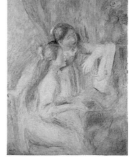

The theme of a woman at the piano often appears in early Impressionist paintings, including Édouard Manet's *Madame Manet at the Piano* of 1867–68 (Musée d'Orsay, Paris), Paul Cézanne's *Girl at the Piano* of 1867–68 (The State Hermitage Museum, St. Petersburg), and Edgar Degas's *Monsieur and Madame Manet* of 1868–69 (Kitakiushu Municipal Museum of Art). In fact, Degas used this theme even earlier, in 1865, as did Henri Fantin-Latour and James Abbott McNeill Whistler as early as the 1850s. Particularly noteworthy is Degas's *Girl at the Piano* of about 1865 (whereabouts unknown; Lemoisne no. 130), in which one girl is shown seated and the other standing.

Renoir, of course, knew at least some of these works when he began his *Woman at the Piano* of 1875 (The Art Institute of Chicago). Through the means of Impressionism he was able to create a fascinating composition in which, avoiding any studied or anecdotal quality, he found the painted equivalent of music. His harmonious combination of colors is indeed "musical." It is not known what prompted Renoir to paint such a work, although unquestionably it was not a commission.

Thirteen years later, the artist once again turned to the piano subject, this time on commission. Catulle Mendès wanted to have a portrait of his three daughters at the piano. The girls were studying music with their mother, a talented pianist. The figures in *The Daughters of Catulle Mendès* of 1888 (Annenberg collection; Daulte no. 545) are not painted at the moment of music making. They are explicitly posed, faces turned to the viewer, as Mendès no doubt desired, since he did not want a genre painting, but a portrait. The work must have brought Renoir pleasure, which at that time happened relatively rarely. It was a moment

of crisis, and Renoir had even refused to take part in the Centennale, the retrospective exhibition of nineteenth-century French art organized as part of the 1889 World's Fair. Sent the following year to the Salon, this portrait was the last canvas he showed there, although it did not receive any particular attention.

Soon after *The Daughters of Catulle Mendès*, Renoir painted the small *Music Lesson* of about 1889 (fig. 1; Joslyn Art Museum, Omaha), in which the right-hand portion of the Mendès composition has been preserved, or to be more precise, the dark piano with the bronze candle holder, the music score spread open, a bouquet, and, in the center, two girls, shown in profile, with golden hair, the color he always favored. One is standing, about to turn the page, and the other is sitting, playing the piano; both are looking at the score. The girls in *The Music Lesson* are sisters. That year they posed again for Renoir, for the painting *The Two Sisters* (private collection; Daulte no. 562).

In late 1891 an event took place that signaled the victory of Impressionism. The Minister of Fine Arts of France, Henri Roujon, a conservative, though not a hopeless one, consented to have a Renoir permanently displayed in the Musée du Luxembourg, the chief museum of contemporary art in Paris. He decided to propose to Renoir the purchase of one of his old paintings. However, Stéphane Mallarmé, a friend of Roujon's, persuaded him that it would be better to have Renoir paint a new work for the Luxembourg, a commission of sorts, which would allow the artist to decide independently what subject he would select.

Renoir chose the motif in *The Music Lesson*. Music and the beauty of the young women combined in one composition symbolizing harmony—in such an idea there could be nothing unacceptable to the

Luxembourg. *The Music Lesson* is a painting imbued with an understanding of the art in museums. Renoir was inspired by the fact that among his predecessors in depicting this subject was his favorite master, Jean-Honoré Fragonard, whose painting *The Music Lesson* of 1755 is in the Louvre. And in Fragonard's decorative panel *Music,* that art form is allegorically personified by a pretty young woman.

Taking as his starting point *The Music Lesson* in the Joslyn Art Museum, Renoir decided to use a substantially larger canvas. Renoir did not finish this painting, now in the Musée de l'Orangerie, Paris (fig. 2), but moved on to another canvas of the same dimensions. However, even the second painting, which was completed, did not satisfy him. One after another, new canvases were placed on his easel, and the same composition was painted. In a series unprecedented for Renoir of six works, four are fully resolved, while the present one, from the Krebs collection, is the least finished canvas in the group. In addition there is a pastel of the same dimensions, executed, most likely, after the oil paintings were completed, and a smaller pastel (The Metropolitan Museum of Art, New York). It is difficult to say in which order the canvases were painted, but the painting from the Musée de l'Orangerie is now generally considered to be the original study.

In contrast to *The Music Lesson,* where the figures were as similar as twins and wore identical red dresses in keeping with the general warm color scheme, in all the versions of *Young Girls at the Piano* the standing girl is a brunette and wears a reddish-colored dress, while the seated girl is a blonde and wears a white dress, the coloration determined by the balance of cool and warm tones.

The suggestion that *Young Girls at the Piano* is a portrait of the daughters of Henri Lerolle, an artist friend of Renoir's, is untenable (D. Mickenberg and G. Szabo, *Impressionism, Post-Impressionism: Nineteenth and Twentieth Century Paintings from the Robert Lehman Collection of The Metropolitan Museum of Art* [Oklahoma Museum of Art, 1983], p. 64). Renoir did indeed paint Yvonne and Christine Lerolle playing the piano, but that was five years later, and, more important, the sisters did not look like the figures in the 1892 series.

There are three major versions. The one that belonged to the Musée du Luxembourg is now in the

Musée d'Orsay (fig. 3). Another was acquired by Durand-Ruel and subsequently, as part of the Lehman collection, entered the Metropolitan Museum of Art, New York. The third was given by Renoir to Gustave Caillebotte and is now in a private collection (see *Renoir* [Hayward Gallery, London, 1985], pp. 260–61, commentary by John House). The fourth in the series (in a private collection) is a sketch, compared to the others. House suggests that it was executed later than the others, but it is more likely that it was painted in two stages. Apparently, this canvas was begun immediately after the one in the Musée de l'Orangerie. (In those two versions only, the left hand of the standing girl is at her cheek, whereas in other versions it hangs over the piano.) Then Renoir left this painting and finished it later for sale. The Lehman and Caillebotte versions clearly followed closely upon one another: the gestures in the two match completely. It is not entirely clear when the painting that went to the Luxembourg was executed, whether before or after them. Most likely it was afterward, because it was the Luxembourg canvas that Mallarmé called "finished." In comparison with the Lehman and Caillebotte versions, small changes are noticeable here.

Renoir seemed to be unsure of himself. An official commission signified a turning point in the biography of an artist who only recently had been fighting against official art, whose citadel still remained the Luxembourg. It forced him to keep seeking a perfection that was indisputable, even by conservative canons.

By mid-April 1892, the basic versions of the composition were completed, and on April 20 Roujon made his choice. The critic Arsène Alexandre, one of the eyewitnesses of these events, wrote the following: "I remember the infinite pains he took in executing the official commission which a well-meaning friend had taken the trouble to gain for him. This was the *Young Girls at the Piano,* a painting delicate and supple in its execution, though its color has yellowed somewhat. Renoir began this painting five or six times, each time almost identically. The idea of a *commission* was enough to paralyze him and to undermine his self-confidence. Tired of the struggle, he finally delivered to the Beaux-Arts the picture which is today at the Museum, which immediately afterwards he adjudged the least good of the five or six" (A. Alexandre, "Renoir sans phrases," *Les Arts,* March 1920). Later, Renoir admitted to Durand-Ruel that the version in the Luxembourg was to some extent "labored"; he had worked on it too much. Perhaps it is not surprising that this version was selected by Roujon, who professed official views on art.

On May 12 Mallarmé wrote a thank-you letter to Roujon. "For myself, and from the unanimous impression gathered around me, I cannot congratulate you enough for having chosen for the museum this definitive canvas, so calm and so free, a work of maturity" (S. Mallarmé, *Correspondance* [Paris, 1981], vol. 5, p. 78).

It should be quite obvious that the painting from the Krebs collection immediately preceded the Luxembourg work. Only in these two can the same gesture be seen. Although the Krebs painting seems not only unfinished but barely begun, Renoir put his signature to it and, consequently, considered it completed. Did he fear that by continuing to work he would make the painting heavier and less charming? Or did he perhaps from the very outset seek the effect of transparency and weightlessness that is so rare in oil paintings? In any case, Renoir made an effort to keep the image from becoming too solidly three-dimensional and/or too material, and sought an effect more like that of a watercolor, so to speak. At the same time, the bouquet that stands on the piano in other versions here becomes a painting within a painting, making the composition flatter. All in all, such a canvas was too free-spirited for the Musée du Luxembourg.

An idea of Michel Hoog's concerning the version in the Musée de l'Orangerie should be noted. He suggested that the entire group of paintings was deliberately promoted as an Impressionistic series, comparable to Claude Monet's series, which in addition to changes of weather could also reflect the artist's changing moods (M. Hoog, *Catalogue de la collection Jean Walter–Paul Guillaume* [Musée de l'Orangerie, Paris, 1984], p. 190). Pursuing this thought, it can be said that the different canvases in Renoir's series each exude their own kind of music. Light as a watercolor, the painting from the Krebs collection can perhaps be compared to Claude Debussy's experiments, as he searched for transparent effects in music during the same years.

The entire series of *Young Girls at the Piano,* or at least the Luxembourg version, had an unexpected

sequel in French painting when, a few years later, Henri de Toulouse-Lautrec produced his parody, *Singing Lesson* of 1898 (Mahmoud Khalil Museum, Cairo), depicting two middle-aged ladies by the piano.

LITERATURE: A. Alexandre, "Renoir sans phrases," *Les Arts,* March 1920.

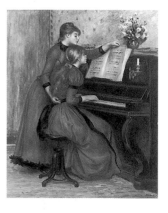

*Fig 1. Pierre-Auguste Renoir. The Music Lesson. c. 1889. Joslyn Art Museum, Omaha. Museum Purchase*

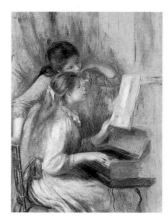

*Fig. 2. Pierre-Auguste Renoir. Young Girls at the Piano. 1892. Musée de l'Orangerie, Paris, Collection Walter–Guillaume*

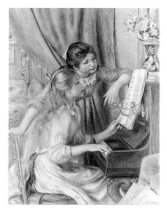

*Fig. 3. Pierre-Auguste Renoir. Young Girls at the Piano. 1892. Musée d'Orsay, Paris*

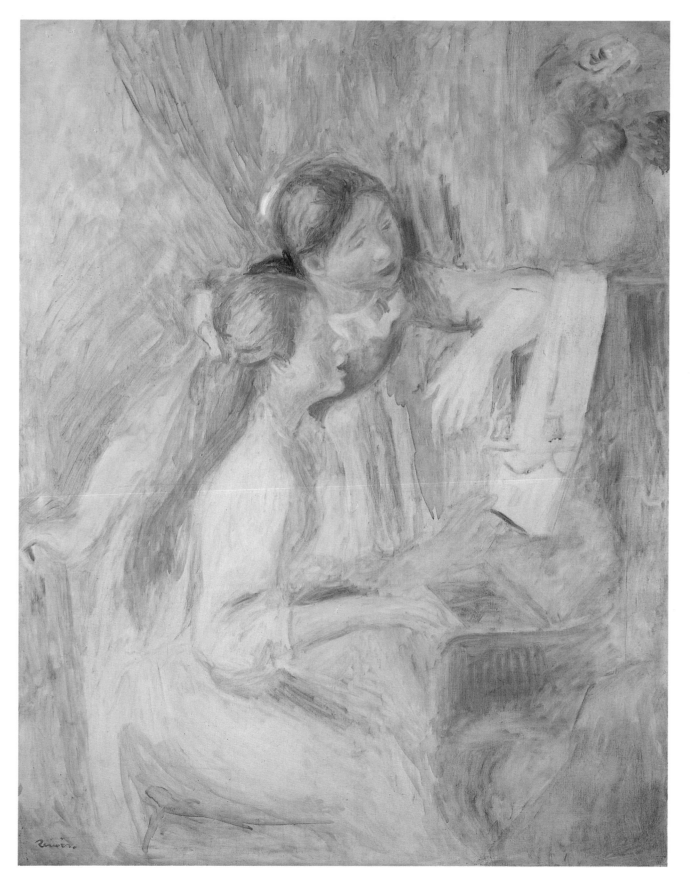

Pierre-Auguste Renoir
## 26. YOUNG GIRLS AT THE PIANO
*Jeunes filles au piano.* c. 1892
Oil on canvas, 45⅞ × 35¼" (116.5 × 89.5 cm). Signed lower left· "Renoir"
No. 3KP 227. Formerly collection Otto Krebs, Holzdorf

# PIERRE-AUGUSTE RENOIR

## YOUNG WOMAN IN A FLOWERED HAT

In the 1890s Renoir frequently painted the subject of a young woman in a hat. The artist had been partial to this theme in the past. It is characteristic that among his very first paintings was *Woman Arranging Her Hat* of about 1860 (Daulte no. 2). The fancy ladies' hats of the end of the century further enlivened Renoir's interest. Suzanne Valadon recalled that Renoir liked them so much that sometimes he ordered especially unusual hats for his models. These *chapeaux fantaisistes* turned out to suit Renoir's women.

At that time Renoir loved to play with the combination of a very bright white or rose dress that was the foundation for the painting's composition and a straw hat with bright flowers, usually red, so that the splash of the flesh tone of the face in the middle would "reconcile" the top and bottom of the painting. On this principle were constructed paintings like *Young Girl in a Red Poppy Hat* of 1889 (fig. 1; private collection; Renoir retrospective [Nagoya City Art Museum, 1988], no. 37). The woman is painted not as a thinker or doer, or a housewife or worker, but as a creation of nature, and its ornament. Therefore, the liveliest colors of nature, luxuriant garden flowers, are quite appropriate here.

Nevertheless, *Young Woman in a Flowered Hat* does not entirely represent the usual Renoir type of woman, who is notable for a soft, oval face with a tiny, round nose. Perhaps this is not the usual portrayal of a model, but the portrait of an unknown lady. The fact that the painting was dated suggests as much, since as a rule pictures of models, unlike portraits, were not dated.

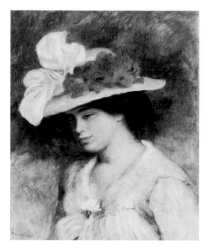

Fig. 1. Pierre-Auguste Renoir. Young Girl in a Red Poppy Hat. *1889. Private collection*

PROVENANCE: Galerie Durand-Ruel, Paris; Galerie Thannhauser, Berlin; Otto Krebs, Holzdorf.

LITERATURE: J. Meier-Graefe, *Renoir* (Leipzig, 1929), p. 363, no. 306 (reprod.).

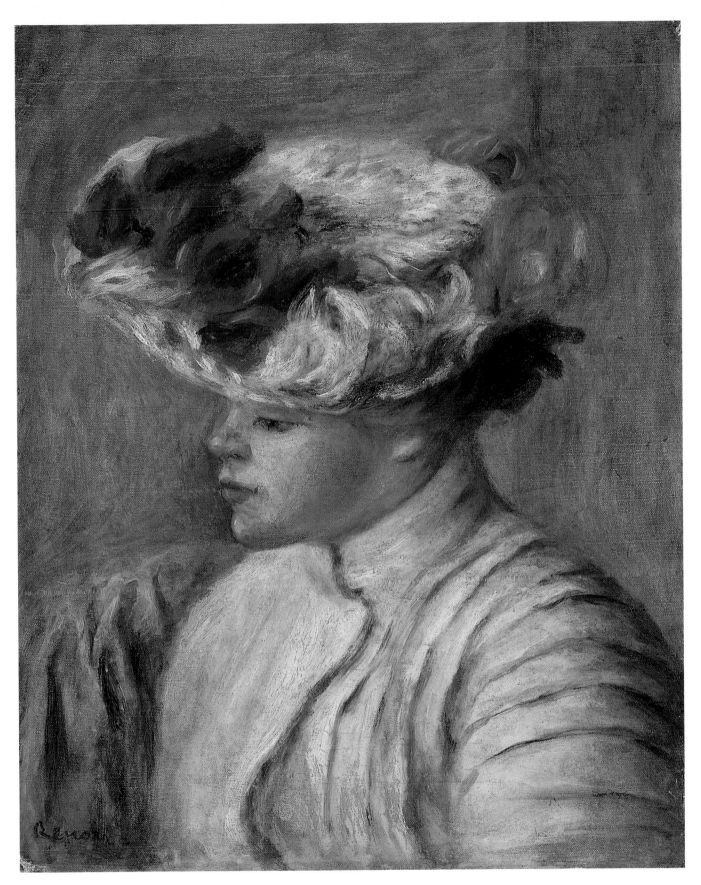

Pierre-Auguste Renoir

## 27. YOUNG WOMAN IN A FLOWERED HAT

*Jeune Femme au chapeau de fleurs.* 1892

Oil on canvas, 16⅜ × 13" (41.5 × 33 cm). Signed and dated lower left: "Renoir 92"

No. 3KP 560. Formerly collection Otto Krebs, Holzdorf

# PIERRE-AUGUSTE RENOIR

## YOUNG GIRL IN A HAT

This painting depicts the same model as *Young Girl in a Charlotte*, which was once in the Durand-Ruel collection and is now in the Galerie Schmit (fig. 1; *Maîtres français, XIX–XX siècles* [Galerie Schmit, Paris, 1994], no. 47). It is not dated, but the Galerie's specialists believe it was executed in 1894. Daulte is intending to include it in the next volume of his catalogue of Renoir's painting. The present painting was clearly painted at the same time as *Young Girl in a Charlotte*.

The charlotte, a hat fashionable in the late nineteenth century, was depicted by Renoir on several occasions during that time in paintings and lithographs. It is difficult to make a precise dating of all these works. Thus, Daulte attributes *Head of a Young Girl, or the Red Hat* (private collection; Daulte no. 644), one of the prototypes for the present painting, to 1890, and it would have been plausible to move this date to a year or two earlier.

During 1892–97, Renoir worked on a series of prints of *Épinglé Hat* (the name of a particular fleecy fabric), using various mediums (etching, dry charcoal, lithography). In this series the portrayal of the two young girls in wide-brimmed hats varies. The subject is simple: one of the girls is pinning flowers to her friend's hat.

The subject of *Young Girl in a Hat* is similar to the left-hand figure in the painting *Young Girls Reading* of about 1892 (Virginia Museum of Fine Arts, Richmond). The catalogue of an exhibition at the Wildenstein Gallery, where the Virginia painting was displayed, advances the supposition that the girls are the daughters of the novelist Paul Alexis, a friend of Paul Cézanne's and a neighbor of Renoir's in Montmartre in the early 1890s (*Renoir: An Exhibition for the Benefit of the American Association of Museums* [Wildenstein Gallery, New York, 1969], no. 74). However, the model also looks like Paule Gobillard, the niece of Berthe Morisot, shown in another painting of approximately the same time, *Two Young Girls Reading* of about 1891 (fig. 2; Los Angeles County Museum of Art).

PROVENANCE: Galerie A. A. Hébrard, Paris (as *Tête de jeune femme*); Otto Krebs, Holzdorf.

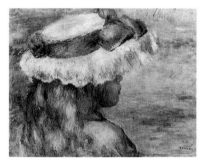

*Fig. 1. Pierre-Auguste Renoir.* Young Girl in a Charlotte. *1894. Private collection, courtesy Galerie Schmit, Paris*

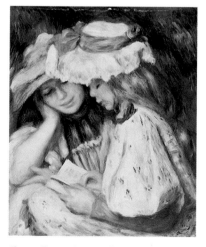

*Fig. 2. Pierre-Auguste Renoir.* Two Young Girls Reading. *c. 1891. Los Angeles County Museum of Art. Gift of Dr. and Mrs. Armand Hammer*

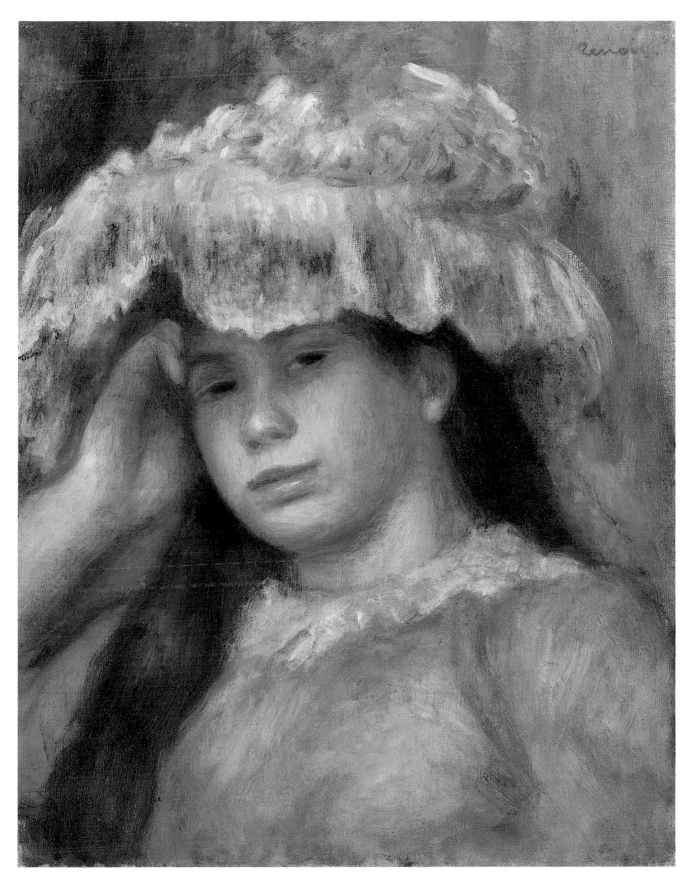

Pierre-Auguste Renoir
## 28. YOUNG GIRL IN A HAT
*Jeune Fille au chapeau.* c. 1892–94
Oil on canvas, 16¼ × 12¾" (41.3 × 32.5 cm). Signed upper right: "Renoir"
No. 3KP 561. Formerly collection Otto Krebs, Holzdorf

# PIERRE-AUGUSTE RENOIR

## APPLES AND FLOWERS

The bouquet in this still life is arranged so that the roses, peonies, and jasmine, similar in coloration, create an unusually subtle range of tones related to white. The chief pictorial effect of the painting emerges from the contrast between these shades of white—symbol of purity and virginity—and the apples, which could relate to the Tree of Knowledge. Renoir was no Symbolist, but he was a product of his time, and in the mid-1890s, when Symbolism was flourishing, he reflected values toward which in his earlier work he had maintained an indifference. There are sensual overtones in the painting that suggest its program was not completely taken up with realist or purely pictorial problems.

The still life also reflects an interest in Paul Cézanne's painting. This is seen most clearly in the selection of objects. The foreground is given to a pile of apples on a plate, as often with the Master of Aix (compare plate 50). Neither in his early work nor in his Impressionist period had the fruit attracted Renoir. But it was Cézanne's example that compelled him to recognize that to create a painting, "an apple on the edge of a table is quite sufficient." In the effort to accentuate the three-dimensionality of the apples, by means of a compact grouping of objects, the further influence of Cézanne can be perceived. Yet this influence manifests itself in an unusual way. Cézanne's rigorous structural quality and his special perspective (*perspective plongeante*) are essentially alien to Renoir, whose work here, as before, is notable for a softness that one wants to call feminine.

Renoir always had the deepest respect for Cézanne. They had worked together in 1882 in L'Estaque, and three years later Cézanne came to visit him in La Roche-Guyon. Renoir spent the summer of 1889 near Aix, renting a house from Cézanne's brother-in-law. In November 1895, Renoir and Degas went to

Cézanne's exhibition organized by Ambroise Vollard. On November 21, 1895, Camille Pissarro wrote his son Lucien: "At that same time at Cézanne's show, when I was so delighted by the surprising and astonishing nature of his works, which had attracted me for many years, Renoir appeared. My admiration was nothing compared to Renoir's delight. Even Degas fell under the charm of the wild and at the same time refined nature of Cézanne, just as Monet and all of us. Are we really mistaken? I don't think so. Those who do not succumb to this charm are those artists and art-lovers who have proved by their mistakes many times that they have no understanding. They very logically cite the shortcomings in Cézanne's work, which we ourselves see, which strike the eye, but the charm . . . they don't see the charm. Renoir has rightly said that there is something analogous to the frescoes of Pompeii in Cézanne's paintings, so archaic and marvelous." And in a letter of December 4, Pissarro added: "Degas and Renoir are enthusiastic about Cézanne's works. Vollard showed me a drawing of some fruit for which they drew lots to see which of them would be the happy owner" (*Camille Pissarro: Lettres à son fils Lucien,* ed. J. Rewald [Paris, 1950], no. 392).

Julie Manet, the daughter of Berthe Morisot (Renoir was her guardian), wrote of the deep impression that Cézanne's still lifes made on Renoir. But, just like his friend Cézanne, Renoir in all instances remained himself. Even when falling under the charm of Cézanne's painting, he was not capable of imitation.

PROVENANCE: Galerie Bernheim-Jeune, Paris; Moderne Galerie (Heinrich Thannhauser), Munich; 1911 or 1912, Bernhard Koehler, Berlin.

EXHIBITIONS: 1912, Paris, "Renoir," Galerie Manzi, Joyant & Cie, no. 176 (?).

LITERATURE: M. Florisoone, *Renoir* (Paris, 1938), p. 155 (under the incorrect title *Framboises et sucrier*).

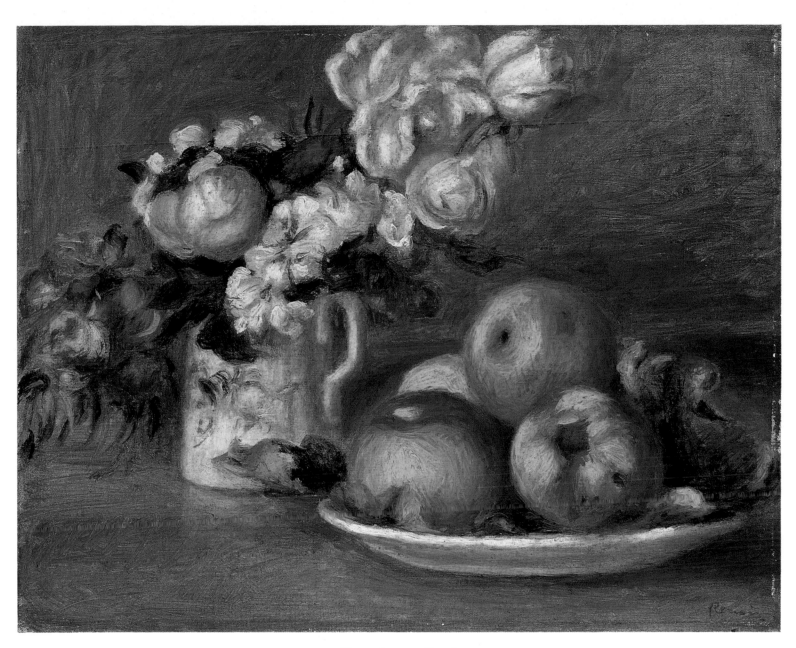

Pierre-Auguste Renoir
## 29. APPLES AND FLOWERS
*Les Pommes et les fleurs.* c. 1895–96
Oil on canvas, 12⅞ × 16¼" (32.8 × 41.4 cm). Signed lower right: "Renoir"
No. 3K 1528. Formerly collection Bernhard Koehler, Berlin

# PIERRE-AUGUSTE RENOIR

## PARTY IN THE COUNTRY AT BERNEVAL

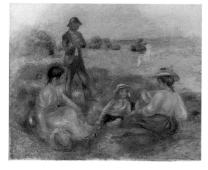

Renoir depicted his first impressions of Berneval, on the Normandy coast near Dieppe, in his painting *Mussel Fishers at Berneval* of 1879 (fig. 1; The Barnes Foundation, Merion, Pennsylvania). He sent this large canvas to the Salon the following spring, but it was displayed poorly and was not successful. Renoir spent the summer of 1879 in Wargemont at the home of his patron Paul Bérard; from there, the trip to Berneval was short. Renoir was able to adapt himself to these places, despite the fact that the rocky beach in *Mussel Fishers* presents a rather stark landscape, hardly Renoiresque in feeling.

In July 1898, Renoir traveled there once again. He had not intended to stay long, but ended up spending the entire summer, yielding to the wishes of his wife, who loved Berneval. He himself found it "a charming place for the first day, too small the second, and intolerable on the third." Nonetheless, by early September, according to Julie Manet, who was in Berneval briefly with the Renoir family, the artist was "content with his stay" (J. Manet, *Journal, 1893–1899* [Paris, 1979], p. 186). When Pissarro happened to be in Berneval two years later, he wrote Durand-Ruel that it was just the sort of place he was looking for: "All around me are beautiful subjects. The beach is marvelous—very Monet!" (letter of July 12, 1900, in L. Venturi, *Les Archives de l'impressionisme* [Paris, 1939], vol. 2).

Renoir did not invent figures for himself: he always made use of nature's inspirations. However, the selection of models was rather limited in remote Berneval. Julie Manet's cousins, Paule and Jeannie Gobillard, came with her to the Renoirs' chalet for a few days' stay. The two girls are shown in the painting's foreground at the right, with Julie Manet at the left. In the center is four-year-old Jean Renoir, the future film

director. Here he could be mistaken for a little girl because of the long locks that his father so loved. To the left stands thirteen-year-old Pierre, the artist's eldest son, who later became a well-known actor. (Both sons figure in *Breakfast in Berneval*, also of 1898 [fig. 3; private collection].) It is not surprising that Renoir kept *Party in the Country at Berneval* until his death, since it portrayed two of his own children and the girls for whom he had a truly paternal feeling.

*Party in the Country at Berneval* interprets a subject that was far from new for French art. The theme of the picnic, of recreation in nature, appeared, on the one hand, in such minor Romantics as Deveria, and on the other hand, in an ironic vein, in Honoré Daumier's lithographs. In the 1860s, it took on great importance for Édouard Manet and Claude Monet in their respective paintings called *Le Déjeuner sur l'herbe*. Renoir turned to the theme only in the 1890s, in such paintings as *Landscape at Pont-Aven* of 1893 (A. André and M. Elder, *L'Atelier de Renoir* [Paris, 1931], no. 77), when it was no longer perceived as current. But in these years, Renoir did not seek current themes and did not strive to be modern, as he had during the rise of Impressionism. He was far more inspired by the painting of Antoine Watteau, François Boucher, and Jean-Honoré Fragonard, their *gallante* scenes played out in nature.

*Landscape with Three Women* (private collection; Renoir retrospective [Nagoya City Art Museum, 1988], no. 39) may be considered a variation of *Party in the Country at Berneval*. In the Nagoya catalogue it is dated 1890, possibly after consultation with François Daulte, who will include it in a forthcoming volume of his Renoir catalogue raisonné. It is more probable, however, that *Landscape with Three Women* was paint-ed at about the same time as *Party in the Country at Berneval,* probably shortly after it. The foreground in *Landscape* is shadowed in a similar way, but the com-position is slightly simpler. A young woman who, like Pierre, has a walking stick is represented instead of him.

PROVENANCE: Galerie Bernheim-Jeune, Paris; Otto Krebs, Holzdorf.

LITERATURE: A. André and M. Elder, *L'Atelier de Renoir* (Paris, 1931), no. 200.

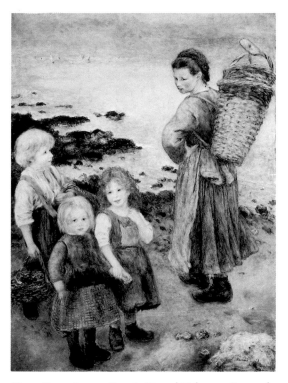

*Fig. 1. Pierre-Auguste Renoir.* Mussel Fishers at Berneval. *1879. The Barnes Foundation, Merion, Pennsylvania.* © The Barnes Foundation

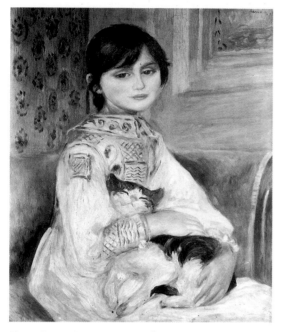

*Fig. 2. Pierre-Auguste Renoir.* Julie Manet. *1887.*
*Private collection*

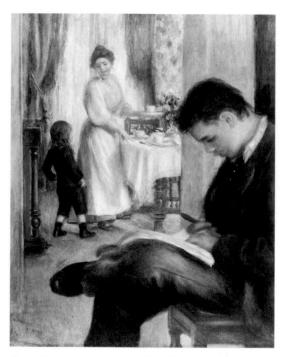

*Fig. 3. Pierre-Auguste Renoir.* Breakfast in Berneval. *1898.*
*Private collection*

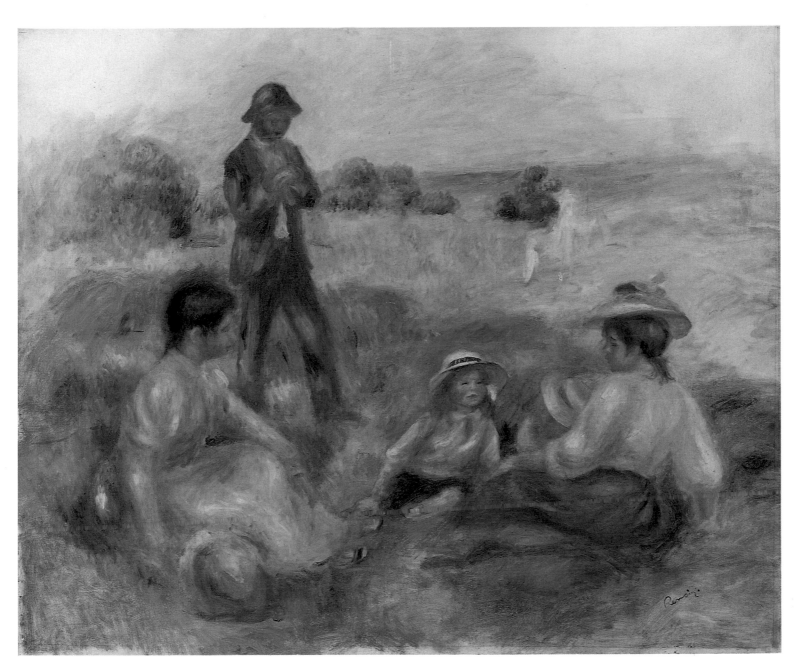

Pierre-Auguste Renoir

30. PARTY IN THE COUNTRY AT BERNEVAL

*Paysage à Berneval avec personnages.* 1898

Oil on canvas, 23¾ × 28¾" (60.3 × 73 cm)

Signed lower right: "Renoir"

No. 3KP 535. Formerly collection Otto Krebs, Holzdorf

# PIERRE-AUGUSTE RENOIR

## LANDSCAPE AT BEAULIEU

The stamp of the Galerie Durand-Ruel with the label *Paysage à Beaulieu* on the painting's stretcher enables us to determine where this canvas was executed.

The little village of Beaulieu, on the Mediterranean near Nice, where Renoir stayed at Villa Quincet, first attracted him in the spring of 1893. He wrote Durand-Ruel from there that although he had arrived tired, he felt marvelous and was satisfied with what he called his "studies." He stayed in Beaulieu again four years later, and there is a painting of a landscape with orange trees in the foreground, dated 1897 (fig. 1; The Fine Arts Museums of San Francisco). Documentary sources do not provide any information about Renoir's working in Beaulieu after that. However, the present painting, which is dated, indicates that he worked there once again in 1899.

The landscape composition arranged by Renoir on this occasion, with a little road running through the middle framed by trees parted like stage curtains, is similar to the painting in San Francisco, except that now a distant ocean view can be seen in the center. The landscape is constructed like a theater set, a far cry from the principles of immediacy and vividness advocated by Impressionism. This is a kind of pastiche, but even when looking back to the eighteenth century, Renoir remained original in his "variations on a Rococo theme."

PROVENANCE: Galerie Durand-Ruel, Paris; Otto Krebs, Holzdorf.

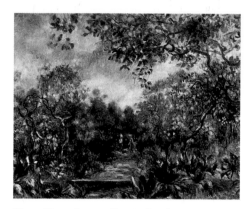

*Fig. 1. Pierre-Auguste Renoir.* Landscape at Beaulieu. *1897. The Fine Arts Museums of San Francisco. Mildred Anne Williams Fund*

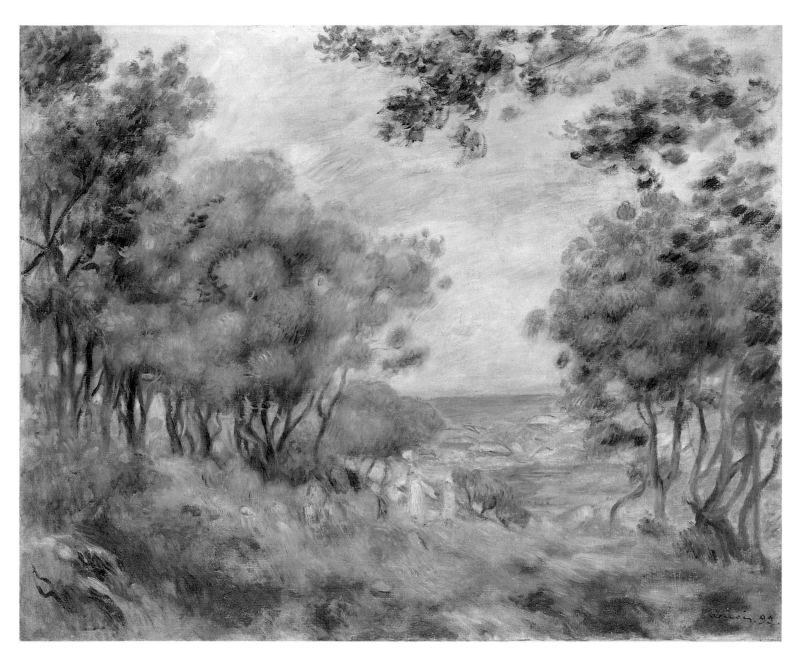

Pierre-Auguste Renoir
31. LANDSCAPE AT BEAULIEU
*Paysage à Beaulieu.* 1899
Oil on canvas, 25¾ × 32" (65.3 × 81.5 cm)
Signed and dated lower right: "Renoir 99"
No. 3KP 518. Formerly collection Otto Krebs, Holzdorf

# PIERRE-AUGUSTE RENOIR

## BOUQUET OF ROSES

In old age, Renoir loved roses as no other flower, painting them enthusiastically and often, especially red roses. By that time, his acuity of perception had lessened somewhat. The delicate nuances characteristic of his early, Impressionist work gave way to a wish to evoke the sheer tangibility of the object. Thus it is no wonder that such still lifes as *Bouquet of Roses* belong to the period of his involvement with sculpture, which began in the summer of 1913. The way he went about executing a painting changed at this time. If before, Renoir had applied color in transparent layers, essential for obtaining many of the subtlest shades, now he felt no such constraint. Painting in layers required an extended time of execution, since a light, transparent layer must be applied on a dried foundation in order to achieve the desired effect. In contrast, the later still lifes are notable for the use of thick brushstrokes, and for objects drawn very quickly, usually in one sitting. The chosen subject necessitated a relatively rapid execution, as cut roses do not last long in water.

Renoir was finding it increasingly difficult to walk, due to his worsening rheumatism, and his hands were affected as well. If the works made at this time lack his previous subtlety, they are perhaps more expressive, and in a different, even expressionistic way. Here, the texture of the roses is boldly re-created with circular strokes that share a single gestural rhythm, the imprint of the artist's action. The principles of an art of painterly abstraction that would arise in the mid-twentieth century were beginning to be established by an artist from whom they might be least expected.

Precise dating of the present still life is rather difficult. Renoir himself did not date these paintings, and in the literature various times of execution are ascribed to them. Thus, the execution of *Vase with Roses* (Renoir family collection; *Monet to Matisse: French Art in Southern California Collections* [Los Angeles County Museum of Art, 1991], p. 66), compositionally very similar but somewhat softer in style, has been dated to about 1890–1900, perhaps an unjustifiably early time frame. Two analogous still lifes with roses in similar globe-shaped vases are dated more convincingly: *Bouquet* to 1909 (A. André and M. Elder, *L'Atelier de Renoir* [Paris, 1931], no. 372) and *Flowers, Bouquet* to 1910 (ibid., no. 410). There is also an undated composition (fig. 1; J. Meier-Graefe, *Renoir* [Leipzig, 1929], p. 328). Yet another bouquet composed in the same fashion and placed in a globe-shaped vase is seen in *Roses with a Blue Curtain* (Gangnat collection, Paris), dated variously from 1890 to 1912. The latter is the more persuasive dating (P. H. Feist, *Auguste Renoir* [Leipzig, 1967], no. 69).

During these years Renoir added rose bouquets to some of his figure compositions. The depiction of roses in *Woman with a Bouquet of Roses* (A. André, *Renoir* [Paris, 1919], no. 21) and *Portrait of the Poetess Alice Vallière-Merzbach* of 1913 (Musée d'Art Moderne, Petit-Palais, Geneva) recalls the present still life.

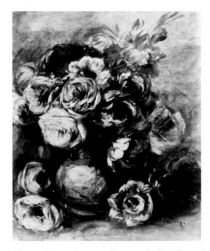

*Fig. 1. Pierre-Auguste Renoir.* Still Life with Roses. *n.d. Whereabouts unknown*

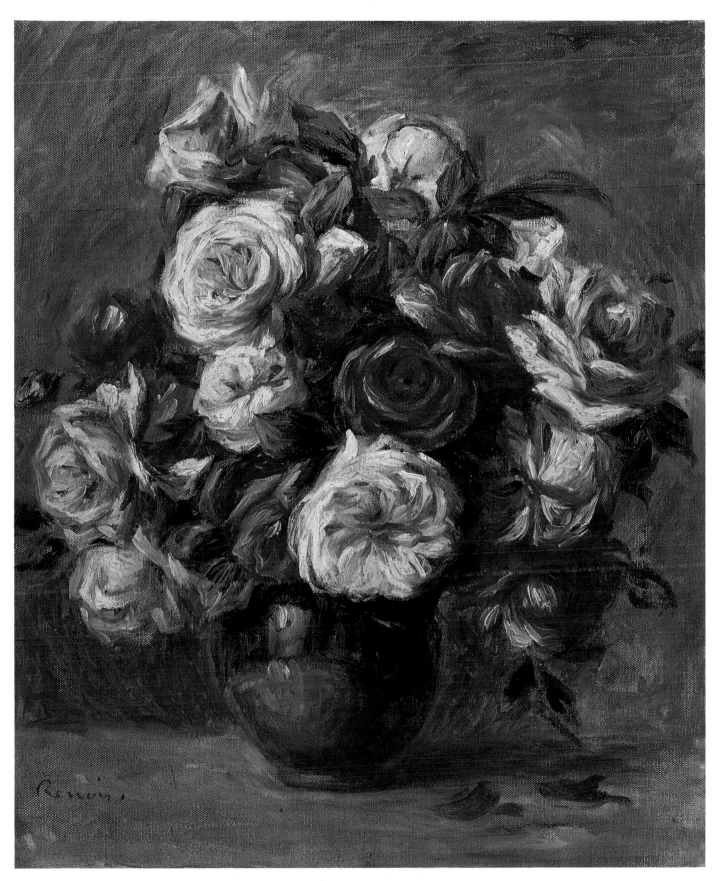

Pierre-Auguste Renoir
## 32. BOUQUET OF ROSES
*Bouquet de roses.* c. 1909–13
Oil on canvas, 18¼ × 15⅛" (46.5 × 38.5 cm)  Signed lower left. "Renoir"
No. 3KP 563. Formerly collection Otto Krebs, Holzdorf

# PIERRE-AUGUSTE RENOIR

## ROSES IN A VASE

This still life is close in style to *Bouquet of Roses* (plate 32) but was probably executed somewhat later. Two analogous paintings published among the works from Renoir's studio, albeit under only approximate dates, support this view: *Study of Flowers* of 1910–14 (A. André and M. Elder, *L'Atelier de Renoir* [Paris, 1931], no. 371) and *Bouquet of Flowers* of 1913–19 (ibid., no. 477). Also to be taken into account is the painting *Roses,* formerly in the Paris collection of Louis Bernard (J. Meier-Graefe, *Renoir* [Leipzig, 1929], p. 329), dated by Meier-Graefe to about 1909 (fig. 2).

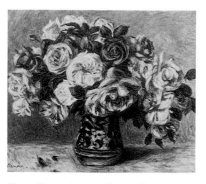

Fig. 1. Pierre-Auguste Renoir. Roses in a Vase. *1910–14. Private collection, Geneva*

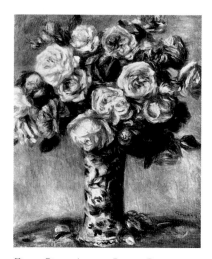

Fig. 2. Pierre-Auguste Renoir. Roses. *1909–12. The Baltimore Museum of Art. The Cone Collection*

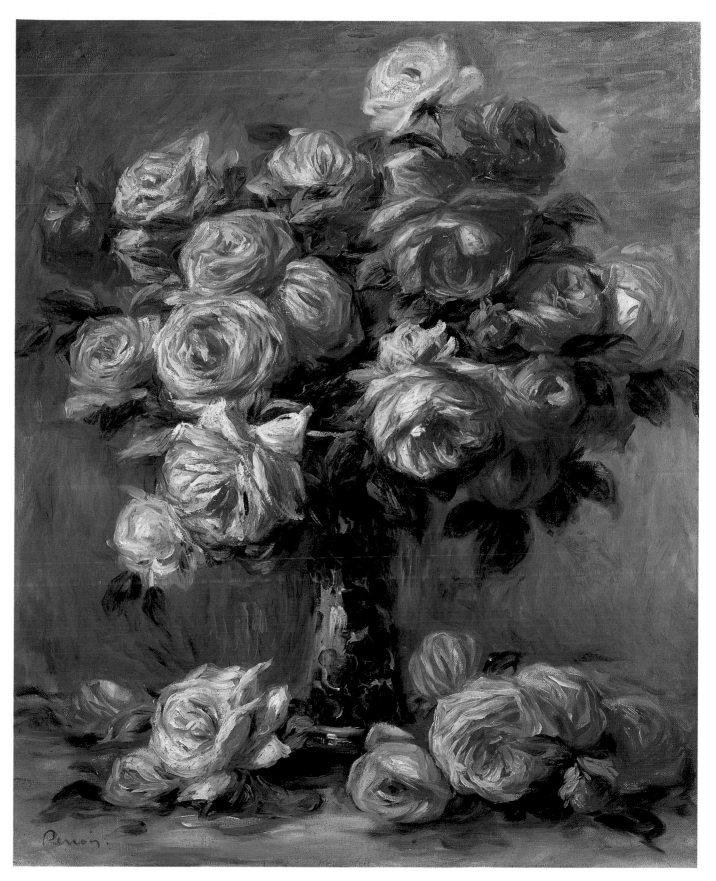

Pierre-Auguste Renoir
### 33. ROSES IN A VASE
*Les Roses dans un vase.* c. 1910–17
Oil on canvas, 24¼ × 20" (61.5 × 50.7 cm). Signed lower left: "Renoir"
No. 3KP 512. Formerly collection Otto Krebs, Holzdorf

# CLAUDE MONET

## THE SEINE AT ROUEN

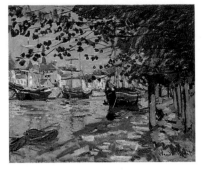

In March 1872, at the insistence of his brother Léon, who lived near Rouen, and who took a lively interest in his work, Claude Monet set off for that city in order to show several paintings at the twenty-third Rouen municipal exhibition. Along with Camille Pissarro, Alfred Sisley, and Edgar Degas, Monet had decided against the idea of sending work to the Salon that spring. The trip to Rouen turned out to be fruitful and yielded several magnificent landscapes.

The main subject that Monet painted in Rouen at this time was sailboats on the Seine, usually moored and with their sails furled. For these, various backgrounds were selected—houses along the embankment, or the famous cathedral in the distance, or the hills on the outskirts of the city. In each instance, Monet was drawn by the effect of open space, as with the painting in the National Gallery of Art, Washington, D.C. (fig. 1). The present painting constitutes an exception. Here, Monet was concerned less to have his sailboats stand out sharply against the water's smooth surface than, as they emerge from the leaves of the foreground trees, to fit them into the general structure of verticals and horizontals. Despite the widespread view that the Impressionists and their leader, Monet, gave little thought to the structure of their landscapes, while concentrating on fleeting impressions, *The Seine at Rouen* is notable for its truly "constructive" composition.

Monet had put his school training to use before, particularly the classical technique of *repoussoir,* as demonstrated by the shadowed foreground of the painting *The Bridge at Bougival* of 1869 (The Currier Gallery of Art, Manchester, New Hampshire; Wildenstein no. 152). At that time, its use was far simpler. Now, however, the *repoussoir* technique is deployed in a masterly fashion, to support the overall impression of a joyful sunny day, with its casual play of light and shadow; the sun's rays, penetrating the foliage, trace intricate designs on the shore that simultaneously echo and contrast with the reflections on the water.

In the early renditions of sailboats executed four or five years before, this motif conveys a strongly Romantic feeling. The churning sea, the ominous sky, and the seagulls, along with the tilted sailboats themselves, define the content of such paintings as *The Mouth of the Seine at Honfleur* of 1865 (fig. 2; The Norton Simon Foundation, Pasadena). White breakers contrast expressively with the dark silhouette of a sailboat in *Seascape: Storm* of about 1866 (Sterling and Francine Clark Art Institute, Williamstown, Massachusetts). Somewhat later, when Romantic impulses yield to the worship of sunny color, the sailboat serves as the best ornament to the calm surface of the sea in *The Beach at Sainte-Adresse* of 1867 (The Metropolitan Museum of Art, New York). In another painting in the Metropolitan Museum executed at the same time, *Terrace in Sainte-Adresse,* Monet waited for the moment when a dark sailboat appeared in silhouette against the sea (our view of which is cut off in the lower half of the picture by the garden terrace), so that the nearly black triangles of sails could resolve the complex interplay of flags, umbrellas, lawn chairs, flowers, and figures, all of which appear as splashes of color in bright sunlight. In these Sainte-Adresse paintings, the water is shown as a light blue mass enlivened by the greenish brushstrokes of delicate waves.

In the late 1860s through early 1870s, the depiction of water played a key role in the establishment of Monet's own style and in the development of Impressionism as a whole. That the reflections on the water

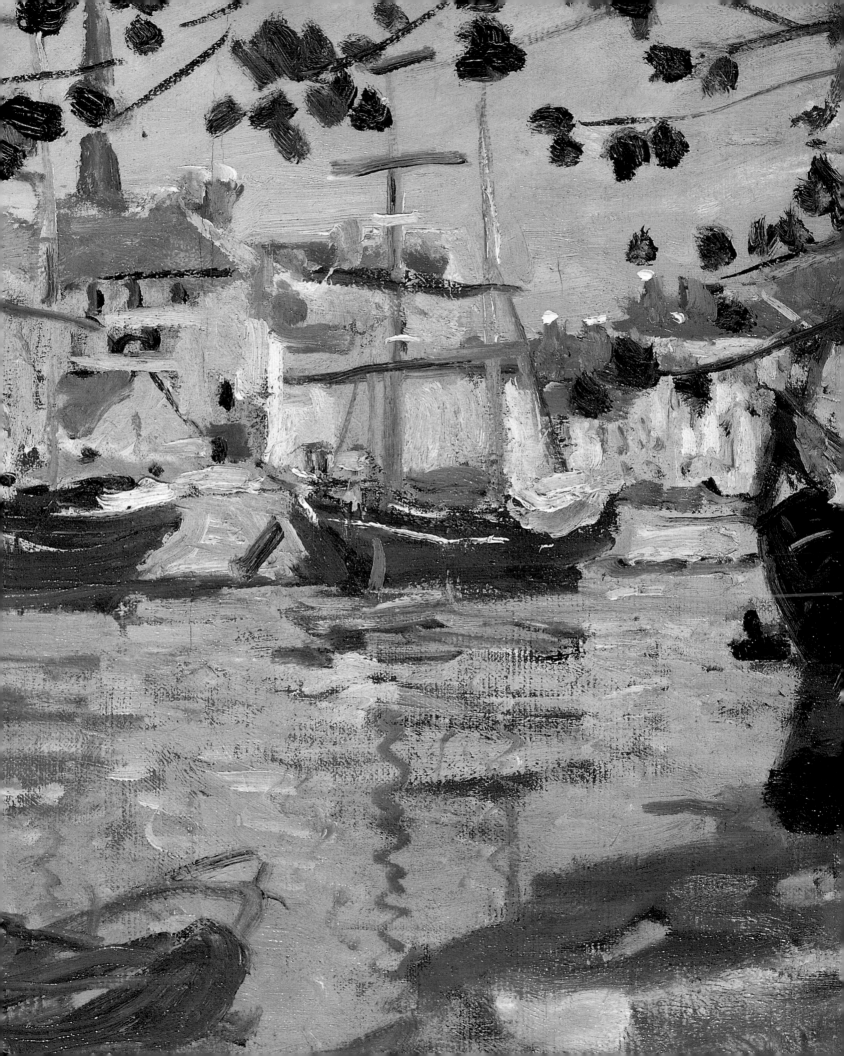

opened up new visual worlds for the artist had to do with the fact that he had for the most part turned his attention from the sea to the river. Having discovered for himself the charm of the Seine, Monet spent many hours by it, either putting up his easel on the banks or, following Charles Daubigny's example, going on short excursions. The landscape along the Seine did not inspire Romantic feelings any more than did the river itself, but it instilled in him a sense of most subtle nuance. Nothing could teach him more about the constant mutability of the natural environment than reflections running and flowing into each other on the river, lessons seen in *The Seine at Rouen* or in the frozen moment of *The River (The Seine at Bennecourt)* of 1868 (fig. 3; The Art Institute of Chicago).

*The River* can be considered the forerunner of such canvases as *The Seine at Rouen*. In this scene of the riverbank at Bennecourt, the foliage of a sturdy tree covers nearly half the painting, while the opposite bank is illuminated by the sun; though separated from the viewer by a strip of river that gives its mirror image, the bank is not far away, but brought up close. Monet thus rejects clear perspective and a gradual recession of planes in favor of a sense of pictorial unity derived from the most diverse details—leaves, shadows on the bank, and fishing boats in the water. Rather than focusing on one thing in particular, his gaze moved rapidly about the scene, but precisely because of this fleeting quality, the impression is bright and coherent.

*The Seine at Rouen* belongs to an early stage of Impressionism, the Argenteuil period of Monet's work (see plate 37). After settling in Argenteuil, he never went away for very long, and when he did, the trips were as a rule connected with the Seine, the river that gave life to this city. In Argenteuil, Monet built himself a studio boat, with a cabin for spending the night and an awning for painting, and would go to Asnières (see plate 35), Poissy, and later even to Vernon and Vétheuil. The characteristic view of a person who would spend time on the water in the middle of the river is anticipated even in such a painting as *The Seine at Rouen*.

PROVENANCE: Sale, Paris, Hôtel Drouot, February 27, 1909, no. 32; Galerie Druet, Paris; Hugo Nathan, Frankfurt; Otto Krebs, Holzdorf.

LITERATURE: G. Swarzenski, "Die Sammlung Hugo Nathan," *Kunst und Künstler*, vol. 15, no. 3 (December 1916), pp. 112 (reprod.), 114; D. Wildenstein, *Claude Monet: Biographie et catalogue raisonné* (Lausanne and Paris, 1974), vol. 1, no. 211.

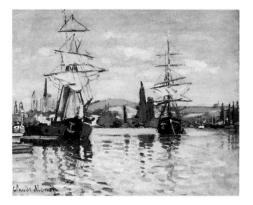

*Fig. 1. Claude Monet.* Ships at Anchor on the Seine at Rouen. *1872. National Gallery of Art, Washington, D.C.*

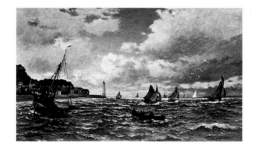

*Fig. 2. Claude Monet.* The Mouth of the Seine at Honfleur. *1865. The Norton Simon Foundation, Pasadena*

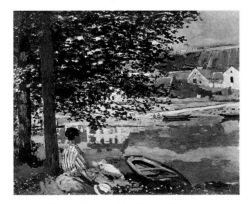

*Fig. 3. Claude Monet.* The River (The Seine at Bennecourt). *1868. The Art Institute of Chicago. Potter Palmer Collection*

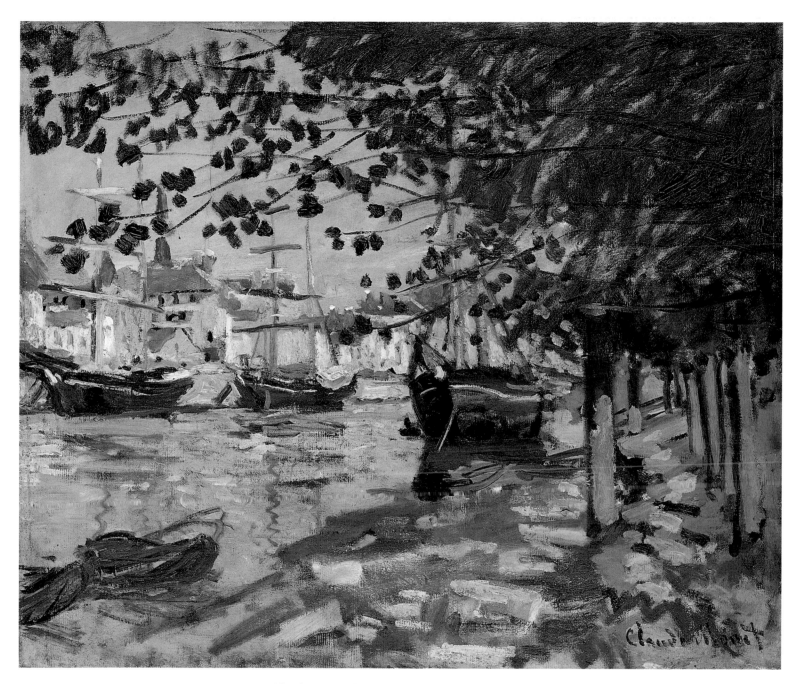

Claude Monet (1840, Paris–1926, Giverny, Eure)

## 34. THE SEINE AT ROUEN

*La Seine à Rouen.* 1872
Oil on canvas, 21¼ × 25¾" (54 × 65.5 cm)
Signed lower right: "Claude Monet"
No. 3KP 506. Formerly collection Otto Krebs, Holzdorf

# CLAUDE MONET

## THE SEINE AT ASNIÈRES

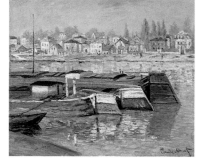

Asnières, long ago made part of Paris, was still an independent community in the mid-nineteenth century, popular for fishing and boating and lauded in songs about such sports as swimming and rowing. As the nearest town to Paris to the north, it often served as a place of recreation for the city's youth. The leisure pursuits of Parisians in Asnières were often depicted in engravings, at times serious, at times ironic, as for example in Gustave Doré's *Arriving at Asnières* and *Leaving Asnières*. The atmosphere of the town was captured also in a novel by Edmond and Jules de Goncourt, *Manette Salomon*, published in 1867. Actors and writers as well as wealthy people from the capital settled here. Later, Argenteuil, further down the Seine, became more popular, not because of the general encroachment of Paris on the countryside but due to the urban-planning reforms of Baron Haussmann: much of the city's sewage had begun to be drained into the Seine in the region of Asnières.

Even with the beginning of industrialization and the subsequent decline of the old Asnières, artists did not forget it. The name of the town would find a permanent place in the history of European art with Georges Seurat's painting *Bathing at Asnières* of 1883–84 (The National Gallery, London), depicting the new, more prosaic character of the place. Paul Signac, Émile Bernard, and Vincent van Gogh also painted here, but Claude Monet was the first among the major painters to do so.

Monet used to come here in the early 1870s, most likely not from Argenteuil, as is usually believed (he had settled there permanently), but from Paris: he viewed Asnières from the Parisian bank of the Seine, from Clichy. When he visited the area, he saw not only the Seine, which never lost its fascination for him, but a row of small, well-built houses. "By the 1870s, these villas stretched all along the banks, accompanied by new or remodeled shops and apartment buildings; the grounds of the old châteaux were being divided up for building lots. Something of the variety of these buildings, like so many weekend revelers in bizarre costumes, can be found in Monet's *The Seine at Asnières* of 1873. Across the massive shapes of commercial barges we see a disconcerting array of buildings, ranging from the grand manor on the right, with its own gate and lawn, to chunky rental buildings and small, gabled villas" (R. L. Herbert, *Impressionism: Art, Leisure, and Parisian Society* [New Haven and London, 1988], pp. 199–200).

Two different realities clash in Monet's painting: the riverbank villas, now so changed as to be unrecognizable, built up untidily yet picturesquely, and the unpretentious workers' barges. With their massive rectangular forms, the magnificent barges set off the evanescent reflections—glimmering, merging, magically alive—that easily and naturally link these two very different worlds. Monet does not emphasize the social aspects; the landscape is not so much a view of some fashionable resort area as it is a poetic image of sunlight—at a time when, shortly before nightfall, the light is especially translucent and golden, becomes luminescent, and is capable of ennobling any natural scene.

In fact, the barge motif had been used even before Monet by Stanislas Lépine and by Alfred Sisley, who in *The Canal Saint-Martin, Paris* of 1870 (Sammlung Oskar Reinhart, Winterthur) gave it a rare expressiveness, juxtaposing the blunt, geometric forms of the barges with the ripples on the water.

The effect of reflections in water had fascinated

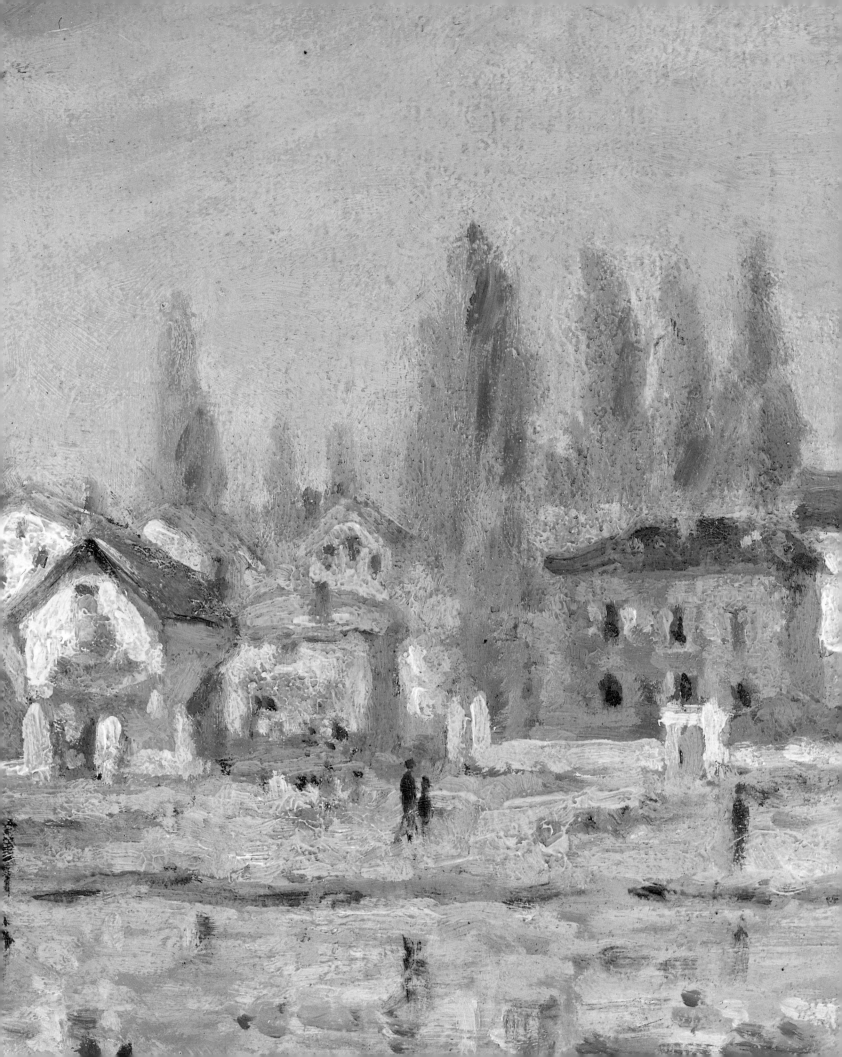

Monet before, but at the time *The Seine at Asnières* was being painted, an intensive investigation of this specific problem opened up for him a larger sense of the mutability of nature in general and taught him how to capture this changeability, which can be known only in fleeting impressions.

The present painting, from the Meyer collection, was not included in the catalogue of Monet's painting compiled by Daniel Wildenstein and until now has been completely unknown to both the public and specialists. There is a version of it, however, in an American private collection (fig. 1; Wildenstein no. 269), with somewhat larger dimensions but the same composition. The differences from the present painting are minimal and not immediately noticeable. For example, in the American version, there are more people strolling on the opposite bank, but they are merely tiny, black spots that do not strike the eye. Carefully comparing the paintings reveals other differences, notably that, aside from the dimensions, the format of the canvases is not the same. In the Meyer collection version, in the left and right sections, there are small areas that have no counterparts in the other canvas, which has somewhat less density of detail. Also, the painterly style is not simply repeated from one picture to the other. Although similar, in each case the brushstrokes do differ; even in dealing with the same composition, and with the same light, the artist does not copy himself, but improvises.

There is no question that the two paintings were created one after the other, but it is impossible to say in which sequence. It may be that one was painted from nature and the other in the studio. In coming back to the same composition, Monet usually chose different lighting, or changed the point of view, and that was enough for a new pictorial structure to emerge. In this case, however, the pictorial structure has been only slightly altered. Perhaps one of the two versions was painted on commission; in great need of money at the time, Monet could have agreed to a collector's proposal that he make another, similar painting, if the first was already spoken for.

Unfortunately, there are many uncertainties regarding the American version of *The Seine at Asnières*. It is no accident that Wildenstein uses question marks in the work's provenance to cover its early existence. Only after the painting wound up in the hands of

Ambroise Vollard at the turn of the century can its disposition be traced. It is therefore difficult to say which version figured in the auction organized by the Impressionists on March 24, 1875 (an event that some art historians equate in significance with the group's regular exhibitions). Twenty of Monet's paintings were in the auction, but it is difficult to identify them precisely.

Yet another variation exists of the same theme, *Barges at Asnières* of 1873 (fig. 2; private collection, United States; Wildenstein no. 270), which at one time belonged to Count Armand Doria and later entered the famous Havemeyer collection. Monet painted it from the same perspective, but altered the right portion of the view and added a sailboat on the Seine.

LITERATURE: D. Wildenstein, *Claude Monet: Biographie et catalogue raisonné* (Lausanne and Paris, 1974), vol. 1, p. 65.

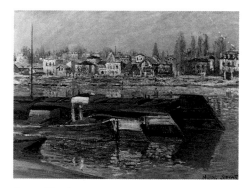

Fig. 1. *Claude Monet.* Barges (The Seine at Asnières). *1873. Private collection, United States*

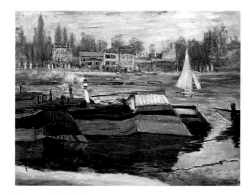

Fig. 2. *Claude Monet.* Barges at Asnières. *1873. Private collection, United States*

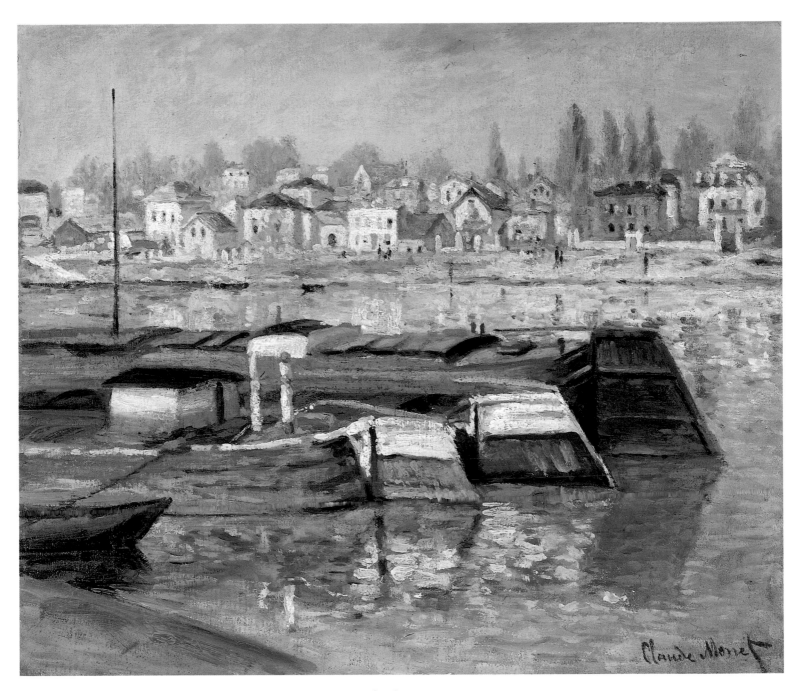

Claude Monet

## 35. THE SEINE AT ASNIÈRES

*La Seine à Asnières.* 1873
Oil on canvas, 18¼ × 21⅞" (46.4 × 55.5 cm)
Signed lower right: "Claude Monet"
No. 3K 1594. Formerly collection Alice Meyer, Berlin

# CLAUDE MONET

## THE GRAND QUAI AT HAVRE

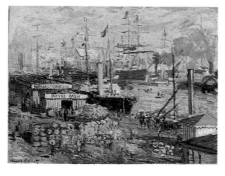

In January 1874, at the height of preparations for the first exhibition of the Société Anonyme, whose chief initiator he was, Monet traveled to his native Havre. His stay on this occasion was short, but it yielded four significant paintings. Their themes were all dictated by the life of the Havre port (Monet stayed nearby at L'Hôtel de l'Amirauté). It is a safe guess that the purpose of the trip was to prepare new works for the forthcoming exhibition. Of course, Monet could not have supposed at the time that the exhibition would provoke a raucous scandal, and that his painting *Impression: Sunrise* (fig. 1; Musée Marmottan, Paris), executed a year earlier at the Havre port, would prompt the naming of a whole group of artists—the leading school in art in the last third of the nineteenth century.

In the first exhibition of the Société Anonyme, at which the members would be dubbed the "Impressionists," Monet decided to represent his work primarily with landscapes, chosen to show their diversity—from the rural landscape of *Wild Poppies* (Musée d'Orsay, Paris) to the noisy Paris street of *Boulevard des Capucines* (The Pushkin State Museum of Fine Arts, Moscow; The William Rockhill Nelson Gallery of Art–Atkins Museum of Fine Arts, Kansas City, Missouri), to views of the mouth of the Seine. To *Impression* he added another canvas from Havre, painted in January 1874, *Havre: Fishing Boats Leaving the Port* (collection Herman, United States; Wildenstein no. 296).

There was a certain logic in Monet's choice of *Fishing Boats* for that first exhibition of the new painting, held in the photographer Nadar's studio; it was a work full of temperament, executed with sweeping brushstrokes. But compositionally, it did not open any

new horizons, as the first of the two works had done.

Not without prompting from Hiroshige's woodcuts, Monet here "carved" his compositional structure, so to speak. The interaction between the horizontals and the verticals is so tight and balanced as almost to put one in mind of Piet Mondrian (though, of course, Monet kept to a specific motif and did not intend to reject it in favor of abstraction). With this forest of masts and smokestacks, and the piles of barrels and bales of goods in the foreground, he conveys the sense of an extremely busy port, with ships departing for the ends of the earth as well as for nearby places such as Caen, the main city of the neighboring *département* of Calvados. Indicative of this in the left portion of the canvas is a sign reading "Havre–Caen" on the building of the shipping office, where a knot of people has gathered on this lovely day. The juxtaposition of the tall smokestacks of the ships in front with the masts of the fishing vessels behind reveals the onset of the industrial age, in spite of Monet's residual Romanticism. Modernity of style is adapted to modernity of subject—the approach Monet shared with his older friend Édouard Manet. It is not by chance that *The Grand Quai at Havre* resembles Manet's *The Port of Bordeaux* of 1871 (fig. 2; Stiftung E.G. Bührle, Zurich).

The work in Havre this time went unevenly. "I work," wrote Monet to Camille Pissarro, "but when I stopped doing the seascapes, it was the devil after that—very difficult. Each moment brings something new, and the weather here changes many times in the course of one day" (D. Wildenstein, *Claude Monet: Biographie et catalogue raisonné* [Lausanne and Paris, 1974], vol. 1, letter 76, p. 429). The painting shows a bright, sunny day. The complexity of the subject prevented the work from being finished in one sitting, and one could not know when precisely the same weather conditions would occur again. *The Grand Quai at Havre* remained not quite finished; the artist evidently did not want to spoil it by trying to bring it to completion without consulting nature.

*The Grand Quai at Havre* can justly be compared with the famous *Impression: Sunrise* shown at the Impressionists' first exhibition. Painted in the same place, the two works form a contrasting pair: one shows morning mist and a few rowboats just beginning to move; the other depicts the height of the workday with an abundance of details. But the differences between the two works are less important than the fact that, in each case, the compositional idea radically contradicted the customary principles. It was obvious that the artist could not hope for an easy victory.

Perhaps Monet himself sensed that to show such a work as *The Grand Quai at Havre* in an exhibition that also included *Impression: Sunrise* would constitute too serious a challenge to the public and critics. Supplied with the subtitle *A Study*, the present painting was first shown three years later, at the third exhibition of the Impressionists.

With thirty canvases, Monet was the artist most heavily represented at that show. He exhibited mostly recent paintings, executed in 1876, but included three or four earlier works, all landscapes, though it is not certain which ones he chose. It is known that *The Grand Quai at Havre* was one of them, but the identities of the other landscapes are in doubt. The titles used in the catalogue could have been changed subsequently, and dimensions were not indicated there. Monet may have believed that *The Grand Quai*, which was ahead of its time in 1874, would seem more accessible after his recent strivings; he could have expected the public to have learned a thing or two.

And, indeed, this time the public was far less hostile toward Monet (it now had its sights on Cézanne). Although many critics continued to exercise their wit at Monet's expense, his defenders also raised their voices. Roger Ballu, a young and ambitious official of the Department of Fine Arts, who in time attained the post of director, subjected Monet to a devastating tirade in *La Chronique des arts* (April 13, 1877, p. 148). Ten days later, his article, "L'Exposition des peintres impressionistes," was reprinted in *Les Beaux-*

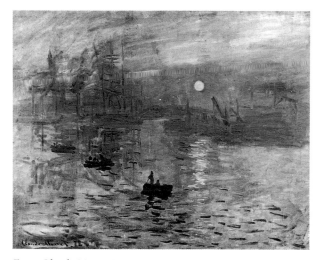

*Fig. 1. Claude Monet.* Impression: Sunrise. *1872. Musée Marmottan, Paris. Bequest of Donop de Monchy*

*Arts illustrées* (April 23, 1877, p. 392). He wrote: "They [Monet and Cézanne] provoke laughter at a time when people should cry over them. They display the most profound illiteracy in drawing, composition, and rendering of color. A child playing with paper and paints does a better job."

Meanwhile, the writer Charles Bigot, although irritated by the audacious, "shouting colors," was nonetheless prepared to admit that in Monet's paintings there was "strength and effect, if you looked at them from a certain distance" (C. Bigot, "L'Exposition des 'impressionistes,'" *La Revue politique et littéraire,* April 28, 1877, p. 1045).

Théodore Duret, a political figure and art critic who became acquainted with Monet and his friends through Édouard Manet, but who until the mid-1870s considered them dilettantes, took their side in a review of their third exhibition. Recalling that Monet and the other exhibitors had now started calling themselves Impressionists, he wrote: "If the term Impressionism was found to be apt and universally accepted to signify a group of painters, it is, of course, precisely because of the features of the art of Claude Monet, whose painting suggested it. Monet is Impressionism *par excellence* because he is able to capture the fleeting impressions that his predecessors had ignored, believing these impossible to reproduce with their brushes. The thousand shades that make up the impression of the water of the sea and rivers, the play of light in the clouds, the vibrating colors of flowers and the dappled shadows of foliage in the rays of the burning sun have been captured by him in all their truth. In preserving in a landscape not only what is immovable and permanent but also the fleeting aspects, caused by irregularities of atmosphere, Monet imbues the scene he has observed with an exceptionally lively and moving feeling" (Th. Duret, *Critique d'avant-garde* [Paris, 1885], pp. 70–71).

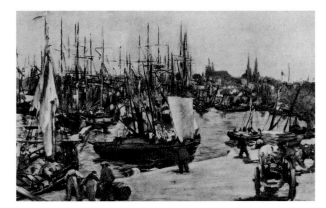

*Fig. 2. Édouard Manet.* The Port of Bordeaux. *1871. Stiftung E. G. Bührle, Zurich*

PROVENANCE: Acquired by Fromenthal from the artist, January 1875; Otto Krebs, Holzdorf.

EXHIBITIONS: 1877, Paris, "Troisième Exposition de peinture," 6, rue Le Peletier, no. III.

LITERATURE: G. Rivière, "Claude Monet aux expositions des impressionistes," *L'Art vivant,* January 1, 1927, p. 18; D. Wildenstein, *Claude Monet: Biographie et catalogue raisonné* (Lausanne and Paris, 1974), vol. 1, no. 295.

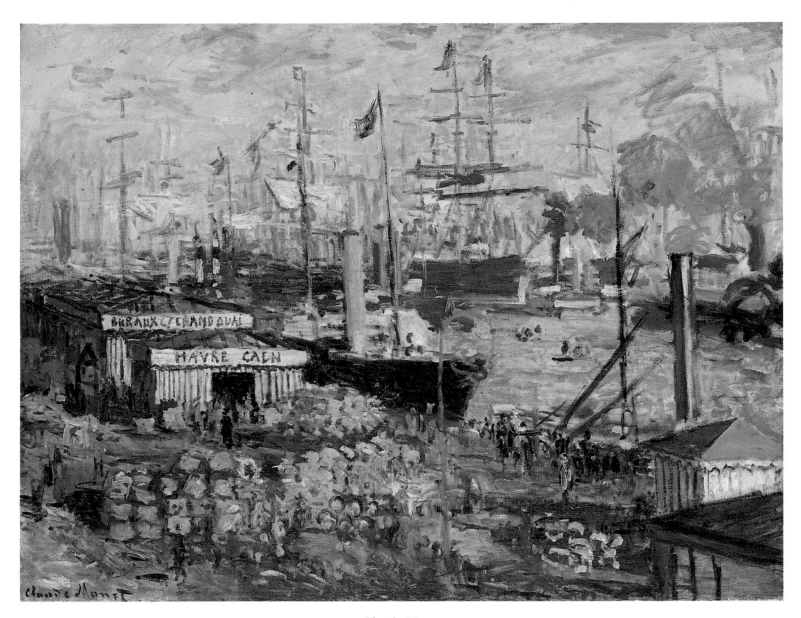

Claude Monet
## 36. THE GRAND QUAI AT HAVRE
*Le Grand Quai au Havre.* 1874
Oil on canvas, 24 × 31⅞" (61 × 81 cm)
Signed lower left: "Claude Monet"
No. 3KP 523. Formerly collection Otto Krebs, Holzdorf

# CLAUDE MONET

## WOMAN IN A GARDEN

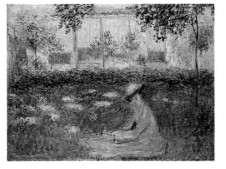

In the background of the painting is depicted Claude Monet's second home in Argenteuil. It still stands, on the corner of the boulevard Saint-Denis (now 21, boulevard Karl-Marx), near the railroad station. From October 1874 to early 1878, Monet lived in this "rose-colored house with green shutters," as it was described by Victor Chocquet, who was once invited there for lunch along with Paul Cézanne. The house figures more prominently in another painting of the same time, *Monet's House at Argenteuil* of 1876 (fig. 1; private collection; Wildenstein no. 406).

In the period when Impressionism was on the rise, Argenteuil became one of the favorite places for the artists of the group. Famous for its vineyards, the village on the Seine attracted them with its proximity to unspoiled nature. In the 1870s, Argenteuil was popular among Parisians in general for recreation, especially at the time when water sports such as rowing and sailing became fashionable (a number of Monet's paintings incorporate such subjects). Only about ten kilometers from Paris, Argenteuil was easy to get to, either by rail or by boat. Édouard Manet, Pierre-Auguste Renoir, and Alfred Sisley came here to see Monet, who lived and worked in the town for much of the 1870s.

In December 1871, Monet had first rented a house in Argenteuil, signaling the end of the somewhat bohemian existence he had previously led. Henceforth, many of his paintings would reflect the life of a family man. Monet enthusiastically painted this first Argenteuil home, its garden, and the little meadow next to it, and at times depicted his wife, alone or with their son, against this backdrop, as in the painting in the Annenberg collection (fig. 2). On warm days Camille would sit on the grass, and is shown this way in two 1874 paintings: in Manet's *The Monet Family in Their Garden* (The Metropolitan Museum of Art, New York) and in Renoir's *Camille Monet and Her Son Jean in the Garden at Argenteuil* (National Gallery of Art, Washington, D.C.). Monet himself had shown her this way even earlier, in his *Camille Reading* (also known as *Woman Reading*) of 1872 (fig. 3; The Walters Art Gallery, Baltimore), the painting that prefigured the present work. Clearly Monet liked this theme, which was inspired by his wife and her characteristic manner. At this time he recorded it in *Rest in the Garden: Argenteuil* of 1876 (private collection, New York; Wildenstein no. 408) and in *Camille in the Grass* (also known as *In the Meadow*) of 1876 (fig. 4; private collection, France; Wildenstein no. 405).

Paul Tucker, who has researched the Argenteuil period of Monet's work, writes: "During all the first half of that year, Monet painted only scenes that were similarly restricted, among them *Camille in the Grass* or *Two Figures in the Garden*. There are ten such garden pictures from these months, more than Monet had done at any other period. They are filled with the beauties of summer sunlight, but nine of them are also limited to the confines of Monet's backyard. The painter of the modern countryside was retreating into a more reassuring world" (P. H. Tucker, *Monet at Argenteuil* [New Haven and London, 1984], p. 158).

PROVENANCE: Galerie Georges Petit, Paris; 1909, Galerie Bernheim-Jeune, Paris; 1914, Goldschmitt; Otto Krebs, Holzdorf.

LITERATURE: D. Wildenstein, *Claude Monet: Biographie et catalogue raisonné* (Lausanne and Paris, 1974), no. 407.

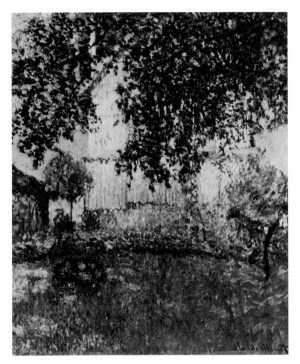

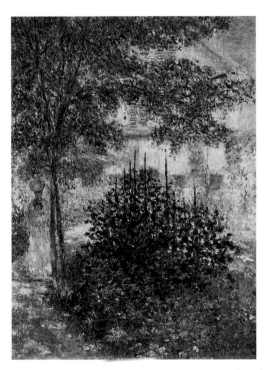

*Fig. 1. Claude Monet*. Monet's House at Argenteuil. 1876.
*Private collection*

*Fig. 2. Claude Monet*. Camille Monet in the Garden of
the House at Argenteuil. *1876. Collection The Hon. and
Mrs. Walter Annenberg*

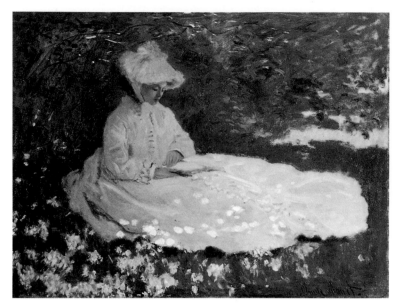

*Fig. 3. Claude Monet.* Camille Reading (Woman Reading). *1872.*
*The Walters Art Gallery, Baltimore*

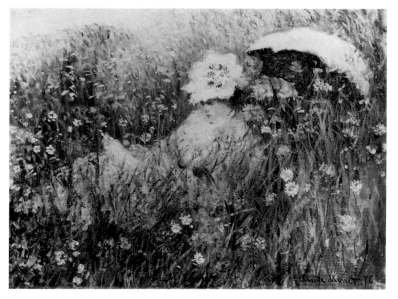

*Fig. 4. Claude Monet.* Camille in the Grass (In the Meadow). *1876.*
*Private collection, France*

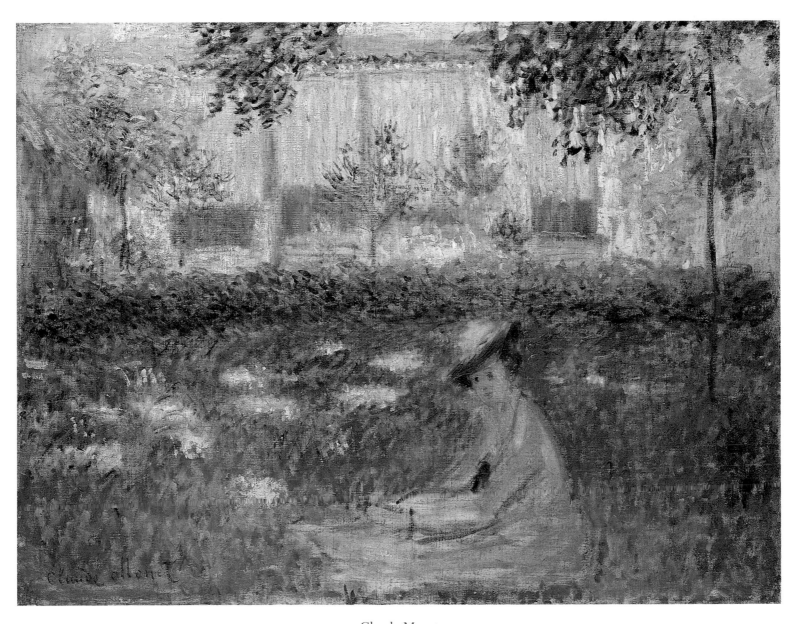

Claude Monet
## 37. WOMAN IN A GARDEN
*Femme dans le jardin.* 1876
Oil on canvas, 32¼ × 25¾" (50 × 65.5 cm)
Signed lower left: "Claude Monet"
No. 3KP 503. Formerly collection Otto Krebs, Holzdorf

# CLAUDE MONET

## THE GARDEN

This painting, like plate 37, depicts the garden of Monet's second home in Argenteuil. After settling here in the fall of 1874, Monet did not immediately turn to this theme. But in the summer of the following year, when the garden behind the home had become overgrown and luxuriant with flowers, time after time Monet set up his easel there, painting five canvases (Wildenstein nos. 382–86). All of these pictures are enlivened by the presence of a female figure, usually recognizable as his wife, Camille.

The garden, which no longer exists, was not especially large. It gave the artist little scope: the bushes and trees were close at hand, so that their tops always reached toward the upper edge of the picture.

In the summer of 1876, Monet painted his beloved garden even more avidly. The ten paintings executed at this time can be divided into two groups, according to the perspective chosen: in some canvases, the house is visible (see plate 37); others are painted looking away from the house. In either case, the garden's untended growth expressed the spontaneous force of nature.

A woman appears in all the landscapes of the second group, depicted always *comme il faut*, as one was expected to appear in public—in a hat, and sometimes even with a parasol. Usually, she is shown strolling, and is sitting only in *The Garden*. This painting picks up the motif of the largest of the garden canvases of 1875, called *In the Garden* (private collection, United States; Wildenstein no. 384), although the seated woman is depicted more casually and abstractly, so that she is not immediately noticed among the burgeoning foliage. Essentially, the artistic idea brilliantly expressed nine years earlier in *Woman in the Garden at Sainte-Adresse* of 1867 (fig. 1; The State Hermitage Museum, St. Petersburg) has been transformed. In the Sainte-Adresse garden, the bright spot of the figure, like other splashes of color in the painting, was delin-

eated with high clarity, and the woman seemed to contrast with the vegetation. Now, in *The Garden*, she merges with it, becoming part of nature. Renoir's idea of woman as flower was not alien to Monet.

PROVENANCE: c. 1896, Galerie Durand-Ruel, Paris; February 1900, Strauss (as *Paysage avec figure*); sale, Hôtel Drouot, Paris, June 23, 1900, no. 75 (Strauss); Galerie Bernheim-Jeune, Paris; 1900, Galerie Durand-Ruel, Paris; 1905, Galerie Cassirer, Berlin; Kunsthalle, Bremen.

EXHIBITIONS: 1910, Bremen, "Internationale Kunstausstellung," no. 190; 1940, Paris, "Centenaire Monet-Rodin," Musée de l'Orangerie, no. 31.

LITERATURE: E. Waldmann, "Die internationale Kunstausstellung in Bremen," *Kunst und Künstler*, vol. 8, no. 7 (June 1910), pp. 371, 374 (reprod.); K. Scheffer, "Deutsche Museen moderner Kunst, III: Die Bremer Kunsthalle," *Kunst und Künstler*, vol. 11, no. 1 (October 1912), p. 94; E. Waldmann, "Bremer Privatsammlungen," *Kunst und Künstler*, vol. 17, no. 5 (February 1919), p. 176; *Katalog der Gemälde in der Kunsthalle in Bremen* (Bremen, 1925), no. 190; H. Tietze, "Les Peintres français du XIXe siècle dans les musées d'Allemagne," *Gazette des beaux-arts*, vol. 17 sér. 5 (February 1928), p. 113; O. Reutersward, *Monet* (Stockholm, 1848), p. 280; M. Bernhard, K. Martim, and K. P. Rogner, *Verlorene Werke der Malerei in Deutschland, 1939–45* (Munich and Berlin, 1965), pp. 78, 214; D. Wildenstein, *Claude Monet: Biographie et catalogue raisonné* (Lausanne and Paris, 1974), no. 411; P. H. Tucker, *Monet at Argenteuil* (New Haven and London, 1984), pp. 163, 168; *Dokumentation der durch Auslagerung im 2. Weltkrieg vermissten Kunstwerke der Kunsthalle Bremen* (Bremen, 1991), no. 29.

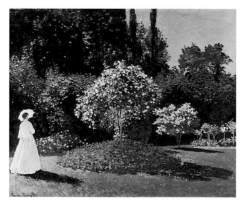

*Fig. 1. Claude Monet.* Woman in the Garden at Sainte-Adresse. *1867. The State Hermitage Museum, St. Petersburg*

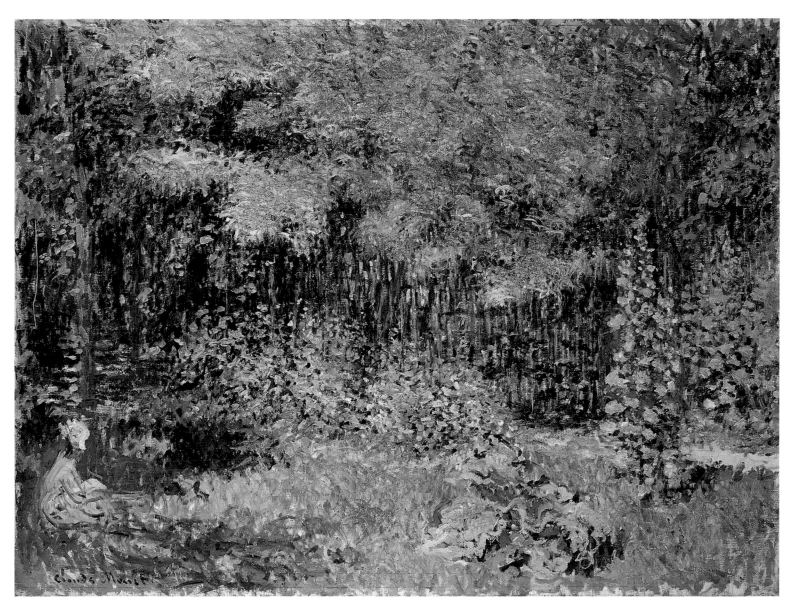

Claude Monet
## 38. THE GARDEN
*Le Jardin.* 1876
Oil on canvas, 29¾ × 39½" (75.5 × 100.5 cm)
Signed lower left: "Claude Monet"
No. 3K 1397. Formerly collection Kunsthalle, Bremen

# CLAUDE MONET

## GARDEN IN BORDIGHERA, IMPRESSION OF MORNING

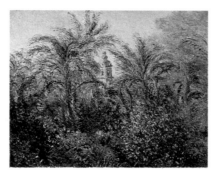

In December 1883, Monet went with Renoir on a brief trip to the Mediterranean. Passing Aix, where they met with Paul Cézanne, both painters proceeded on to Italy, finally reaching Genoa. Monet returned to Paris at the end of the month.

On January 12, 1884, Monet wrote to Paul Durand-Ruel from Giverny:

*I ask you as well to reserve for me for Wednesday a 500-franc note; I will come to Paris for it, since I have decided to travel to Italy immediately. I want to spend a month in Bordighera—one of the most beautiful places that we saw during our trip. I hope to bring you back a number of new things from there.*

*I ask you also not to tell anyone of my plans. I am not saying this because I intend to make a secret of it, but I feel like traveling alone: pleasant as it was to travel with Renoir as a tourist, it was confining for me to travel with him for the purposes of work. I have always worked better alone and in accordance with my own personal impressions.*

*So, until new instructions, keep my intention a secret. If Renoir finds out that I am planning to travel, he will immediately want to accompany me, and that would be just as harmful for me as for him. I think you will agree with me.*
(D. Wildenstein, *Claude Monet: Biographie et catalogue raisonné* [Lausanne and Paris, 1976], vol. 2)

On January 23, Monet wrote Durand-Ruel from Bordighera (on the Italian Riviera, close to the French border) that he had begun to paint the previous evening: "The results as always are at first mediocre, but I am sure that I will bring home some interesting things since it is very beautiful here and the weather is superb. I am planning to spend about three weeks here

and somewhere else close by, in order to bring some different sorts of things. I think I will work on some palms here and several exotic views."

Monet wrote a postscript to the same letter, asking Durand-Ruel to obtain a letter of introduction to "a certain M. Moreno from Marseilles"; evidently, it was impossible to get into his fabulous estate without such a letter. Five days later, he once again reminded Durand-Ruel of his request, adding that M. Moreno "had the most superb palms growing in Bordighera—a marvelous motif!" A week after that, on February 5, Monet wrote: "I received the splendid letter for M. Moreno, who gave me a very warm welcome there: he handed me the key and permitted me to come to the estate when I saw fit, and, just as I had supposed, there are scenes in the estate such as an artist can only dream of."

The stay at Bordighera turned out to be very fruitful, and far longer than Monet had planned at first: it produced some fifty landscapes, such as the one in the Metropolitan Museum of Art, New York (fig. 1). "You ask me if I am happy with Bordighera. Yes, and in fact I am more and more delighted with it and am working a lot" (letter to Durand-Ruel, February 9, 1884).

Monet stayed at the Pension Anglaise. Sometimes he worked in the countryside, and sometimes in the gardens of Moreno. On this estate, which Monet called "an earthly paradise," he painted five landscapes. In a letter of February 5, he told his wife: "How delightedly I stroll in the most secluded corners of these incomparable properties. It is a pity to start other studies. The garden is like no other: it is pure fairyland. Here vegetation from all over the world grows luxuriantly and without any pruning, it seems; it has entire groves of palms of all sorts, all types of oranges and mandarins" (Wildenstein, letter 407).

On March 31, not long before his departure, Monet once again wrote Durand-Ruel: "The first steps were rather torturous because of the frequent changes in the weather; but in the end, though it was hard for me and I made some bad things, nonetheless I suppose there are also some good ones. Perhaps it will cause the enemies of blue and rose to wail, because it is just that radiance, that fairylike light, that I am striving to render, and those who have not seen these places or have seen them poorly, I am certain, will begin to howl about the lack of resemblance, although I do not even come near the tone. All of these iridescent colors are delightful and each day nature becomes even more beautiful, and I am enchanted with this country" (Wildenstein, letter 442).

Without any doubt, *Garden in Bordighera, Impression of Morning,* from the Krebs collection, ought to be included among the "good things" of which Monet wrote. The effect of morning is superbly conveyed with a harmony of blue and rose hues produced by the color of the rising sun. These shades, interlacing with the green of the palms, almost subduing it, create a rare rainbow coloration.

The particular light of this landscape is interesting to compare with the other Bordighera paintings, above all *Moreno Gardens in Bordighera* of 1884 (fig. 2; Norton Gallery and School of Art, West Palm Beach, Florida; Wildenstein no. 865), where the same view is depicted, although somewhat closer—an elevated section of the Moreno gardens in the twilight. In both cases the campanile of the Church of Santa Maria Magdalena della Città Alta looms in the background.

On June 10, 1884, Monet sent Durand-Ruel some paintings along with a letter from Giverny enumerating the works and their prices. He valued *Garden in Bordighera* at 900 francs (Wildenstein, letter 503, p. 253).

The format of the present painting was altered after it was finished. A strip of the canvas along the right side at least 6 centimeters wide has been folded behind the stretcher. In addition, canvas was cut off in the same place (not preserved). The original, wider composition must have had a more extended, perhaps almost panoramic character.

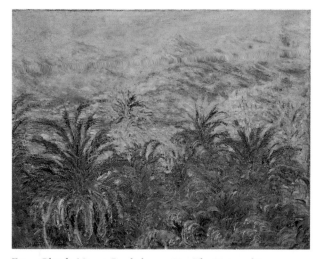

*Fig. 1. Claude Monet.* Bordighera. *1884. The Metropolitan Museum of Art, New York. Bequest of Miss Adelaide Milton de Groot*

PROVENANCE: Purchased by Durand-Ruel, June 1884; Galerie Durand-Ruel, Paris; 1929, Hugo Perls, New York; Otto Krebs, Holzdorf.

EXHIBITIONS: 1895, New York, "Monet," Galerie Durand-Ruel, no. 36 (?); 1896, St. Louis, "Thirteenth Annual Exhibition," no. 353; 1900, New York, "Monet and Renoir," Galerie Durand-Ruel, no. 21; 1901, Syracuse, N.Y., "Inaugural Exhibition of the Syracuse Museum of Fine Arts," no. 27; 1915, New York, "Monet and Renoir," Galerie Durand-Ruel, no. 1; 1923, New York, "Monet," Galerie Durand-Ruel, no. 12.

LITERATURE: L. Venturi, *Archives de l'impressionisme* (Paris, 1939), vol. 1, p. 281; D. Wildenstein, *Claude Monet: Biographie et catalogue raisonné* (Lausanne and Paris, 1976), vol. 2, no. 866 (letter 503).

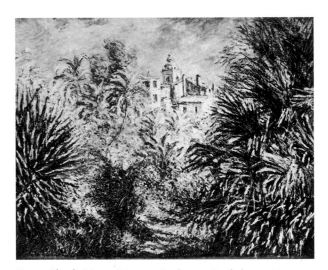

*Fig. 2. Claude Monet.* Moreno Gardens in Bordighera. *1884. Norton Gallery and School of Art, West Palm Beach, Florida*

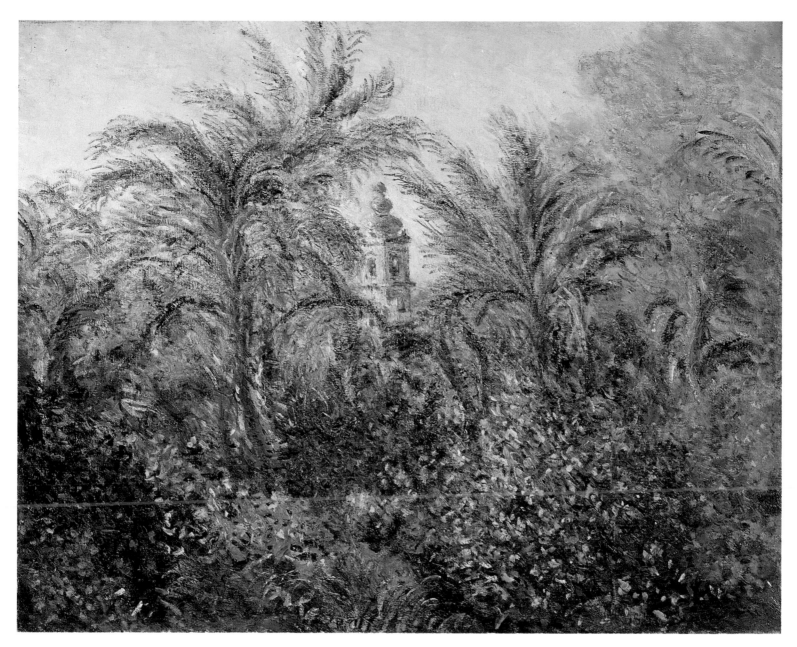

Claude Monet

### 39. GARDEN IN BORDIGHERA, IMPRESSION OF MORNING

*Jardin à Bordighera, effet du matin.* 1884
Oil on canvas, 25 ¾ × 32" (65.5 × 81.5 cm)
Signed lower right: "Claude Monet"
No. 3KP 522. Formerly collection Otto Krebs, Holzdorf

# ALFRED SISLEY

## BARGES AT BILLANCOURT

Billancourt, now an industrial zone occupied by Renault automobile factories, was a small village when Alfred Sisley and Armand Guillaumin painted there. The changes began with the construction of a railroad bridge across the Seine, linking Billancourt to Issy on the right bank of the river: in Sisley's landscape the smokestacks of Issy can be seen in the distance.

Sisley often painted in Billancourt during 1877–79, especially in the early part of that brief period. The work in Billancourt was related to his move in 1877 from Marly-le-Roi to Sèvres. At that time, Sisley was having difficulty making ends meet. The publisher Georges Charpentier, along with the pastry chef Eugène Murer, another lover of the Impressionists' painting, had rescued him from his impatient creditors. Murer organized a lottery in early November 1877 to help Sisley by selling one of his paintings. Nevertheless, no matter how difficult Sisley's financial situation remained, it did not influence the mood of his painting. It seemed as if nothing but the changing sky over Paris concerned him. His work is notable for an incomparable sensitivity to the subtlest nuances of weather and sunlight, a superb example of which is the present painting, *Barges at Billancourt*.

In his catalogue of Sisley's painting, François Daulte records a number of views of Billancourt and the Seine painted in 1877 (Daulte nos. 251, 252, 266, 268). Several additional canvases, showing a barge at the bank, form a group (nos. 273–76), and among them is *Barges at Billancourt*. Of the three other works in the group, the one most similar to this landscape is *Unloading the Barges* of 1877 (fig. 1; National Museum, Belgrade; Daulte no. 276), where the same view is shown, with some alterations.

Sisley had a persistent fascination with painting barges, which may seem somewhat strange for such a poet of the sky and untouched nature. He first turned to this subject in the Paris landscapes of 1870, *View of the Canal Saint-Martin* (Musée d'Orsay, Paris) and *Barges on the Canal Saint-Martin* (Sammlung Oskar Reinhart, Winterthur). Some recent commentators note, perhaps with justification, that the frequent depiction of such a subject as barges indicated the wish to be contemporary, common to all the Impressionists. Yet there does remain one other simple but important reason for an artist to return to such a theme so persistently: for Sisley, as for Claude Monet in Argenteuil, the masts of the barges served as convenient reference points in arranging the pictorial structure of the landscape, which only to an untrained eye could seem to be an accidental, unplanned view of the Seine. Here, as in the other Billancourt canvases, the construction is accurate and flawless; the foremost barge anchors the composition, and its mast effectively denotes the center line.

PROVENANCE: Comtesse de Chaulnes, St. Petersburg; Galerie Étienne Bignou, Paris; Alexandre Reid; Lefevre Gallery, London; Otto Krebs, Holzdorf.

EXHIBITIONS: 1923, London, "Exhibition of French Art," Lefevre Gallery, no. 1.

LITERATURE: F. Daulte, *Alfred Sisley: Catalogue raisonné de l'oeuvre peint* (Lausanne, 1959), no. 275.

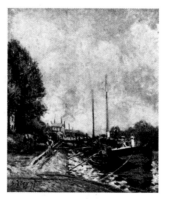

*Fig. 1. Alfred Sisley. Unloading the Barges. 1877. National Museum, Belgrade*

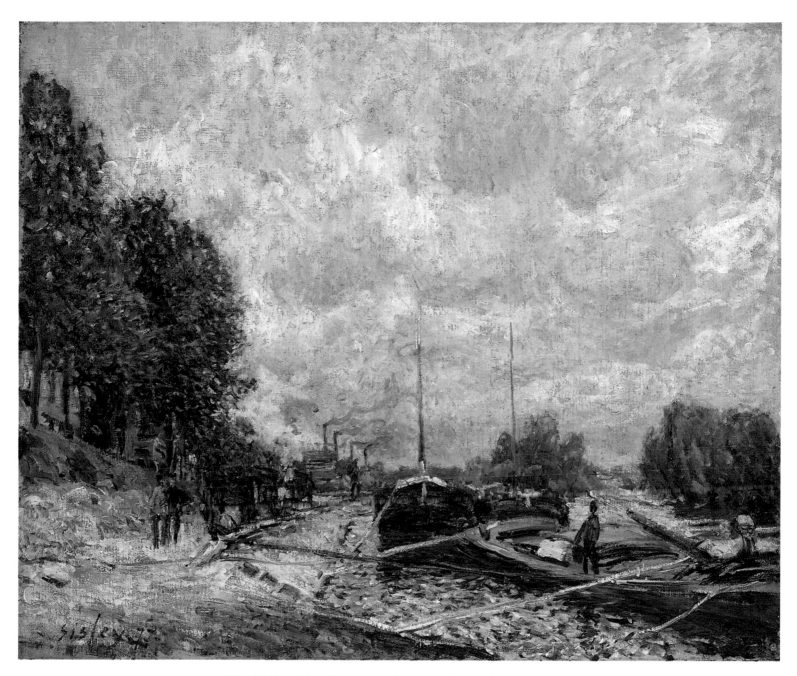

Alfred Sisley (1839, Paris–1899, Moret-sur-Loing, Seine-et-Marne)
40. BARGES AT BILLANCOURT
*Les Peniches à Billancourt*. 1877
Oil on canvas, 18¼ × 22⅛" (46.5 × 56.3 cm)
Signed and dated lower left: "Sisley 77"
No. 3KP 515. Formerly collection Otto Krebs, Holzdorf

# CAMILLE PISSARRO

## Town Park in Pontoise

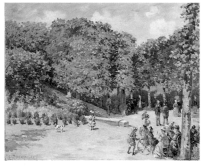

Pontoise, a small town on the river Oise about thirty kilometers from Paris, is very closely connected to Camille Pissarro's work. He lived there, or near-by, during 1866–69 and 1873–84, alto-gether almost fifteen years. It was in Pontoise that the largest number of his Impressionist-period paintings were done. Friends would often come to visit him there, particularly Armand Guillaumin and Paul Cézanne. From time to time, Cézanne, who settled nearby in Auvers, worked with Pissarro in Pontoise. According to the memoirs of Pissarro's son Lucien, Cézanne would walk three kilometers in order to paint with his father. The small town on the Oise played almost as impor-tant a role in the history of Impressionism as Argenteuil on the Seine.

The Oise and the hills and glades around Pontoise provided fine opportunities for the landscape painter, but there was another, more prosaic reason for the attachment: Pontoise was not very far from Paris, so that one could visit and keep abreast of the goings-on in the art world. Moreover, life in the provinces for a man with a wife and three children was far cheaper than in the capital—an important factor for an artist with modest and very erratic earnings.

Pissarro did not live in Pontoise itself but in its out-skirts, in a rural district called L'Hermitage, and for the most part this is where he painted. He was not tempt-ed by any of the local sights in the center of the town, such as the Place de l'Hôtel de la Ville, or Notre-Dame, or the famous Saint-Maclou church with its portal and bell tower in florid Gothic style. Pissarro was most drawn by nature. It was characteristic that in Pontoise itself he found a motif that was essentially nat-ural: the Jardin Publique, with its green wall of lush chestnut trees. This town park, near the Saint-Maclou

church, exists to this day, although the town suffered greatly during World War II.

Pissarro painted the town park twice. Another canvas with the same name and the same dimensions (fig. 1; private collection, Honolulu; Pissarro/Venturi no. 257), dated 1874, shows a broad lawn with a solitary tree in the middle and a fence in the distance. Both landscapes are notable for their careful construction. Clearly, Pissarro thought out in advance the disposition of elements in his work. In the present painting, from the Krebs col-lection, the tree at the right forms a sort of curtain, and to the left, to give a kind of closure to the compo-sition, Pissarro took pains with the shading necessary for overall balance. The middle ground is defined by the figure of a young girl. Finally, the dense clumps of trees, form a firm backdrop to the whole scene. It is a mise-en-scène staged by a confident director. Through his work in Pontoise, Pissarro gained greater assurance in the art of arranging figures in a landscape. Although Venturi believed that the figures introduce a useless distraction in both town-park pictures (L. Venturi, "L'Art de Camille Pissarro," in L.-R. Pissarro and L. Venturi, *Camille Pissarro: Son Art, son oeuvre* [Paris, 1939], vol. 1, p. 43), this cannot be conceded.

The motif of both town-park paintings harks back to the Rococo period, when artists loved to depict soci-ety in a park; of course, it was society of a special type, a company of fine ladies and their cavaliers. In the nineteenth century, such personages were replaced by the ordinary heroes of the bourgeois world. They are to be found, for example, in Louis-Léopold Boilly's paint-ing *The Politicians in the Tuileries Gardens* of 1832 (fig. 2; The State Hermitage Museum, St. Petersburg). Then the theme was completely transformed by

Édouard Manet in *Concert in the Tuileries Gardens* of 1862 (The National Gallery, London). Finally, we must recall such early garden and park compositions by Claude Monet as *Woman in the Garden at Sainte-Adresse* of 1867 (The State Hermitage Museum, St. Petersburg) and *Women in the Garden* of 1867 (fig. 3; Musée d'Orsay, Paris). Monet's approach in these paintings, in which forms are sharply accented by bright sunlight, and confident brushstrokes seize each detail at a touch, must have made a strong impression on Pissarro, and it is with such works that his *Town Park in Pontoise* should be compared.

In his two variations on the park theme, Pissarro depicts the modest provincial leisure of a small town that does not want to lag behind Paris. Not surprisingly, therefore, both canvases display a genre quality unusual for Pissarro, more strongly expressed in the present painting.

It was as if Pissarro had set himself the task of showing various types of recreation in the park at one time. In the center, where the incline begins, a man in a blue suit moves along at a slow pace. Perhaps he is heading for one of the viewing stands depicted in the other painting of the park. Further right, from behind the trees, two ladies out for a stroll are accompanied by a cavalier. Even further to the right, two men have stopped and are having a discussion; in such a town, or at least among those that gather in the park, it seems that everyone knows one another. And in the front there is a lively company, seated on rented garden chairs. The women are deep in one conversation, the men in another. While the two women, oblivious of those around, are exchanging news, another woman, holding up a parasol against the sun, is watching the approach of a little girl with a hoop, probably her daughter.

Although he had in mind the Honolulu version of *Town Park in Pontoise,* Richard Brettell's comment could equally apply to the Krebs collection *Park*: "There are virtually never bourgeois figures where there ought *not* to be bourgeois figures. They are seen, most often, against the appropriate background of the town itself. They stroll, gossip, and stand idly along the road in *Le Tribunal de Pontoise, Place Saint-Jean* [Pissarro/Venturi no. 211; collection Peter Salm, New York] of 1873. Children play together while their mothers chat and watch in the pictorially fascinating *Le*

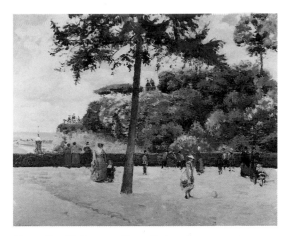

*Fig. 1. Camille Pissarro.* Town Park in Pontoise. *1874. Private collection, Honolulu*

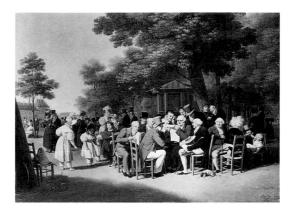

*Fig. 2. Louis-Léopold Boilly.* The Politicians in the Tuileries Gardens. *1832. The State Hermitage Museum, St. Petersburg*

*Jardin de la Ville, Pontoise*. The figures are absolutely 'at home' in their town setting. They belong as the rural workers belong in the market, on the road, or in the field" (R. R. Brettell, *Pissarro and Pontoise: The Painter in a Landscape* [New Haven and London, 1990], p. 130).

Children figure in each of Pissarro's park paintings. Such details may explain the origin of paintings so unusual for Pissarro. His own children, his son Lucien or daughter Jeanne, could have persuaded him to go to the park. For them such outings promised games and talk with their friends, especially attractive after the monotony of rural L'Hermitage. It is possible that the little girl with the doll in the center of the painting is Jeanne (her full name was Jeanne-Rachel, but she was called Minette at home). She is of about the right age and appearance.

Minette was born in 1865 and died on April 6, 1874. On April 15 of that year, an exhibition opened on the boulevard des Capucines in Paris that was destined to become a landmark in the history of European art, the first exhibition of the Impressionists, who at that time still called themselves the Société Anonyme des Artistes. Pissarro chose five paintings for this exhibition, including *Town Park in Pontoise*. All the works were landscapes of various kinds. The present painting is of special note: it is not a pure landscape, but rather a combination landscape and genre composition. Aside from artistic considerations, Pissarro may have had personal reasons for showing a painting that put him in mind of his deceased daughter.

The catalogues of the Impressionists' exhibitions do not indicate the dimensions or provide other information that would enable us to identify each of the paintings with certainty. It has been asserted that the *Town Park in Pontoise* shown at the first Impressionist exhibition was the painting now in Honolulu (see *The New Painting: Impressionism, 1874–1886* [The Fine Arts Museums of San Francisco, 1986], p. 122, in the chapter on the 1874 exhibition by Paul Tucker). Such a supposition is completely untenable. The Honolulu version is dated 1874 and depicts a summer day, whereas the exhibition opened in mid-April, and a painting with the name *Town Park in Pontoise* (*Jardin de la ville de Pontoise*) could only have been the composition of the preceding year; that is, the one in the Krebs collection. This is precisely what is indicated in

the catalogue of Pissarro's paintings compiled by his son Ludovic-Rodolphe with Lionello Venturi.

Old nail holes along the back edges suggest that the painting was executed without a stretcher and was mounted on one only later, after the work was completed. Consequently, it was painted not *en plein air* but in the studio, using drawings made in the park. The arrangement of the painting, especially the grouping of figures in it, would also indicate that it was not painted outdoors.

PROVENANCE: Private collection, Paris; sale ("vente de la collection d'un amateur"), Paris, Hôtel Drouot, June 23, 1900, no. 84; Galerie Paul Rosenberg; collection Cazalens; Otto Krebs, Holzdorf.

EXHIBITIONS: 1874, Paris, "Société Anonyme des Artistes Peintres, Sculpteurs, Graveurs, etc.: Premiere Exposition," no. 139.

LITERATURE: L.-R. Pissarro and L. Venturi, *Camille Pissarro: Son Art, son oeuvre* (Paris, 1939), no. 231.

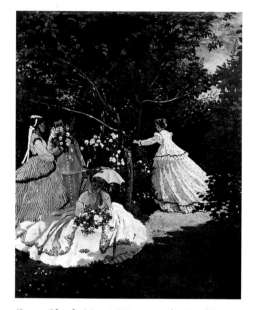

*Fig. 3. Claude Monet.* Women in the Garden. *1867. Musée d'Orsay, Paris*

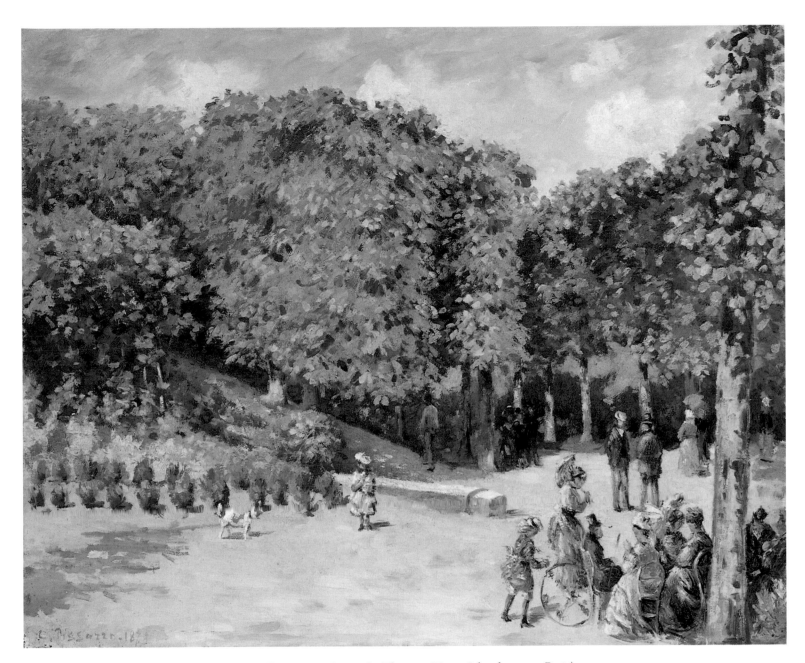

Camille Pissarro (1830, St. Thomas, Virgin Islands–1903, Paris)
41. TOWN PARK IN PONTOISE
*Le Jardin de la ville à Pontoise.* 1873
Oil on canvas, 23½ × 28⅞" (59.5 × 73.3 cm)
Signed and dated lower left: "C. Pissarro 1873"
On the reverse side of the upper bar of the stretcher,
probably in the artist's hand: "Jardin de la ville, Pontoise"
No. 3KP 517. Formerly collection Otto Krebs, Holzdorf

# CAMILLE PISSARRO

## STILL LIFE WITH A COFFEEPOT

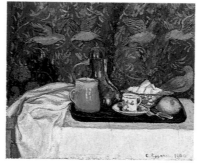

Camille Pissarro painted relatively few still lifes in his long career. Of the 1,316 paintings recorded by Ludovic-Rodolphe Pissarro and Lionello Venturi in their catalogue of his works, only seventeen are still lifes.

John Rewald once remarked that in order to paint still lifes, an artist needed rainy weather that kept him from going outside (J. Rewald, *Camille Pissarro* [New York, 1974], p. 90). Not a single still life has been preserved dating from between 1872 and 1898, the years of Pissarro's most intensive work *en plein air*. It is hard to say what inspired him to paint still lifes. Perhaps he hoped that such paintings would more easily find admirers. It is more likely, however, that the still life could serve as a means for resolving specific artistic problems. It is noteworthy that Pissarro never repeated his still lifes, whereas in his landscapes a repeated composition could serve as a reliable basis for an entire series.

Most often, Pissarro painted flowers in his still lifes, for which his wife, who had been a florist in her youth, sometimes selected the bouquets. But probably the most interesting among the paintings under this rubric are those that show other kinds of objects.

Two still lifes particularly stand out among Pissarro's later paintings: *Still Life with Spanish Peppers* of 1899 (fig. 1; Pissarro/Venturi no. 1069) and the present *Still Life with a Coffeepot*. Both were selected by the artist for a solo show at the Galerie Durand-Ruel in January and February 1901. Pissarro wanted that exhibition to show the latest developments in his painting, which these two still lifes turned out to exemplify perfectly. They cannot help but be compared, since they have identical dimensions and similar compositional features. Each work makes use of an ornamental background, provided by wallpaper or decoratively painted fabric. Against this background is a table spread with a white tablecloth. In the middle of the table in each picture there are several objects, associated with each other not only by an artistic principle but by everyday use: along with the bright peppers in a bowl there is a hefty bottle of peasant wine; the coffeepot is accompanied by a cup and a sugar bowl. Of the two pictures, *Spanish Peppers* is the more traditional, giving greater attention to conveying the depth of space.

*Still Life with a Coffeepot* is more intricately arranged and flatter. The background is very active. No other painting by Pissarro, before or after, shows the decorative fabric used in this work. Such fabrics, some of which were woven in a textile mill in Lyons, were fashionable at the turn of the century due to Japanese influence. Their design harks back to the studies of birds from Hokusai's *Manga*. Another japonaise note is added by the black lacquered tray. Pissarro always had a sincere interest in Japanese art. Like all the Impressionists, he was enamored of Japanese woodcuts and, following their example, had worked a great deal on painting fans.

*Still Life with a Coffeepot* is without a doubt Pissarro's most decorative painting. The objects have been selected and arranged with great care in order to interact with the patterns on the fabric. Thus, the rounded contours of the birds are echoed by the lines of the handles of the milk pitcher, coffeepot, and cup. Nevertheless, Pissarro does not at all succumb to stylization. The fashionable fabric combines quite naturally in his painting with the coarse, rustic-looking ceramic pitcher, which in turn combines with the porcelain cup. Incidentally, the juxtaposition of diverse items in the still life, including some rather plain

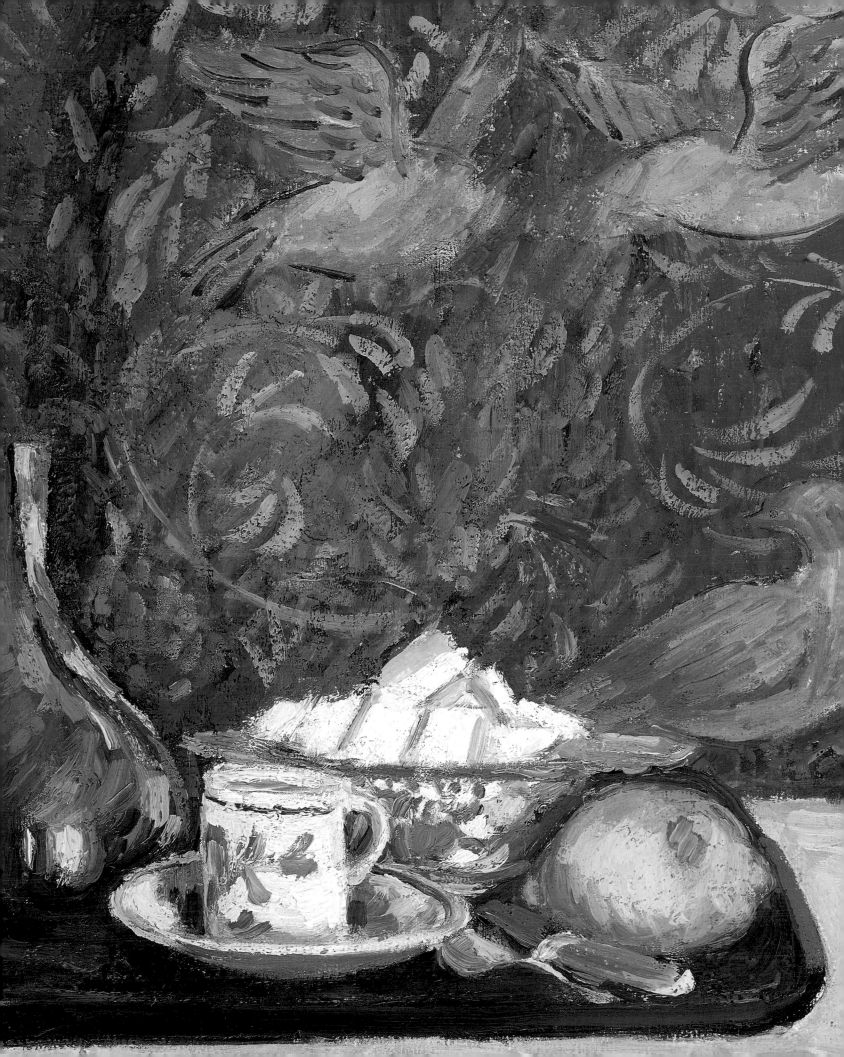

objects, hints that perhaps the painting was executed not in Paris but in Normandy, or Dieppe, or in Berneval, where Pissarro spent the summer of 1900.

Apparently, *Still Life with a Coffeepot* was preceded by *Still Life with a Cup and Teapot* (Pissarro/Venturi no. 1070), which is sketchier and freer, and includes the same cup.

It is worth noting that certain details of the present work are reminiscent of Cézanne: the wrinkled white tablecloth, the gleaming white cup, and the bowl. Pissarro did not try to compose his paintings like the Master of Aix, though to some extent he considered himself his student; Cézanne's methods of constructing forms and delineating space remained alien to him no matter how much he admired them in his friend's canvases. But he could not resist the temptation of using Cézanne's color harmonies, and the affinities between the two artists are apparent. The old Pissarro remembered with pleasure how he had discerned the talent of the "wonderful Provençal" early on, back in 1861 (letter to Lucien Pissarro, December 4, 1895). In another letter to his son (November 22, 1895), concerning Cézanne's exhibition at Ambroise Vollard's gallery, Pissarro recalled a period of mutual influence: "In Pontoise I influenced him and he influenced me. Remember the speeches of Zola and Beliar in this regard? They were certain that painting is invented anew each time and only the artist who does not look like anyone else is original. Interestingly, at Cézanne's exhibition at Vollard's gallery the similarity between his landscapes of Auvers and Pontoise and mine was visible. It is not surprising; we were always together. But it is true, and easily proved, that each had his own 'feeling,' and that is the most valuable thing." That individuality of "feeling"—to which in the end any impressions, whether from objects or the works of other painters, are subordinated—can be seen as well in *Still Life with a Coffeepot*.

It is thought that Henri Matisse knew this painting, having seen it when he visited the old painter. Some recollection of this work can be postulated in Matisse's famous *Still Life with a Blue Tablecloth* of 1909 (fig. 2; The State Hermitage Museum, St. Petersburg), in which an analogous composition, echoing the rhythms of printed fabric in the contours of objects, was constructed by the leader of the Fauves.

This painting was known as *Copper Coffeepot (Cafetière à cuivre)* at the Galerie Durand-Ruel, Paris.

PROVENANCE: Galerie Durand-Ruel, Paris; 1907, Galerie Bernheim-Jeune, Paris (gallery imprint on reverse side of stretcher); Otto Krebs, Holzdorf.

EXHIBITIONS: 1901, Paris, "Camille Pissarro," Galerie Durand-Ruel, no. 42.

LITERATURE: *L'Art et les artistes*, February 1928 (reprod.); L.-R. Pissarro and L. Venturi, *Camille Pissarro: Son Art, son oeuvre* (Paris, 1939), no. 1116.

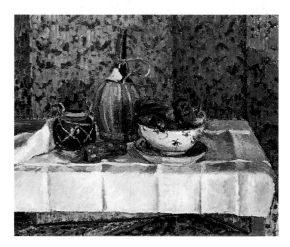

Fig. 1. *Camille Pissarro.* Still Life with Spanish Peppers. *1899. Private collection, Texas*

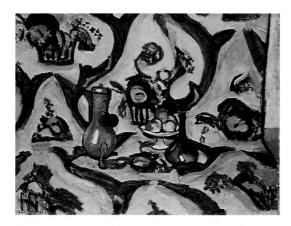

Fig. 2. *Henri Matisse.* Still Life with a Blue Tablecloth. *1909. The State Hermitage Museum, St. Petersburg*

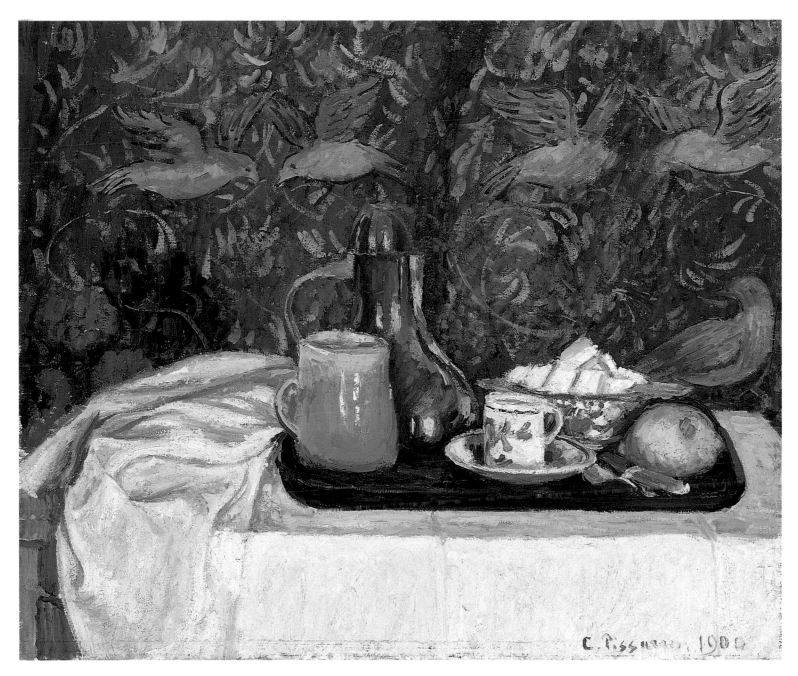

Camille Pissarro
### 42. STILL LIFE WITH A COFFEEPOT
*Nature morte, la cafetière.* 1900
Oil on canvas, 21½ × 25¾" (54.5 × 65.3 cm)
Signed and dated lower right: "C. Pissarro 1900"
No. 3KP 527. Formerly collection Otto Krebs, Holzdorf

# CAMILLE PISSARRO

## THE TUILERIES GARDENS

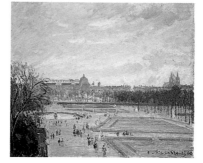

Pissarro was not the first among the Impressionists to paint the Tuileries Gardens. In 1876, Claude Monet had painted four canvases showing the view from Victor Chocquet's apartment, which was on an upper floor (Wildenstein nos. 401–4; see fig. 1). They were well known to Pissarro, since three of them were shown the following year at the third Impressionist exhibition. The one called *The Tuileries* (Wildenstein no. 401), showing a corner of the Place du Carrousel, is particularly noteworthy. Émile Zola had that painting in mind when ten years later he described one of the works of his fictional character Claude Lantier in *L'Oeuvre*, a novel that brought about a change in the Impressionists' attitude toward Zola: Monet, Pissarro, Renoir, and Cézanne began to avoid him. But perhaps if we were to look among the four Monets for the painting that led to Pissarro's *The Tuileries Gardens*, we would have to choose the one from the Musée d'Orsay (Wildenstein no. 403); the painting has all the airiness and freedom of style that are suggested by its subtitle, *Sketch*.

Pissarro took steps toward creating a series of paintings of the Tuileries Gardens in late 1898. Earlier, for a series devoted to the boulevard Montmartre or the avenue de l'Opéra and the Place du Théâtre-Français, he had taken care to find hotel windows with an unobstructed view (an eye ailment prevented him from working *en plein air*). Now, on December 4, 1898, he wrote to his son Lucien: "We have rented an apartment on the rue de Rivoli, 204, across from the Tuileries, with a superb view of the garden. To the left is the Louvre; beyond the trees in the garden, the houses on the embankment can be seen; to the right is the dome of the Invalides and beyond the massive chestnut trees is the bell tower of Sainte-Clotilde. It is

very beautiful. I can make a good series. It will cost me dearly, but I hope to pull through with the help of the series" (J. Bailly-Herzberg, *Correspondance de Camille Pissarro*, vol. 4: *1895–1898* [Paris, 1989], p. 522).

Pissarro's apartment on the rue de Rivoli was at the corner of a small street now called the rue du 29 Juillet. Its windows looked out on the Bassin of the Tuileries, which in the present painting from the Krebs collection can be seen on the left. The Bassin was a convenient reference point for taking spatial bearings, and it is depicted in twelve other paintings from the series. Next to it, the pathways and vendors' stalls in the gardens provide a ready-made geometrical foundation for the composition, giving structure to these paintings focused on shimmering atmospheric effects. Monet operated in similar fashion in his series devoted to the Gare Saint-Lazare or the Rouen Cathedral. The church tower of Sainte-Clotilde also became an important reference point.

The opportunity to view the city not from a hotel room, as before, but from his own windows, from a fairly spacious—and highly elevated—apartment, gave the painter great advantages. The view was panoramic, and he could examine particular details by going from one window to the next. Pissarro generally preferred horizontal formats, and in the Tuileries series they were used to good advantage. With a series of open, panoramic views at his disposal, the artist could move freely to the left, toward the Louvre, or to the right, toward the stalls in the Tuileries.

The beginning of the work on the Tuileries series was noted in Paul Signac's diary, in rather strong terms. The leader of the Neo-Impressionists clearly could not forgive the old painter for abandoning their doctrine:

*I was with Louis at Pissarro's apartment on the rue de Rivoli, from whose window he is painting the Tuileries Gardens. His earlier works hang on the walls of the room, making it plain how much these new ones yield to them. Truly, in these dirty, cloudy tones we can no longer see what a wonderful colorist Pissarro was, and they fail to convey the charm and magnificence of the beautiful sight lying before him. On this marvelous winter day, the orange afternoon light tinged the whole landscape with gold; long blue shadows contrasted with the hot shades of color, or paled alongside them. Within these wonderful surroundings were the multicolored splashes of the crowd. And all of this corresponded to the "Impressionist" understanding of the life of the world and color! Then, stepping away from the window, with dismay you see the gloomy interpretation of the scene by the old artist. His character, however, has remained the same and his health is strong.*

*It is surprising that Impressionism ends with darkness. Everything the Impressionists fought against since their youth, to all this they seem to come again at the end of their work. What is it—exhaustion, weakness, or the urge for novelty, which in fact leads back to the past?* (February 21, 1899; from "Extraits du journal inédit de Paul Signac, 1897–1898, 1898–1899," *Arts de France*, nos. 11–12 [1947])

Pissarro, who was nearly tempted by the Neo-Impressionist system, returned to the precepts that he himself had developed two or three decades previously; compared to the methods of Signac and his associates, they were more effective for depicting a modern city. Pissarro sacrificed the vividness of tone and a decorative quality for the sake of an impression of the spirit and atmosphere of the city. But it is interesting that even in Signac's subjective words an admission of an attempt at synthesis can be detected ("the urge for novelty, which in fact leads back to the past").

The Tuileries landscapes can be divided into two separate series, each containing fourteen canvases. The first series was executed in 1899 and the second in 1900. The present painting is from the 1900 series and was preceded by at least six similar views of this garden, all dated 1899 (Pissarro/Venturi nos. 1097–1102). Four of those six were painted in the winter (see figs. 2,3), the other two with the onset of spring. In four further paintings, executed in the winter of 1900,

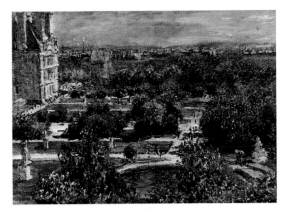

Fig. 1. *Claude Monet.* View of the Tuileries. *1876. Musée Marmottan, Paris. Bequest of Donop de Monchy*

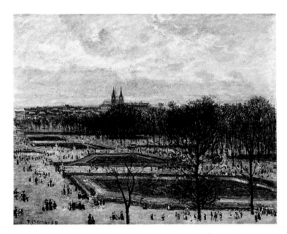

Fig. 2. *Camille Pissarro.* The Tuileries Gardens on a Winter Afternoon, I. *1899. The Metropolitan Museum of Art, New York. Gift of Katrin S. Vietor in loving memory of Ernest G. Vietor*

and which include the present *Tuileries Gardens,*
Pissarro returned to the same perspective. Of these,
one canvas (fig. 4; private collection, Japan;
Pissarro/Venturi no. 1123) is of far greater size, while
the other two are the same. Most likely, the painting
from the Krebs collection was the last in this cycle. In
it, to the left of center, the framework of the huge
Gare d'Orsay shed, then under construction for the
World's Fair, can be seen clearly. In other works in the
series, in particular the one from the Japanese collection, building cranes have been drawn at the site of the
great railroad shed. Pissarro, of course, could not imagine that in a later time the Musée d'Orsay would be
housed under this roof, and would contain the greatest
collection of his own works.

PROVENANCE: André Teissier, Mâcon; Otto Krebs, Holzdorf.

EXHIBITIONS: 1930, Paris, "Centenaire de la naissance de l'artiste,"
Musée de l'Orangerie, no. 102.

LITERATURE: L.-R. Pissarro and L. Venturi, *Camille Pissarro: Son Art,
son oeuvre* (Paris, 1939), no. 1126.

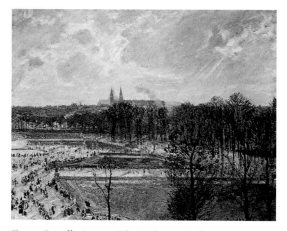

*Fig. 3. Camille Pissarro.* The Tuileries Gardens on a Winter
Afternoon, II. *1899. The Metropolitan Museum of Art,
New York. Gift from the collection of Marshall Field III*

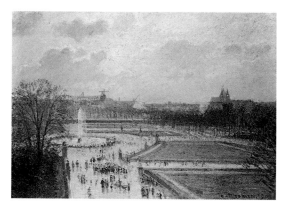

*Fig. 4. Camille Pissarro.* The Pool in the Tuileries:
Afternoon. *1900. Private collection, Japan*

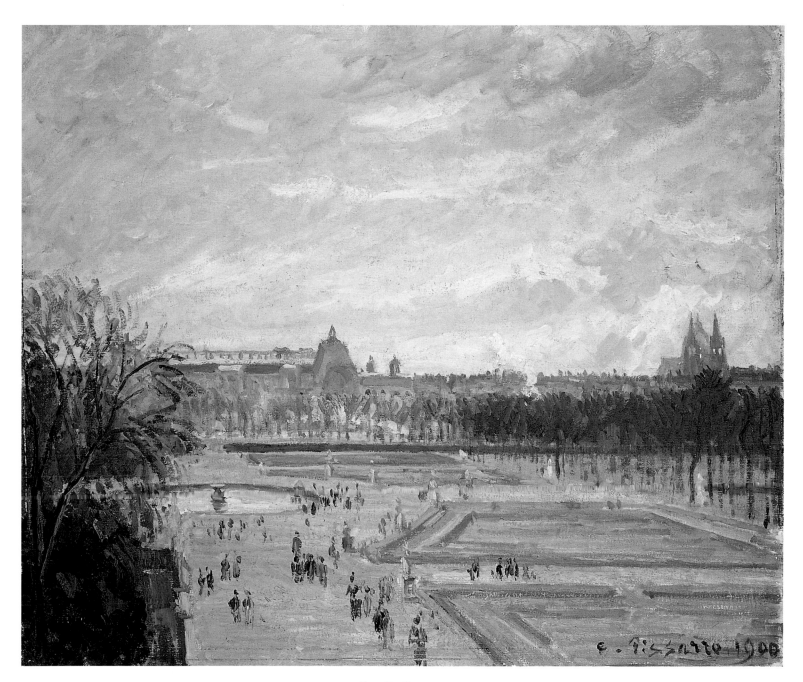

Camille Pissarro
### 43. THE TUILERIES GARDENS
*Jardin des Tuileries.* 1900
Oil on canvas, 21 ¼ × 25 ¾" (54 × 65.3 cm)
Signed and dated lower right: "C. Pissarro 1900"
No. 3KP 509. Formerly collection Otto Krebs, Holzdorf

# CAMILLE PISSARRO

## The Fair in Dieppe, Sunny Morning

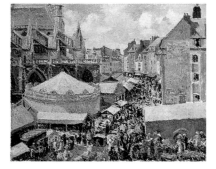

On July 19, 1901, Camille Pissarro wrote to his son Lucien from Eragny: "I am going to Dieppe tomorrow and am staying at the Hôtel du Commerce, on Place Duquesne. My window will look out on the market; to the left, the portal of the Church of Saint-Jacques, towers, and quite picturesque homes can be seen" (J. Bailly-Herzberg, *Correspondance de Camille Pissarro,* vol. 5: *1899–1903* [Saint-Ouen-L'Aumone, 1991], p. 188). A week later there was another note: "So, I've settled in here in a small hotel room across from the Church of Saint-Jacques and the market. I have already begun several paintings with rain. I decided to paint the rain, figuring that after the tropical heat sent down to us, the rainy weather would start—to the great consternation of the local shopkeepers."

When Pissarro settled into the hotel to start what he called his "summer campaign," he did not paint the market yet; that subject appeared later. The first thing he painted was the empty square under the rain and the enormous bulk of the church. The Church of Saint-Jacques, Dieppe's main sight, is a remarkable Gothic structure built in the thirteenth and fourteenth centuries with later alterations. Pissarro always had a lively interest in the Gothic. In October 1889, he wrote to his son Georges that he "could gain great benefit from comparing nature with the works of the Gothic masters, artists with incomparable boldness who, in general, derived their elements from nature" (J. Bailly-Herzberg, *Correspondance de Camille Pissarro,* vol. 2: *1886–1890* [Paris, 1986], p. 306).

Although the precise sequence of the works in the series at Dieppe is not entirely certain, in all likelihood the first canvas was *The Church of Saint-Jacques in Dieppe in Rainy Weather, Morning* (Pissarro/Venturi no. 1194). Two other scenes followed, both showing a sunny morning (Pissarro/Venturi nos. 1193, 1196). From a different vantage point, Pissarro painted *Portal of the Church of Saint-Jacques in Dieppe* (Pissarro/Venturi no. 1199).

From time immemorial the square next to the church had been used as a market. Pissarro's paintings show how lively the trading would become on Sundays in the town. The space around the Gothic monument would rapidly fill up with a motley assortment of tents, booths, and pavilions. In *The Market at the Church of Saint-Jacques, Dieppe* (fig. 1; private collection; Pissarro/Venturi no. 1196), the medieval cathedral looks like a cliff towering over a whirlpool.

At some point during the summer, probably in August, the market would expand into a fair, with entertainment added to the trading. In *The Fair at the Church of Saint-Jacques in Dieppe, Sunny Morning* (fig. 2; private collection; Pissarro/Venturi no. 1197), a round pavilion with a dome appears, apparently a traveling circus. As if wishing to view this new scene closer, the artist "changes the focus" (to use a photographer's term), and thus we have the present work, *The Fair in Dieppe, Sunny Morning.*

The series created in Dieppe between July and September 1901 consists of eight canvases (Pissarro/Venturi nos. 1194–1200, plus a painting from the Musée d'Orsay, *The Church of Saint-Jacques in Dieppe,* which did not get into the Pissarro/Venturi catalogue). On August 28, 1901, the artist wrote to his son Lucien: "I have made four canvases of [format] 30, one of 25, one of 15, and a gouache" (*Correspondance de Camille Pissarro,* vol. 5, p. 192). The painting from the Krebs collection is of format 25. Unquestionably, it is one of the two canvases that were still not finished when Pissarro wrote at the end of August.

Pissarro had begun to paint markets in 1881 in Pontoise and Gisors, reflecting a wish to turn once again to figure compositions. He started with such gouaches as *Grain Market in Pontoise* of 1881 (Pissarro/Venturi no. 1347) and *The Market Woman* (no. 1348). The latter work is the only one of the market scenes shown by the artist during the Impressionist era (seventh Impressionist exhibition, no. 126). On the whole, Pissarro explored the market theme more enthusiastically in gouaches, at times even engaging to a degree in genre painting. A series of such works (Pissarro/Venturi nos. 1387–90) is dated 1883–84.

In the very first painting on this subject, *Poultry Market in Pontoise* of 1882 (The Norton Simon Foundation, Pasadena; Pissarro/Venturi no. 576), the artist's attention was concentrated on the fleeting and essentially insignificant everyday impressions received in a crowd. The artist wants to feel like the man in this picture who glances from behind the backs of the peasants gathered at the Sunday market.

Such compositions of the 1880s on the market theme were a continuation of Pissarro's peasant subjects. He considered it essential to portray peasants' labor, including the sale of their produce. By the end of the 1890s, however, his approach to the subject had changed. In part this resulted from the altered circumstances under which Pissarro now worked; unable to paint under the open sky and view the scene up close, he sees it from a window, from somewhere above, and refrains from depicting figures on a large scale. *Grocers' Street in Rouen* of 1898 (The Metropolitan Museum of Art, New York; Pissarro/Venturi no. 1036) begins to prepare the way for the Dieppe series: the foreground is filled by a crowd at the height of market day, and further back the towers of the famous Rouen Cathedral are outlined behind the roofs of some buildings. The stone towers and walls losing their materiality in the bright sunlight, the brick roofs, the billboards, the colorful awnings over the store windows, and the teeming humanity—all are subsumed into a single impression of the general flow of life.

This tendency finds a convincing embodiment in the paintings done at the Hôtel du Commerce. In *The Fair in Dieppe, Sunny Morning* from the Krebs collection, the artist discovered a way not only to convey the impression of busy town life, but to create an unusually integrated rhythmic structure through a flawlessly

calculated interplay of geometric details. "Dieppe gave him a new strength," wrote Lionello Venturi. "*Fair in Dieppe, Sunny Morning* is a masterpiece of pictorial energy: the ensemble created by the church, the buildings, the barracks, and the crowd is full of movement, yet everything contributes to one grand and unified effect" (L. Venturi, "L'Art de Camille Pissarro," in L.-R. Pissarro and L. Venturi, *Camille Pissarro: Son Art, son oeuvre* [Paris, 1939], vol. 1, p. 65).

PROVENANCE: Galerie Bernheim-Jeune, Paris; Otto Krebs, Holzdorf.

EXHIBITIONS: 1902, Paris, "Camille Pissarro et nouvelle série de Claude Monet," Galerie Bernheim-Jeune, no. 2; 1908, Paris, Galerie Bernheim-Jeune, no. 23.

LITERATURE: L.-R. Pissarro and L. Venturi, *Camille Pissarro: Son Art, son oeuvre* (Paris, 1939), no. 1198; J. Bailly-Herzberg, *Correspondance de Camille Pissarro*, vol. 5: 1899–1903 (Paris, 1991), pp. 192, 219.

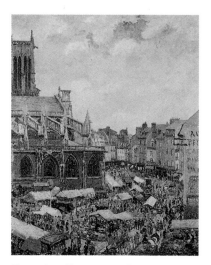

*Fig. 1. Camille Pissarro.* The Market at the Church of Saint-Jacques, Dieppe. *1901. Private collection*

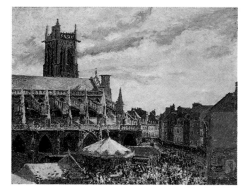

*Fig. 2. Camille Pissarro.* The Fair at the Church of Saint-Jacques in Dieppe, Sunny Morning. *1901. Private collection*

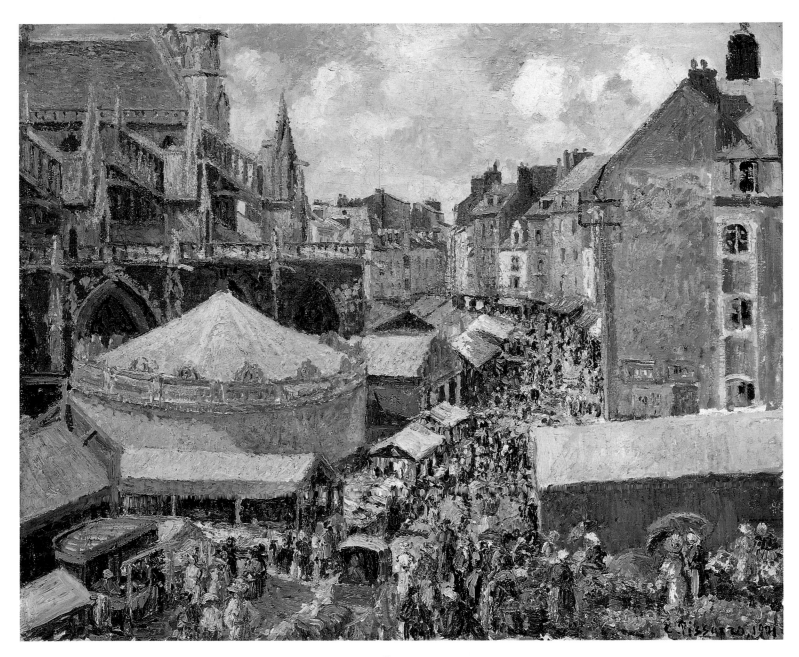

Camille Pissarro

## 44. THE FAIR IN DIEPPE, SUNNY MORNING

*La Foire à Dieppe, matin, soleil.* 1901
Oil on canvas, 25 ¾ × 32" (65.3 × 81.5 cm)
Signed and dated lower right: "C. Pissarro 1901"
No. 3KP 525. Formerly collection Otto Krebs, Holzdorf

# CAMILLE PISSARRO

## QUAI MALAQUAIS, SUNNY AFTERNOON

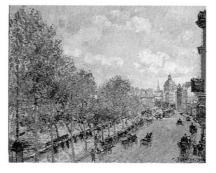

On March 30, 1903, Pissarro wrote to his son Lucien: "I am now working on a series of canvases in the Hôtel du Quai Voltaire: Pont Royal and Pont du Carrousel, and also the perspective of the Quai Malaquais with the Institut [de France] and the background to the left of the Seine banks—superb motifs of light" (J. Bailly-Herzberg, *Correspondance de Camille Pissarro*, vol. 5: *1899–1903* [Saint-Ouen-L'Aumone, 1991], p. 329–30).

Pissarro painted four scenes of the Quai Malaquais from the same perspective (Pissarro/Venturi nos. 1289–92; see fig. 1). The largest and most significant of them is the present canvas, from the Krebs collection. The view portrayed here by the artist has survived to the present day; even the booksellers' stalls still stand along the embankment, although automobiles have taken the place of the horses and carriages.

Such themes had played a significant role in early Impressionism, in Renoir's *Pont-Neuf, Paris* of 1872 (National Gallery of Art, Washington, D.C.) and the even earlier *Pont-des-Arts* of 1867 (The Norton Simon Foundation, Pasadena), where the Institut de France is visible in the right portion of the painting. Monet's *Quai du Louvre* of 1867 should also be recalled (Gemeentemuseum, The Hague). In those days, Pissarro preferred far more modest subjects. His first quai painting, *The Pontoise Bridge* of 1878 (Pissarro/Venturi no. 443), naturally lacks the excitement with which the later Paris landscape is charged. Genre elements like those in *Town Park in Pontoise* (plate 41) are accorded a similar place, as residents of the town casually stroll and exchange bows with each other. Several years later, in the depictions of the Rouen embankments—for example, *Quai Napoléon at Rouen* of 1883 (Pissarro/Venturi no. 606) and *Lacroix*

*Island at Rouen* of 1883 (Pissarro/Venturi no. 607)—the accent shifts to convey the busy atmosphere of the port district.

In the later Parisian series devoted to the boulevard Montmartre or the avenue de l'Opéra, Pissarro strove to express the spirit of the great European capital and its incessant bustle. He made a point of staying at a hotel or settling in a place from which he could constantly see his favorite motifs. In 1900, he rented an apartment in one of the older houses on the Île de la Cité near the Pont-Neuf, which enabled him to paint a series of thirteen canvases. In that series, Pissarro was concerned not so much to render the beauty of the oldest bridge in the city as to depict the constant movement of pedestrians, carriages, and omnibuses, and to show that this was one of the nerve centers of contemporary Paris.

From there, it was not far to the Quai Voltaire, where Pissarro decided to paint his next series. His interest shifted from the Right Bank of the Seine to the Left, and the works consequently differed in character from the preceding pictorial ensembles. It was to be his last Parisian cycle. Although active, the banks of the Seine were among the less noisy and congested transportation arteries of Paris. Looking out the window of his hotel to the cobblestone street running into the distance, Pissarro, a true Impressionist, was charmed by the mutability of everything that fell within his field of vision. But here, the motif of actual physical activity, in particular, the motion of the carriages, is less important. Instead, Pissarro, by various means, chiefly through the diagonals and curves in the composition and the vibration of the brushstrokes, creates the sense of a dynamic Paris street at midday. At the same time, there is a feeling of equilibrium, and it

is noteworthy that the entire series is distinguished by the centralized, even stagelike nature of the arrangement. In the painting from the Krebs collection, the canopies of the trees to the left and the corner of the building to the right frame this outdoor stage.

During this time, Pissarro was experiencing some financial difficulties. These are reflected in the fact that he moved into the second-rate Hôtel du Quai Voltaire. Both of his dealers, Durand-Ruel and Bernheim, offered prices that seemed too low to him, and he was forced to reduce his regular support to his three eldest sons. Pissarro decided to start a new series and on July 3 departed for Dieppe, from where he soon moved on to Havre. At the end of October he returned to Paris and once again settled at the same hotel.

Probably at that moment he once again turned to *Quai Malaquais, Sunny Afternoon*. The rather pasty texture of the painting suggests that it was worked on at different times. Other canvases in this series were definitely painted in the spring; they show almost bare trees with only the remnants of the previous year's leaves. Unlike those pictures, the dense but already yellowing foliage of the present landscape suggests that the scene took place in the fall.

Pissarro's last stay at the Hôtel du Quai Voltaire lasted only a few days. His prostate disease, which doctors had tried to treat without success, led to blood poisoning and ultimately to his death, on November 13. Thus, *Quai Malaquais, Sunny Afternoon* was one of the artist's last works.

LITERATURE: L.-R. Pissarro and L. Venturi, *Camille Pissarro: Son Art, son oeuvre* (Paris, 1939), no. 1291.

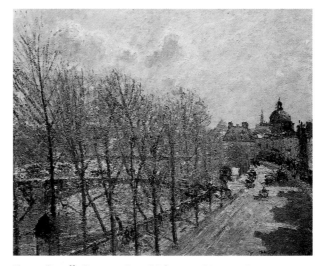

*Fig. 1. Camille Pissarro.* Quai Malaquais: Morning Sun. *1903. Private collection*

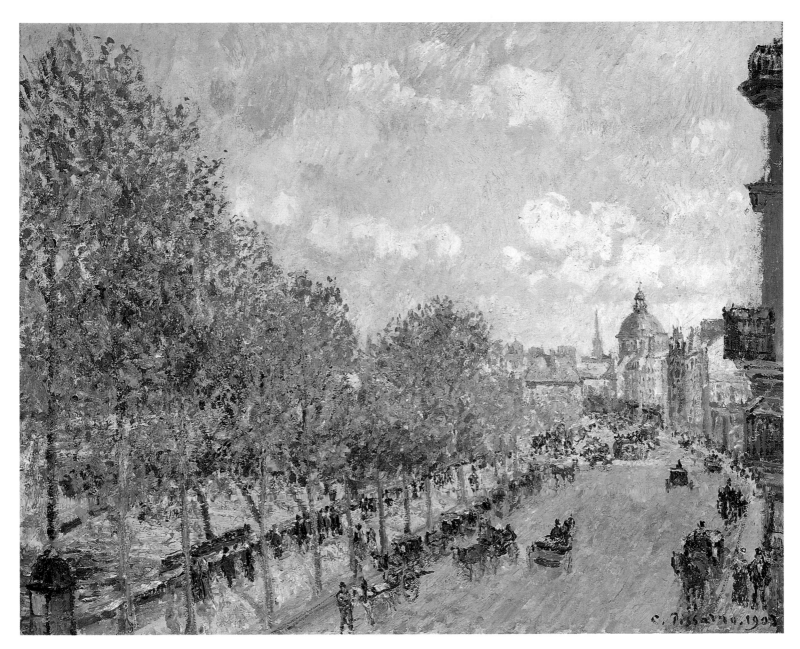

Camille Pissarro

45. QUAI MALAQUAIS, SUNNY AFTERNOON

*Quai Malaquais après-midi, soleil.* 1903
Oil on canvas, 25 ¾ × 32" (65.3 × 81.5 cm)
Signed and dated lower right: "C. Pissarro 1903"
Notation on stretcher crossbar, apparently by the artist:
"Quai Malaquais après-midi (Soleil)"
No. 3KP 531. Formerly collection Otto Krebs, Holzdorf

# PAUL CÉZANNE

## JAS DE BOUFFAN, THE POOL

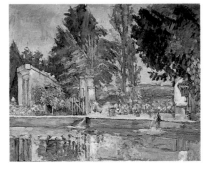

Jas de Bouffan was the estate on the outskirts of Aix-en-Provence acquired by Louis-Auguste Cézanne, the artist's father, in 1859 (the name is from the Provençal, meaning "Residence of Winds"). Its vineyards seemed like a very promising investment to the banker. The historical buildings on the property perhaps concerned him less, although possessing them undoubtedly flattered his pride. A three-story mansion from the time of Louis XIV which once served as a residence for the governor of Provence survived at Jas de Bouffan. In the summers, the Cézanne family came out to the estate on Sundays (eventually they settled there more permanently). Jas de Bouffan was indeed open to all the winds and gave respite from summer's sweltering heat. The mansion was in a state of disrepair and many rooms were closed, but bedrooms were arranged on the second floor. Trying to preserve his independence, Cézanne worked for hours at a stretch.

Cézanne deeply loved Jas de Bouffan, which for forty years remained a refuge for his restless spirit. He painted the home several times, but these works, the best of which is in the Národni Galeri, Prague (Venturi no. 460), belong to a later period, the 1880s, when he was striving to build a firmer pictorial structure in his art; the geometry of the great stone edifice suited his studies.

One of the first subjects Cézanne painted at Jas de Bouffan was the large pool surrounded by shrubs and trees and by decorative sculptures of lions and dolphins. Cézanne did not at first paint the sculptural and architectural beauties of the pool. In the early views of this part of the estate, rather dramatic in mood and dark in coloration, attention is focused instead on the trees, as with *The Pool at Jas de Bouffan* of 1869–70

(Venturi no. 40) and *The Chestnut Trees and the Pool at Jas de Bouffan* (Tate Gallery, London). In *The Pool at Jas de Bouffan* from the Sheffield City Art Galleries (Venturi no. 160), probably painted at the same time, the energy of the brushstrokes is somewhat subdued and an overall dark green tone fills almost the entire canvas.

*Jas de Bouffan, the Dolphin* of about 1878–79 (fig. 1; Venturi no. 166) shows the pool as only a narrow strip of water, while the artist concentrates on the abundant foliage: the white marble dolphin stands out sharply against the backdrop of greenery. Nature is presented almost in the Impressionist style, reminiscent of similar landscapes of Camille Pissarro, such as *Quarry near Pontoise* of about 1874 (Kunstmuseum, Basel; Pissarro/Venturi no. 251). Cézanne learned a great deal from working with Pissarro in Pontoise, above all, the advantages of painting *en plein air* and maintaining a pure palette. He considered Pissarro his tutor, and the older artist advised him to paint more often under the open sky in Aix.

In the present painting from the Krebs collection, from the general period of *Jas de Bouffan, the Dolphin*, the pool is shown in its most attractive form, since, in addition to the greenery, which provides the overall color scheme, the architectural and sculptural appointments are also visible: the somewhat comical lion of yellow sandstone; the dolphin, playfully flipping its tail; the gates; and an old building with paired columns. The blue fence erected by Louis-Auguste Cézanne to protect his property and the wooden gate do not clash with the old sculptures or buildings.

A curious detail is included in the painting, one quite unusual for Cézanne: the pool is being filled with water. Concentrating on fleeting moments, pursuing

the rapid and the transient, the Impressionists tried to capture such effects as moving water. Alfred Sisley, for example, a relatively short time before, painted a frothing stream of water in *Molesey Weir, Hampton Court* of 1874 (National Gallery of Scotland, Edinburgh). In depicting the water flowing from two pipes or the reflections distorted by the ripples, Cézanne seems to succumb to the temptations of Impressionism; ordinarily he would have portrayed the mirrorlike smoothness of still water. Nevertheless, the painting is far from Impressionist.

The depictions of the pool at Jas de Bouffan made in the mid-1870s may appear to verge on the methods of Impressionism; in *The Pool at Jas de Bouffan* (fig. 2; Albright-Knox Art Gallery, Buffalo; Venturi no. 417), for example, the influence of the Impressionists is felt in the seemingly unpremeditated choice of point of view. As if accidentally, in the spirit of Claude Monet, part of the shrubbery is glimpsed in the foreground, not entirely within the frame of the picture, with a corner of the pool behind it. The nominally Impressionist composition, however, turns out to contain a solid structure within it, and the large, orderly brushstrokes are alien to Impressionist mobility. Not surprisingly, Venturi dated this painting to the artist's "constructive" period, to 1882–85. Götz Adriani believes that it was painted in 1876–78 (G. Adriani, *Cezanne: Gemälde* [Kunsthalle Tübingen, 1993], no. 20), probably a more accurate view. Most likely the Albright-Knox landscape was executed at the beginning of the period indicated by Adriani; in other words, at approximately the same time as the painting from the Krebs collection, perhaps a little after it.

Each new approach to the same subject taught Cézanne how better to reveal the structural elements within it; this is where he went beyond Pissarro. Concern with compositional coordination, balance, the ordering of planes was naturally not foreign to a major landscape painter like Pissarro. But Cézanne's pictorial construction is a phenomenon of a different order. Distinguished by a more complex and integrated rhythmic organization, it is drawn from nature while at the same time seeming to exist independently of it. In this respect, the structural quality of *Jas de Bouffan, the Pool* is more strongly evident than that of *The Dolphin* or even the Albright-Knox painting. The work is painted in a format close to the "golden section," its propor-

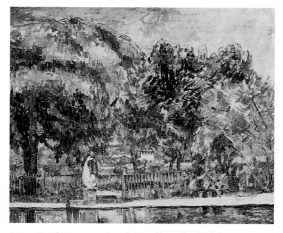

*Fig. 1. Paul Cézanne.* Jas de Bouffan, the Dolphin. *1878–79. Whereabouts unknown*

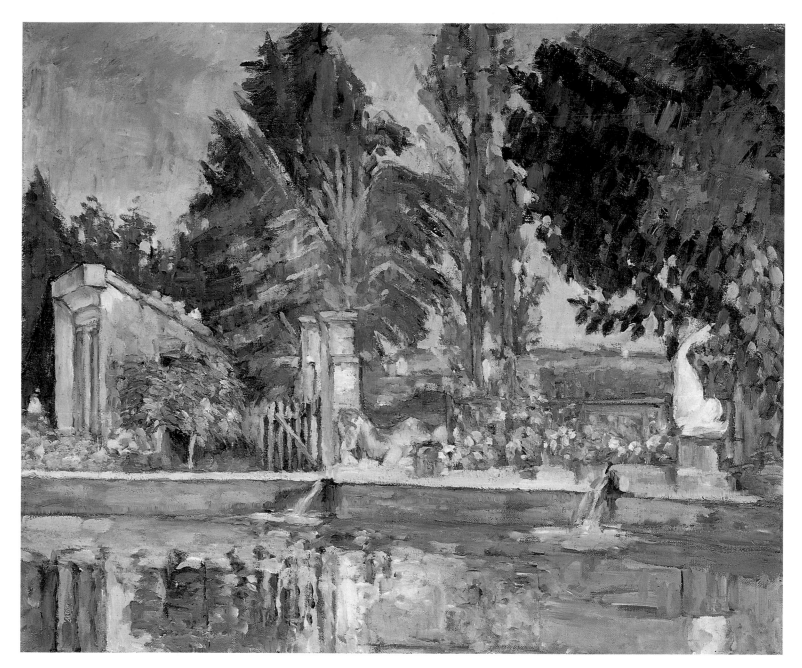

Paul Cézanne (1839, Aix-en-Provence–1906, Aix-en-Provence)
### 46. JAS DE BOUFFAN, THE POOL
*Jas de Bouffan, le bassin.* c. 1876
Oil on canvas, 18⅛ × 22⅛" (46.1 × 56.3 cm)
No. 3KP 530. Formerly collection Otto Krebs, Holzdorf

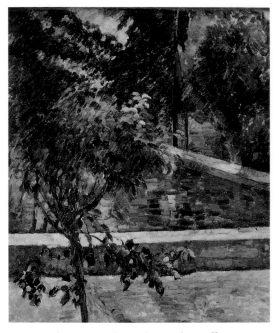

Fig. 2. *Paul Cézanne.* The Pool at Jas de Bouffan. *1876–78. Albright-Knox Art Gallery, Buffalo*

tions ruled by a mathematical formula. Yet, at the same time, this canvas from the Krebs collection, despite all its rational calculation, derives a good deal of its effect from color harmonies, and is far from being dry in any way.

The element of calculation can be described as follows. The edge of the pool, the trunks of the trees, the sculpture of the dolphin, the gates, and part of the dilapidated building form a solid system of compositional fulcrums that govern the landscape. Most likely Cézanne began with the sculpture of the lion, which determined the center of the landscape. The sides were obtained from the paired columns to the left and the dolphin to the right. However, the composition is not constructed around a central axis, and, not surprisingly, the lion is overshadowed in the painting and is not even immediately noticeable. The line of the pool's border, running from one edge of the painting to the other, and which also reiterates the lines of the fence and the horizon, provides a very strong horizontal pull. It is balanced by the verticals of the columns, the gates, and the tree trunks. But the picture's composition is not only a matter of the sum of the horizontals and verticals balancing one another; it is a question of a particular organization of space. The upper portion of the painting is organized as two overlapping squares, the bases of which are the line of the water. The trunk of the poplar tree forms the right side of one square and the pylon of the gates forms the left side of the other. It should be noted that Cézanne placed the gates to the left of center; otherwise, the composition would have lost its marvelous solidity. All the elements of the composition are structured on such precisely calibrated interrelations, and, most remarkably, this is done so subtly that what results may seem only a spontaneous depiction of nature.

The landscape was indeed painted from life, which accounts for why the gray-blue tone of the southern sky, the green of Provence, and its yellow soil have been conveyed so exactly. The combination of green and blue is one of the most difficult problems for any painter. In *Jas de Bouffan, the Pool*, the harmony of these tones, strengthened by a sprinkling of bright ocher, displays a masterly grasp of color.

The painting was dated by the artist's son to 1885 (photograph in the Ambroise Vollard archive). Georges Rivière supported this dating. Monnière attributes the canvas to 1874. Lionello Venturi was inclined to believe that it was painted about 1875–76. John Rewald believed that the time of execution was about 1876.

PROVENANCE: Paul Cézanne fils, Paris; June 21, 1913, Galerie Bernheim-Jeune, Paris; April 4, 1914, Galerie Paul Cassirer, Berlin; Neumann, Bremen; August 19, 1924, Galerie Thannhauser, Lucerne; February 15, 1926, Galerie Bernheim-Jeune, Paris; J. K. Thannhauser, Berlin; Otto Krebs, Holzdorf.

EXHIBITIONS: 1899–1900, Paris, "Exposition centennale de l'art français," no. 88; 1914, Bremen, "Internationale Ausstellung," Kunsthalle, no. 74; 1926, Paris, "Paul Cézanne: Exposition rétrospective," Galerie Bernheim-Jeune, no. 44; 1927, New York, "The Classics of Modern Painting," De Hauke & Co., no. 7.

LITERATURE: T. Duret, "Paul Cézanne," *Kunst und Künstler*, vol. 5, no. 3 (November 1906), p. 100 (reprod.); G. Rivière, *Le Maître Paul Cézanne* (Paris, 1923), pp. 57, 216 (as *Mon Jardin*); *Bulletin de la vie artistique*, 1926, p. 179; K. Pfister, *Cézanne: Gestalt, Werk, Mytos* (Potsdam, 1927), p. 47 (as *Landschaft*); E. Waldmann, *Die Kunst des Realismus und des Impressionismus* (Berlin, 1927), p. 501; G. Rivière, *Cézanne, le peintre solitaire* (Paris, 1933), p. 129; G. Mack, *Paul Cézanne* (New York, 1935), pl. 8; "Recueil important des oeuvres de Cézanne," in *Paysage*, vol. 1 (Tokyo, 1935), pl. 8; L. Venturi, *Cézanne: Son Art, son oeuvre* (Paris, 1936), no. 167; A. Vollard, *Paul Cézanne: His Life and Work* (New York, 1937), pl. 31; F. Novotny, *Cézanne und das Ende der wissenschaftlichen Perspektive* (Vienna, 1939), p. 199, illus. 28, 29; B. Dorival, *Cézanne* (Paris, 1948), pl. 34; J. Rewald, in collaboration with W. Feilchenfeldt and J. Warman, *Paul Cézanne: The Paintings—A Catalogue Raisonné* (New York, forthcoming), no. 278.

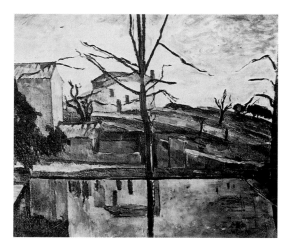

Fig. 3. *Paul Cézanne*. The Pool at Jas de Bouffan in Winter. *c. 1878. Private collection*

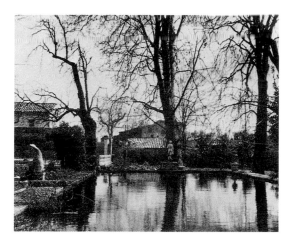

Fig. 4. *The Pool at Jas de Bouffan. Photograph by John Rewald. c. 1935*

# PAUL CÉZANNE

## APPLES, PEACHES, PEARS, AND GRAPES

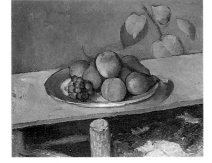

Cézanne's still lifes were "democratic" from the outset, even more so than those painted by the adherents to the realist doctrine of François Bonvin or Augustin Ribot. Bread, eggs, onions, a cheap, thick glass on a plain napkin make up the contents of one of his first works on this subject, *Still Life: Bread and Eggs* of 1865 (Cincinnati Art Museum; Venturi no. 59). Although to some extent the painting reflects the artist's impressions of Jean-Baptiste Chardin's paintings in the Louvre, it lacks the Chardinesque elegance that Cézanne's contemporaries valued and tried unsuccessfully to imitate. In Cézanne's early still lifes there is an unresolved contradiction: the idea of still life presupposes calm and tranquility, which clashes with his artistic temperament and with his thick, heavy brushstrokes. The pears, for example, in *Sugar Bowl, Pears, and Blue Cup* of about 1865 (Musée d'Orsay, Paris; Venturi no. 62) are sculpted out of several energetic blows of the brush; "sculpted" is indeed the right word, since the paint is applied so thickly as to remind one of a sculptor modeling in clay. Gradually, however, Cézanne in the early 1870s developed a calmer manner.

A significant number of still lifes appeared in the period of Cézanne's Impressionism (1872–77). They can be divided into two groups: bouquets of flowers (the smaller group) and compositions with fruit (the larger group). Small paintings in the second group depicting fruit on a plate, such as *Peach and Grapes* of 1873–77 (fig. 1; Venturi no. 192) and *Apples, Orange, and Lemon* of 1873–77 (Venturi no. 201), undoubtedly prepared the way for the present still life from the Koehler collection.

Though he worked to achieve greater subtlety, a still life such as this shows us a Cézanne constitution-

ally incapable of mere prettiness. This we see in the very selection of the setting: a bare, wooden plank, a plain background with unpretentious leafy wallpaper—nothing to indicate even the slightest wish to interest the viewer in the beauty of the setting or the rarity of the objects.

By the 1880s, when the public demanded a more finished quality in still lifes than in any other subject, Joris-Karl Huysmans gave the following characterization of Cézanne's paintings of fruit: "Pears and apples covered with bright light in porcelain dishes or scattered on a white tablecloth are coarse and chiseled as if hewn out of plaster by a trowel and adjusted by a thumb. If you come up close, before your eyes are savage heaps of brushstrokes of cinnabar and yellow, green and blue; if you step back to a distance to focus, you see fruit worthy of the showcases of the best store, juicy, ripe, and appetizing. Now you see what you had failed to notice up to now: the strange and at the same time real tones, the swatches of color unexpected in their authenticity, the delightful light blue shadows in the folds of the wrinkled tablecloth and around the fruit scattered upon it. Comparing these canvases with ordinary still lifes executed in unsightly gray tones and on an inexpressive background, you sense all of their novelty with a particular clarity" (J.-K. Huysmans, *Certains* [Paris, 1889]).

The blue border of the plate creates a wonderful frame for the fruit and gives more resonance to the green, yellow, and orange hues. The leaves in the design of the wallpaper are introduced as an element of artistic play; there is a slight ambiguity about whether these leaves are printed on paper pasted to the wall, and are part of a mechanical pattern, or whether they belong with the fruit. One branch, with four leaves, is emphasized and brought up close to the fruit, and the leaves are those of an apple tree; however, they are not green but bluish gray. By this means, Cézanne distinguished between this background element and the dish but at the same time allowed it to play a role in the composition.

At a preliminary stage, there was much more blue in the painting. One can see the blue coming through the ocher brushstrokes of the board on which the plate rests. It appears that the whole canvas was painted in a blue almost the same as the border of the plate. Cézanne used modern factory-made paints and therefore could not work in the manner of the Old Masters, who created inimitable effects by adding one transparent layer of paint on top of another. However, to the extent he could, Cézanne emulated their practice and employed preliminary color preparations. "The thought can be expressed in full only through different paints," said Cézanne before Veronese's *Marriage at Cana* in the Louvre. "He first laid one color on his canvas—the way they all did in their era—embracing the entire painting at once, which at that moment looked like the earth not yet lit by the rays of the rising sun. . . . Nowadays, artists apply a thick layer of paint on their canvas; they do it in a rough manner, like masons, and imagine that this is very powerful and very sincere. The art of preparation is now forgotten, and the paintings no longer have the fluidity and the impact that the undertones used to create" (J. Gasquet, *Paul Cézanne* [Paris, 1921])

Different scholars dated this still life differently. The artist's son indicated 1875–80 on the photograph preserved in Ambroise Vollard's archives. Lionello Venturi shifted the date to 1879–82. He placed this canvas with a group of paintings that all show wallpaper with a leafy pattern in the background. This, together with peculiarities of style, makes it possible to determine more precisely when such still lifes were created. Venturi believed that the wallpaper belonged either in Melun, where Cézanne lived from April 1879 to March 1880, or the rue de l'Ouest in Paris, where the artist had an apartment in 1881–82. At a later date, scholars tried to correct this method of grouping the paintings, arguing that wallpaper with both leafy and geometric patterns reproduced by Cézanne at that time could have been found elsewhere than the rue de l'Ouest. Charles Sterling, Lawrence Gowing, Georges

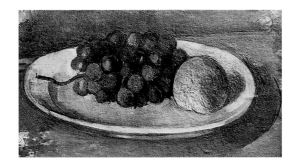

*Fig. 1. Paul Cézanne.* Peach and Grapes. *1873–77. The Barnes Foundation, Merion, Pennsylvania. © The Barnes Foundation*

Rivière, and John Rewald tried to narrow the date of the still lifes with wallpaper; summing up the opinions of these experts on Cézanne, Rewald decided on 1879–80, which seems convincing.

Usually, the artist placed the objects of his still lifes on a table or a chest, and sometimes, which he did in this case, on a simple board. Next to the painting from the Koehler collection, we should place two small works undoubtedly created at the same time and depicting the same plate with a blue border and the leafy wallpaper: *Still Life* of 1879–80 (Národni Galeri, Prague; Venturi no. 348) and *Blue Plate* of 1879–80 (Venturi no. 353), which belonged to Octave Mirbeau.

The painting is also known under the titles *Plate with Fruit (Assiette de fruits)* and *Blue Plate (Assiette bleu)*.

PROVENANCE: Galerie E. Druet, Paris; April 20, 1909, Galerie Bernheim-Jeune, Paris; March 20, 1911, Bernhard Koehler, Berlin.

EXHIBITIONS: 1912, Cologne, "Sonderbund Internationale Kunstausstellung," Städtische Ausstellunghalle, no. 128.

LITERATURE: Vasily Kandinsky and Franz Marc, eds., *Der Blaue Reiter Almanach* (Munich, 1912), p. 55 (reprod.); K. Scheffer, "Die Jungsten," *Kunst und Künstler*, vol. 11, no. 8 (May 1913), p. 392 (reprod.); L. Venturi, *Cézanne: Son Art, son oeuvre* (Paris, 1936), no. 345; J. Rewald, in collaboration with W. Feilchenfeldt and J. Warman, *Paul Cézanne: The Paintings—A Catalogue Raisonné* (New York, forthcoming), no. 432.

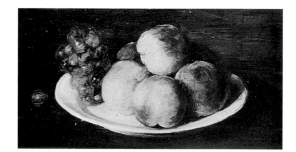

*Fig. 2. Henri Fantin-Latour. Still Life: Peaches and Grapes. 1863. Paisley Museum and Art Gallery, England*

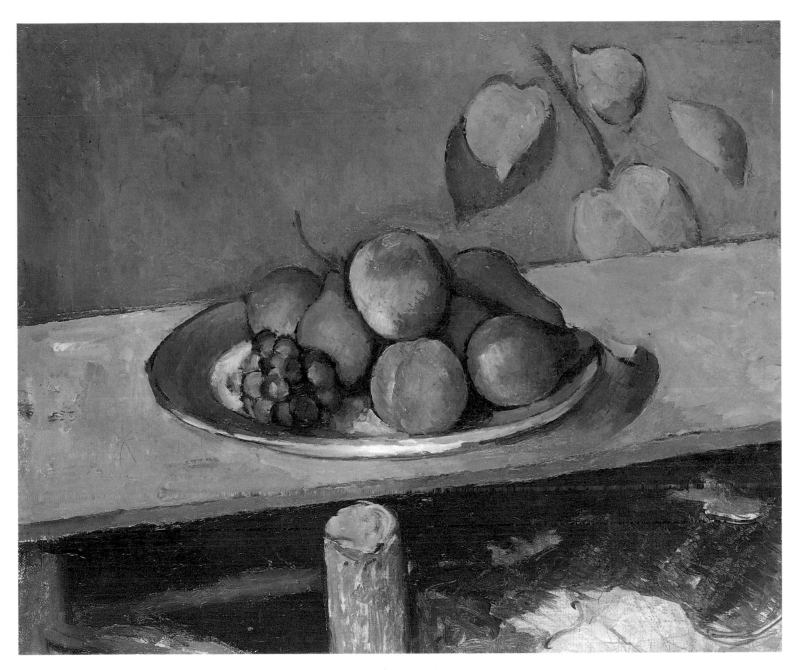

Paul Cézanne
47. APPLES, PEACHES, PEARS, AND GRAPES
*Pommes, pêches, poires et raisins.* c. 1879–80
Oil on canvas, 15⅛ × 18¼" (38.5 × 46.5 cm)
No. 3K 1580. Formerly collection Bernhard Koehler, Berlin

# PAUL CÉZANNE

## HOUSES ALONG A ROAD

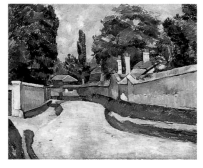

The theme interpreted in this painting runs like a thread through all of Cézanne's work, from *Turn of the Road in Provence* of 1867–68 (The Montreal Museum of Fine Arts; Venturi no. 53) to *Blue Landscape* of 1904–5 (The State Hermitage Museum, St. Petersburg; Venturi no. 793). In the latter case, the motif of a turn in the road concealed in the thickets reflects not so much his impressions from walks in the outskirts of his native Aix as his deep and dramatic reflections upon a life's path coming to an end. At earlier stages, matters were far simpler. From his youth, Cézanne would walk a great deal and did not drop this habit even later in life, sometimes hiking from Auvers to Pontoise in order to meet or work with Pissarro, or sometimes heading off to Mont Sainte-Victoire.

Shortly before *Houses along a Road* was painted, Cézanne wrote to Émile Zola: "Of course, as you say, my stay in Pontoise does not prevent me from seeking you; on the contrary, I am even thinking of going to Médan on my own two feet and I think I'll be able to stand the exertion" (letter of May 20, 1881; in J. Rewald, *Cézanne: Sa Vie, son oeuvre, son amitié pour Zola* [Paris, 1939], p. 246; and *Cézanne: Correspondance*, ed. J. Rewald [Paris, 1937]).

The motif of a turn in the road played a particularly important role in Cézanne's painting in the late 1870s and early 1880s. Even before, it enabled the artist to capture his own impressions expressively and simply, while serving as an effective means to organize the painting. In a natural fashion, a road ties together various planes within a work. Furthermore, Cézanne, with all his concerns about the rendering of space, wanted to avoid perspectives that were too deep; the bend in the road provided him with a convenient way to limit himself to the foreground and middle ground. As if inviting the viewer to stroll deeper into the landscape, a painting would begin with a road branching off, but the road never runs far. Either it almost runs into a house (a technique used in the famous *House of the Hanged Man at Auvers* of 1873 (Musée d'Orsay, Paris; Venturi no. 133) or it disappears, skirting the house, as in *Home of Doctor Gachet at Auvers* of 1873 (Musée d'Orsay, Paris; Venturi no. 145). Although all these landscapes are devoid of people, they remain related to the sphere of human activity; the small houses and bare stone walls along passageways (Cézanne loved to paint them in Pontoise) create a sense that people live behind these walls.

Aside from *Houses along a Road*, Cézanne painted two other landscapes in Pontoise similar in theme and style of execution: *Turn in the Road* of 1881 (fig. 1; Museum of Fine Arts, Boston; Venturi no. 329) and *Houses at the Edge of the Road* of 1881 (Wildenstein collection, New York; Venturi no. 328). His persistent painting of this part of the town can be explained by a correlation between the natural scene and a creative surge that appeared distinctly about 1881. The rhythmic system of composition became clearer and the drawing cleaner and more integrated. The sharp lines of the road, the stone walls, and the roofs of the houses suggest a search for simpler, purer structures in painting.

This Cézanne landscape can be seen on the wall in the background of a portrait of Jos Hessel by Édouard Vuillard, painted in 1905, which supports the hypothesis that the work belonged to Hessel at the time.

Venturi dated the work to 1879–82, Rivière to about 1880, and Rewald to about 1881.

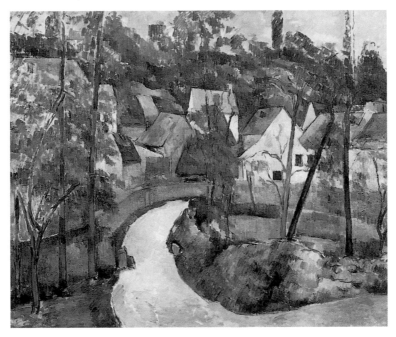

*Fig. 1. Paul Cézanne.* Turn in the Road. *1881. Museum of Fine Arts, Boston. Bequest of John T. Spaulding*

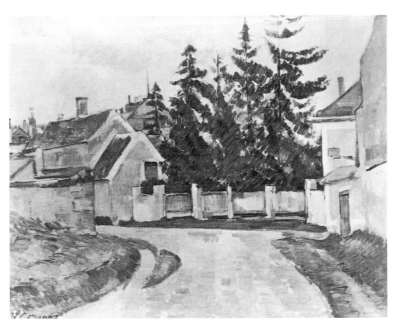

*Fig. 2. Paul Cézanne.* Turn in the Road. *1879–82. The Kreeger Museum, Washington, D.C.*

PROVENANCE: Galerie Bernheim-Jeune, Paris; Jos Hessel, Paris; July 18, 1907, Galerie Paul Cassirer, Berlin; November 24, 1907, Theodor Behrens, Hamburg; Baroness M. von Koenig, Berlin; Galerie Thannhauser, Berlin; Otto Krebs, Holzdorf.

EXHIBITIONS: 1904, Berlin, Galerie Paul Cassirer; 1906, Paris, Salon d'Automne, Grand Palais, no. 326; 1920, Paris, "Cézanne" (catalogue text by O. Mirbeau); Galerie Bernheim-Jeune, no. 10 (as *La Route*); 1921, Berlin, "Paul Cézanne: Werke in deutschen Privatbesitz," Galerie Paul Cassirer, no. 7.

LITERATURE: E. Bernhard, "Erinnerungen an Paul Cézanne," *Kunst und Künstler*, vol. 6, no. 12 (September 1908), p. 523 (reprod.); J. Meier-Graefe, *Paul Cézanne* (Munich, 1910), p. 69 (reprod.); J. Meier-Graefe, *Paul Cézanne* (Munich, 1913), p. 69 (dated 1880; Th[eodor] Behrens collection); M. Deri, *Die Malerei im XIX. Jahrhundert* (Berlin, 1919), pl. 41; A. Popp, "Cézanne: Elemente seines Stiles, anlässlich einer Kritik erörtert," *Die bildenden Künste*, vol. 2 (1919), p. 177; F. Burger, *Cézanne und Hodler* (Munich, 1920), pl. 105; J. Meier-Graefe, *Ein Betrag zur Entwicklung Geschichte der moderne Malerei* (Munich, 1920), pl. 501; A. Zeisho, *Paul Cézanne* (Tokyo, 1921) (in Japanese); F. Ahlers-Hestermann, "Von den Wandlungen der neueren Kunst," *Kunst und Künstler*, vol. 19, no. 10 (July 1921), p. 361; J. Meier-Graefe, *Cézanne und sein Kreis* (Munich, 1922), p. 147; E. Waldmann, *Die Kunst der Realismus und der Impressionismus* (Berlin, 1927), p. 497; K. Scheffler, *Geschichte der Europaeischen Malerei und Plastik* (Berlin, 1927), p. 93; K. Pfister, *Cézanne: Gestalt, Werk, Mytos* (Potsdam, 1927), pl. 45; E. Waldmann, *Paul Cézanne: Acht farbige Gemälde* (Leipzig, 1930), pl. 1; G. Rivière, *Cézanne, le peintre solitaire* (Paris, 1933), p. 27; M. Peschke-Koed, "Den perverse Stil," *Samleren*, 1934, p. 122; L. Venturi, *Cézanne: Son Art, son oeuvre* (Paris, 1936), no. 330; P. Feist, *Paul Cézanne* (Leipzig, 1963), pp. 16, 28, pl. 32; J. Rewald, in collaboration with W. Feilchenfeldt and J. Warman, *Paul Cézanne: The Paintings—A Catalogue Raisonné* (New York, forthcoming), no. 486.

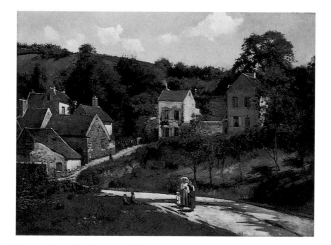

*Fig. 3. Camille Pissarro. L'Hermitage at Pontoise. c. 1867. Solomon R. Guggenheim Museum. Justin K. Thannhauser Collection*

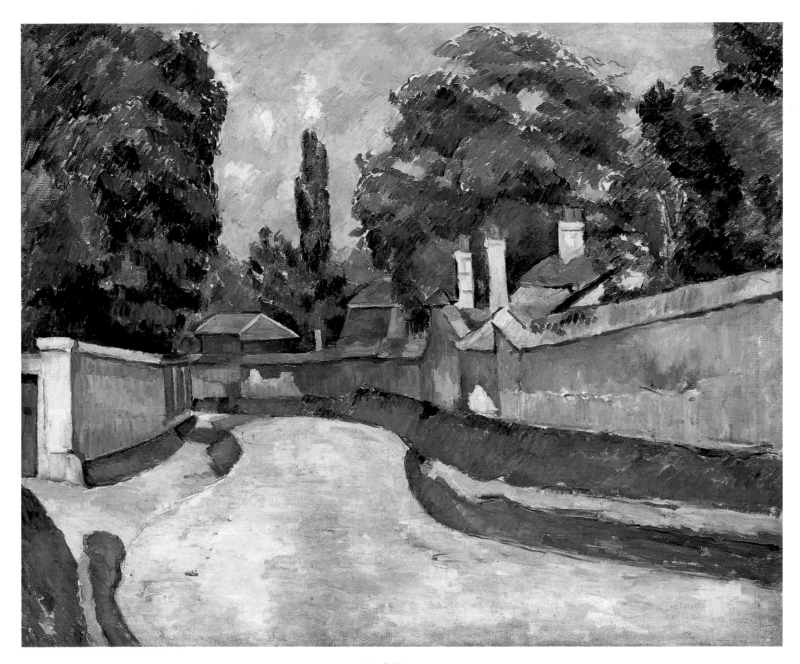

Paul Cézanne
## 48. HOUSES ALONG A ROAD
*Maisons au bord d'une route.* c. 1881
Oil on canvas, 23⅝ × 28⅞" (60 × 73.5 cm)
No. 3KP 502. Formerly collection Otto Krebs, Holzdorf

# PAUL CÉZANNE

## SELF-PORTRAIT

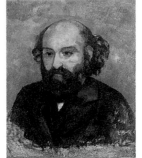

Among Cézanne's self-portraits—and there are more than two dozen of them—this work occupies a quite unusual place because, unlike the others, it was painted without the use of a mirror. In this painting, Cézanne made a variation of the portrait of himself done by Pierre-Auguste Renoir. Lionello Venturi noted the singularity of the painting, although his characterization leaves something to be desired: "unique of its kind because it is a copy or at least an imitation of the portrait of Cézanne done by Renoir in pastel."

Despite the dissimilarity in temperaments and the differences in their creative personalities, a deep friendship united the two artists. "It was in 1863 that I met Cézanne. At that time I had a small studio which I shared with Bazille. One day Bazille came in with two young fellows. 'I have brought you two first-rate recruits!' he said. They were Cézanne and Pissarro." At that time Cézanne and Pissarro, who were studying at the Académie Suisse under Charles Gleyre, became acquainted with Renoir as well as with such other fellow students as Claude Monet and Alfred Sisley. Thus were laid the foundations for the future alliance that enabled them to gather together in 1874 for the first Impressionist exhibition.

Renoir made his pastel portrait of Cézanne in 1880 in his Paris studio on rue Norvins (fig. 3; private collection; see F. Daulte, *P.-A. Renoir: Watercolours, Pastels and Drawings in Colour* [London, 1959]). It is justly considered one of the finest depictions of the Master of Aix. Later, in 1902, Renoir duplicated this pastel in a lithograph (L. Delteil, *Pissarro, Sisley, Renoir: Le Peintre-graveur illustré*, vol. 17 [Paris, 1932], no. 34), and later still, in 1915–17, Ginot used the portrait to make a sculpted medallion following his directions; one of the castings decorates a fountain in Aix.

Renoir dated his portrait, enabling us to date, at least approximately, the version executed soon afterward by Cézanne. To be sure, the opinions of scholars differ slightly: Venturi believed the portrait to have been painted in 1880–81 and John Rewald in 1881–82.

In creating his variation, Cézanne borrowed the pastel he admired either from Renoir himself or, more likely, from Victor Chocquet, upon whose commission it was made. While preserving the dimensions and composition of the portrait, Cézanne infused it with a different, more severe spirit. It lacks the rose tones that define the color scheme of Renoir's portrait, using in their place a more prosaic bright ocher. In method, Cézanne's work also differs quite substantially from Renoir's: instead of the soft touches of the pastel chalks that create a homogenized surface, here there are broken, energetic brushstrokes whose dynamic is reinforced by their diagonal direction. Overall, the painting is distinguished by its greater terseness and generality: instead of the separate strands of hair in Renoir's pastel, there is a dense mass of color. Barbara White appropriately noted: "While Renoir's portrayal is mild, with eyes meditating off into space, Cézanne's version is harsh and withdrawn."

N. V. Yavorskaya, a Russian scholar of Cézanne's work, has precisely characterized the difference between the two painters' approach to portraiture. Her remarks about their portraits of Victor Chocquet are quite applicable to their two versions of Cézanne's portrait: "The fluffy hair painted by Renoir takes on a certain form in Cézanne, and the softness of the modeling of the face has disappeared. The psychological significance of the portrait is also different. Renoir renders an objective image, more lively and optimistic but also more external; Cézanne's version is more severe, meaningful, and energetic. In the Renoir it is easy to imagine that the person depicted will make another gesture, will turn his head another way, whereas in the Cézanne this is hard to imagine" (N. V. Yavorskaya, "Cezann v krugu svoikh sovremennikov" ["Cézanne in the Circle of His Contemporaries"], in *Pol Cezann: Perepiska—Vospominaniya sovremennikov* [*Paul Cézanne: Memoirs of His Contemporaries*] [Moscow, 1972], p. 17).

It is their portrayal of space and volume that makes the two portraits antipodes. Cézanne translated Renoir into his own language, concentrating only on the problem that concerned him, rendering volume with color. His painting became not so much a variation as a reminiscence: interpreting his own skull as a globe, with shadings of ocher, greenish and grayish blue tones, he relied on the experience acquired in working with a mirror in such works of the same time as *Self-Portrait* (fig. 1; The Pushkin State Museum of Fine Arts, Moscow). The spherical contours of the forehead are rendered more delicately and precisely there.

In the lower portion of the figure's chest an old tear has been restored, its length almost 30 centimeters. It probably appeared when the painting was still in Cézanne's studio. It is known that Cézanne was rather careless with his works, often losing interest in them when they were finished. Worse, it sometimes happened that he took out his feelings of dissatisfaction or irritation on them. The gap in this canvas was caused by a sharp blow and necessitated remounting the painting on board. It is hard to say when this happened; most likely, it was before the painting went to Camille Pissarro, its first owner. After Pissarro's death, it became the property of Octave Mirbeau, the novelist, playwright, and art critic who defended the new art.

Given the deep friendship between the two painters, it can be surmised that the portrait was given as a present to Pissarro, making a worthy addition to the group of portraits of Cézanne executed by Pissarro in 1874 (a pencil drawing, an engraving, and an oil).

PROVENANCE: Camille Pissarro; Octave Mirbeau, Paris; February 24, 1919, Mirbeau collection sale; Madame Mirbeau, Paris; November 4, 1920, Galerie Bernheim-Jeune, Paris; January 3, 1920, Georg Caspari, Munich; Galerie Hugo Perls, Berlin; Otto Krebs, Holzdorf.

EXHIBITIONS: 1920, Paris, "Cézanne" (catalogue text by Octave Mirbeau), Galerie Bernheim-Jeune, no. 21; 1925, Berlin,

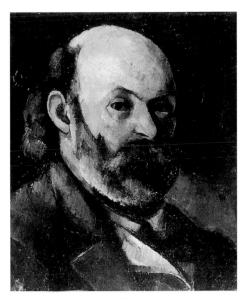

*Fig. 1. Paul Cézanne. Self-Portrait. 1879–85. The Pushkin State Museum of Fine Arts, Moscow. Shchukin Collection*

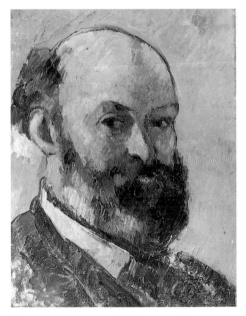

*Fig. 2. Paul Cézanne. Self-Portrait. 1880. Sammlung Oskar Reinhart, Am Römerholz, Winterthur*

"De Delacroix à Picasso," Galerie Hugo Perls, no. 4.

LITERATURE: *Catalogue de la vente d'Octave Mirbeau* (Galerie Durand-Ruel, Paris, February 24, 1919), no. 2 (reprod.); A. Ades, "Mirbeau, critique d'art et collectionneur," *La Renaissance*, 1919, 2, p. 55; H. von Wedderkop, *Paul Cézanne* (Leipzig, 1922); *Kunst und Künstler*, vol. 23 (1924–25), p. 285; *Bulletin de la vie artistique*, 1925, p. 361 (reprod.); M. Raynal, *Cézanne* (Paris, 1936), pl. 61; L. Venturi, *Cézanne: Son Art, son oeuvre* (Paris, 1936), no. 372; J. Rewald, "Sources d'inspiration de Cézanne," *Amour de l'art*, vol. 17 (May 1936), pp. 189–95, fig. 94; A. Vollard, *Recollections of a Picture Dealer* (Boston, 1936), p. 188; G. Jedlicka, *Cézanne* (Bern, 1949), fig. 24; W. Andersen, *Cézanne's Portrait Drawings* (Cambridge, Mass., and London, 1970), fig. 21; F. Elgard, *Cézanne* (New York, 1975), fig. 49; B. E. White, *Renoir: His Life, Art, and Letters* (New York, 1984), p. 102; J. Rewald, "Chocquet and Cézanne," in *Studies in Impressionism* (London, 1985), pp. 173–74; S. de Vries Evans, *The Impressionists Revealed: Masterpieces from Private Collections* (Aukland, 1992), p. 90; J. Rewald, in collaboration with W. Feilchenfeldt and J. Warman, *Paul Cézanne: The Paintings—A Catalogue Raisonné* (New York, forthcoming), no. 446.

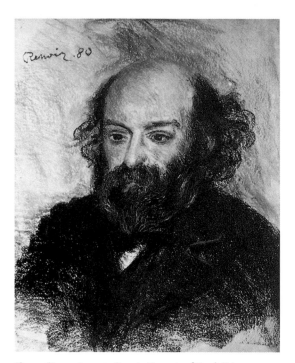

*Fig. 3. Pierre-Auguste Renoir.* Portrait of Paul Cézanne. *1880. Private collection*

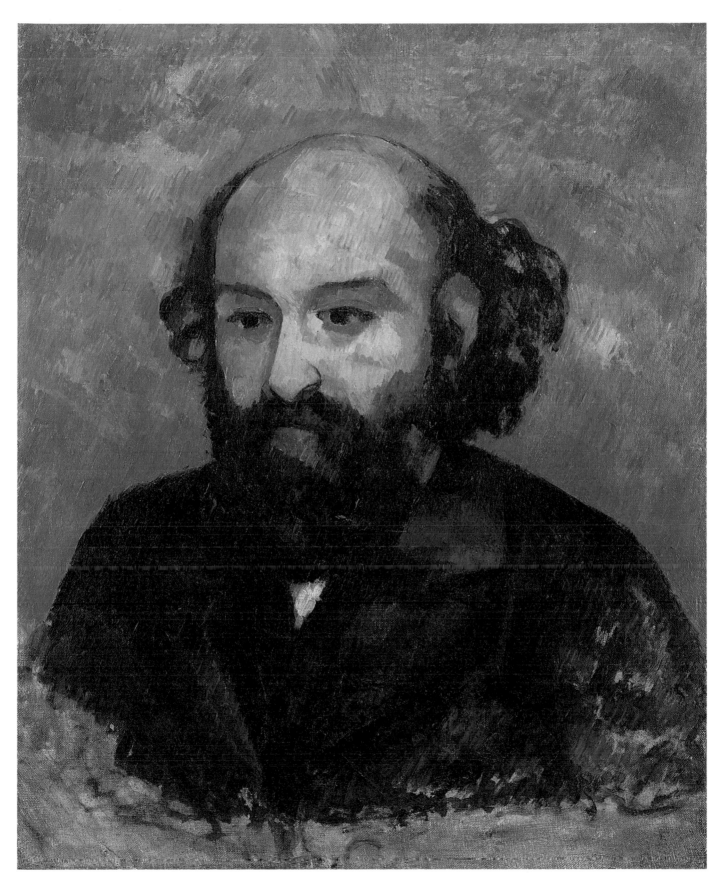

Paul Cézanne
## 49. SELF-PORTRAIT
*Portrait de l'artiste par lui-même.* c. 1880–81
Oil on canvas mounted on wood, 21¾ × 17⅞" (55.5 × 45.5 cm)
No. 3KP 513. Formerly collection Otto Krebs, Holzdorf

# PAUL CÉZANNE

## STILL LIFE WITH APPLES

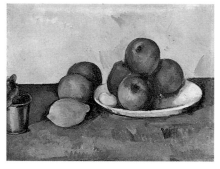

Among Cézanne's many paintings with apples, this still life occupies a special place as one of the culminating treatments of the subject: "I am astonishing Paris with my apples," said Cézanne when he met Gustave Geffroy.

Green and red apples establish the color scheme of the painting. The contrast of these two complementary colors played a key role in the color schemes of Eugène Delacroix, who was Cézanne's favorite painter and whom he called a great master. Cézanne himself had already used apples to create such a contrast in his earlier still lifes, painted at the end of the 1870s, in particular *Fruit Dish, Wineglass, and Apples* of 1879–80 (private collection; Venturi no. 341). *Still Life with Apples and Pear* appeared later, in 1885–87 (National Gallery of Art, Washington, D.C.; not in Venturi). The small Washington painting, sometimes mistakenly called *Still Life with Three Peaches*, can be seen as a prototype of the present *Still Life with Apples*, except that a green pear serves as the contrast to a pile of yellow-red apples on a plate.

Apples were at the center of Cézanne's attention for a number of reasons. Not only are they beautiful in color, but in comparison with other fruit they are more varied, a fact that works to advantage in the present painting from the Krebs collection. Above all, Cézanne was attracted to the simplicity and completeness of their form. He was striving to attain first principles, revealing primal forms. At the same time, he preferred to investigate the relationships between color and spatial and material values by using the simplest examples. There was also a practical reason important for Cézanne: apples do not spoil quickly. With his intensive and prolonged work, he had to take this quality into consideration.

According to Joachim Gasquet, Cézanne said to him: "In school Zola and I were considered phenomena. I could learn hundreds of Latin verses by heart in two tries; I was quite industrious when I was young. Zola was not interested in anything. He daydreamed. He was absolutely uncommunicative, a sort of melancholy, poor soul. You know, the kind that the other kids usually hate. Without any reason they harassed him. And that was when our friendship began. The entire school, the older kids and the younger, once gave me a thrashing for not taking part in their ostracism. I scorned them and went and talked to him as always. He was a wonderful friend. The next day he brought me a basket of apples. That's where Cézanne's apples came from! They go back to an ancient time" (J. Gasquet, *Cézanne* [Paris, 1921]).

Today, Gasquet's memoirs are not always considered reliable, and various inaccuracies have been found in them. Nevertheless, the episode with the basket was hardly invented. To be sure, it is naïve to use it to explain Cézanne's predilection for painting apples. Yet, obviously, it is not enough to cite the practical or artistically formal reasons for such a preoccupation. At some level the motivating factor for the use of the apples was the meaning hidden in the depicted object itself. The apple is, after all, a symbol of Venus and an attribute of Eve. The passions that had from youth tormented Cézanne, a fear of women that was almost pathological, found expression in a number of early works, gloomily Romantic in mood and erotic in subject. In the context of these works, the symbolism of the apple is unambiguous. Paris hands an apple to the most beautiful of the nude goddesses in *The Judgment of Paris* of 1862–65 (private collection; Venturi no. 16), a painting that tells more about the erotic misery of the artist than about the famous myth. In the later *L'Éternel féminin* of 1875–77 (fig. 1, watercolor, private collection, Zurich; oil, J. Paul Getty Museum, Malibu, Venturi no. 247), in which the artist included his own portrayal as well, in the center on a bed reclines a nude woman, as a symbol of eternal temptation; she is being served golden apples on a dish. Although it may be pointless to look for an equivalent degree of symbolism in Cézanne's fruit still lifes, we cannot overlook the primordial impulses that underlie his characteristic themes.

In the painting from the Krebs collection, along with the apples and the lemon an object is shown that is not encountered in any other work: a small metal flowerpot that looks like a can, with earth and some wilted plant. The thematic reasons for the presence of this pot are not entirely clear, but the formal ones are. Among the spherical objects another primal form is introduced, the cylinder, and another color, gray, setting off the pure tones of the apples and the lemon.

The period to which *Still Life with Apples* belongs, the last in Cézanne's creative work, has been considered a "synthetic" period by art historians. The still lifes of this period, more complex in their settings as a rule and more dynamic in construction, in the volumes of objects and the space they inhabit, are rendered with more confidence than previously. By comparison with other paintings of the same period, *Still Life with Apples* is uncommonly laconic in composition and simple in rhythm, and all the more definitively and effectively are problems of form resolved here.

"Black lines," wrote R. P. Rivière and J. F. Schnerb after Cézanne's death, "often bordering the objects in his paintings, were not an additional element to the color but were applied in order to capture the form in its entirety before modeling it with color" (R. P. Rivière and J. F. Schnerb, "L'Atelier de Cézanne," *Grande Revue*, December 25, 1907). Because color and the construction of form were inseparable for Cézanne, this was the aspect of painting technique that showed him to be a true master.

Émile Bernard, in his memoirs of Cézanne, recollected some words of his that would have an enormous resonance among young painters and which are ideally suited to such paintings as *Still Life with Apples*: "You must see in nature the cylinder, the sphere, the cone,

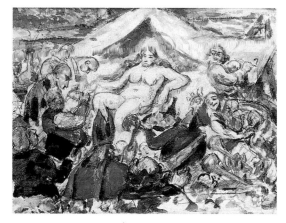

*Fig. 1. Paul Cézanne. L'Éternel féminin. 1875–77. Private collection, Zurich*

and above all an artist must learn from these simple figures, and only later do what he wants" (É. Bernard, "Souvenirs sur Paul Cézanne et lettres inédites," *Mercure de France*, October 1907). In this regard, the apple was a perfect exemplar of a pure spherical object seen in nature.

For reasons such as these, Paul Sérusier claimed, "Of an apple by an ordinary artist, people say, 'I feel like eating it.' Of an apple by Cézanne they say, 'How beautiful!' You would not peel his apple; you would like to copy it" (M. Denis, "Cézanne," *L'Occident*, September 1907; also in *Théories, 1890–1910: Du symbolisme et de Gauguin vers un nouvel ordre classique* [Paris, 1920]).

Lionello Venturi dated this still life to 1883–87, then narrowed the time of execution to 1883–86. John Rewald proposed dating the painting to about 1890, which is stylistically more appropriate to the canvas. Rewald also considered that *Still Life with Apples* came to the Galerie Ambroise Vollard fairly early, and was sold by the dealer to Gustave Geffroy in 1895. Compositionally, this work is very similar to *Apples,* a still life of the same dimensions (fig. 2; Venturi no. 501) in which the plate is shown at the left.

The painting was not executed on a prefabricated canvas but on a canvas primed and prepared by Cézanne himself. The format of the painting has been changed. At the bottom, canvas was cut off after the completion of the work, and part of the picture surface was folded behind the lower edge, upon which remains the edge of the reddish brown plank of the table where the still life was arranged. Incidentally, this plank can be seen in the *Apples* mentioned earlier.

PROVENANCE: Galerie Ambroise Vollard, Paris; December 24, 1895, Gustave Geffroy, Paris (?); Daber, Paris; Galerie Tanner, Zurich; Karl Haberstock, Berlin; Georg Caspari, Munich; Galerie Hugo Perls, Berlin; Otto Krebs, Holzdorf.

LITERATURE: L. Venturi, *Cézanne: Son Art, son oeuvre* (Paris, 1936), no. 1518; J. Rewald, in collaboration with W. Feilchenfeldt and J. Warman, *Paul Cézanne: The Paintings—A Catalogue Raisonné* (New York, forthcoming), no. 674.

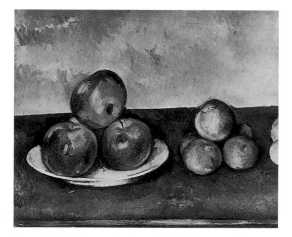

*Fig. 2. Paul Cézanne.* Apples. *1885–87. Private collection, Paris*

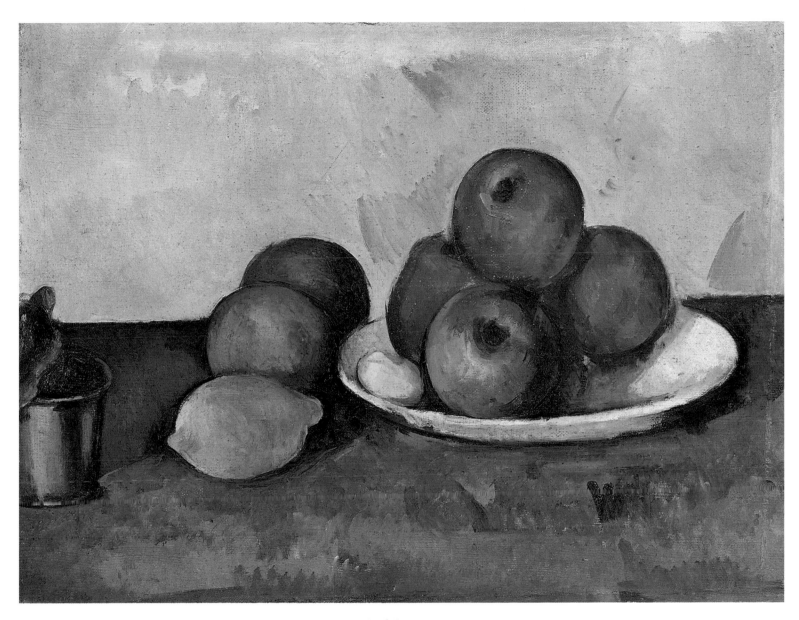

Paul Cézanne

50. **STILL LIFE WITH APPLES**

*Nature morte: Les Pommes.* c. 1890

Oil on canvas, 13¾ × 18⅛" (35.2 × 46.2 cm)

No. ZKP 558. Formerly collection Otto Krebs, Holzdorf

# PAUL CÉZANNE

## BATHERS

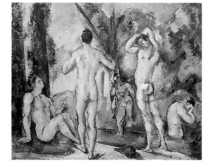

Of the almost two hundred drawings and paintings of male and female bathers by Cézanne, this work from the Krebs collection is among the finest.

Unlike his Impressionist friends (with the exception of Pierre-Auguste Renoir), Cézanne considered the creation of monumental compositions with nude figures a most important task of painting. His paintings of this subject continued the venerable tradition of European art, his bow to the Old Masters, whether Titian or Poussin, but at the same time they were an open challenge to the academic nudes of the Salon. The fortunate idols of the Salon created visions of paradise as idealized as they were lifeless, yet they, too, considered themselves descendants of the masters. Adolphe William Bouguereau, hated by Cézanne, and the other leading lights of official art would have thought it inconceivable that Cézanne was the true heir to the tradition of the Old Masters.

With rare exceptions, Cézanne's paintings of nudes did not refer to ancient mythology, and even when he dealt with mythological themes, such as the Judgment of Paris, his work remained free of any illustrative quality, implying instead a personal subtext. Cézanne, who treated even Jean-Auguste-Dominique Ingres with irony, rejected all the more the standardized visions of the Golden Age that regularly appeared at the Salons. *Bathers* to a certain extent does embody the idea of a lost age of innocence—not the saccharine prehistoric and ancient eras lauded in the Salon "machines," but his own time, his own youth. Over and over again he was inspired by memories of how, with his closest school friends Émile Zola and Baptistin Baille, he went on expeditions outside the city, to the countryside, where the chief delight was playing games under the open sky and swimming in the Arc River.

Cézanne's entire group of Bather paintings is devoid of any idyllic quality. Georges Rivière, defending Cézanne during the third Impressionist exhibition, in *L'Impressioniste*, the journal he published, wrote that ignoramuses who cackled when they looked at the Bathers seemed to him to be barbarians criticizing the Parthenon. "Those who have never held a brush or pencil in their hands claim that he does not know how to draw and reproach him for his 'imperfections,' which in fact are the refined method of an astonishingly sophisticated master. I know that despite this, Cézanne will never achieve the success won by the young artists. Who will hesitate about what he prefers, *The Bathers* or Épinal's little soldiers? Naturally, everyone likes the latter more. The lady clutching the strapping young blond man by the arm will never exclaim in front of Cézanne's painting, rolling her eyes, 'How delightful!'" (in Lionello Venturi, *Les Archives de l'impressionisme* [Paris, 1939]).

Maurice Denis called the style of Cézanne's Bather compositions "awkwardly Poussinesque." Denis ascribed almost the same significance to the notion of *gaucherie* as to the idea of style. Because Cézanne strove to express his sensations immediately, refusing to follow conventional formulas, his painting became "awkward," like the painting of "primitives" (M. Denis, *Théories, 1890–1910: Du symbolisme et de Gauguin vers un nouvel ordre classique* [Paris, 1920], pp. 251, 254–55). In those terms, Cézanne had become a "primitive," a herald of the new art, in the development of which compositions such as *Bathers* played an enormous role.

The first composition in the enormous cycle, *Male and Female Bathers* of about 1870 (Richardson collection; Venturi no. 113), is one of the few works where

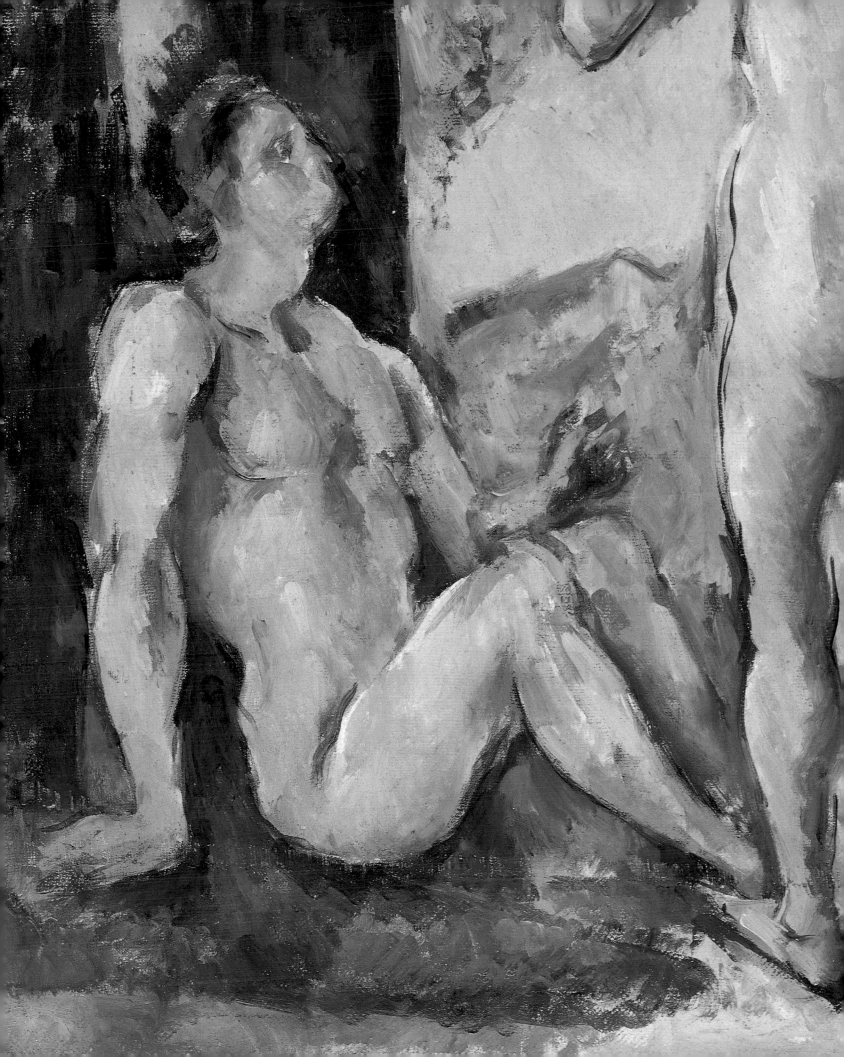

nude figures of both sexes are shown together. We can suppose that here the theme of the Judgment of Paris is transformed, having already been interpreted by Cézanne in one of his earliest paintings, from 1862–65 (private collection). The two bacchanalian scenes called *La Lutte d'amour* are dated to 1875–76 (private collection and National Gallery of Art, Washington, D.C.; Venturi nos. 379, 380). The first version belonged to Camille Pissarro, the second to Renoir. Later, the erotic elements obvious in these paintings disappear altogether. The composition becomes even more abstract, to the point where the differentiation between male and female is not rigidly maintained. Though Cézanne may have feared accusations of immorality, at least when he was in Aix, more important, such a lack of strict demarcation reflected the logic of his creative evolution—toward a more philosophical view of things, toward a greater concentration on formal similarities. By not combining figures of opposite sexes within the confines of one work, Cézanne created compositions very similar in spirit and equally abstract. Not surprisingly, the pose in which a male bather was depicted could then be used in a painting of female bathers.

The first groups of male and female bathers appeared in Cézanne's work toward the end of his Impressionist period. But even in his landscapes painted from nature such as *Jas de Bouffan, the Pool* (see plate 46), Cézanne did not completely share the views of the leaders of the Impressionist movement, and in compositions that were entirely invented he departed from them a great deal, though still valuing their advances in the area of color and artistic signature. Together with Claude Monet and Camille Pissarro, Cézanne defended the right to use pure paint colors and liberal brushstrokes against the demand for a naturalistic understanding of authenticity. But with the Bathers, Cézanne's philosophy of art sought something like the opposite of the fleeting moments of Impressionism. Whereas the Impressionist painters were devoted to the reproduction of real, immediate impressions, Cézanne proceeded like a good builder, concerned above all with firmness of construction. His composition cannot be mentally taken apart, as is easy to do with the painting of Monet or Pissarro. The Bather paintings, including the canvas from the Krebs collection, are solid pyramidal structures expressing an

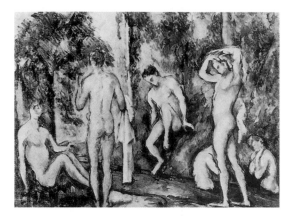

*Fig. 1. Paul Cézanne.* Bathers. *1883–84. Private collection, Paris*

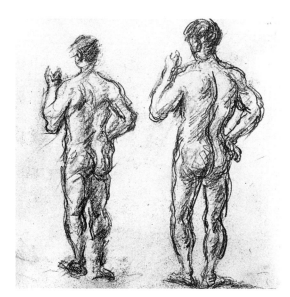

*Fig. 2. Paul Cézanne.* Bather, Seen from the Back. *c. 1879–82. Whereabouts unknown*

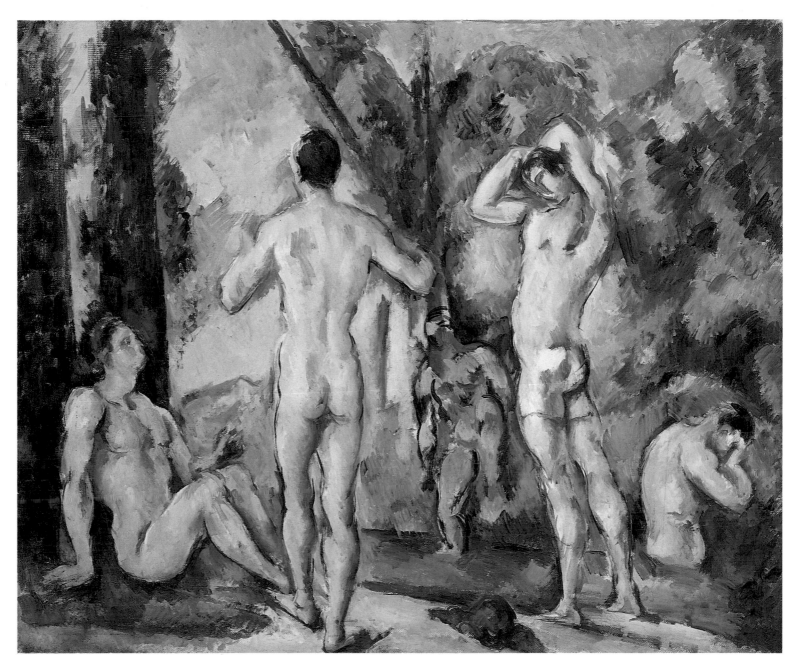

Paul Cézanne
51. BATHERS
*Bagneurs en plein air.* c. 1890–91
Oil on canvas, 21⅜ × 26⅛" (54.2 × 66.5 cm)
No. 3KP 536. Formerly collection Otto Krebs, Holzdorf

idea of firmness without which the dynamic world cannot survive. It is logical that the greater portion of Bathers belong to the artist's "constructive" period (1878–87).

A subordination of details does not exist in such paintings; it cannot be said that the figures, which provided the original impulse for the painting's entire construction, are more important than the trees or the sky. As Cézanne said to Joachim Gasquet, " 'You see, a motif is this . . .' He put his hands together . . . drew them apart, the ten fingers open, then slowly, very slowly brought them together again, clasped them, squeezed them tightly, meshing them. 'That's what one should try to achieve. . . . If one hand is held too high or too low, it won't work. Not a single link should be too slack, leaving a hole through which the emotion, the light, the truth can escape. You must understand that I work on the whole canvas, on everything at once. With one impulse, with undivided faith, I approach all the scattered bits and pieces' " (J. Gasquet, *Cézanne* [Paris, 1926], p. 131).

As if summarizing this, Cézanne said that art is harmony, a parallel nature. There is nothing strange in the fact that his compositions with male and female bathers are only loosely tied to real models. Although Gasquet said that Cézanne made drawings of soldiers swimming in the Arc, these sketches have not survived, and most likely they did not play a substantial role in work on the Bathers.

"Standing before *Bathers*," recalled Francis Jourdain, "he explained to us that he was rejecting models because the Jesuits had long been following after him like a Catholic observing rituals, and that sometimes he felt like painting with a nude model, but that strictly speaking, his recollections from the Académie Suisse were sufficient. 'Painting is here, inside,' he said, pointing to his forehead" (F. Jourdain, "À propos d'un peintre difficile: Cézanne," *Art de France*, no. 5, 1946). The German collector Karl-Ernst Osthaus told how Cézanne complained to him of the narrow provincial views that forced him to make do with the services of an old invalid who posed for the female bathers. Both of these accounts refer to the period shortly before Cézanne's death. In those later years, he painted female bathers far more often than male. However, his creative method had been the same even a decade and a half earlier, when the

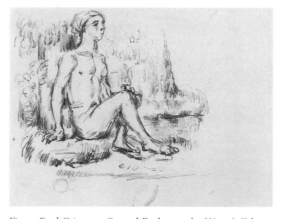

Fig. 3. *Paul Cézanne.* Seated Bather at the Water's Edge. *1877–80. Öffentliche Kunstsammlung Basel, Kupferstichkabinett*

painting from the Krebs collection was done.

It is true that Cézanne made use of drawings dating from his youth in Paris, sometimes from a model but more frequently from sculpture, whether antiques or the works of Michelangelo. Such drawings served as nothing more than an expedient. There were other drawings, however, in which he sought a more accurate formulation of the thought that then found expression in the painting.

The prototype for the youth seated to the left in the present painting is *Seated Bather at the Water's Edge* of 1877–80 (fig. 3; Öffentliche Kunstsammlung Basel, Kupferstichkabinett). Another drawing from Basel,

*Bather with Arms behind Head*, corresponds to the figure on the right side of the painting but belongs to a later time (about 1900). Several sheets with figures from the painting in the Krebs collection can be found in Cézanne's sketchbook published by John Rewald (*Paul Cézanne: Carnet de dessins—Préface et catalogue raisonné par John Rewald* [Paris, 1951], pp. 107, 108, 110).

In the catalogue of an exhibition devoted to Cézanne's Bathers (*Paul Cézanne: The Bathers* [Kunstmuseum, Basel, and New York, 1989], p. 183), in a chapter entitled "The Paris *Baigneurs*," Mary Louise Krumrine notes that the central figure shown from the back is reminiscent of Cleomenes's *Roman Orator* at the Louvre. The same marble sculpture served as a model for the statue in Thomas Couture's *Romans of the Decadence* of 1847 (Musée d'Orsay, Paris), a painting Cézanne knew and admired. This figure appears in several of Cézanne's paintings: in *Bathers* of 1879–82 from the Detroit Institute of Arts (Venturi no. 389) and from a private collection (Venturi no. 390), and also compositions from the Pushkin State Museum of Fine Arts in Moscow dated to 1890–94 (Venturi no. 588) and the Art Institute of Chicago (Venturi no. 589). It appears as well in several drawings, notably *Standing Bather* from the Wadsworth Atheneum, Hartford. Krumrine calls some of the other figures "decorative afterthoughts," which is, of course, not entirely accurate. Although they do not have such elaborate lineage, these figures in the painting have equal rights in that silent dialogue conducted in the language of form and color.

After the painting from the Krebs collection, there followed two complicated and less expressive compositions with a large number of figures, in 1892–94 (The St. Louis Art Museum and the Musée d'Orsay, Paris; Venturi nos. 581, 580). The Paris work is the largest and most elaborate painting of the group that contains also the two small canvases from Moscow and Chicago mentioned earlier. It is very difficult to say in which sequence the works of the group were painted. Due to a lack of confirming documentation, dates can be assigned only on the basis of stylistic features.

In terms of coloration, all the Bathers of the early 1890s are quite different from one another. Whereas the painting from the Krebs collection is restrained, with a cool range of colors, in those from the Musée d'Orsay and St. Louis warm tones prevail. They also differ in the degree of their finish. In this regard, the painting from the Krebs collection is particularly interesting in that it reveals some of Cézanne's methods and allows us to sense how the painting progressed. Thus, it is evident, for example, that the figure in the center, the bather entering the water, appeared later than the others. Apparently, Cézanne originally planned a composition with four figures. The fifth figure was sketched in on top of the landscape and is less developed than the others.

Venturi first dated the painting to 1888–90, then decided that it had been painted earlier, in 1885–88; Georges Rivière believed that it was done even earlier, in 1884. Theodore Reff dates it to before 1890, and Rewald to 1890–91.

PROVENANCE: Galerie Ambroise Vollard, Paris; November 1911, Marczell de Nemes, Budapest; de Nemes sale, Paris, June 18, 1913; Galerie Bernheim-Jeune, Paris; Baron Maurice de Herzog, Budapest; October 22, 1929, Galerie Paul Cassirer, Berlin; Otto Krebs, Holzdorf.

EXHIBITIONS: 1904, Paris, Salon d'Automne, Petit Palais, no. 27; 1911, Budapest, "Collection Nemes," Musée des Beaux-Arts; 1912, Düsseldorf, "Collection Nemes," Städtische Kunsthalle, no. 116; 1921, Berlin, "Paul Cézanne: Werke in deutschen Privatbesitz," Galerie Paul Cassirer, no. 36; 1925, Vienna, "LXXXII-te Ausstellung der Sezession: Führende Meister der Französischen Kunst im XIX. Jahrhundert," no. 87.

LITERATURE: *Vente de Marczell de Nemes* (Galerie Manzi-Joyant, Paris, June 18, 1913), no. 88 (reprod.); *Cicerone*, 1913, p. 383; A. Vollard, *Paul Cézanne* (Paris, 1914), p. 45; G. Coquiot, *Paul Cézanne* (Paris, 1919), p. 176; G. Rivière, *Le Maître Paul Cézanne* (Paris, 1923), pp. 187, 212; T. Klingsor, *Cézanne* (Paris, 1923), pl. 17; *L'Art vivant*, May 1, 1925, p. 19; E. Faure, *Paul Cézanne* (Paris, 1926), pl. 55; J. Mauny, "Cézanne: The Old Master," *Drawing and Design*, January 1927, p. 18; E. d'Ors, *Paul Cézanne* (Paris, 1930), no. 36; R. Rey, *La Renaissance du sentiment classique: Degas, Renoir, Gauguin, Cézanne, Seurat* (Paris, 1931), p. 88; G. Mack, *Paul Cézanne* (New York, 1935), pl. 34; N. V. Yavorskaya, *Cézanne* (Moscow, 1935), illus. 23; L. Venturi, *Cézanne: Son Art, son oeuvre* (Paris, 1936), no. 582; L. Guerry, *Cézanne et l'expression de l'espace* (Paris, 1940), p. 112; *Paul Cézanne: Carnets de dessins—Préface et catalogue raisonné par John Rewald* (Paris, 1951), pp. 107, 108, 110; T. Reff, "Cézanne's Late Bather Paintings," *Arts Magazine*, vol. 52, no. 2 (October 1977), p. 118; T. Reff, "The Pictures within Cézanne's Pictures," *Arts Magazine*, vol. 53, no. 10 (June 1979), p. 100, fig. 29; M. L. Krumrine, *Paul Cézanne: The Bathers* (Kunstmuseum, Basel, and New York, 1989), pp. 167–96 (reprod. p. 190, dated c. 1888); J. Rewald, in collaboration with W. Feilchenfeldt and J. Warman, *Paul Cézanne: The Paintings—A Catalogue Raisonné* (New York, forthcoming), no. 748.

# PAUL CÉZANNE

## MONT SAINTE-VICTOIRE

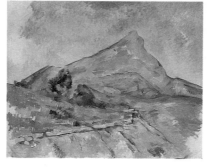

Along with the Hermitage painting (Venturi no. 663), this is one of the largest of Cézanne's paintings of Mont Sainte-Victoire and among the most outstanding in execution of the motif.

Cézanne painted Mont Sainte-Victoire tirelessly, from different points of view, and it dominates his later work. Looming over the outlying regions of Aix, the mountain most fully embodied for the artist the grandeur, simplicity, and indestructibility of nature—everything that remained most important in his worldview. Sainte-Victoire became a kind of religion for the old painter.

As Denis Coutagne, the organizer of a unique exhibition of works devoted to Mont Sainte-Victoire, wrote: "The painter needed time to become aware of the meaning of this mountain. If Cézanne had died in 1886, his name would not have been connected with Sainte-Victoire. As far as is known, Sainte-Victoire was established as a motif only beginning in 1885–86. Then how tenaciously did Cézanne cling to this motif! To paint Sainte-Victoire until his eyes went dark! Because of the mountain, once in October 1906 he was caught in a thunderstorm outside his studio in Lauves. Because of this stubbornness he collapsed with his brush in his hand, only to meet death a few days later! Cézanne must have clung to this motif for some important reason. Not even a subject in 1870, the mountain became the most important embodiment of nature. Moreover, it became the goal of painting itself and a reply to the Bathers as well as to the Apple" (D. Coutagne, "Cézanne, tradition et modernité," in *Sainte-Victoire: Cézanne, 1900* [Musée Granet, Aix-en-Provence, 1900], p. 85).

It would seem that those who consider 1886 an important landmark in Cézanne's biography are cor-rect. At that time Cézanne, who always felt the despotic hand of his father, whom he feared yet respected, finally reconciled with him. When Louis-Auguste died in October of that year, Paul gained a material independence that he had previously never had. It would be pointless to look for an immediate reflection of the events of Cézanne's life in his art, but the changing circumstances should nonetheless be taken into account. Now he no longer needed to struggle to support his wife and son, whose existence he had carefully concealed from Louis-Auguste. Life began to settle down. The passionate impulses that had been boiling to the surface began to quiet. Cézanne became wiser, but his character did not change. The conflict between an intense temperament and the yearning for harmony constantly reflected in his painting found a new focus in the motif of Mont Sainte-Victoire.

The mountain can be seen easily from Jas de Bouffan, although in painting the nooks and crannies of the estate, Cézanne seemed for a long time to take no notice of it. The cone of the mountain pushing up behind the trees in *Chestnut Trees of Jas de Bouffan* of 1885–87 (Minneapolis Institute of Arts; Venturi no. 476) attracted the artist only when the mountain became an *idée fixe*, a special object of fascinated attention, in a whole group of paintings now preserved in the museums of Moscow, Merion, Washington, Amsterdam, and elsewhere (Venturi nos. 423, 435, 424, 456).

In fact, in his youth Cézanne often went climbing on Mont Sainte-Victoire. Émile, the son of Philippe Solari, an old friend of Cézanne's, described how the three of them, along with Achille Emperaire, made an excursion to the mountain in the fall of 1895, "not dangerous, but quite tiring, requiring at least three hours." Cézanne was almost fifty-seven years old and suffering from diabetes. "Cézanne and my father reminisced about their youth, reliving it anew. . . . On the descent, Cézanne wanted to prove to himself that he had kept his former agility, and tried to climb a pine tree at the side of the road. But the long hike had exhausted him, and the attempt was unsuccessful. 'Don't you remember, Philippe, how easily we used to do that!'" (G. Mack, *La Vie de Paul Cézanne* [Paris, 1939], p. 281).

Cézanne was not, of course, the first to paint this magnificent aspect of the Aix landscape, although no one else adopted such an all-consuming attitude toward it. Cézanne's studio was decorated with an engraving by Deviller of Bertin's painting *The Crowning of Aristide;* the silhouette of the mountain against the background is very reminiscent of Mont Sainte-Victoire as it appears in the present painting, from the Koehler collection. Cézanne undoubtedly knew the large painting by an unknown artist, dated 1686, *La Chartreuse Sainte-Marthe d'Aix-en-Provence,* which remains to this day in the Monastère de la Grande Chartreuse in the western part of Aix. The painting depicts the interior of a church, and through the open portal can be seen Mont Sainte-Victoire. F.-M. Granet's watercolor *Mont Sainte-Victoire in Clear Weather from the Malvalat Quarter* (Musée Granet, Aix-en-Provence), with which Cézanne was familiar, was painted from approximately the same point of view.

Unquestionably, Cézanne also knew another work by Granet, a study for *The Death of Poussin* of 1849, also in the Musée Granet. There, above his deathbed, as the master's last testament, was hung Nicolas Poussin's painting *"Et in Arcadia ego."* This Poussin masterpiece, one of the treasures of the Louvre, was greatly admired by Cézanne. He often made use of its lessons, with its pyramidal composition and astonishing tonal balance, in his own work (as can be seen, for example, in *Bathers,* plate 51). The landscape background of *"Et in Arcadia ego"* is crowned by Mont Sainte-Victoire (see fig. 1). Its silhouette is approximately that of the Cézanne painting from the Koehler collection, only from a greater distance. Poussin always remained for Cézanne an irreproachable authority. His study of Poussin can be seen not only from his draw-

ings after Poussin's painting but also from his compositional borrowings (see D. Coutagne, *Régard sur Poussin,* op. cit., pp. 111–19). Cézanne's well-known aim of "redoing Poussin after nature" meant combining the fundamentals of the master's paintings with the discoveries of contemporary art that would arise from the most intimate contact with nature. *"Et in Arcadia ego"* signified for Cézanne something greater than simply a painting. Incorporating within itself the image of Mont Sainte-Victoire, Poussin's painting itself became a kind of icon, sanctifying the use of a motif that in the eyes of the Provençal Cézanne was almost sacred.

If the French iconographic sources of the motif of Mont Sainte-Victoire are more or less obvious, it is more difficult to determine to what extent acquaintance with Japanese woodcuts, which influenced the painting of the Impressionists and their followers, was reflected in Cézanne's work.

Although it would seem that Cézanne's art was untouched by the Japanese influences that so affected his Impressionist friends, the example of Hokusai may be reflected in the portrayal of Mont Sainte-Victoire. In this case, it is apparently not accidental that the image created by Cézanne echoes Hokusai's *Red Fuji.* Hokusai's work was reproduced in *Paris illustré* on May 1, 1886, and thus may have been known to Cézanne.

The painting was done from the Bibémus quarry beneath the mountain. In their younger days, Cézanne and Émile Zola used to go hunting and hiking in this area. Returning after almost forty years, the artist rented a small hut here, a *cabanon,* to do his work. Usually, Cézanne would paint Mont Sainte-Victoire from a more remote distance, which would allow him to capture the stone blocks of Bibémus at the foot of the mountain and thus work on rendering space, taking the division into planes indicated by nature as a point of departure. However, any mention of division into planes with regard to this painting must be made with caution. Here, one plane elides with another, so that the eye, encountering no obstacles, quickly runs the whole distance up to the peak. The painting is notable for its lightness, a sense reinforced by both the details of the mountain cone and the pure line capturing its silhouette, as well as by the light rose colors from the morning sun.

The painting contains a fair amount of unpainted primer, in the lower part on the left, and on the right, especially in the sky, the painting is very light and fluid. Cézanne probably found the right tonality immediately and "drove" the painting almost at Impressionist speed.

In the upper portion of the mountain there is a dab of the undiluted madder that Cézanne combined with whitewashes to achieve the rose tint of early morning. It fell on the canvas accidentally, but he did not remove the spot, either thinking that he would get back to the painting later or else not seeing it as a problem. If we take the work as pure painting, this dab is appropriate to the color scheme of the canvas.

A similar composition, with Mont Sainte-Victoire depicted from approximately the same perspective, was subsequently developed in Cézanne's watercolors, in 1900–1902 (Venturi nos. 1022, 1560, 1562). The last work, in the Louvre, is particularly close to the painting from the Koehler collection, although blue shades predominate.

There is disagreement in the literature about the dating of this landscape. Venturi originally dated the painting to 1894–1900, then believed that it was executed earlier in 1890–95; John Rewald's point of view is more certain—about 1895; Theodore Reff estimates that the painting was done in the late 1890s.

PROVENANCE: July 25, 1908, Galerie Ambroise Vollard, Paris; Bernhard Koehler, Berlin.

EXHIBITIONS: 1912, Cologne, "Sonderbund Internationale Kunstausstellung," Städtische Ausstellunghalle, no. 141; Frankfurt, Städelsches Kunstinstitut, no. 56 (?); Berlin, Kunstausstellung, Galerie Gustave Knauer (?).

LITERATURE: P. Mahlberg, "Die internationale Sonderbund-ausstellung in Köln," *Kunst und Künstler*, vol. 10, no. 10 (July 1912), p. 511 (reprod.); L. Venturi, *Cézanne: Son Art, son oeuvre* (Paris, 1936), no. 664; J. Rewald, in collaboration with W. Feilchenfeldt and J. Warman, *Paul Cézanne: The Paintings—A Catalogue Raisonné* (New York, forthcoming), no. 762.

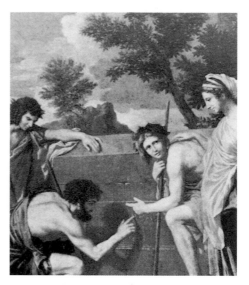

*Fig. 1. Nicolas Poussin. "Et in Arcadia ego" (detail). 1638–39. Musée du Louvre, Paris*

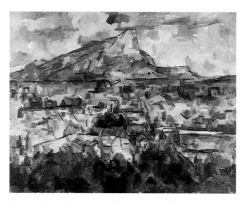

*Fig. 2. Paul Cézanne. Mont Sainte-Victoire. 1902–4. Philadelphia Museum of Art. George W. Elkins Collection*

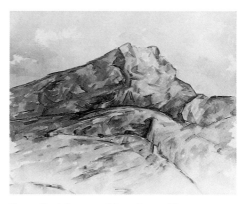

*Fig. 3. Paul Cézanne. Mont Sainte-Victoire. c. 1904. Edsel and Eleanor Ford House, Grosse Pointe Shores, Michigan*

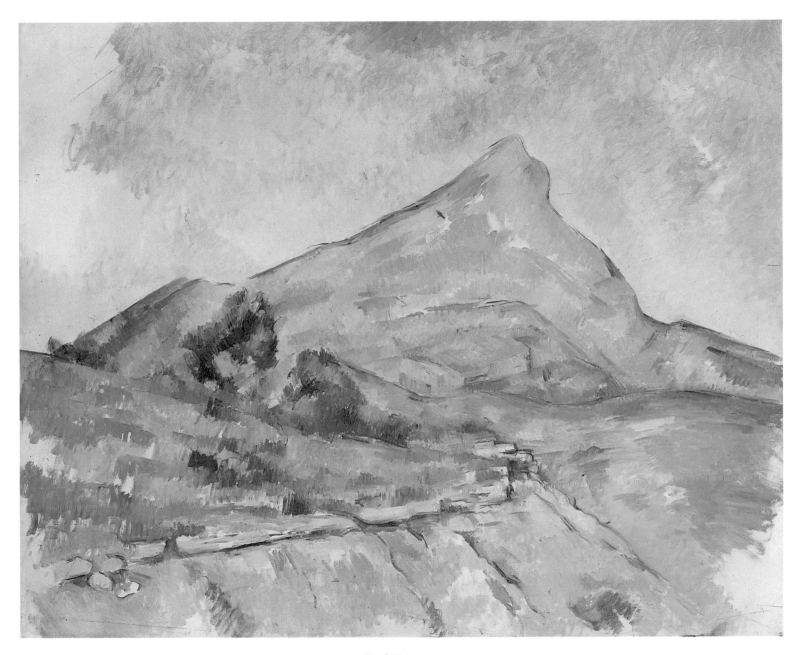

Paul Cézanne
## 52. MONT SAINTE-VICTOIRE
*La Montagne Sainte-Victoire.* c. 1897–98
Oil on canvas, 31⅞ × 39½" (81 × 100.5 cm)
No. 3K 1395. Formerly collection Bernhard Koehler, Berlin

# GEORGES-PIERRE SEURAT

## VIEW OF FORT SAMSON

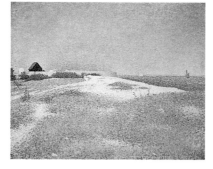

The Seurat scholar Alain Madeleine-Perdrillat, believing that this painting had been lost forever and describing it only from photographs, nevertheless gave it a wonderful and precise characterization: "Having seen this majestic work, we can only regret the loss of the *View of Fort Samson*, which today can be admired only in photographic reproductions, and whose softness and undisturbed immensity must have been its pure counterpoint. The sea, set back in the distance, leaves room for a stretch of sand dunes in the center of the composition; they are bare of vegetation and describe a superb lozenge of light which catches the eye. . . . It almost makes us lose sight of the horizon, which is already interrupted by the shoreline and the walls of the fort. Even when it is checked in its expansion, this vast space in the foreground, which opens out onto space and nothing else, unsupported by any verticals, often appears in the painter's seascapes. One could say that their particular quality of emptiness, silence and suspended time, even more than the immobility of the figures in the large painting, are the hallmark of Seurat's art" (A. Madeleine-Perdrillat, *Seurat* [New York, 1990], p. 78).

Here in essence is unfolded and translated into the language of modern concepts a characterization that was given to Seurat's paintings back in 1886, when *View of Fort Samson* was first shown to the public. Wrote Félix Fénéon, spokesman and defender of the new movement, which he had dubbed Neo-Impressionism, "Seurat's seascapes radiate calm and melancholy, monotonously receding into the remote horizon."

In the spring of 1885, Seurat first went to paint the sea, staying for several weeks at Grandcamp, a Normandy village on the coast of La Manche. His stay at Grandcamp turned out to be fruitful: Seurat returned to Paris with twelve studies and six paintings (see figs. 1, 2). In subsequent years, he would travel to the coast in the summer, always to the north. The choice of Grandcamp was easily explained; his family had spent its summer vacation here four years previously. A small fishing port in the district of Bayeux, Grandcamp was not rich in sights. Fort Samson or Fort-Sanson (or simply *l'ancien fort*, as it was called in the guidebooks of the time) was a fifteen-minute walk from Grandcamp. At low tide, clam digging was good near the old fort, for which the spot was famous.

The main event in 1886 for Seurat was the opening of the eighth Impressionist exhibition. The group now rejected its previous labels—Independents, Impressionists—but everyone knew that this was their exhibition, and it turned out to be their last. Its composition was rather unusual. The leaders of the movement, Claude Monet, Pierre-Auguste Renoir, and Alfred Sisley, refused to submit their paintings. The friction between the members of the group during the preparation of the exhibition worsened, and one of the chief points of dispute was whether to admit Seurat and Paul Signac into the circle. Neither artist would ever have been accepted without the energetic support of Camille Pissarro. The Neo-Impressionists were given a separate gallery, the last one, which nevertheless attracted the most attention from the public and the press, reminiscent of the worst days of the first Impressionist exhibition. As an eyewitness, George Moore, recounted, in front of Seurat's paintings there was "boisterous laughter, exaggerated in the hope of giving as much pain as possible" (G. Moore, *Confessions of a Young Man* [London, 1888], p. 29).

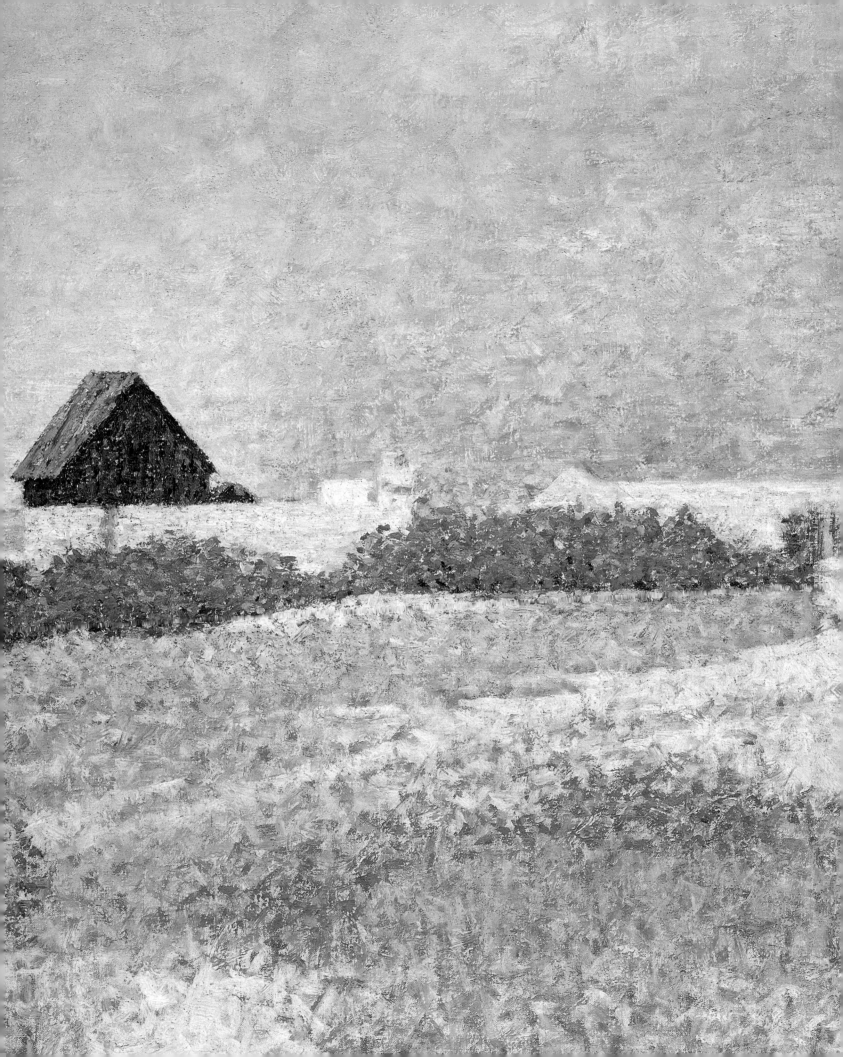

Seurat's position at that moment was not favorable. Even the leading critics, such as the influential Octave Mirbeau and Teodor de Wyzewa, who supported the Impressionists, dismissed the paintings of Seurat and Signac. Amid the hostile chorus, the voices of those who tried to take a different view were only faintly heard. Émile Hennequin mildly praised *View of Fort Samson* (while garbling its name)—"*Fort Lansac* and *Le Bec du Hoc* are among the good things that we saw"—but at that time his reaction to *A Sunday Afternoon on the Island of La Grand Jatte* was sour, and he said that he could hardly have imagined anything grayer or with poorer light (É. Hennequin, "Les Impressionistes," *La Vie moderne*, June 19, 1886, p. 390).

Maurice Hermel, a bolder and more insightful critic, also picked out *View of Fort Samson*: "Seurat is a radical reformer, not one of these semi-innovators who timidly attempt to use complementary colors. He breaks up the prism with implacable logic, and introduces *petit-point* needlework to painting. . . . Thus, in his landscapes *Le Bec du Hoc*, *Le Fort-Samson*, *La Rade de Grandcamp*, *La Seine à Courbevoie*, even though the use of pointillist technique still seems to me too prominent, there is a vibration of light, a richness of color in the shadows permeated with light, a sweet and poetic harmony, an inexpressibly milky, flowered quality that voluptuously caresses the retina. Seurat has the stuff of a superb artist. One only wishes he spread out the tricks of his art with a little less ostentation" (M. Hermel, *La France Libre*, May 28, 1886).

Seurat's landscapes found support as well in Jules Vidal, who wrote that they had been made with a confident technique and were imbued with "an enchanting impression of sadness" (J. Vidal, *Lutèce*, May 29, 1886).

However, while artists, or at least those who considered themselves innovators, were excited about Seurat's discoveries, whether accepting or rejecting them, the public did not display any noticeable interest in the exhibition. In June, Pissarro wrote to his son Lucien: "The exhibition is going badly, and there are no visitors paying to enter" (*Lettres de Camille Pissarro à son fils Lucien* [Paris, 1950], p. 104).

The main attraction and object of outrage became *A Sunday Afternoon on the Island of La Grand Jatte*. Seurat placed two Grandcamp landscapes, *View of Fort*

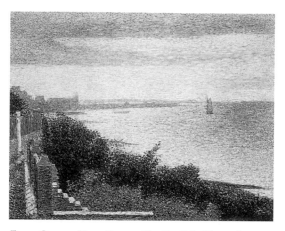

Fig. 1. *Georges-Pierre Seurat*. The English Channel at Grandcamp. *1885. The Museum of Modern Art, New York. Estate of John Hay Whitney*

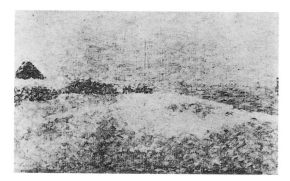

Fig. 2. *Georges-Pierre Seurat. Fort Samson at Grandcamp. 1885. Private collection, Paris*

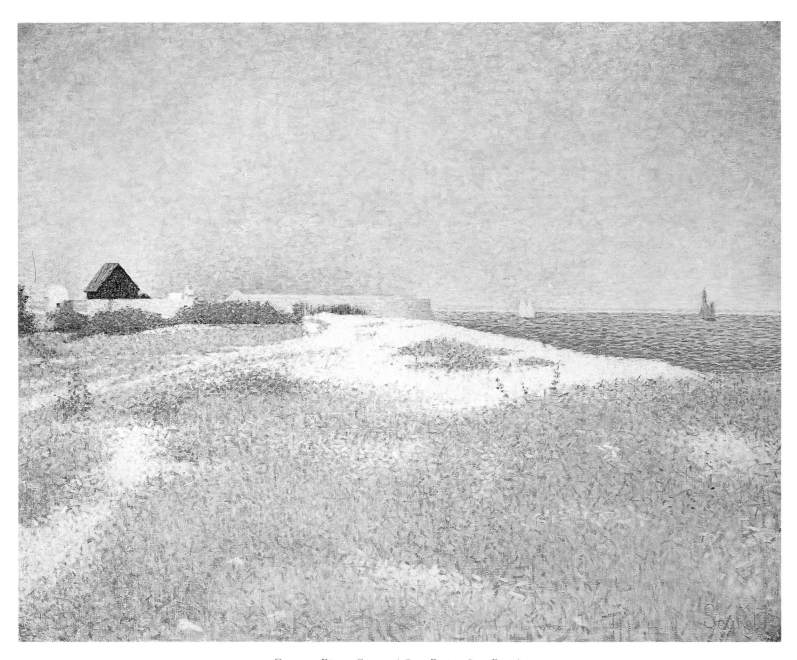

Georges-Pierre Seurat (1859, Paris–1891, Paris)
## 53. VIEW OF FORT SAMSON
*Fort Samson, Grandcamp.* 1885
Oil on canvas, 25⅝ × 32" (65 × 81.5 cm)
Signed lower right: "Seurat"
No. 3KP 1577. Formerly collection Bernhard Koehler, Berlin

*Samson* and *Le Bec du Hoc* alongside that enormous canvas, two views that formed a contrasting pair. Tranquility predominates in the first, while the second provokes a more complicated feeling: the composition itself, where a large, beak-shaped cliff looms, aggressively thrusting out into space, elicits a certain uneasiness, although it is subordinate to the disciplined clarity of vision without which Seurat's art is unthinkable.

In themselves, the motifs of Seurat's landscapes did not seem fundamentally new in comparison with the old Impressionists; in the early 1880s, Claude Monet painted many cliffs. It is not hard to find precedents for *View of Fort Samson* either; in particular, we can look to Renoir's *Low Tide at Yport* (plate 23), painted only two years earlier. But the differences, in both mood and the application of paint, are enormous. While Monet and Renoir, the "romantic Impressionists," as they were called at that moment, painted with little reflection on the structure of the brushstroke—which could be either large or small, aimed in any direction, existing separately or merging with neighboring strokes—the methods proposed by Seurat presupposed greater homogeneity and orderliness.

The composition of *View of Fort Samson* immediately gives a sense of Seurat's superior academic training. In placing the line of the horizon in the painting a little higher than the middle, he attains a correlation between the earth and the sky that best expresses a feeling of tranquility. The highlighting of the rhomboidal plot of land separates the middle ground of the composition from its center. The apex of the rhombus, somewhere beyond the right extremity of the wall of the fort, is the point toward which the lines of the foreshortening strive. Without meeting any obstacles, the eye quickly runs from the foreground to that point and comes up against the wall of the fort, a gray strip of stone, sufficient to introduce a note of mystery into this melancholy landscape.

It is remarkable how, without concealing the construction of his perspective, Seurat avoids any studied quality, by finding the foundations of the construction within the elements already in the landscape: the upper right border of the rhombus is the line of the bank and the left is a path. The lines are so natural that the geometric armature can be discovered only

through analysis. Seurat was not satisfied with a studied perspective. If a horizon curves in his painting, it is because it proceeds not from the drawing, but from real experience: straight lines become distorted in the eye.

Seurat's painting immediately began to be called both divisionist (he preferred this term to all others), since it was based on separated brushstrokes, and pointillist, because the strokes were individual dots or points of paint. Most often, however, it was called Neo-Impressionist, because of its complex relationship with the art of Monet and Renoir. And a scientific doctrine was soon seen as forming the basis of the technique of Seurat and Signac. In a century that deified science, this helped the style to spread rather quickly throughout Europe; from France to Belgium to Russia, canvases began to be covered with carefully separated strokes of paint. Many followers of Seurat, not emulating his manner but adapting it to their own temperament and sense of color, did not understand the spirit of his art. In speaking of the similarity between Seurat and Fra Angelico, Lionello Venturi noted that the decorative motif emerged in the French painter with immediacy, and at the same time in complete separation from reality, as a creation of pure poetry. He was writing about the Grandcamp landscapes, which respond to purely intuitive needs. Simple, banal views of the sea, of little houses and white sails, provoked in the artist only a feeling of endless delight, with no hint of irony.

It would be hard to find a better illustration than *View of Fort Samson* of Seurat's remarks on his aesthetics in a letter to the writer Maurice Beaubourg:

*Art is Harmony. Harmony is the analogy of contrary and of similar elements of* tone, *of* color, *and of* line *considered according to their dominants and under the influence of light, in gay, calm, or sad combinations.*

*The contraries are: for* tone: *a more luminous, or lighter, shade against a darker; for* color: *the complementaries, i.e., a certain red opposed to its complementary, etc.; for* line: *those forming a right angle.*

*Gaiety of* tone *is given by the luminous dominant; of* color, *by the warm dominant; of* line, *by* lines *above the horizontal.*

*Calmness of* tone *is given by an equivalence of light and darkness; of* color, *by an equivalence of warm and*

cold; and of line, by horizontals. . . .
(Félix Fénéon, *Oeuvres plus que complètes* [Geneva and Paris, 1970], vol. 1)

Fénéon, in publishing this characteristically terse document, supposed that such a theory acquires efficacy only when something specific guides it. At any rate, this aesthetic tract of Seurat, who was sparing of words, does not "explain" his paintings; the reason for their unique merits is the artist's genius.

It was Fénéon himself who identified the differences between the Impressionists and the new school and, having in mind mainly the Grandcamp landscapes, formulated the essence of the Neo-Impressionist doctrine:

*The phenomenon of the sky, of water, of shrubbery, varies from second to second, according to the original Impressionists. To cast one of these fugitive aspects upon the canvas—that was the goal. Hence the necessity to capture a landscape in one sitting and hence an inclination to make nature grimace in order to prove conclusively that the moment is unique and will never occur again. To synthesize landscapes in a definite aspect which will preserve the sensation implicit in them is the Neo-Impressionists' endeavor. Moreover, their procedure makes haste impossible and necessitates working in the studio. . . . Objective reality is for them a simple theme for the creation of a higher and sublimated reality into which their personalities are transfused.*
(F. Fénéon, "Le Néo-impressionisme," *L'Art moderne*, May 1, 1887; in Fénéon, *Oeuvres plus que complètes*)

The same year as the eighth Impressionist exhibition, Seurat sold *View of Fort Samson*, which then disappeared from the art world for a quarter of a century. Most likely, Fénéon, who directed the Bernheim-Jeune gallery, had something to do with its acquisition.

"Fénéon," wrote one of Seurat's contemporaries, Charles Angrand, "will undoubtedly show you *Fort Samson*, which has recently returned to Bernheim. It is a very beautiful canvas which can be placed, at least in my view, next to any new landscape at the Louvre" (letter of July 4, 1912, from Angrand to Lucie Cousturier, printed in *La Vie*, October 1, 1936, p. 248).

A small study for the painting (fig. 2; 15.2 by 24.7 centimeters; Dorra/Rewald no. 156), done from nature and executed on board, belonged to Paul Signac (now in a private collection, Paris). Compared with the study, the canvas has been expanded on three sides, adding earth and sky and bringing its format closer to the proportions of the golden section. The differences between the study and the painting, which was not done outdoors, lie not only in the composition but in the manner of execution: the painting is calmer, softer, and more confident.

PROVENANCE: 1886, Behrend; 1912, Galerie Bernheim-Jeune, Paris; Bernhard Koehler, Berlin.

EXHIBITIONS: 1886, Paris, "Huitième Exposition des peintures impressionistes," Maison Dorée, no. 177; 1921, Berlin, Kronprinzen Palast Exposition; 1925, Vienna, "Französischen Meister der XIX. Jahrhundert," no. 55; 1927, Hamburg, "Europäische Kunst der Gegenwart," no. 230; 1930, Düsseldorf, no. 81.

LITERATURE: Darzens, *Pléiade* (Paris, May 1886); É. Hennequin, "Les Impressionistes," *La Vie moderne*, June 19, 1886, p. 390 (with incorrect title); Ajalbert, *Revue moderne*, June 20, 1886, p. 393; "Vingtistes Parisiens," *Art moderne*, June 27, 1886, p. 204; L. Cousturier, *Georges Seurat* (Paris, 1921), pl. 25; G. Coquiot, *Seurat* (Paris, 1924), pp. 220, 246; "Lettre d'Angrand à L. Cousturier (4 July 1912)," *La Vie*, October 1, 1936; J. Laprade, *Georges Seurat* (Monaco, 1945), p. 4, no. 35; L. Venturi, *Impressionistes et symbolistes* (Paris, 1950), p. 151; J. Laprade, *Seurat* (Paris, 1951), p. 14, no. 34; L. Venturi, *De Manet à Lautrec* (Florence, 1950), p. 200; H. Dorra and J. Rewald, *Seurat* (Paris, 1959), no. 157; C. de Hauke, *Seurat et son oeuvre* (Paris, 1961), no. 157; *L'Opera completa di Seurat* (Milan, 1971), no. 157; C. Grenier, *Seurat: Catalogo completo* (Florence, 1990), no. 156; A. Madeleine-Perdrillat, *Seurat* (New York, 1990), pp. 78–79.

# PAUL SIGNAC

## THE LARGE PINE, SAINT-TROPEZ

This work is a nature study for the painting *Italian Pine on the Road to Saint-Tropez* of 1893 (Jacques Caroli collection, Paris), which Paul Signac gave at one time to his friend the Belgian artist Teo van Rijsselberghe. The reverse side of the study bears an old label, "St. Tropez. Le Pin." The canvas from the Caroli collection is also known under the titles *The Bonaventure Pine (Pin de Bonaventure)* and *Umbrella Pine (Pin parasol)*. This pine—or one quite similar to it—also figures in the painting *The Golden Age* (another name is *In the Time of Harmony*). Both works, executed in a careful pointillist manner, unlike the study, were dated to 1892 by Signac's granddaughter Françoise Cachin (see F. Cachin, *Signac* [Paris, Musée du Louvre, 1963], pp. 44–54, and F. Cachin, *Paul Signac* [New York, 1971], p. 65).

Compared to the study, the silhouette of the pine in the paintings is far more formalized and suggests Japanese influence, in particular such Hiroshige woodcuts as *Oji Falls and Asukayama Hills* of 1857.

Signac painted similar pines later, as in *The Pines of Cannoubiers* of 1897 (Musée de l'Annonciade, Saint-Tropez) and *The Pine at Bertaud, Saint-Tropez* of 1909 (fig. 1; The Pushkin State Museum of Fine Arts, Moscow).

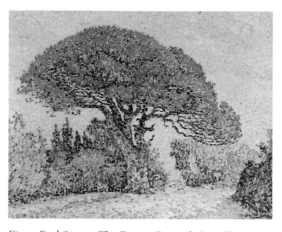

Fig. 1. *Paul Signac.* The Pine at Bertaud, Saint-Tropez. *1909. The Pushkin State Museum of Fine Arts, Moscow. Shchukin Collection*

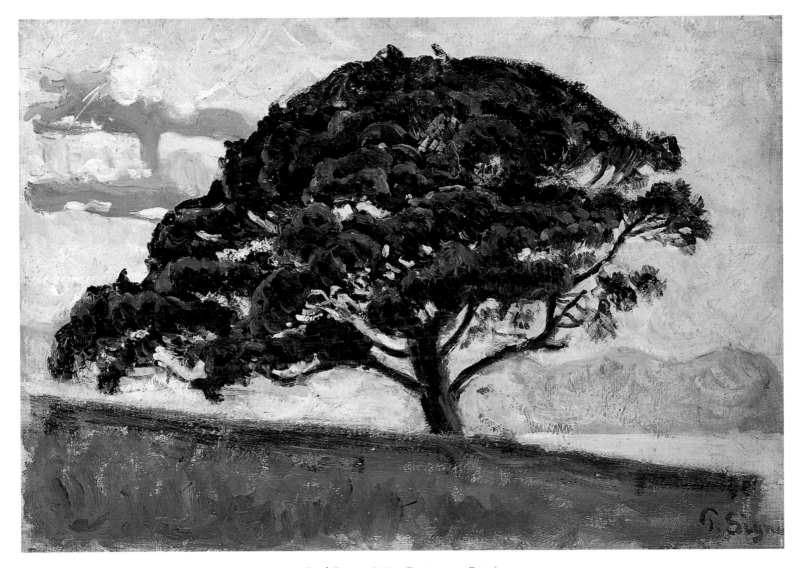

Paul Signac (1863, Paris–1935, Paris)
**54. THE LARGE PINE, SAINT-TROPEZ**
*Le Grand Pin, Saint-Tropez.* c. 1892–93
Oil on canvas, 7½ × 10⅝" (19 × 27 cm)
Signed lower right: "P. Signac"
No. 3KP 542. Formerly collection Otto Krebs, Holzdorf

# PAUL GAUGUIN

## AT THE WINDOW

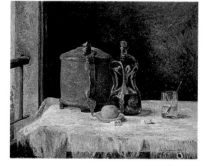

The combination of objects in this still life is quite unusual (there is no other like it in Gauguin's painting), but apparently it resulted not only from the logic of formal juxtapositions but also from thematic considerations. For example, the lemon in the center is the bright spot upon which the whole composition hangs, but, like the other items on the table, it is also needed to prepare grog. (Grog is a delicious hot drink that originated in England, often used as a home remedy for colds.) Thus, next to the lemon are a bottle of very strong wine, sugar cubes, a glass for hot water, and a spoon for mixing. The large mug with a lid to the left is probably being used as a container for the sugar.

Gauguin placed two of the objects next to each other with a certain note of irony: the intricately curved bottle and the massive mug of a most simple form. The cylindrical mug is the largest and most noticeable item in the painting. It first appeared in Gauguin's work in 1880, in the still life *Iron and Clay Pots* (private collection; Wildenstein/Gauguin no. 47). The mug can easily be taken for a ceramic one, although in fact it is made of wood. A close inspection of *At the Window* reveals the uneven texture of this object and the marks left by a chisel. The mug, either Danish or Norwegian, was made in the eighteenth century and most likely appeared in Gauguin's home along with the Danish woman Mette Gad, who later became his wife. Gauguin himself loved to carve wood and certainly valued this unusual mug, a beautiful example of old folk art. Its traditional medieval form was of the kind Gauguin admired. This tankard can now be found in the Trafalgar Galleries, London.

Gauguin included the tankard again in the *Sleeping Child* of 1884 (fig. 1; Josefowitz collection, Lausanne; Wildenstein/Gauguin no. 81), a painting that caused

consternation among the critics with its seeming illogical combination of details, some remarking that "this juxtaposition is humorous in a fantastic way" (see *The Art of Paul Gauguin* [National Gallery of Art, Washington, D.C.; The Art Institute of Chicago, 1988], p. 13). The painting will indeed seem strange if Gauguin's tankard is perceived as a vessel for alcohol, but it is wooden and cannot hold liquids. If it was used as a sugar bowl, however, then the image of the sleeping boy almost clinging to the enormous mug perhaps does contain some humor, but of a very ordinary human type. The tankard reappears in *Still Life in an Interior* of 1885 (fig. 2; private collection, United States; Wildenstein/Gauguin no. 176), probably painted in Copenhagen.

*At the Window* most likely depicts a corner of Gauguin's Paris apartment on the rue de Carcel, where he had moved in 1880. Early 1882, the year this picture was painted, was a critical time for Gauguin. Shortly before, he had written to Camille Pissarro that he did not want to remain a dilettante artist and had decided to give up his career as a broker: "You cannot paint only at your leisure." Gauguin was undoubtedly pushed into a decisive move by his personal financial failures, exacerbated by the collapse of the Bank of Lyons and Loire and the devaluation of the stock of L'Union Générale in January, when he once again lost a lot of money. The fall of the stock market made further financial speculation impossible and cut off forever his way back to the life of a prosperous businessman fascinated by art, who bought and painted paintings not to earn a living, but for pleasure. In this distressing situation—after all, he had a family with many children to support—he dared to take the decisive step and became a professional artist.

Gauguin had never felt his loneliness so acutely, though his paintings do not betray the doubts that gripped him: he sought and found reassurance in painting. Nevertheless, the still life *At the Window*, partly, perhaps, in its subject matter, but more in its restrained coloring, reflects the internal state of an artist who will stubbornly go his own way.

There are not many paintings from 1882, only about a dozen in all, if we do not count another half dozen small studies. They include landscapes of Paris and Pontoise, portraits, and three still lifes, two of them with flowers. Naturally, compared with *At the Window*, they are livelier in color and more cheerful in mood, and they seem to have been painted very quickly. *At the Window* is different not only from the other still lifes, but from all other works executed at the time. Besides the wish to keep up with the Impressionists in conveying the effects of light, the lessons of the Old Masters, above all Jean-Baptiste Chardin, are keenly felt here.

Most likely this painting was shown at the seventh Impressionist exhibition in 1882, under the title *At the Window: Still Life (À la fenêtre: Nature morte)*. In his catalogue of Gauguin's work, Georges Wildenstein suggested that it was *Vase with Flowers at the Window (Vase de fleurs à la fenêtre)* of 1881 (Musée des Beaux-Arts, Rennes; Wildenstein/Gauguin no. 63) that was shown at the exhibition under that title. Gauguin showed four still lifes at that show, and they are rather difficult to identify by the titles alone, the names themselves not being sufficiently specific. If the Rennes painting was shown at the seventh Impressionist exhibition, it could just as easily have been entitled *Flowers: Still Life*, a title in fact used for Gauguin's canvas no. 18. Wildenstein did not know the Krebs collection *At the Window* and accompanied the publication of the Rennes painting with the comment that "this is the only known painting that could have corresponded to this name."

Meanwhile, there is still one more consideration. The Rennes painting is only a small study (19 by 27 centimeters) that does not make any new advances. The still life *At the Window* is a more considerable work, noted not only for its Impressionist interest in reproducing light but for its strong composition. It is easy to suppose that Gauguin would have chosen this work first for this exhibition (if, of course, it existed at

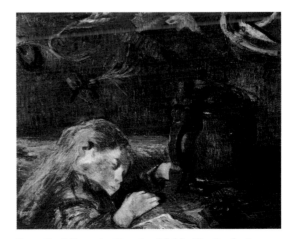

*Fig. 1. Paul Gauguin.* Sleeping Child. *1884. Josefowitz Collection, Lausanne*

the time). It was important for him to establish himself among the Impressionists, especially because in 1882, almost all the founders of the movement, except Degas, were once again gathered together. But Gauguin's hopes for success were dashed this time. Joris-Karl Huysmans, who had only recently encouraged him, now saw him making no progress and commented on the "dirty and flat coloration." The critic Hepp called his paintings hieroglyphs in white frames.

Another title for this painting, under which it appeared in the Krebs collection, is *Still Life with Bottle, Mug, and Lemon*.

PROVENANCE: Galerie Matthiesen, Berlin; Otto Krebs, Holzdorf.

EXHIBITIONS: 1882, Paris, "Septième Exposition des artistes indépendants," no. 23 (?).

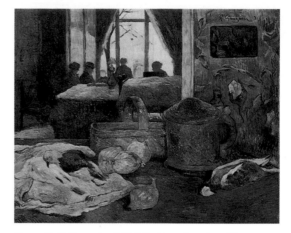

*Fig. 2. Paul Gauguin.* Still Life in an Interior. *1885. Private collection, United States*

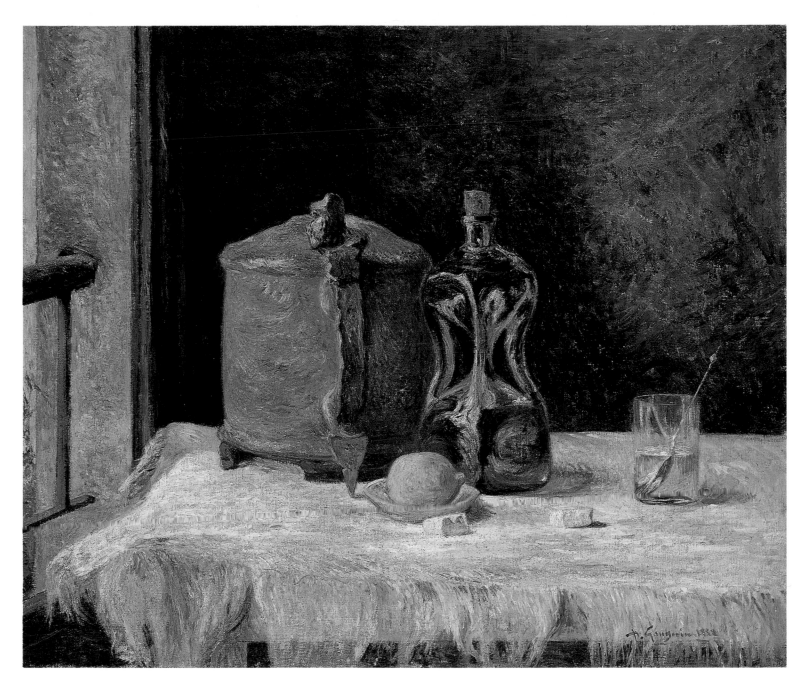

Paul Gauguin (1848, Paris–1903, Atuana, Dominica, Marquesas Islands)
**55. AT THE WINDOW**
*À la fenêtre.* 1882
Oil on canvas, 21¼ × 25¾" (54 × 65.3 cm)
Signed and dated lower right: "P. Gauguin 1882"
No. 3KP 641. Formerly collection Otto Krebs, Holzdorf

# PAUL GAUGUIN

## BOUQUET

At the time *Bouquet* was painted, Gauguin was mainly painting landscapes in the Impressionist manner. The still lifes of 1884, among which *Bouquet* is the largest, are few in number but are accorded special significance. Of the three paintings shown by Gauguin in the fall of 1884 in Kristiania (now Oslo), two were still lifes. By depicting flowers or fruit, the artist was perhaps hoping to find a potential buyer.

Gauguin very much needed some success, just to make a living. In December 1883, his wife Mette gave birth to their fifth child. In the birth certificate, the father's occupation is listed as *artiste-peintre*. In January 1884, Gauguin and his family moved to Rouen, where living was cheaper than in Paris. He was hoping to find buyers for his paintings there but was soon to meet with disappointment. The somewhat gloomy mood of *Bouquet* may thus be explained by the situation in which he found himself, difficulties that were to accompany the artist after he left Rouen.

The red spots of the berries glimmer prettily in this painting, but ominously. They can easily be taken for inflorescence. Gauguin did not strive for botanical accuracy and was entirely unconcerned about correctly depicting each berry. Although the rowan berry is rendered exactly, the color selected does not match that of the actual berry. It takes on a certain autonomy and acquires new functions here. The dark background and the hazy reflections in the mirror bring an element of mystery to the painting, which the rounded, soothing lines of the vase, the century plant, and the oval mirror are designed to subdue.

It is difficult to determine with complete certainty where the painting was executed—in Rouen, in the apartment that Gauguin had rented there at 5, impasse Malherne, or in Copenhagen. He had spent the greater part of the year in Rouen; the rowan berry ripens in the fall and would seem to suggest that Gauguin was still in Rouen at that time. In November he joined his family, who had gone ahead to Denmark. Even that late, he could still find there ripe berries that had not yet fallen. The vase depicted in *Bouquet* is easier to tie to Copenhagen. It figures in two canvases painted in the Danish capital: *Still Life with Japanese Peonies and Mandolin* of 1885 (fig. 1; Musée d'Orsay; Wildenstein/Gauguin no. 173) and *Vases and Fan* of 1885 (Winthrop collection, New York; Wildenstein/Gauguin no. 178). In the Musée d'Orsay painting, essentially the same compositional principle is employed—the juxtaposition of a bouquet in a vase with an object on the wall—except that instead of an intricate oval mirror there is a painting of Gauguin himself, in a white frame.

PROVENANCE: Galerie Matthiesen, Berlin; Otto Krebs, Holzdorf.

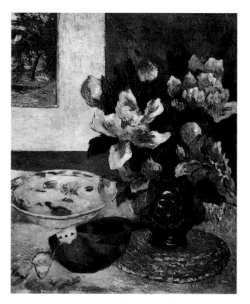

*Fig. 1. Paul Gauguin.* Still Life with Japanese Peonies and Mandolin. *1885. Musée d'Orsay, Paris*

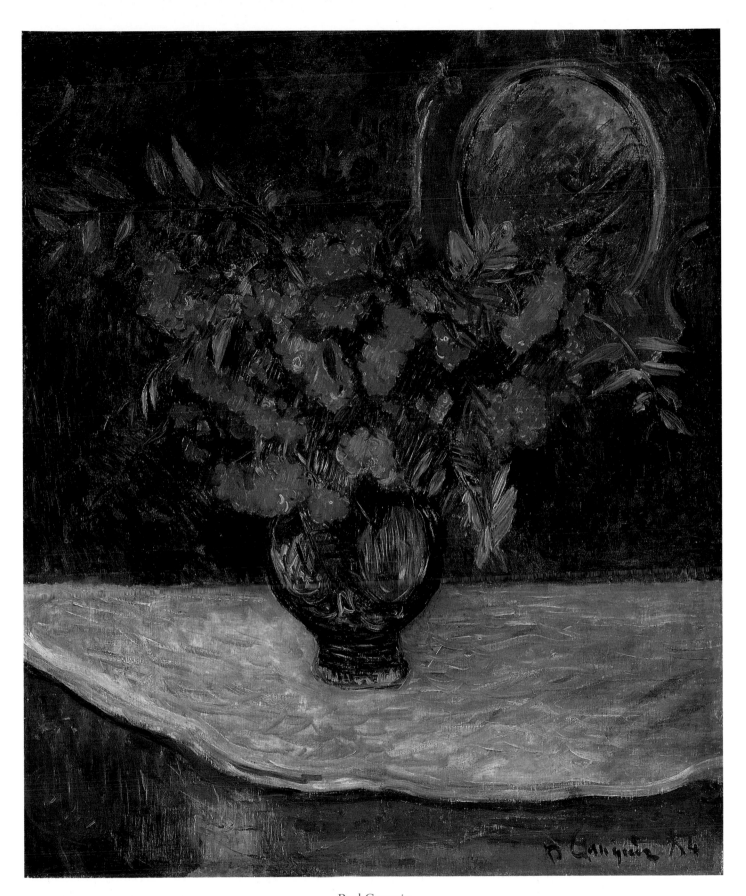

Paul Gauguin
## 56. BOUQUET
*Bouquet.* 1884
Oil on canvas, 25½ × 21½" (65.3 × 54.5 cm)
Signed and dated lower right: "P. Gauguin 84". No. 3KP 510. Formerly collection Otto Krebs, Holzdorf

# PAUL GAUGUIN

## PITI TEINA (TWO SISTERS)

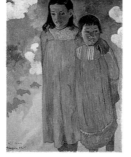

Gauguin loved to paint children, beginning with his own. Thus, in one of his first paintings, from 1875 (whereabouts unknown; Wildenstein/Gauguin no. 10), he depicted his firstborn son, Emil. Then once again he painted Emil, then Aline, then Jeanne, at first alone, and then in pairs, as in *Clovis and Aline* of about 1883 (private collection, Switzerland; Wildenstein/Gauguin no. 82) and *Aline and Pola* of 1885 (private collection; Wildenstein/Gauguin no. 135).

Separation from his family led Gauguin to create other children's portraits, particularly in Brittany in 1888–89, such as *Round Dance of Little Bretons* of 1888 (National Gallery of Art, Washington, D.C.; Wildenstein/Gauguin no. 251), *Young Breton Bathers* of 1888 (Josefowitz collection, Lausanne), *Fighting Children* of 1888 (Kunsthalle, Hamburg), and others. Gauguin preferred to portray the boys nude and the girls in long, baggy dresses. One of the more expressive compositions was *Two Breton Girls by the Sea* of 1889 (painting in the National Museum of Western Art, Tokyo [fig.1], and a smaller pastel in a private collection, London; Wildenstein/Gauguin nos. 340, 341).

In late 1889, Gauguin wrote to Vincent van Gogh: "This year I'm mostly painting simple farm children strolling beside the sea with their cows. Only, because I don't like *tromp-l'œil* landscapes or *trompe-l'œil* anything else, I try to infuse these desolate figures with the wildness that I see in them, and which is also in me. Here in Brittany the country people have something medieval about them" (D. Cooper, ed., *Paul Gauguin: 45 Lettres à Vincent, Theo, et Jo van Gogh* [The Hague and Lausanne, 1983], 36.3).

One of Gauguin's first works in Tahiti was a study of a neighbor boy, *Creole Child* of 1891 (private collection; Wildenstein/Gauguin no. 416). It contains noth-

ing of what would become typical of the style of Gauguin's Tahitian paintings. Gauguin quickly realized that Papeete, the main settlement of Tahiti, where he first landed, was more a French province than the remote place he dreamed of, untouched by civilization. Moving then to the village of Mataheya, he tried to become closer to the natives, who received him very gladly. In such canvases from the early part of his stay in Tahiti as *Meal, or Bananas* of 1891 (Musée d'Orsay, Paris; Wildenstein/Gauguin no. 427), the style of the Tahitian period emerges fairly definitely; the fruit and utensils of Oceania and the little islanders at the table depict a nature to which the means capable of conveying the charm of *Noa-Noa (Fragrant Earth)* must learn to correspond. True, in *Meal* it is not the figures but the exotic still life that takes precedence, pushing into the background the two little boys and girl, who probably did not elicit deep interest from the artist.

Two little Tahitian girls did provoke his interest, however, the sisters in *Piti teina* (the Tahitian name of the painting is translated as "Two Sisters"), arguably Gauguin's finest images of children. Perhaps it reflects his recollection of his own younger daughter, Pola—who was eight years old at the time, about the same age as the younger of the two little girls—although Gauguin was not noted for sentimentality. No doubt he did recall *Two Breton Girls by the Sea*, since he employed the same composition, but now with greater mastery and ease. Looking at *Piti teina* puts one in mind of Gauguin's lines from *Noa-Noa* about the "Women-girls, in whose rhythm of body movements, [and in whose] eyes, penetrating and clear, [and] in the amazing stillness there is something ineffably ancient, lofty and religious."

In the Tahitian album of sketches that is preserved

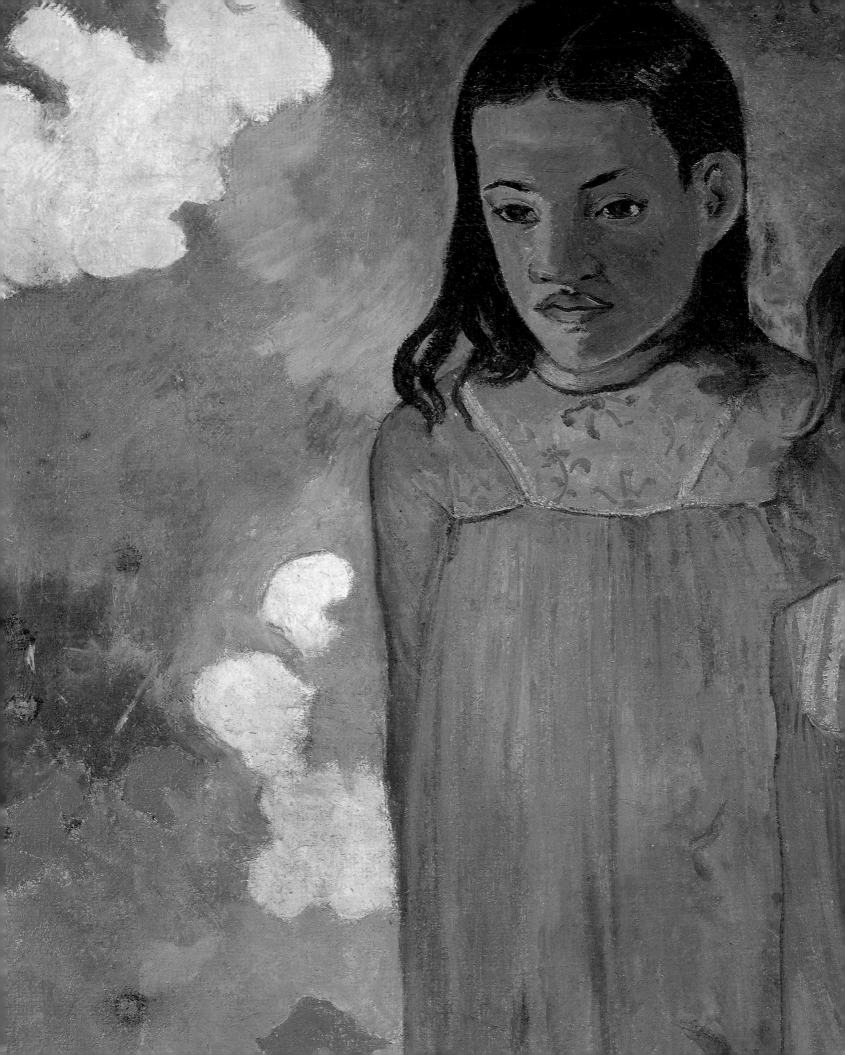

in the Louvre's Cabinet des Dessins, there are two preparatory pencil drawings for the painting, undoubtedly from life (fig. 2; B. Dorival, *Carnet de Tahiti* [Paris, 1954], p. 41). After sketching the head of each girl separately, the artist wrote their names next to the drawings. The elder one was named Tetua and the younger Tehapai. Most likely Gauguin asked the girls their names after making the drawings. Perhaps the younger girl's pronunciation was not clear, or her name was difficult for the European ear; at first, Gauguin wrote only "Tapai," then added another letter to make "Taapai," then crossed that out and wrote "Ehapai," and finally crossed it out again and put down "Tehapai." In looking at the inscribed drawing, you seem to hear the artist asking his model: "What was it? Say it once more."

In the beautifully edited and annotated *Carnet de Tahiti*, only the drawings with the heads of Tetua and Tehapai receive no critical commentary, which is not surprising: *Piti teina* was never reproduced and remained unknown, and is not mentioned in Wildenstein's catalogue of Gauguin's paintings. The remarkable scholar Bernard Dorival, who published the Tahitian sketchbook, had no information with which to place the drawings of the two girls in the general sequence of Gauguin's work.

Wildenstein's catalogue, incidentally, cites the study *Little Tahitian Girl in Red* (fig. 3; The Museum of Modern Art, New York; Wildenstein/Gauguin no. 425), accompanied by the following commentary: "a study that cannot be related to any of Gauguin's known works." The girl in the red dress with the raised hands is, of course, Tetua. Here, too, in the corner, the head of her younger sister, Tehapai, is shown in profile. Tetua's unusual gesture might lead one to suppose that Gauguin intended to paint a symbolic composition. *Ia orana Maria (Hail Mary)* of 1891 (The Metropolitan Museum of Art, New York) became such a composition, a painting very rare among the canvases of Gauguin's first year in Tahiti, which were mainly portraits, landscapes, or genre subjects.

It is possible that the idea of a symbolic painting with the two girls arose when *Piti teina* was finished. The drawings from the *Carnet de Tahiti* were a kind of act of acquaintance with them, and no doubt *Piti teina* was executed immediately after the drawings, it is so closely related to them. *Little Tahitian Girl in Red* is not dated. Wildenstein placed it among the works of

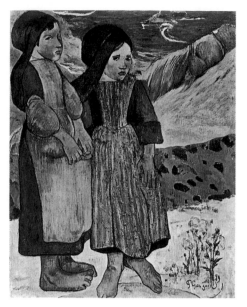

*Fig. 1. Paul Gauguin.* Two Breton Girls by the Sea. *1889. National Museum of Western Art, Tokyo*

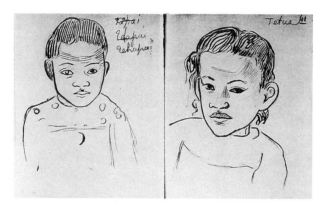

*Fig. 2. Paul Gauguin.* Two Tahitian Children: Tehapai, Tetua. *n.d. Cabinet des Dessins, Musée du Louvre, Paris*

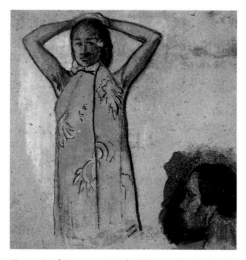

*Fig. 3. Paul Gauguin.* Little Tahitian Girl in Red. *1891. The Museum of Modern Art, New York. The William S. Paley Collection*

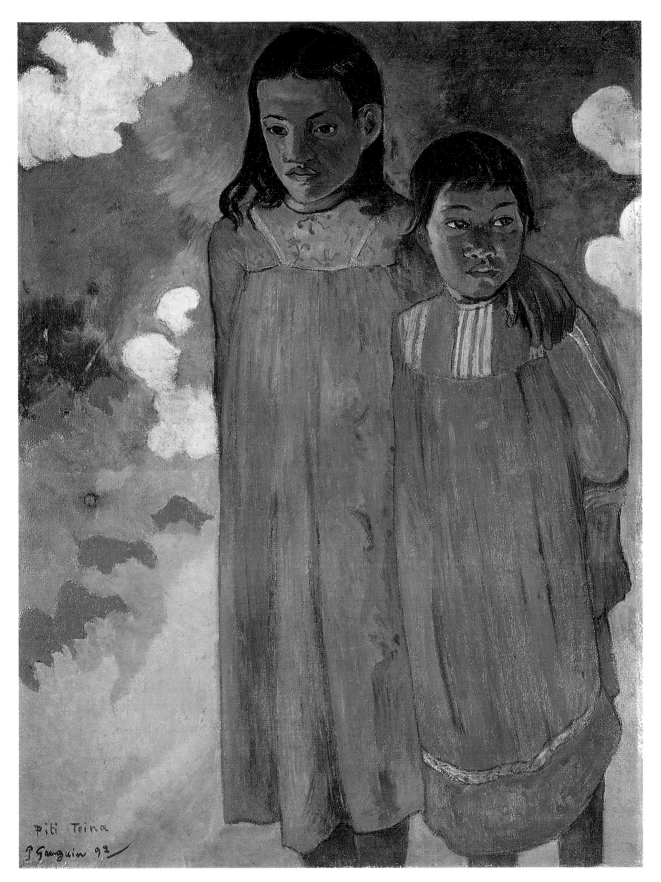

Paul Gauguin

**57. PITI TEINA (TWO SISTERS)**

1892. Oil on canvas, 35 ⅝ × 26 ⅝" (90.5 × 67.5 cm)

Signed and dated lower left with notation: "Piti Teina / Paul Gauguin 92"

No. 3KP 522. Formerly collection Otto Krebs, Holzdorf

1891, sensing the similarity of this study to such a semi-symbolic work, shown next to it, as *Meal*, although it is clear that this study could not have been executed at the same time.

A curious detail is that the dress in *Little Tahitian Girl in Red* is sewn from material with large decorative designs quite popular in Tahiti (*Ia orana Maria* provides an example of such dresses). The depiction of such fabrics enabled Gauguin not only to portray the characteristic feature of Tahitian crafts and native life but, employing the designs on the material, to introduce into the painting unique decorative links, whereby the whirls of the ornament on the dress rhyme with elements in the landscape. The abstract details of the background in *Piti teina* could very well echo the fabric design in *Little Tahitian Girl in Red*, but, unlike the study, in the painting Tetua's dress is made of a simple coarse material reminiscent of the clothing of the little Bretons. The mysterious background contrasts with the single silhouette of the children's figures. A noble simplicity and monumentality is combined here with the delicacy and even vulnerability peculiar to childhood. *Piti teina*'s uniqueness is in just this contrast.

Although much commentary has been devoted to Gauguin, modern scholars have somehow overlooked the traces of *Piti teina*. The painting figured in the famous sale undertaken in 1895 to finance Gauguin's second trip to Tahiti. The list of the sales, which had long been a bibliographic rarity, was republished by René Huyghe in the catalogue for the Gauguin retrospective in Paris in 1949, and contains as item no. 14: "Piti teina. 430 francs à M. Slewinski."

Thus, the painting belonged to Wladyslaw Slewinski (1854–1918), a Polish artist who was in the Pont-Aven group. After fleeing from his creditors in Poland, he turned up in Paris in 1888 and began studying at the academies of Julian and Colarossi. Slewinski became a habitué of the restaurant Charlotte and decorated its colorful awning with his work. At this restaurant he regularly met not only with his compatriots the artist Wyspianski and the writer Przybyszewski, but also with August Strindberg, Edvard Munch, and Alphonse Mucha. Gauguin, who met Slewinski, persuaded him to become a professional painter. In Paris and Brittany, where Slewinski traveled in 1890, the two were on very good terms. It was said that Gauguin, who loved to emphasize his own aristocratic back-

ground, was impressed by his Polish friend's aristocratic and somewhat adventuresome nature. He recognized in him "un parfait gentilhomme," as he remarked. Gauguin was hoping to go with him to Tahiti, but this plan fell through. Slewinski, with his fine apartment and studio in Paris and his villa in Brittany, was not a man to share the hardships of island existence. Gauguin's letters to Slewinski sent from Tahiti have been lost, but a portrait of Slewinski survives (fig. 4; National Museum of Western Art, Tokyo; Wildenstein/Gauguin no. 386). Wildenstein dated the portrait to 1890, based on Jean Leymarie's commentary in the catalogue for the Gauguin retrospective: "In the spring of 1894, Gauguin went to Pouldu, but Mlle Henry no longer possessed the cottage. It was the painter Slewinski . . . who offered him his villa. . . . Perhaps Gauguin made this portrait as a sign of gratitude, although in style it appears more like the works of 1889–90" (J. Leymarie, *Paul Gauguin* [Paris, Musée de l'Orangerie, 1949], no. 43). Back in Poland, from 1905 Slewinski was a member of the Mloda Polska artists group; through him, French influence, especially that of the Pont-Aven group, spread to Poland.

Slewinski was a capable but not very profound artist, imitating first Émile Bernard, then Paul Sérusier, but most of all Gauguin. The influence of *Piti teina*, which belonged to him, can be sensed in several of his depictions of children, such as *Orphan from Poronine* of 1906 (Muzeum Narodowe, Warsaw).

PROVENANCE: Wladyslaw Slewinski, Paris; 1895, Paul Gauguin sale, Hôtel Drouot, Paris: Otto Krebs, Holzdorf.

LITERATURE: *Paul Gauguin: Vente 1895* (Paris, Hôtel Drouot, 1895), no. 430; B. Dorival, *Carnet de Tahiti* (Paris, 1954), p. 41; *Kindlers Malerie Lexicon* (Zurich, 1968), vol. 5, p. 370.

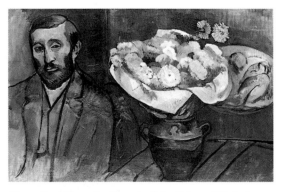

*Fig. 4. Paul Gauguin.* Portrait of the Painter Wladyslaw Slewinski. *1890. National Museum of Western Art, Tokyo. Matsukata Collection*

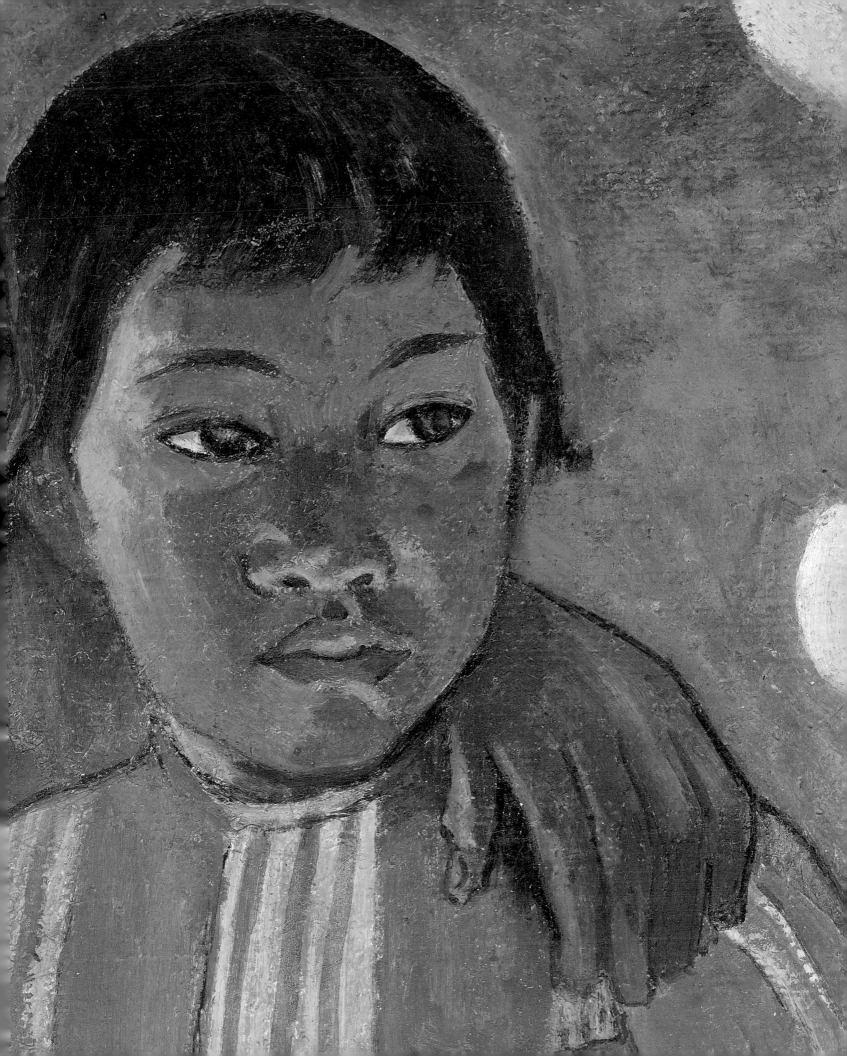

# PAUL GAUGUIN

## TAPERAA MAHANA (LATE AFTERNOON)

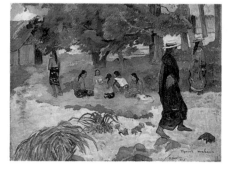

A hut with a dark doorway, trees in front, women seated in the shadows under the trees—such a theme, which immediately reflected village life on Tahiti, began to be developed by Gauguin soon after he settled in Mataheya. One of the first embodiments of this theme was *Te raau rahi* (*Great Tree*) of 1891 (Griesinger collection, United States; Wildenstein/Gauguin no. 437). The time is toward evening, when the Tahitian women gather on an open field and the village seems to be coming back to life after the midday heat. Gauguin chose precisely this time for *Taperaa mahana*. The Tahitian title can be translated as "Approaching Evening." Without seeing the painting, Wildenstein translated the phrase as "Sundown," but that is imprecise: the colors on the canvas correspond to an earlier hour. However, he could judge the painting only from the black-and-white reproduction in the catalogue of an exhibition in Germany. (It is not clear what exhibition he had in mind when he recorded that the work was no. 11 in the catalogue; the painting may have been exhibited in Berlin in 1928 at the Thannhauser gallery.) The correct translation of the name of the painting, "Late Afternoon," was given by Richard Field, in his essay on Gauguin's first trip to Tahiti, who noted that the painting had never been exhibited and was known to him only from an old photograph kept in the Courtauld Institute, London.

Gauguin was fascinated by the theme of women who have gathered in a circle and are having a leisurely conversation; for the artist it was the characteristic embodiment of the rhythm of Oceanic life. The first development of this theme was the painting *Parau parau (Whispered Words)* of 1891 (The State Hermitage Museum, St. Petersburg; Wildenstein/Gauguin no. 435).

In an accompanying letter to Daniel de Monfried, Gauguin gave the translation of the name as "Conversation, or Gossiping." The following year, he returned to the motif of the conversation circle. In *Parau parau (Whispered Words), II* of 1892 (fig. 1; Yale University Art Gallery, New Haven, Connecticut; Wildenstein/Gauguin no. 472), the circle of women sitting on the grass has moved into the background, and the landscape elements have begun to play a far greater role.

*Taperaa mahana* was probably painted at this same time. It has the same landscape background, the same circle of Tahitian women, along with a hut on the left side. The women have arranged themselves under the canopy of the trees, where it is cooler, a detail intended to reflect Tahitian habits, dictated by the climate. The figures are largely indistinguishable from the natural backdrop against which they are placed. Delicately, but very effectively, Gauguin used the method of similarity, so that the tussocks and clumps of grass in the foreground merge into the configurations that are then used to depict the women in the central part of the painting. Another aspect of this assimilation links the silhouettes of the walking Tahitian women and the trunks of the trees.

In his figure compositions, Gauguin juxtaposed the static and the dynamic, although it is a measured dynamic. Gauguin was very wary of rendering motion, saying, "Avoid poses in movement." The movement of figures in the landscape is supported by landscape details: the orange spots of clay at the feet of the Tahitian woman in a black dress are perceived if not as footprints, then as marks of a trail. In the same way, to the left, where a Tahitian woman is depicted walking away, a path is indicated leading to the hut.

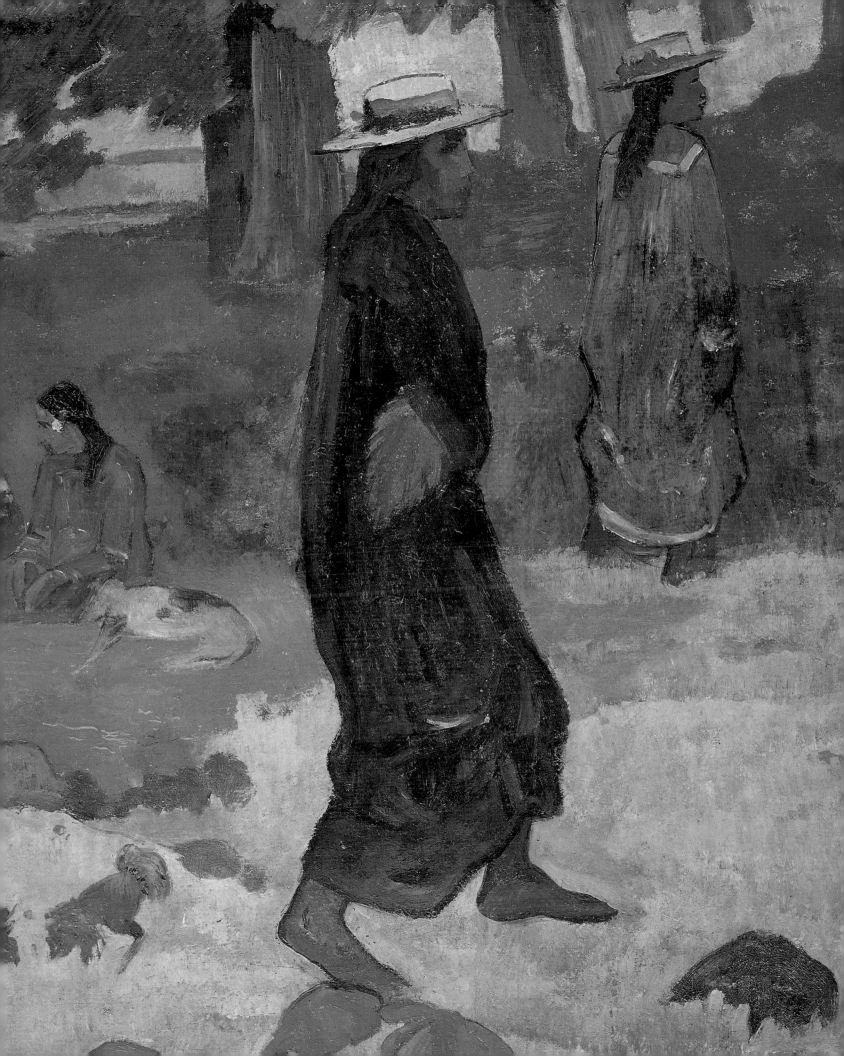

The combination of figures in *Taperaa mahana* seems to symbolize the passing of one era into another on Tahiti. The two Tahitian women to the right, possibly going out on a visit (as may be suggested by the bundle under the arm of one of them) have put on hats with colored ribbons and wear their best dresses, which are a curious mixture of Tahitian and European fashion. Black dresses had become common across the island by the time of Gauguin's arrival, due to the influence of missionary preachers, and they can often be seen in his paintings. The gray-blue costume of the Tahitian woman to the far right, decorated with a turned-down sailor's collar, is a further example of cultural mixing. Whether accidentally or not, these more Westernized representatives of native society are walking away from the circle of village gossips. Another village woman is moving away from them, too, but she is dressed, on the contrary, in a traditional Tahitian skirt.

Regarding the hut, Bengt Danielsson, an expert on Tahitian ethnography and a student of Gauguin's life in Oceania, claims that this was Gauguin's kitchen, next to his home (B. Danielsson, *Gauguins soderhavsar* [Stockholm, 1964]). This bamboo shack can be seen in another painting of 1892, *Tahitian Village with Walking Woman* (fig. 2; Ny Carlsberg Glyptotek, Copenhagen; Wildenstein/Gauguin no. 480). The woman at the extreme left is shown in other canvases as well, such as *Te fare (The House)* (private collection; Wildenstein/ Gauguin no. 474). The details of one painting carry over to another, sometimes even to a third, often with scarcely any alteration, since, even when depicting a specific locality and Tahitian women that he saw from his home, Gauguin was not trying to capture them as in life. He wanted to combine images and memories. At the same time, the artist here used several drawings from his Tahitian sketchbook now in the Louvre (see B. Dorival, *Carnet de Tahiti* [Paris, 1954]).

Gauguin's painting is paradoxical. On the one hand, this is purely a genre composition, stitched together from various details of everyday life: the women are having a leisurely conversation, a dog is napping nearby, and two roosters are fighting. Yet, on the other hand, all of these details show no true absorption with genre: the accent is not on narrative but on the suggestive, hypnotizing power of pure color.

*Taperaa mahana* is a hymn to the glory of Tahitian flora. Luscious green, in places verging on a greenish

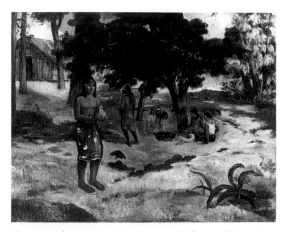

*Fig. 1. Paul Gauguin. Parau parau (Whispered Words), II. 1892. Yale University Art Gallery, New Haven, Connecticut. John Hay Whitney, B.A. 1926, Hon. M.A. 1956, Collection*

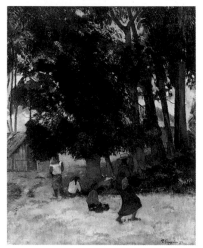

*Fig. 2. Paul Gauguin.* Tahitian Village with Walking Woman. 1892. *Ny Carlsberg Glyptotek, Copenhagen*

yellow, is the predominant color of the painting. Supported by complementary contrasting tones, it is powerfully expressive. A subtly balanced color contrast is provided by the middle part of the canvas portraying the clay soil of Mataheya. Under Gauguin's brush, the red-brown tone of this soil can flame to a pure cinnabar.

The format of the painting has been altered somewhat. A strip of canvas about 2 centimeters wide was folded back on all sides along the edges. Apparently, the work was sent rolled from Tahiti and was mounted on a stretcher later, in France.

PROVENANCE: 1928, Knoedler Gallery, London; Otto Krebs, Holzdorf.

LITERATURE: G. Wildenstein, *Paul Gauguin* (Paris, 1964), no. 473; G. M. Sugana, *L'Opera completa di Gauguin* (Milan, 1972), no. 297 (with the incorrect title *Tramonto del sole*); R. Field, *Paul Gauguin: The Paintings of the First Voyage to Tahiti* (New York and London, 1977), p. 422, no. 77.

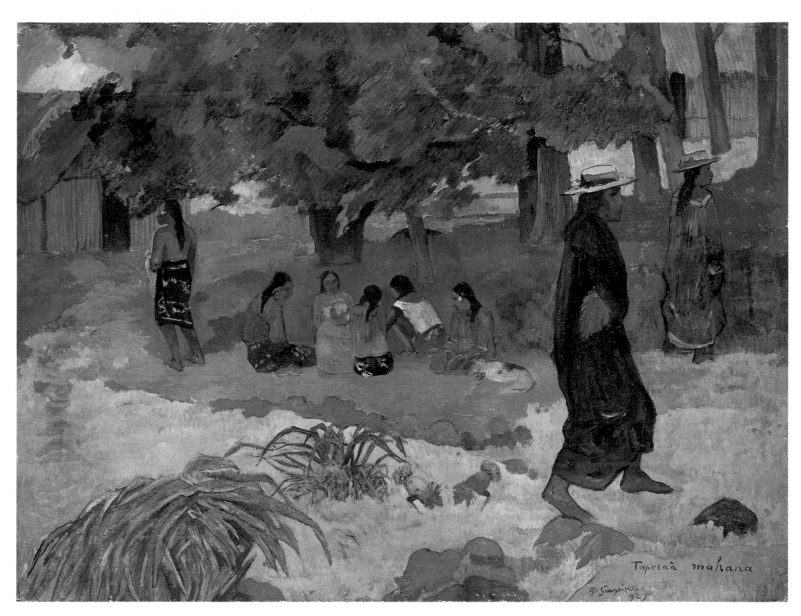

Paul Gauguin
## 58. TAPERAA MAHANA (LATE AFTERNOON)
1892. Oil on canvas, 28½ × 38⅜" (72.3 × 97.5 cm)
Signed and dated lower right with notation: "Taperaa mahana/P. Gauguin 92"
No. 3K 533. Formerly collection Otto Krebs, Holzdorf

# VINCENT VAN GOGH

## PORTRAIT OF MADAME TRABUC

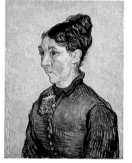

In early September (about the 6th) of 1889, Vincent van Gogh sent his brother Theo a letter from the asylum in Saint-Rémy. It was to become one of the most important pieces of evidence of the artist's understanding of his tragic fate:

*Life passes by, and you cannot undo it, but precisely for that reason I am working without sparing any effort: the opportunity to work may not present itself again. This is so much more the case with me: after all, an unusually strong attack could destroy me as an artist forever.*

*During the attacks I fear the suffering and torture, and fear more what follows, and perhaps it is this cowardliness that now forces me to eat like two, work a lot, and have less to do with the other patients for fear of a relapse; while before I did not have the wish to get better, now I am trying to get well—like someone who has tried to drown himself, but finding the water too cold, now struggles to reach the shore. . . .*

*I, of course, am mentally ill, but I tirelessly repeat to myself that many other artists also suffered from mental imbalance and nevertheless, as if nothing were wrong, practiced the painter's craft. When I see that the attacks evoke in me ridiculous religious sentiments, I am almost convinced of the necessity of returning to the north. Do not talk about this with the doctor too much, but I suspect that such moods are a direct consequence of the many months of staying in the two veritable monasteries—the Arles hospital and this asylum. In a word, such an environment is not suitable for me—it would be better to go without a roof over my head, although I myself am hardly indifferent to questions of faith, and religious thoughts often bring me relief even during the attacks.*

*. . . I am irritated every minute by the sight of all these kind women believing in Our Lady of Lourdes and making up other such tales, and I am burdened by the consciousness that I am a prisoner of an establishment where sick religious errors are cultivated, instead of being treated. That is why I say that it would be better for me to end up in forced labor or, at least, in military service! . . .*

*Now if Père Pissarro or say Vignon were to agree to take me in—that would be something else. Perhaps it could be arranged—I am an artist too. Let the money that is spent on my confinement go to artists, and not to nuns!*

*. . . I finished the portrait of the head attendant and copied it for you. It is a curious contrast with my self-portrait: my expression is veiled and withdrawn, but the warden has something military about him; his eyes are black, small and alive.*

*I gave him the portrait and will also paint his wife if she agrees to pose. She is an unhappy, faded, and quiescent woman, so inconsequential and unnoticeable that I felt an acute wish to paint on canvas this dusty blade of grass.*

*I spoke with her several times when I was painting the olive trees that grow behind their little house, and she tried to convince me that she does not believe I am ill. In fact, you would say the same thing if you could see me now at work: my thoughts are clear, and my hand is so sure that I copied Delacroix's* Pietà *without taking a single measurement, although the poses and gestures in that painting, where the hands stand out in the foreground, are not so easy or simple to reproduce* (LT 605).

Van Gogh's confession enables us to better understand the portraits of two people alien to him in all respects, but nevertheless among the rare individuals with whom he communicated and who personified for him features of human nature. Even the "dusty blade of grass" was for him more interesting than the self-satisfied nuns—whom he never painted. It cannot be said that he identified himself with the wife of the warden, Madame Trabuc, but a certain empathy cannot be denied either: under the conditions of the mental hospital, the artist could not help but liken his fate to that of the blade of grass, especially because he perceived the woman's husband, who possessed a strong nature, as completely opposite to himself. It is impossible not to sense some relationship when comparing the self-portraits van Gogh painted in September in Saint-Rémy with *Portrait of Madame Trabuc*.

On one of the first days of September, van Gogh began the portrait of Charles-Elzéard Trabuc (sometimes spelled "Trabu"), the head warden of the Saint-Paul-de-Mausole hospital in Saint-Rémy (fig. 1). In a letter that Ronald Pickvance dated September 3 (R. Pickvance, *Van Gogh in Saint-Rémy and Auvers* [New York, 1986], p. 127), the artist told his brother: "Yesterday I began the portrait of the head attendant; perhaps I shall paint his wife too, for he is married and lives in a little house a few steps away from the establishment. A very interesting face; there is a fine etching by Legros, representing an old Spanish grandee, if you remember it, that will give you an idea of the type. He was at the hospital in Marseilles through two periods of cholera; altogether he is a man who has seen an enormous amount of suffering and death, and there is a sort of contemplative calm in his face, so that I can't help being reminded of Guizot's face—for there is something of that in his head, but different. But he is of the people and simpler. Anyway, you will see it if I succeed with it and if I make a duplicate" (LT 604).

Most researchers consider *Portrait of Trabuc* of September 1889 (Kunstmuseum, Solothurn) to be a duplicate made in the absence of a model, but within five days of the first version. The version from the model has not survived. Most likely the same is true of *Portrait of Madame Trabuc*. To be sure, in this case it is difficult to say which of the versions, made one right after the other, survived—the one from the model or the duplicate. The woman's portrait is less stylized than the man's. Although they have identical dimensions and are analogous bust portraits, they are not a true pair in the pictorial sense. Most likely the artist did not set himself such a task. Each stands as an independent work, and is not part of a diptych. In Pickvance's opinion, the first version of *Portrait of Madame Trabuc* and the duplicate for Theo were painted between September 7 and 19, 1889.

This is what Vincent said about the painting in his next letter to his brother, on September 19: "I also painted a woman's portrait—the wife of the attendant. I think you'll like it. I made a duplicate of it, but it turned out worse than the original. I'm afraid that the model will take that one away from me, and I'd like for you to have it. It was made in both rose and black" (LT 607). In a letter to his sister Wilhelmina, Vincent fur-

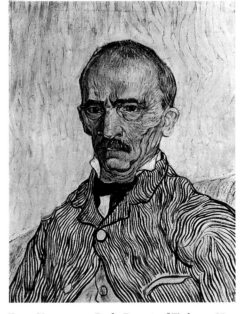

*Fig. 1. Vincent van Gogh. Portrait of Trabuc. 1889. Kunstmuseum, Solothurn. Dübi-Müller-Stiftung*

ther specified: "The withered face is tired, pock-marked—a sunburned, olive-colored complexion, black hair. A faded black dress relieved by a geranium of a delicate pink, and the background in a neutral tone, between pink and green" (W 14).

Although van Gogh selected a rather standard composition for a bust portrait, the painting has its own kind of energy. It has a sense of intricacy common to the Baroque era and, later, to Delacroix, who used the experience of the seventeenth century in his Romantic compositions. It is significant that when intending to paint the portrait of the wife of the head attendant, van Gogh recalled Delacroix's *Pietà*. He owned a lithograph by Celestin Nanteuil after Delacroix's painting and very much regretted that it was damaged during one of his attacks. Van Gogh decided to remedy the situation by making a copy of it, or rather a variation. In working on the variation he was fascinated by motifs of spiral movement. Some of the energetic nature of the brushstrokes that distinguishes his *Pietà* (fig. 2; Rijksmuseum Vincent van Gogh, Amsterdam) are conveyed in *Portrait of Madame Trabuc*.

Jeanne Lafuye Trabuc (1834–1903) was fifty-five years old when she posed for van Gogh. Aside from the characterization he gave of her in his letters, little is known of her. For the artist she remained, to an even greater degree than her husband, a representative of the people. Her portrait is similar to the heads of peasant women that van Gogh painted in his Holland years. Pickvance, speaking about *Portrait of Trabuc*, ties that work to the tradition of the "Heads of the People," images of working people drawn in the 1870s by illustrators for the British weekly *The Graphic* (Pickvance, *Van Gogh in Saint-Rémy and Auvers*, p. 128). Van Gogh admired these pictures and collected them. Pickvance's observation is no less applicable to *Portrait of Madame Trabuc*.

The portrait is painted on a very thin canvas, which has tears in the lower portion that made remounting necessary. The new mounting on a redwood board was done long ago, most likely when the painting was in Amsterdam.

PROVENANCE: Johanna van Gogh-Bonger, Amsterdam; V. W. van Gogh, Amsterdam; Galerie Thannhauser, Berlin; Otto Krebs, Holzdorf.

EXHIBITIONS: 1910, Berlin, "III. Ausstellung," Galerie Paul Cassirer, no. 1 (as *Portrait of a Woman*); 1911, Hamburg, Commeter'sche Kunsthandlung, no. 39; 1914, Berlin, "Van Gogh," Galerie Paul Cassirer, no. 41 (as *Portrait of a Woman*); 1926, London, Leicester Galleries, no. 18; 1926, Munich, Exposition Glastpalast, no. 2068; 1927, Berlin, Galerie Thannhauser; 1928, Berlin, Galerie Paul Cassirer, no. 63; 1928, Frankfurt, Galerie J. S. Goldschmidt, no. 39.

LITERATURE: Vincent van Gogh, letters to his brother Theo (see *The Complete Letters of Vincent van Gogh* [London and New York, 1958]), nos. LT 604, LT 605, LT 607; J. Meier-Graefe, in *Der Cicerone* vol. 12, no. 2 (January 1927), p. 55 (reprod.); *Kunst und Künstler* vol. 25, no. 6 (March 1927), p. 227 (reprod.); F. Fels, *Vincent van Gogh* (Paris, 1928), p. 114; J.-B. de la Faille, *L'Oeuvre de Vincent van Gogh: Catalogue raisonné* (Paris and Brussels, 1928), no. 631; W. Scherjon and W. J. de Gruyter, *Vincent van Gogh's Great Period: Arles, Saint-Rémy, and Auvers-sur-Oise (Complete Catalogue)* (Amsterdam, 1937), pp. 34, 35; *L'Opera completa di van Gogh* (Milan, 1966), no. 684; P. Lecaldano, *L'Opera pittorica completa di van Gogh e i suoi nessi grafici* (Milan, 1971), no. 684; J. Hulsker, *The Complete van Gogh: Paintings, Drawings, Sketches* (New York, 1980), no. 1777; R. Pickvance, *Van Gogh in Saint-Rémy and Auvers* (The Metropolitan Museum of Art, New York, 1986), pp. 45, 127 (reprod.); W. Feilchenfeldt, *Vincent van Gogh and Paul Cassirer: The Reception of van Gogh in Germany from 1901 to 1914* (Zwolle, 1988), p. 108; P. Bonafoux, *Van Gogh* (Paris, 1989), p. 155; G. Testori and L. Arrigoni, *Van Gogh* (Florence, 1990), no. 685; *Vincent van Gogh and the Modern Movement, 1890–1914* (Museum Folkwang, Essen; Rijksmuseum Vincent van Gogh, Amsterdam, 1990), p. 152; I. F. Walther and R. Metzger, *Vincent van Gogh: The Complete Paintings* (Cologne, 1993), vol. 2, p. 538.

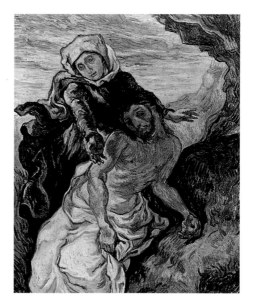

*Fig. 2. Vincent van Gogh.* Pietà (after Delacroix). *1889. Rijksmuseum Vincent van Gogh, Amsterdam*

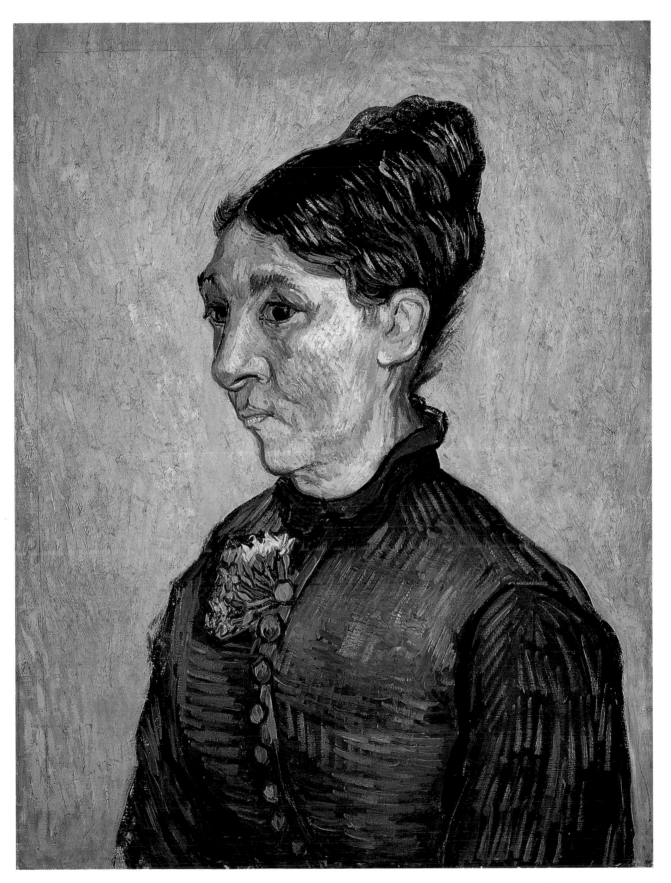

Vincent van Gogh (1853, Groot-Zundert, Holland–1890, Auvers-sur-Oise, France)
59. PORTRAIT OF MADAME TRABUC
*Portrait de Madame Trabuc.* September 1889
Oil on canvas mounted on wood, 25 × 18⅞" (63.7 × 48 cm)
No. 3KP 521. Formerly collection Otto Krebs, Holzdorf

# VINCENT VAN GOGH

## LANDSCAPE WITH HOUSE AND PLOUGHMAN

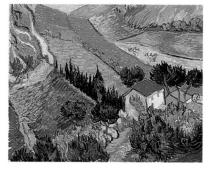

A half a month after arriving in Saint-Rémy, Vincent van Gogh wrote his brother: "Since I arrived here, the desolate garden . . . has been sufficient for my work and I have not yet been outside. Nevertheless, the scenery at Saint-Rémy is very beautiful, and sooner or later I shall probably spend some time there" (LT 592; May 25, 1889). Doctor Peyron, the director of the hospital for the insane, reported at the same time to Theo: "He spends the whole day drawing in the park here, but as I find him entirely tranquil I have promised to let him go out in order to find scenery outside this establishment" (J. Hulsker, "Vincent's Stay in the Hospitals at Arles and Saint-Rémy: Unpublished Letters from the Reverend Mr. Salles and Doctor Peyron to Theo van Gogh," *Vincent* 1, no. 2 [1971], p. 39).

The Saint-Paul-de-Mausole hospital, located about three kilometers from the little town of Saint-Rémy, was surrounded by fields, vineyards, and olive groves. Van Gogh's bedroom window looked out on a field with mountaintops in the distance. In June, he obtained permission to work outside the confines of the asylum. However, his condition did not inspire confidence in him: "My health is so-so, but thanks to work I feel happier in the asylum than I did in freedom. If I stay here longer, I will become accustomed to the regimen, which means that subsequently I will start to lead a more ordered life and will become less impressionable. That's already something. Moreover, I do not have sufficient courage now to begin life on my own. Once, when I went out to the village, accompanied by an attendant, I fell ill from the mere sight of people and things. In the bosom of nature I am supported by the awareness that I am working" (LT 594; June 9, 1889).

This same letter contains a line in which, in a paradoxical way, the germ of the idea for *Landscape with House and Ploughman* may be present: "The local landscape is very reminiscent of Ruysdael—only the laborers are missing." In fact, the scenery of Provence, and in particular, the area around the asylum, does not look much like the views captured by Jacob van Ruysdael, but van Gogh, yearning for the north in his forced confinement, wanted to sense some similarity. Laborers are not typical of Ruysdael's landscapes, and it is not clear what picture van Gogh had in mind.

Indeed, we cannot help but see the present painting as the antithesis of the classic painter of the Dutch landscape: we can barely tell the peasant and the plough apart, and the bristling countryside seems ready to swallow him up. The landscape is so active and dynamic that it seems as if some tectonic process is occurring before our eyes. Any comparisons with the landscapes of classical European art becomes impossible. For the Old Masters, mountains were only a part of the world, usually the most remote part, and were to be drawn at some distance. In van Gogh's work, however, the mountains are practically upon us, and they take up almost the whole space. There is something vertiginous about *Landscape with House and Ploughman*.

In order to paint such a work, real impressions of mountains were required, especially for such a passionate native of the Dutch flatlands as van Gogh. Such an opportunity seems to have arisen in the fall of 1889. But first he had to become stronger physically and be prepared psychologically to withstand the experience of a mountain hike. Characteristically, in a letter dated June 19, he reassured his brother: "Don't be afraid, I will never voluntarily climb up to dizzying heights and will not risk myself: after all, we are all unfortunately children of our age and suffer from its ills" (LT 595).

In July, while van Gogh was painting in the fields, his first serious attack at Saint-Rémy began, and it lasted five weeks. Van Gogh himself admitted that he "had been in *total dérangement*, the same, or perhaps worse than in Arles" (LT 601). A letter written on one of the last days of August (Pickvance believes about the 30th), shows that his condition had somewhat improved: "Yesterday I began to work a little again—on something I see from my window—a field of yellow stubble that they are ploughing, the contrast of the violet-tinted ploughed earth with the strips of yellow stubble, background of hills" (LT 602).

The letter was accompanied by a small sketch of the field with a laborer. In an earlier letter, from May 25, van Gogh, after describing his new residence, added: "Beyond the window with its iron bars I can see an enclosed field of wheat . . . above which I see the sun rise in the morning in all its glory" (LT 592). However, *Enclosed Field with Ploughman* of late August 1889 (fig. 2; private collection, United States; de la Faille no. 625) was not painted from nature, as one might think from van Gogh's description, but, as Pickvance has convincingly shown (*Van Gogh in Saint-Rémy and Auvers* [New York, 1986], pp. 124–25), from memory. Landscape suited van Gogh's art, precisely because it can be simultaneously realistic and symbolic. Thus, all of the elements in this painting—the rising sun, the solitary cottage in the distance, the earth being readied for the next harvest—express the passionate hope of the artist that change is for the best. That van Gogh did not lose interest in this motif is shown by his later variation, *Enclosed Field with Ploughman and Mill* of October 1889 (Museum of Fine Arts, Boston; de la Faille no. 706).

In the first half of November, van Gogh made a two-week trip to Arles. In addition to the wish to buy paints and visit the Ginoux, a couple who were very friendly to him, it was as if he wanted to test himself and see if such a strain would provoke a new attack. The rest of that month he worked mainly in the olive groves next to the hospital, but he was pursued by the idea of other motifs for which he needed more strength On November 26 van Gogh asked his brother to send him another 10 meters of canvas at the first opportunity, so that he could "attack the cypresses and the mountains. I think that this will be the core of the work that I have done here and there in Provence" (LT 615).

De la Faille may have relied on that letter to determine the time the painting was executed as December 1889. Next to it he placed *Landscape on the Outskirts of Saint-Rémy* (whereabouts unknown; de la Faille no. 726), which most likely depicts the same location. Both landscapes, identical in size and seemingly similar in manner (although it is difficult to judge this from the black-and-white photograph), are dated to December 1889 by de la Faille.

However, the idea of "attacking the cypresses and the mountains" did not come to van Gogh at the end of November, but most likely earlier, and in *Landscape with House and Ploughman* he could have been approaching this idea. The painting does not look like

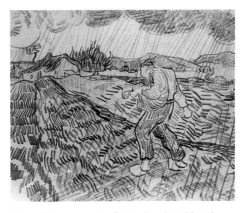

*Fig. 1. Vincent van Gogh.* Enclosed Field with Sower in the Rain. *1889. Rijksmuseum Vincent van Gogh, Amsterdam*

something created within the walls of the asylum. It is a study from nature, displaying a very rapid, even passionate grasp of a natural subject. But if the landscape was executed *en plein air*, what do the figures signify? Field labor is not done in December. Another, usually unnoticed detail is interesting in this regard: there is a woman at a well in the left part of the painting. Although, like the laborer, she is indicated by only a few white brushstrokes, van Gogh conveys the sense that she is leisurely, not the way a person would behave in December, but in a warmer time. The yellow light of the afternoon sun on the wall of the house with the red room is also not a December light. The coloring of the painting, the action of the figures, and finally the circumstances of the artist's work as we know them from letters and other evidence—all these compel us to move the date of the landscape's execution to October, a time when van Gogh worked not only on the hospital grounds, but outside them as well.

*Landscape with House and Ploughman* is unusual in its elevated, almost bird's-eye point of view. Such an angle can be seen as an attempt to look at the world in the Japanese way, natural for an artist obsessed with Japan. However, we cannot speak of serious influence here: van Gogh's view was individual and came from his own personal impressions. The dynamism distinguishing this little painting is alien to Far Eastern landscapes. The painting has such enormous internal energy that it could easily have been executed on a much larger scale. The crossing diagonals forming the borders of the fields and the ploughed furrows, the contours of the roofs, the row of cypresses—such vectors strain the composition, but not so much as to disturb the unity of the whole.

PROVENANCE: Paul Gachet, Auvers-sur-Oise; Paul Cassirer, Amsterdam; October 24, 1928, Paul Cassirer, Berlin; Otto Krebs, Holzdorf.

LITERATURE: J.-B. de la Faille, *L'Oeuvre de Vincent van Gogh: Catalogue raisonné* (Paris and Brussels, 1928), no. 727; J.-B. de la Faille, *Vincent van Gogh* (Paris, London, and New York, 1939), p. 567; J.-B. de la Faille, *The Works of Vincent van Gogh: His Paintings and Drawings* (Amsterdam and New York, 1970), no. 727 (as *A Spot of Greenery: Valley with Ploughman Seen from Above*); P. Lecaldano, *L'Opera pittorica completa di van Gogh e i suoi nessi grafici* (Milan, 1971), no. 778; J. Hulsker, *Van Gogh en sijn weg* (Amsterdam, 1977), no. 1877; J. Hulsker, *The Complete van Gogh: Paintings, Drawings, Sketches* (New York, 1980), no. 1877; G. Testori and L. Arrigoni, *Van Gogh* (Florence, 1990), no. 756; I. F. Walther and R. Metzger, *Vincent van Gogh: The Complete Paintings* (Cologne, 1993), vol. 2, p. 591.

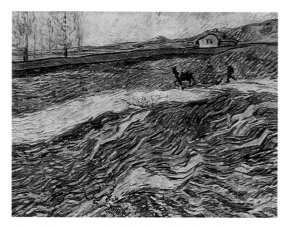

Fig. 2. *Vincent van Gogh.* Enclosed Field with Ploughman. *1889. Private collection, United States*

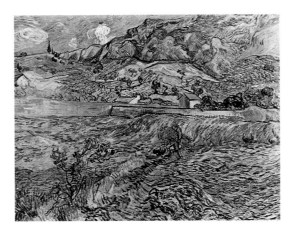

Fig. 3. *Vincent van Gogh.* Enclosed Field with Peasant. *1889. Indianapolis Museum of Art. Gift in memory of Daniel W. and Elizabeth C. Marmon*

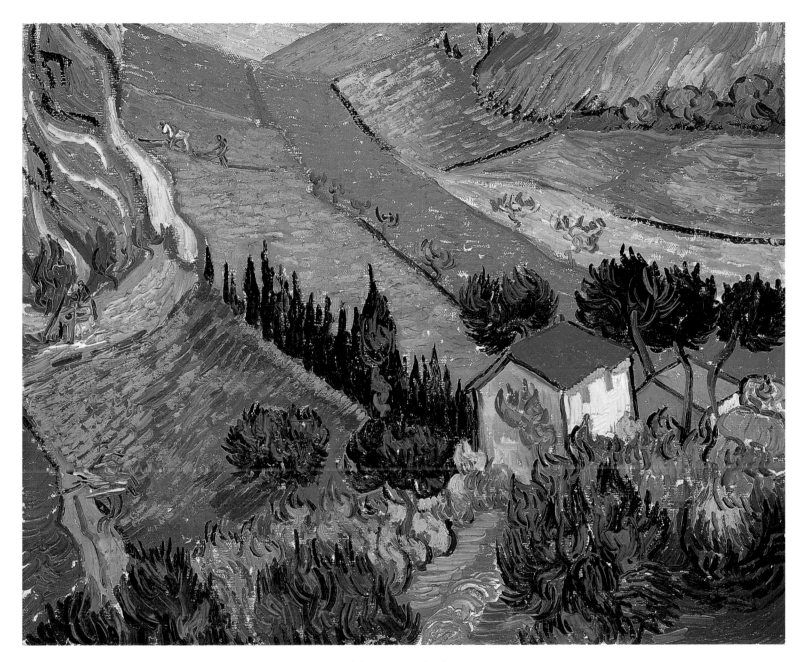

Vincent van Gogh
## 60. LANDSCAPE WITH HOUSE AND PLOUGHMAN
*Paysage avec une maison et un laboureur.* October 1889
Oil on canvas, 13 × 16¼" (33 × 41.4 cm)
No. 3KP 562. Formerly collection Otto Krebs, Holzdorf

# VINCENT VAN GOGH

## MORNING: GOING OUT TO WORK (AFTER MILLET)

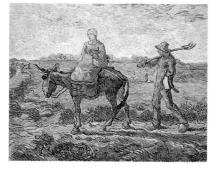

Jean-François Millet was a master to whose works Vincent van Gogh constantly returned, reflecting on them, studying and copying them. In a letter to his brother Theo, Vincent named Millet first among the artists he loved: "Yes, Millet's painting *The Angelus* is real, it is richness, it is poetry" (January 1874; LT 13). The tone of a letter sent a year and a half later from Paris is even more reverent: "There was a sale of Millet's drawings here. . . . When I went into the room in the Hôtel Drouot where they were exhibited, I was seized by a feeling something like this: Take off your shoes; you are standing on holy ground" (LT 29).

In 1880, when van Gogh had only just decided to become an artist, he asked his brother to send to him in the village of Cuesmes reproductions of Millet's series *The Labors of the Field* (August 20). On September 7 he reported that he had made sketches from ten works in Millet's series (they have not been preserved). "In addition, I have drawn *The Angelus* from the engraving that you sent me" (LT 135). Much later, in a letter sent from Arles, describing how he had decorated his studio with Japanese prints and reproductions of paintings by Honoré Daumier, Théodore Géricault, and Eugène Delacroix, van Gogh added: "I want terribly to have in my studio Millet's *Labors of the Field* and Le Rat's etching after *The Sower*, which is being sold at Durand-Ruel for about a franc and a quarter" (LT 542).

Van Gogh admired Alfred Sensier's book *La Vie et l'oeuvre de J.-F. Millet* (Paris, 1881). In 1882 he borrowed a copy of it for a while from the artist Théophile de Bock. He mentioned the book in a letter to his brother Theo (LT 180), and in the summer of 1884 Theo sent him a copy as a gift, much to Vincent's delight. The Sensier book includes the engraving *Morning,* after Millet (see fig. 1). Subsequently, a drawing of the figure on the right appeared in van Gogh's Nuenen sketchbook (fig. 2; SB 1/9).

*The Labors of the Field*, which served van Gogh as an inexhaustible source of inspiration, is a series of ten wood engravings made by Jacques-Adrien Lavieille after Millet's compositions. They show a peasant man or woman at work, sometimes with a sickle, sometimes with a scythe or rake, and so on.

In the second half of September 1889, van Gogh wrote his brother from the asylum in Saint-Rémy:

*I have already copied seven of Millet's ten* Labors of the Field. *. . . I assure you that I am extremely interested in making copies because I don't have models now, and with the help of these copies I won't have to abandon figure work. Furthermore, they will serve as decoration for the studio where I or anyone else will work. I would also like to copy* The Sower *and* Laborers. *There is a photograph of* Laborers *made from a drawing. And from* The Sower, *which is at Durand-Ruel, there is Le Rat's etching.*

*He also has* The Four Hours of the Day—*corresponding copies can be found in the collection of wood engravings. I would very much like to have all of that or at least etchings and wood engravings. They are essential help for me: I want to learn. Copying is considered an old-fashioned method, but I don't care about that. . . .*

*You'd be surprised at the impression that* The Labors of the Field *makes in color. It is a very heartfelt series. I will try to explain to you what I am looking for in them and why I considered it a good thing to copy them.*

*From us painters it is demanded that we always arrange things ourselves and that above all we be mas-*

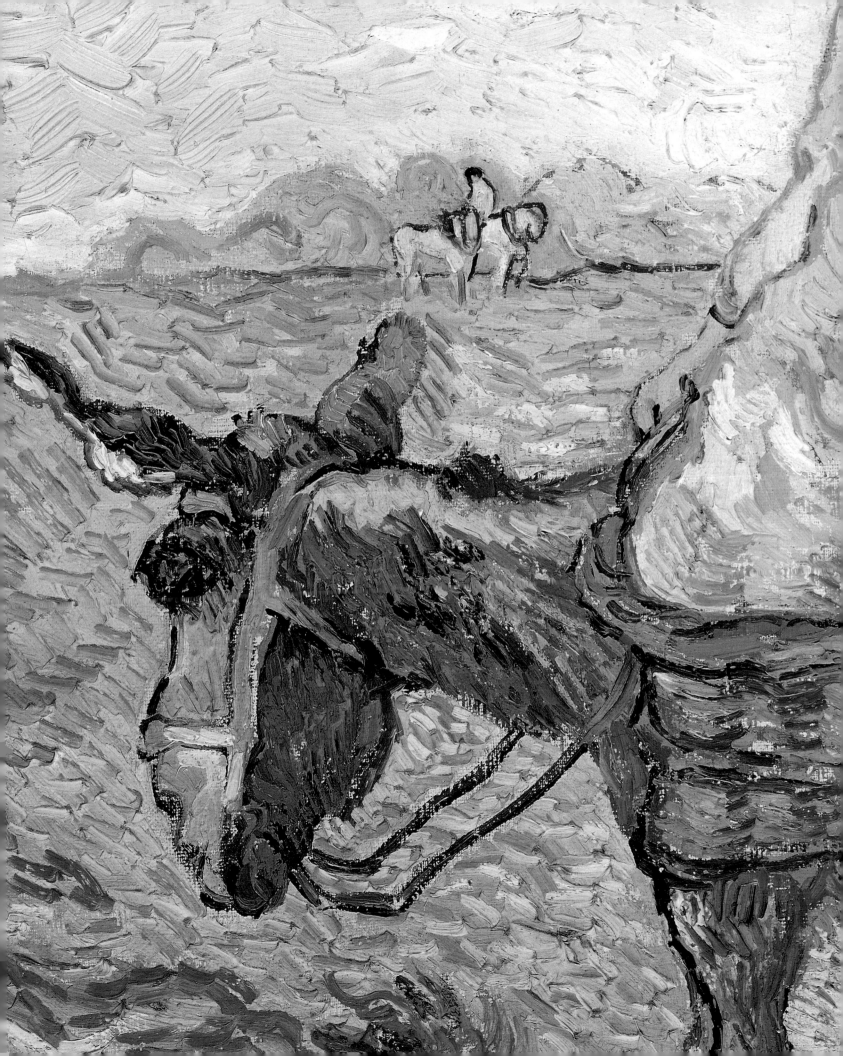

ters of composition. *Let us suppose this is correct. However, in music it is different. In playing Beethoven, the performer interprets a thing in his own way, and after all, in music, and especially in singing, interpretation also means something, because the composer hardly performs his own works all the time.*

*So now that I am ill, I am trying to create something that will soothe me and bring pleasure to me personally. I am using the black-and-white reproductions of Delacroix or Millet as subjects.*

*And then I improvise the color, although, of course, not entirely as if I were doing it myself, but trying to recall the pictures. However this "recollection" may be, the indefinite harmony of their paints, though not exact, is still sensed in my interpretation.*

*Many people do not accept copying; others, just the opposite. I came to it accidentally, but I find that it teaches me a lot and—this is the main thing—sometimes soothes me. In such instances, the brush plays in my hand like a bow on a violin and I work exclusively for my own enjoyment* (LT 607).

"It seems to me," van Gogh wrote on November 2, "that making paintings from Millet's drawings means rather to *translate them into another language* than to copy them" (LT 613). In the same letter he thanked his brother for sending the "Millet reproductions." "I am working on them intensively and that cheers me: I had begun to slowly deteriorate without the opportunity of seeing works of art. I finished *La Veillée.* . . . *La Veillée* was done in a range from violet to soft mauve, the light of the lamp is pale lemon-yellow, the glow of the fire is orange, and the man is red ocher."

On January 10 van Gogh replied to the letter Theo had sent after receiving *La Veillée:*

*I was very heartened by your opinion of my copy of Millet's* La Veillée. *The more I think of all this, the more clearly I see how justified it was to copy those works of Millet that he did not manage to do in oil. Moreover, working on his drawings and wood engravings cannot be considered copying in the strict sense of the word. It is rather translation into another language, the language of paints, of impressions created by the black-and-white light and shadow.*

*I finished three new copies from the series* The Four Hours of the Day *from Lavieille's wood engravings. They*

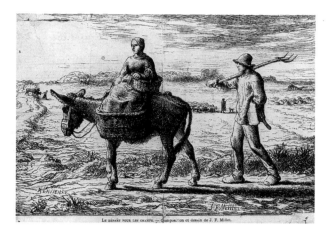

*Fig. 1. Jacques-Adrien Lavieille after Jean-François Millet.* Morning: Going Out to Work. *1860. Rijksmuseum Vincent van Gogh, Amsterdam*

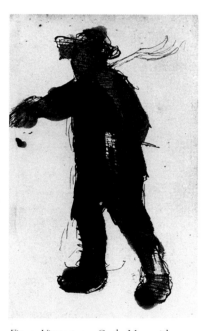

*Fig. 2. Vincent van Gogh.* Man with a Pitchfork. *1889. Rijksmuseum Vincent van Gogh, Amsterdam*

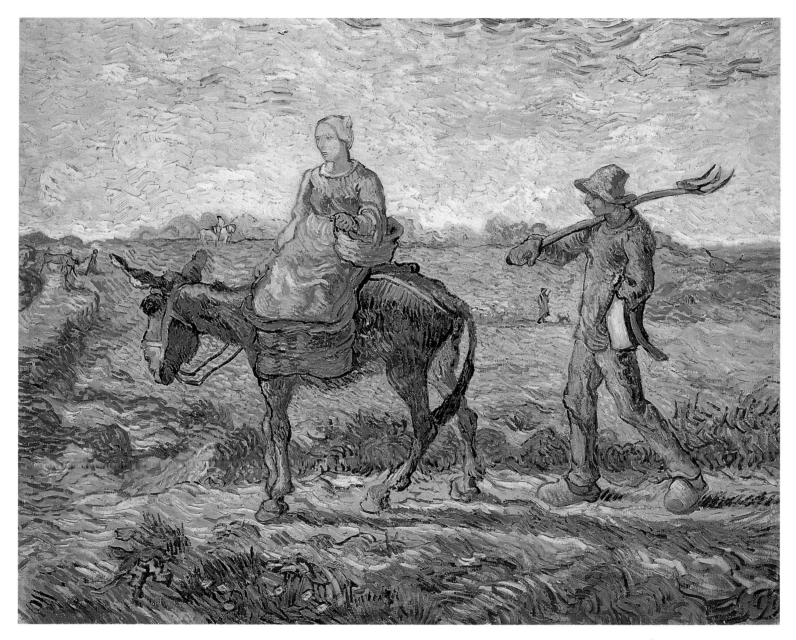

Vincent van Gogh
## 61. MORNING: GOING OUT TO WORK (AFTER MILLET)
*Le Matin, le départ au travail.* January 1890
Oil on canvas, 28¾ × 36¼" (73 × 92 cm)
No. 3KP 532. Formerly collection Otto Krebs, Holzdorf

*gave me some work and took up a lot of time. You proba-
bly remember how I copied* The Labors of the Field *last
summer. I did not send the latter to you, although I will
send it later, because they were searches in the dark, by
touch. Nevertheless they helped me a great deal in working on* The Four Hours of the Day. . . . *These three canvases will dry for another month, but once you see them
you will be convinced that I took up copying from a sincere and deep admiration of Millet. Even if they are crit-
icized and considered worthless as copies, that does not
shake my confidence in the fact that the attempt to make
the legacy of Millet more accessible for the ordinary public at large is intelligent and justified* (LT 623).

The thought of popularizing Millet through such
paintings as *Morning: Going Out to Work* was of
course naïve, especially because the demands of the
"ordinary public at large" were well known to him.
"Delacroix," he wrote four years later, "also tried to
arouse in people a belief in the symphony of color. And
I tried in vain, perhaps it can be said, if you recall that
almost everyone understands 'good color' to mean
correctness of local color, pedantic exactness, to which
neither Rembrandt, nor Millet, nor Delacroix, nor
Manet, nor Courbet, nor Rubens, nor Veronese—in
short, no one attempted" (LT 443).

The full title of Lavieille's series of wood engravings
printed in 1860 was *The Four Hours of the Day: Rural
Scenes Engraved by Adrien Lavieille after Original
Drawings of J.-F. Millet.* The drawings had been made
two years earlier. The motif of *Morning: Going Out to
Work* was first developed by Millet in a vertical format:
a drawing done about 1850 shows a peasant couple
heading out to the fields. The same composition
appears in the paintings in the Glasgow City Art
Gallery (c. 1850–51) and the Cincinnati Art Museum
(c. 1851–53), and later in an etching of 1863. Van Gogh
knew this composition. It was a loose variation of its
peasant with a pitchfork that appeared in the Nuenen
sketchbook, SB 1/9 (fig. 2; see J. van der Wolk, *The
Seven Sketchbooks of Vincent van Gogh: A Facsimile
Edition* [New York, 1987], p. 283). As for the composition in a horizontal format, where the peasant woman
is riding a donkey, besides the drawing used by
Lavieille for the wood engraving (fig. 1), there is also a
pastel (formerly in the Helen Clay Frick collection).

Thus, one way or another, Millet's *Four Hours of the*

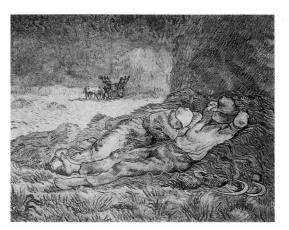

*Fig. 3. Vincent van Gogh.* Noon: Rest (after Millet). *1890.
Musée d'Orsay, Paris*

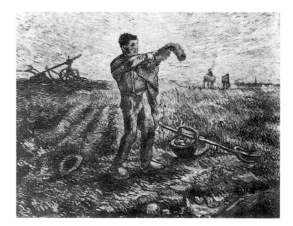

*Fig. 4. Vincent van Gogh.* Evening: The End of the Day
(after Millet). *1890. Menard Art Museum, Komaki, Japan*

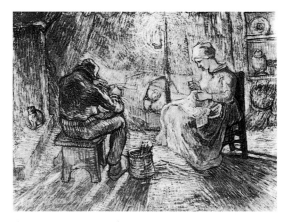

*Fig. 5. Vincent van Gogh.* La Veillée: The Family at Night
(after Millet). *1889. Rijksmuseum Vincent van Gogh,
Amsterdam*

*Day* was constantly in van Gogh's sight, at least after 1875. On July 6 of that year van Gogh, describing the room he had rented in Montmartre in detail, lists *The Four Hours of the Day* among the engravings he has chosen to decorate it.

The entire series of paintings from *The Four Hours of the Day,* to which van Gogh undoubtedly ascribed great significance, was made on the largest canvases he had available—about format 30; most often he worked with a ready-made canvas and cheap, standard stretchers. Subsequently, the series was broken up and never shown all together. In addition to the present painting, *Morning: Going Out to Work* (de la Faille no. 684), it is comprised of *Noon: Rest* (fig. 3; Musée d'Orsay, Paris; de la Faille no. 686), *Evening: The End of the Day* (fig. 4; Menard Art Museum, Komaki, Japan; de la Faille no. 649), and *La Veillée: The Family at Night* (fig. 5; Rijksmuseum Vincent van Gogh, Amsterdam; de la Faille no. 647).

Three paintings from *The Four Hours of the Day* are dated by scholars to January 1890. It is possible to be more precise and date them to early January. Evidence of this is, first, van Gogh's own comment, in the letter of January 10, about the paint still needing to dry on the three canvases, and second the fact that, in the last week of December, when van Gogh had an attack, he did not paint anything. The remark that they "took up a lot of time" should most likely be understood in the sense that the work was especially intense. It is possible that one of the paintings, *Evening: The End of the Day,* was only reworked in early January, having been executed in November. Heughten and Conisbee suggest that *Morning,* too, was executed in November. The nature of the paint on this canvas, however, does not support the idea that the time of execution stretched to two months, which was a fairly long period for van Gogh.

PROVENANCE: Johanna van Gogh-Bonger; February 1906, Karl-Ernst Osthaus, Hagen; Museum Folkwang, Hagen; A. Mack, Amsterdam; Galerie Paul Cassirer, Berlin; Galerie J. S. Goldschmidt, Frankfurt; Otto Krebs, Holzdorf.

EXHIBITIONS: 1905, Amsterdam, "Vincent van Gogh," Municipal Museum, no. 175 (as *Returning from the Field*); 1905, Hagen, Museum Folkwang (sold under the name *Return from the Market*); 1912, Hagen, "Moderne Kunst," Museum Folkwang, no. 134 (as *Return from the Field [after Millet]*); 1928, Frankfurt, "Vincent van Gogh," Galerie Goldschmidt, no. 41 (reprod.).

LITERATURE: Vincent van Gogh, letter to his brother Theo (see *The Complete Letters of Vincent van Gogh* [London and New York, 1958]), no. LT 623; *Beeldende Kunst,* vol. 10, no. 91 (reprod.); *Maandschrift voor Beeldende Kunsten* vol. 1, no. 2 (color reprod.); J. Meier-Graefe, *Vincent van Gogh* (Munich, 1910), p. 71; *Der Cicerone* 12, 3 (February 3, 1920) (reprod.); G. Hartlaub, *Vincent van Gogh* (Leipzig, 1922); J. Meier-Graefe, *Vincent: A Biographical Study* (London and New York, 1922), vol. 2, pl. 85; A. Mack sale, D. Komter Galerie, Amsterdam, October 27, 1925, no. 123; J.-B. de la Faille, *L'Oeuvre de Vincent van Gogh: Catalogue raisonné* (Paris and Brussels, 1928), no. 684 (as *Le Retour de champs*); W. Scherjon and W. J. de Gruyter, *Vincent van Gogh's Great Period: Arles, Saint-Rémy, and Auvers-sur-Oise (Complete Catalogue)* (Amsterdam, 1937), p. 282, no. 88 (as *Setting Out for the Fields*); J.-B. de la Faille, *Vincent van Gogh* (Paris, London, and New York, 1939), no. 676; *L'Opera completa di van Gogh* (Milan, 1966), no. 758; J.-B. de la Faille, *The Works of Vincent van Gogh: His Paintings and Drawings* (Amsterdam and New York, 1970), no. 684; P. Lecaldano, *L'Opera pittorica completa di van Gogh e i suoi nessi grafici* (Milan, 1971), no. 758; J. Hulsker, *The Complete van Gogh: Paintings, Drawings, Sketches* (New York, 1980), no. 1880, p. 432; J. Van der Wolk, *De schetsboeken van Vincent van Gogh* (Amsterdam, 1986), pp. 280–81; J. Van der Wolk, *The Seven Sketchbooks of Vincent van Gogh: A Facsimile Edition* (New York, 1987), p. 282; W. Feilchenfeldt, *Vincent van Gogh and Paul Cassirer: The Reception of van Gogh in Germany from 1901 to 1914* (Zwolle, 1988), p. 112; L. van Tilborgh, ed., S. van Heughten, and P. Conisbee, *Van Gogh and Millet* (Amsterdam, 1989), no. 32, pp. 95–98 (as *Morning: Peasant Couple Going to Work*); I. F. Walther and R. Metzger, *Vincent van Gogh: The Complete Paintings* (Cologne, 1993), vol. 2, p. 605.

# VINCENT VAN GOGH

## THE WHITE HOUSE AT NIGHT

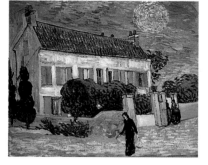

On May 21, 1890, Vincent van Gogh came to Auvers-sur-Oise and immediately expressed his impressions of the new place in a letter to his brother and his sister-in-law: "Auvers is very beautiful, among other things a lot of old thatched roofs, which are getting rare. . . . Truly it is profoundly beautiful, it is the real country, characteristic and picturesque" (LT 635). By the next letter, van Gogh reported that he was painting some old, straw-thatched houses. The painting he describes is undoubtedly *Thatched Cottages in Auvers* (fig. 1; The State Hermitage Museum, St. Petersburg). Homes with straw, brick, or iron roofs appear time after time in his canvases. He had happened to paint some buildings in the past, but far fewer than in the two months he spent at Auvers.

In the earliest paintings of the Dutch period, the house he depicts is the dark silhouette of a peasant cottage, not so much a domicile standing on the ground as a part of the soil, a feature of the landscape, and, consequently, a symbol of the peasant's lot.

In the Nuenen years (1883–85), the motif acquires new resonance. The previously indistinguishable mass is replaced by a structure with clearly defined details—walls, windows, and roof. Earlier, if windows or doors were indicated at all, it was only by dark splashes, and did not make one wish to enter. The Nuenen homes take on a different nature; they become more attractive. The windows are enlivened with a dim glow from within, or a shimmer of light appears on the glass from either moonlight or the setting sun.

Formally, the Nuenen paintings belong under the rubric of landscape, yet they are also metaphors for the condition of the artist and his relations with his own family, which were, as he put it, in a deliberately understated way, "somewhat strained." These metaphors can only be understood within the context of the other symbols with which van Gogh's painting is preoccupied. There is a difference between a mere house and a true home—the latter traditionally embodied by the family hearth. In this regard, however, van Gogh proposes a new and entirely private symbolism: the symbols of comfort whose depictions are supposed to express a yearning for one's own home contain no joy, and are filled instead with inexplicable alarm. Did he realize that he had fallen into a contradiction? Apparently he did, but he could not paint otherwise, because each image had to reflect honestly the state of his soul.

In Nuenen, the home was shown in various forms: on the one hand, as a residence or haven; and on the other, as a kind of anthropomorphic creature. The artist's personal drama—his terribly complex relationships with other people, first and foremost with his father and relatives—was projected onto it. The home in the Nuenen period was above all the home of his father.

In a letter to his brother Theo, van Gogh wrote of his parents: "Letting me into the family is as terrible for them as letting in a large, shaggy mutt. It tracks mud in the rooms with its wet paws—and besides, it's so shaggy. It gets underfoot everywhere. And it *barks so loudly*. In short, it's a nasty animal. I agree. Still, this mutt has a human life and soul and is even so perceptive as to understand what they think of him—mutts usually aren't able to do that. The mutt sees that if he isn't kicked out, it is only because people are reconciled to him, that he is tolerated '*in this home*'" (LT 346). The notion of the home cannot be removed from van Gogh's dramatic metaphor; he emphasized it him-

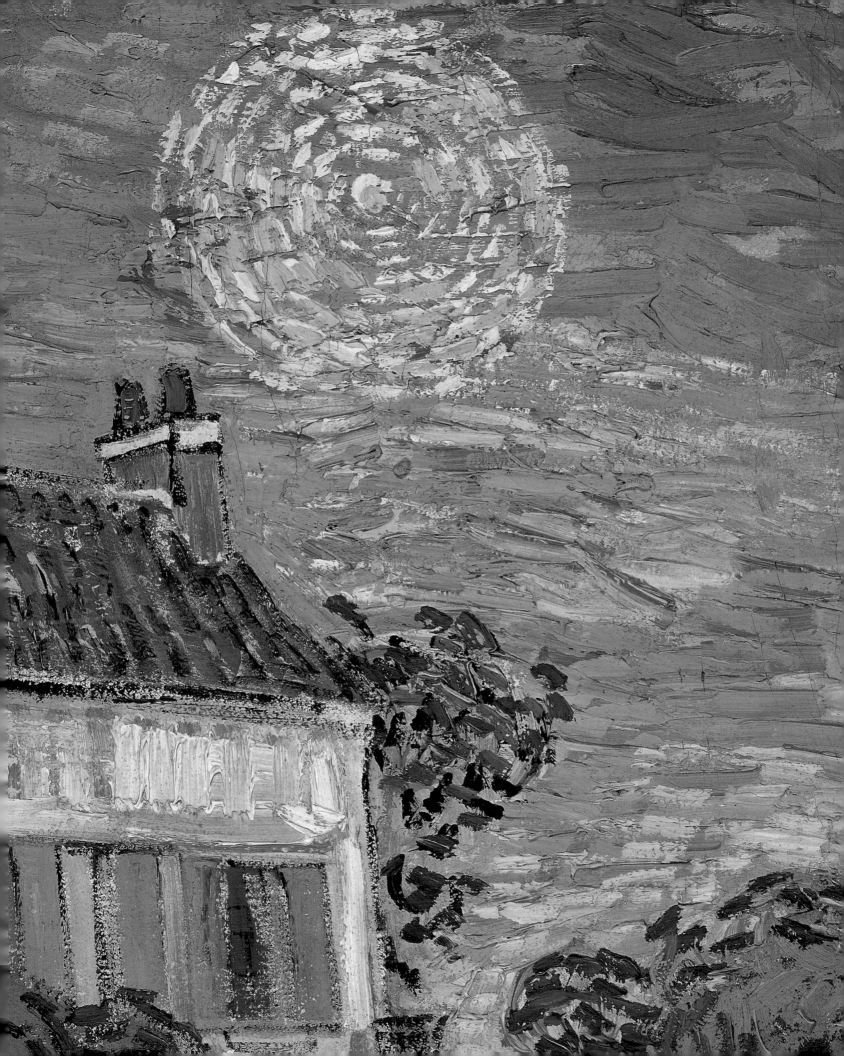

self. In the next letter (LT 347), van Gogh returns to his metaphor, which is more than a figure of speech: "I tell you that I am deliberately choosing *the lot of a dog*: I will remain a mutt, I will be *destitute,* I will be *an artist,* I want to remain *a human*—a human amidst nature." The idea of home is not mentioned here, but it is implied, because the "destitute" are homeless, and because "nature," which signifies the condition of freedom, is restrained by the confines of a home.

Van Gogh twice painted the parsonage in Nuenen (de la Faille nos. 182, 183), once in twilight and once in moonlight. The times chosen were, of course, not accidental. Each of the paintings gives a sense of the alienation of the artist, who compares himself to a dog kicked out of the house at night. It is characteristic that van Gogh does not even think of painting an interior; the gloomy two-story structure with the high roof is drawn only from the outside. There is a kind of distance between the artist and the home that does not enable him to be with his parents.

It is astonishing how much *The White House at Night* looks like *The Parsonage at Nuenen* of October 1885 (fig. 2; Rijksmuseum Vincent van Gogh, Amsterdam; de la Faille no. 182). It is slightly wider (having two more windows), but quite a number of elements coincide: the general construction of the house, the low stone wall, the gate to the right, and the dark silhouette of a woman in front of the house. Most likely, parsonages tended to be of similar size and of similar design, simple and severe. Van Gogh's father's former home in Etten also had two stories and seven windows, like the one in *The White House.* It is depicted in van Gogh's early drawing *The Parsonage at Etten* of 1881 (Rijksmuseum Vincent van Gogh, Amsterdam; see M. E. Tralbaut, *Vincent van Gogh* [New York, 1969], pp. 76–77). But, of course, even though there is a striking outward similarity between *The Parsonage at Nuenen* and *The White House at Night,* which most likely provoked the artist's sorrow, the later painting possesses a different mood.

Van Gogh's French period was notable for the accentuation of artistic elements that had a lesser role in the Dutch years. Chief among these elements is pure light, which he learned from both the Impressionists and the masters of Japanese woodcuts. In a letter to his brother sent from Auvers, he himself explained his trip to the south by the wish to learn "to

feel and paint like the Japanese" (LT 605). Japanese art was also the source of quite a few motifs. Among van Gogh's possessions was a work very similar to *The White House at Night*, the woodblock print *View of the Saruwokacho: Theater Street at Night* of 1856 from the series *One Hundred Famous Views of Edo* by Hiroshige (*Vincent van Gogh and Japan* [Kyoto, 1992], p. 204). A woodcut like *British Delegation in Yokohama* was also known in France, and had a similar theme. Nevertheless, the new impressions, including the Japanese ones, did not mean a rejection of the original, Dutch principles.

The hold of the symbolic qualities of the early work was reinforced by homesickness. This nostalgia can be clearly seen in Arles, when van Gogh painted the L'Anglois bridge, which reminded him of the bridges of Holland, or in the Arles composition *Women of Arles (Memory of the Garden at Etten)* of November 1888 (The State Hermitage Museum, St. Petersburg). In the last, Auvers period, reminiscences of the north color many of his works.

The Auvers period ended with van Gogh's death, but it had begun with the hope of a new life and the recovery of health. This sense of hope is expressed in the Hermitage *Thatched Cottages in Auvers* and other works that followed, painted after his arrival in Auvers in May 1890: *House at Auvers with a Figure* (Museum of Fine Arts, Boston; de la Faille no. 805), *The House of Père Eloi* (private collection, Switzerland; de la Faille no. 794), *The House of Père Pilon* (collection S. Niarchos; de la Faille no. 791), *Village Street in Auvers* (Ateneumin Taidemuseo, Helsinki; de la Faille, no. 802), and other landscapes. Van Gogh had never painted so many houses, and what is more, in such a short time. More than a third of the Auvers works are devoted to this motif. Without a doubt, van Gogh was painting landscapes with specific addresses. Sometimes the identity of the residents was lost (for example, it is not known who owned the "white house"), but the houses still became landmarks.

In the June paintings, the motif of the home remained at the center of the artist's attention, but its emotional range expanded greatly—from gloomy foreboding to conciliation. Since the emotion was expressed by the artist less through the subject itself than through his manipulation of the very methods of painting, the structure of his compositions changed

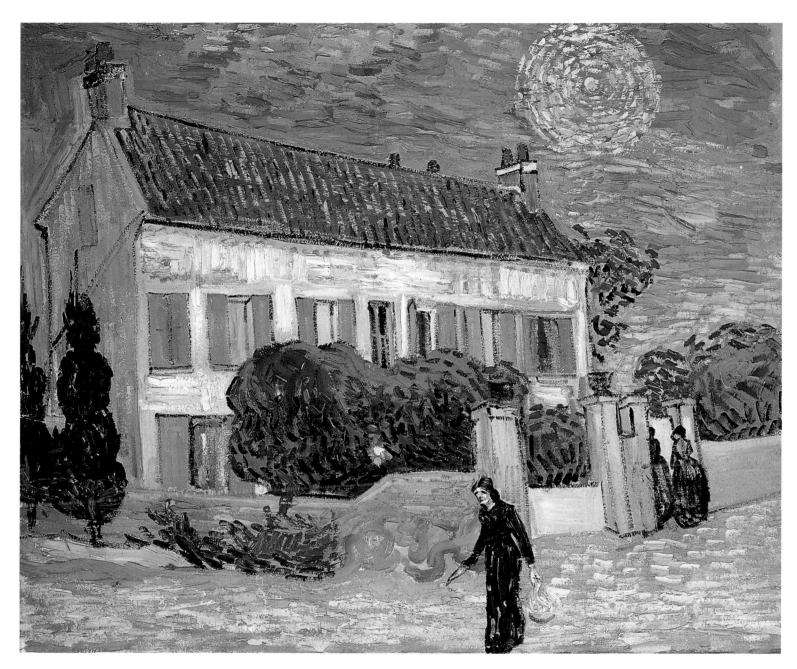

Vincent van Gogh

## 62. THE WHITE HOUSE AT NIGHT

*La Maison blanche au nuit.* June 1890
Oil on canvas, 23¼ × 28½" (59 × 72.5 cm)
No. 3KP 511. Formerly collection Otto Krebs, Holzdorf

each time. In this regard, *The White House at Night* is the antithesis of *Thatched Cottages*. There, the green colors of hope prevailed, and the whole painting, an avalanche of diagonal brushstrokes, was remarkable for motion, tension, and forward thrust.

In *The White House at Night,* however, a frozen quality prevails, and the chief lines are stable horizontals and verticals. Straight lines and corners are needed to draw a house, but they can turn it into a prison; memories of Holland merge with real expectations of possible trouble. No other Auvers painting gives such attention to windows, the "eyes" of a home. The home seems more alive than the three dark figures before it. The red splashes of the windows to the right are alarming; the red color of the houses he had painted in May (needed to depict the red tiles of the roofs) had been joyfully passionate and did not contain any hidden fear.

A star appears twice in the paintings of the Auvers period: in *Road with Cypress and Star* of May 1890 (Rijksmuseum Kröller-Müller, Otterlo; de la Faille no. 683) and in *The White House at Night*. The two works are among the most dramatic of this period. Van Gogh would draw a star, a sign of fate, at moments of greatest anguish.

On June 17, 1890, he wrote to his brother Theo: "At the moment I am working on two studies, one a bunch of wild plants, thistles, ears of wheat, and sprays of different kinds of leaves—the one almost red, the other bright green, the third turning yellow. The second study is a white house among the trees, with a night sky and an orange light in the window and dark greenery and a note of somber pink. That is all for the moment."

The "study" on which van Gogh was working simultaneously, *Meadow Flowers and Thistles in Vase* of June 1890 (private collection, Japan; de la Faille, no. 763)—the most angular still life of the Auvers period—like *The White House at Night*, expresses (albeit with less power) the great psychological tension under which van Gogh found himself.

The letter was no doubt written before finishing work on *The White House at Night*. There are not one but two colorful windows in the painting, and the orange light shades into redness. Such changes increased the dramatic element. The dark rose note has essentially disappeared. More important, the

house, though "among the trees," is not covered with foliage. On the contrary, it dominates the greenery. In *Daubigny's Garden,* by comparison, the house is indeed covered with foliage.

The latter composition is known to exist in two versions (Kunstmuseum, Basel [fig. 3], and Hiroshima Museum of Art; de la Faille nos. 777, 776). The first was done from nature, and the second is a variation done at home. The two versions complete a long series of depictions of homes, and van Gogh's comment about Auvers is applicable to them: "Everywhere I feel—or it seems to me that I feel—the calm à la Puvis de Chavannes. No factories are to be seen, although beautifully, neatly trimmed foliage is in abundance" (LT 637). In painting *Daubigny's Garden,* van Gogh worked from nature, although, as in all his works, he strove not so much to capture it as to express himself, his feelings, and his beliefs. His dream of a harmonious coexistence with nature is embodied in this painting. *Thatched Cottages, The White House at Night,* and *Daubigny's Garden* can be imagined as a three-act play; after a powerful finale, there is not calmness as painted by Puvis de Chavannes, but reconciliation as painted by van Gogh. This new image of a different white house, truly white under the rays of the midday sun, signified the overcoming of a crisis.

In May 1994, in London's *The Art Newspaper,* an article calculated to cause a sensation appeared: "Where Is the Real van Gogh's *White House at Night*?" The doubts of readers of *The Art Newspaper* were provoked by the fact that a certain Gerhard Novak approached a representative of Christie's with an offer to sell *The White House at Night* and even showed a photograph of it. The canvas itself, however, was never displayed. It is difficult to tell what Novak's motives were: an attempt to pass off and sell as an original an old copy, or perhaps a fresh copy prepared from photographs of the original, a work that was published and had never been a secret? Moreover, there were photographs of paintings from the former Krebs collection in Germany that could have been used in this instance. Whatever the case, that was the end of the affair.

The painting was not executed on the standard manufactured canvas usually sent by Theo, but on a fine fabric with the foundation prepared by the artist himself. It was hard for such fabrics to withstand the load of van Gogh's heavy brushstrokes. The fragility of the very thick layer of paint apparently forced one of the former owners, many years ago, before the painting was acquired by Krebs, to reline it. Furthermore, the relining was not done very professionally; instead of a special canvas for relining, a manufactured one of the kind for painting was used. In relining, some of the textured strokes that were not sufficiently hard were flattened.

Thanks to special conservation methods, the painting has retained much of the freshness of its colors, but some of the tones have nonetheless changed. De la Faille, in describing the painting in the 1928 catalogue, stated that the clothing on the woman in the foreground was painted in ultramarine; these ultramarine strokes have now darkened a good deal— a natural result of the chemical processes that have affected several other canvases by van Gogh.

PROVENANCE: Johanna van Gogh-Bonger; September 1908, C. M. van Gogh, The Hague; F. Meier-Fierz, Zurich; Fred. Muller, Amsterdam; 1926; Sale Fred. Muller & Co., Amsterdam; Galerie Paul Cassirer, Berlin; Galerie J. S. Goldschmidt, Berlin; Otto Krebs, Holzdorf.

EXHIBITIONS: 1905, Amsterdam, Stedelijk Museum, no. 217 (as *White House*); 1908, Paris, "Vincent van Gogh," Galerie Bernheim-Jeune, no. 83; 1908, Munich, Moderne Kunsthandlung, no. 66; 1908, Dresden, Emil Richter Galerie, no. 64; 1908, Frankfurt, Kunstverein, no. 75; 1908, Zurich, Kunsthaus, no. 38; 1924, Basel, Kunsthalle, no. 77; 1924, Zurich, Kunsthaus, no. 39.

LITERATURE: Vincent van Gogh, letter to his brother Theo (see *The Complete Letters of Vincent van Gogh* [London and New York, 1958]), no. LT 642; *Wissen und Leben* 17, 1 (October 1, 1923), p. 22 (reprod.); sale, Fred. Muller & Co., Amsterdam, July 13, 1926, no. 11; J.-B. de la Faille, *L'Oeuvre de Vincent van Gogh: Catalogue raisonné* (Paris and Brussels, 1928), no. 766; W. Scherjon and W. J. Gruyter, *Vincent van Gogh's Great Period: Arles, Saint-Rémy, and Auvers-sur-Oise (Complete Catalogue)* (Amsterdam, 1937), p. 324, no. 132; J.-B. de la Faille, *Vincent van Gogh* (Paris, London, and New York, 1939), no. 78; *L'Opera completa di van Gogh* (Milan, 1966), no. 845; J.-B. de la Faille, *The Works of Vincent van Gogh: His Paintings and Drawings* (Amsterdam and New York, 1970), no. 766; P. Lecaldano, *L'Opera pittorica completa di van Gogh e i suoi nessi grafici* (Milan, 1971), no. 845; J. Hulsker, ed., *Van Gogh door van Gogh: De brieven als commentaar op zijn werk* (Amsterdam, 1973), p. 842; J. Hulsker, *Van Gogh en sijn weg* (Amsterdam, 1977), no. 2031; J. Hulsker, *The Complete van Gogh: Paintings, Drawings, Sketches* (New York, 1980), no. 2031; R. Pickvance, *Van Gogh in Saint-Rémy and Auvers* (The Metropolitan Museum of Art, New York, 1986), p. 209 (reprod.); W. Feilchenfeldt, *Vincent van Gogh and Paul Cassirer: The Reception of van Gogh in Germany from 1901 to 1914* (Zwolle, 1988), p. 118; G. Testori and L. Arrigoni, *Van Gogh* (Florence, 1990), no. 821; I. F. Walther and R. Metzger, *Vincent van Gogh: The Complete Paintings* (Cologne, 1993), vol. 2, p. 654; M. Bailey, "Where Is the Real van Gogh's *White House at Night?*," *The Art Newspaper*, vol. 5, no. 38 (May 1994), p. 4.

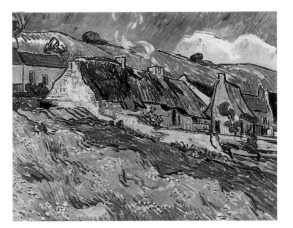

*Fig. 1. Vincent van Gogh. Thatched Cottages in Auvers. 1890. The State Hermitage Museum, St. Petersburg*

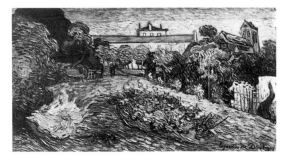

*Fig. 2. Vincent van Gogh. The Parsonage at Nuenen. 1885. Rijksmuseum Vincent van Gogh, Amsterdam*

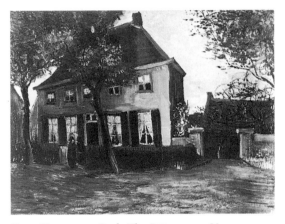

*Fig. 3. Vincent van Gogh. Daubigny's Garden. 1890. Kunstmuseum, Basel. On loan from the Rudolf Staechlin Collection*

# HENRI DE TOULOUSE-LAUTREC

## WOMAN WITH AN UMBRELLA
### (BERTHE THE DEAF IN THE GARDEN OF MONSIEUR FOREST)

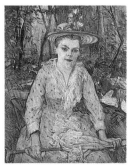

In cases where ordinary cabaret actresses or prostitutes posed for the artist, many of his models are known only by their first names. Of the woman in this picture, we know a little more: her nickname. In the well-known photograph (fig. 1; Musée Toulouse-Lautrec, Albi), Berthe, posing for the artist, leans forward a little, possibly listening hard to what the artist is saying, the way people who are partially deaf sometimes do. This photograph is a remarkable document. It attests to Lautrec's precision in conveying natural detail, from the garden chair's armrest to the wide-brimmed flowered hat—and it attests as well to how merciless he could be in portraying a woman. Compared to what we see in the photograph, Berthe's chin in the painting is a bit heavier, the nose more turned up. The only detail that seems inconsistent with nature is the green brim of the hat, necessary to tie the figure to the background. Its very pronounced oval shape is not without an ironic undertone, reminiscent as it is of halos in paintings of holy martyrs, but now introduced into a portrait of a prostitute.

The garden where Berthe's portrait was painted no longer exists. In its place in lower Montmartre, where the rue Forest and the rue Caulaincourt feed into the boulevard de Clichy, later came racetracks, then the Gaumont movie theater. In the 1880s and early 1890s, it was a quiet, almost rural neighborhood. The garden belonged to the rich Père Forest, a former photographer, who was on friendly terms with Lautrec. Two or three times a week, Forest brought his friends over to this unruly, overgrown garden for some archery, or even for archery contests, the kind of sporting pastime he loved. The rest of the time the garden was deserted. Lautrec obtained Forest's permission to work there whenever the mood struck him. In the photograph,

we can see, behind the artist, a small shed where he kept his paints, other materials, and a small stock of wine.

Here, in this garden, several excellent paintings were created: *Red-haired Woman in the Garden of Monsieur Forest* of 1889 (private collection; Dortu no. P343), portraits of Justine Dieuhl (Musée d'Orsay, Paris; Dortu no. P394) and Désiré Dihau (Musée Toulouse-Lautrec, Albi; Dortu no. P381), and *The Streetwalker (Casque d'or)* of 1890 (Annenberg collection; Dortu no. P407), among others. Toulouse-Lautrec preferred that the models who posed for him in Forest's estate be redheads. He found that this particular hair color was a splendid accent against the fresh green of the garden. Berthe was not a redhead, though, so he looked for another, subtler color combination: lilac-pink and green. Apparently, the artist's desire to get a special clarity and lightness of color scheme encouraged him to turn to water-soluble paints, watercolors, and gouache, whereas working on other garden pictures, he as a rule used oils.

"By 1890," wrote Gerstl Mack, "Lautrec has cast off the direct influence of the Impressionists, and in this portrait, as well as in many others of the period, his individual technique is clearly apparent. The picture is painted on cardboard in the very thin, slightly chalky medium that is characteristic of so much of Lautrec's work. Brushstrokes are free yet placed with extreme care; the composition is a masterpiece of refined boldness" (G. Mack, *Toulouse-Lautrec* [New York, 1938], p. 77).

No doubt Lautrec was well aware of the way his forerunners the Impressionists developed motifs like this. Pictures like Claude Monet's *In the Park* of about 1874 (Tate Gallery, London) served as a starting point for Lautrec's portrait of his mother sitting on a garden

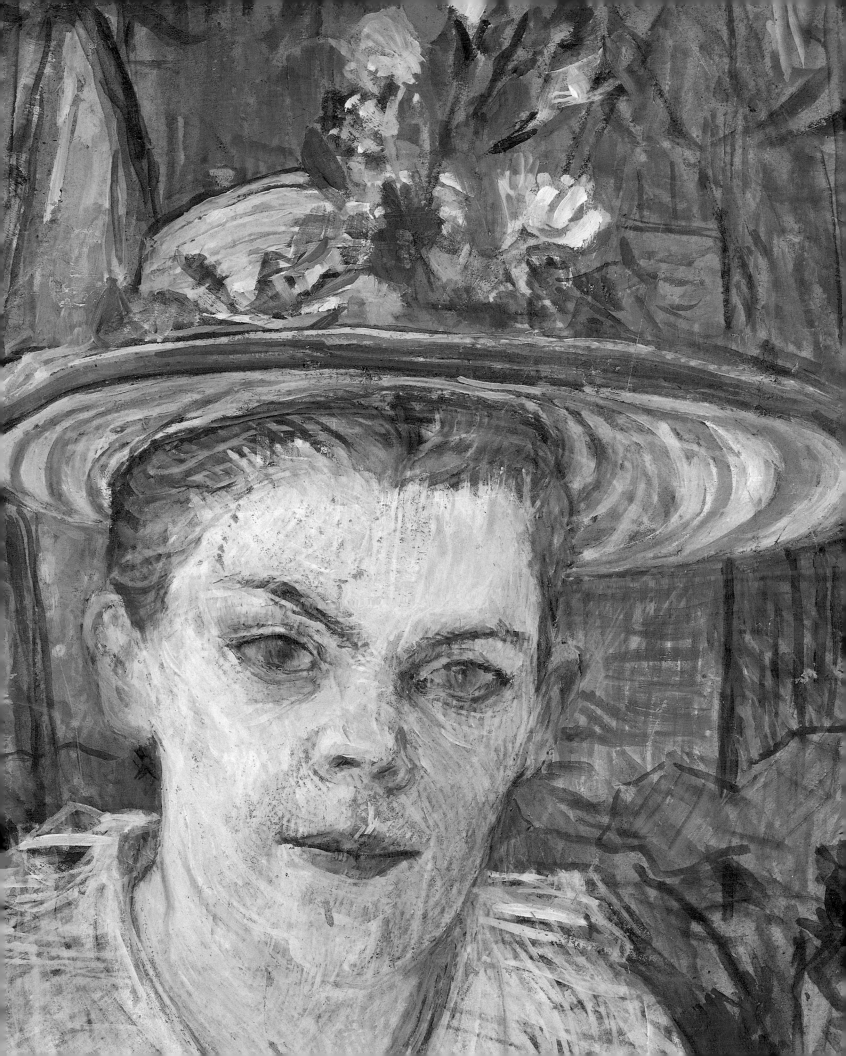

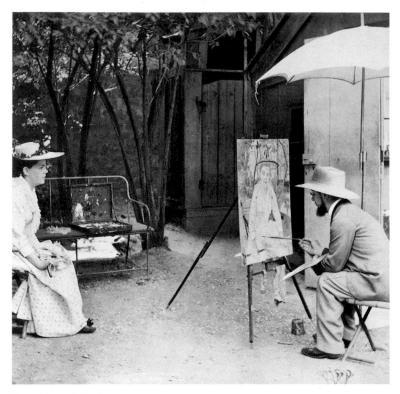

*Fig. 1. Henri de Toulouse-Lautrec painting* Woman with an Umbrella. *1889. Musée Toulouse-Lautrec, Albi*

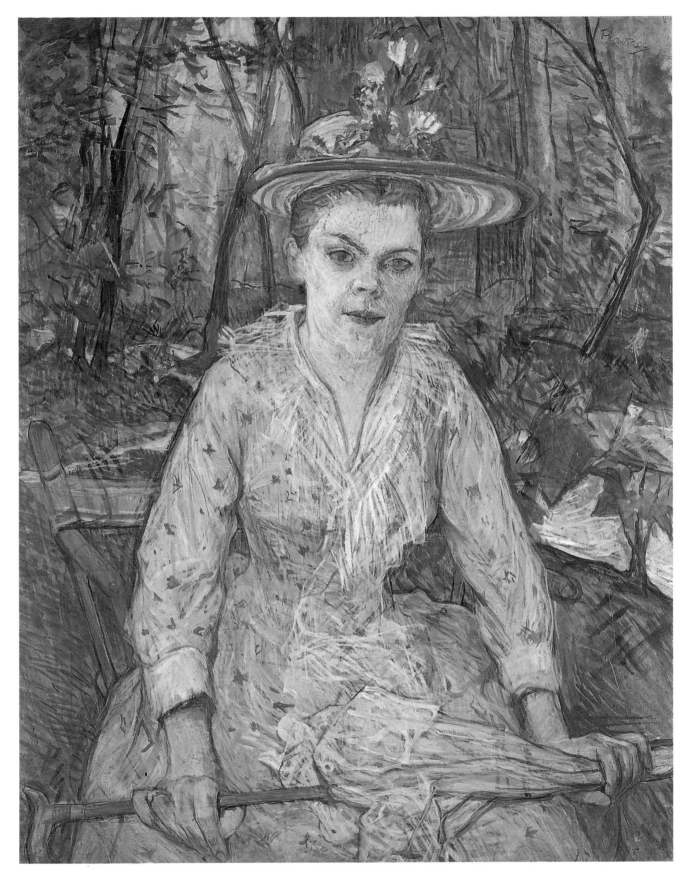

Henri de Toulouse-Lautrec (1864, Albi, Tarn–1901, Malromé, near Bordeaux)
## 63. WOMAN WITH AN UMBRELLA (BERTHE THE DEAF IN THE GARDEN OF MONSIEUR FOREST)
*Femme à l'ombrelle, dite Berthe la Sourde, assise dans le jardin de Monsieur Forest.* 1889
Gouache, watercolor, and tempera on cardboard, 30⅛ × 22⅝" (76.6 × 57.5 cm)
Signed upper right: "H.T-Lautrec." No. GR 155-97. Formerly collection Otto Krebs, Holzdorf

bench holding an umbrella, *Madame la Comtesse A. de Toulouse-Lautrec* of 1882 (Musée Toulouse-Lautrec, Albi; Dortu no. P180). Lautrec was truly taken by the play of the light coming through the leaves: the whole surface of the canvas turns into a dance of color spots. Seven years later, when the artist addressed the same theme in *Woman with an Umbrella*, he did not give light as prominent a part as before, assigning it only a secondary role. The figure itself is painted with only a hint of chiaroscuro, with no Impressionist liberties whereby this or that part of the body would be randomly highlighted so as to convey the momentary impression. *Woman with an Umbrella* from the Krebs collection is not the fruit of fleeting impressions. The image is synthetic and well balanced, as remarkable for its severe pyramidal structure as for its psychological insight.

*Woman with an Umbrella* is noticeably different from most of the portraits of women painted in Forest's garden in a number of representative details. In other instances, Lautrec's models let their hair down and wear plain dresses. Berthe, however, looks as if she dressed up for a formal portrait, with an expensive two-tone hat of fine straw, an umbrella (or parasol), and a gown with lace trimming. Moreover, the artist did not attempt to emulate the natural look of a moment captured accidentally. Instead, Berthe is obviously and patiently posing for a portrait that is supposed to be her best ever. She undoubtedly wants to look like a lady of society, and she almost succeeds, except the artist could not resist adding irony, however benign or sympathetic. Berthe looks as if she is part of a masquerade here. Notice how she clutches the umbrella; there is none of the finesse about the hands of this daughter of a peasant that would have been characteristic of a lady of a higher society. But seldom can such wide-open eyes, shining with genuine interest in life, be seen in Lautrec's bordello dwellers.

Berthe, who came from Brittany to make a living in Paris, wound up in the Green Parrot whorehouse that Lautrec used to visit. It was not hard to persuade her to pose: one of her lovers was an artist by the name of Rachou. For some time Lautrec and Berthe were closer to each other than was usual in Parisian bordellos.

Herbert Schimmel, in his recent edition of Toulouse-Lautrec's letters, supposes that a letter to an unknown addressee, which the artist mailed in January

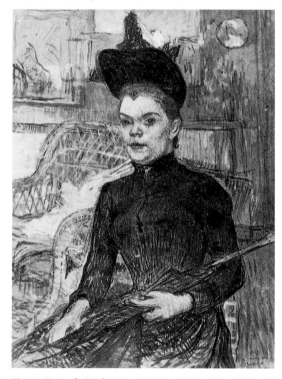

*Fig. 2. Henri de Toulouse-Lautrec.* Woman in a Black Hat. *1890. Private collection*

1893, concerned *Woman with an Umbrella*, although he does not exclude an alternative possibility, *Portrait of Jane Avril* (Dortu no. P418). Lautrec mentions a conversation with the talented champion of the new school of painting, critic Roger Marx: "Marx did in fact talk to me about your desire to have the mauve lady with the black hat. You can collect it at my studio next Monday . . . on rue Caulaincourt. All I ask is that you do not show the picture until a month from now" (*The Letters of Henri de Toulouse-Lautrec*, ed. H. Schimmel [Oxford, 1991], letter 266, p. 196). This raises a few questions, however. Berthe's hat is not black. On the other hand, Jane Avril was too famous an actress to be called "the mauve lady."

There is another letter that Lautrec sent to his gallery in August 1890 that undoubtedly mentions the *Woman with an Umbrella*: "The other day I forgot two pictures, one showing a 'seated woman in pink, full-face, leaning forward a little,' the other 'a red-haired woman seated on the floor, seen from the back, nude.' These two pictures were shown this year in Brussels at the Vingtiste exhibit" (*The Letters of Henri de Toulouse-Lautrec*, letter 177, p. 134). For the seventh exhibition of Les Vingt, Lautrec selected five paintings: *The Ball at Moulin de la Galette, Woman Reading, The Redhead,* and two studies. From his letter, one of the "studies" is easily identifiable as *Woman with an Umbrella*. It is curious that Lautrec, sending Berthe's portrait to the exhibition, avoided giving it a specific title. Since we know that the exhibition in Brussels opened in mid-January 1890, *Woman with an Umbrella* obviously could not have been painted the same year, as has sometimes been stated in the literature. There is no doubt that it was completed in 1889.

Lautrec painted Berthe twice. Her second portrait, *Woman in a Black Hat* (fig. 2; private collection; Dortu no. P373), was done at a later date (the artist himself dated it 1890) and also shows the model seated, holding an umbrella, but in an interior. This time she has on a dark dress and a black hat. This detail might have been the reason why the subjects were confused when Lautrec wrote about "the mauve lady with the black hat." The second portrait differs significantly from the first one in atmosphere: Berthe has a wooden expression and her eyes are dull and puffy. The tall hat of exquisite design contrasts sharply with the model.

PROVENANCE: Barincourt, Paris; Galerie Paul Rosenberg, Paris; Otto Krebs, Holzdorf.

EXHIBITIONS: 1890, Brussels, "VIIe Exposition des Vingt," no. 4 (as *Etude*); 1914, Paris, "Toulouse-Lautrec: Rétrospective," Galerie Manzi-Joyant, no. 30; 1924, Chicago, The Art Institute of Chicago, no. 8; 1926, Amsterdam, "Rétrospective d'art français," no. 109; 1931, New York, "Toulouse-Lautrec and Redon," The Museum of Modern Art, no. 14.

LITERATURE: G. Coquiot, *Lautrec* (Paris, 1913), pp. 76, 77 (reprod.); T. Duret, *Lautrec* (Paris, 1920), p. 61; G. Coquiot, *Lautrec* (Paris, 1921), pp. 78, 129; A. Astre, *Henri de Toulouse-Lautrec* (Paris, 1925), p. 78; M. Joyant, *Henri de Toulouse-Lautrec, 1864–1901, peintre* (Paris, 1926), pp. 103, 268; Lapparent, *Toulouse-Lautrec* (1927), p. 21; Mac Orlan, *Lautrec* (Paris, 1934), p. 37; E. Schaub Koch, *Psychoanalyse d'un peintre moderne: Henri de Toulouse-Lautrec* (Paris, 1935), pp. 186–87; G. Mack, *Toulouse-Lautrec* (New York, 1938), p. 77; J. Rinaldini, *Toulouse-Lautrec* (Buenos Aires, 1942), pp. 14–15; J. Lassaigne, *Toulouse-Lautrec* (Paris, 1945), pl. 11; T. Natanson, "Toulouse-Lautrec, the Man," *Art News Annual*, 1951, p. 79; F. Jourdain and J. Adhémar, *Toulouse-Lautrec* (Paris, 1952), p. 119, no. 36; J. Lassaigne, *Lautrec* (Geneva, 1953), p. 36; L. and E. Hanson, *The Tragic Life of Toulouse-Lautrec* (London, 1956), pp. 102, 142, 172; E. Julien, *Lautrec* (Paris, 1959), pp. 18, 86; *L'Opera completa di Toulouse-Lautrec* (Milan, 1969), no. 251; M. G. Dortu, *Toulouse-Lautrec et son oeuvre* (New York, 1971), vol. 2, no. P360; J. Milner, *The Studios of Paris: The Capital of Art in the Late Nineteenth Century* (New Haven and London, 1988), p. 44; G. Murray, *Toulouse-Lautrec: The Formative Years, 1878–1891* (Oxford), pp. 186, 189, 250; *The Letters of Henri de Toulouse-Lautrec*, ed. H. Schimmel (Oxford, 1991), pp. 128, 131, 134, 196.

# ÉDOUARD VUILLARD

## Young Woman in a Room

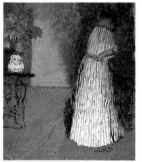

In dating this picture, it is useful to compare it with *Woman Reading* (fig. 1; private collection; C. Freches-Thory and A. Terrasse, *The Nabis: Bonnard, Vuillard, and Their Circle* [Paris, 1990], p. 80), which the artist himself dated 1893. This small composition against a gray door undoubtedly shows the same woman in a light blouse with blue stripes. There is also reason to link *Young Woman in a Room* with *The Dressmaker's Shop*, a decorative five-part screen made for Desmarais, also in 1893. The picture is closely related to the studies for *The Dressmaker's Shop*, particularly *The Dressmaking Studio, I* of about 1892 (fig. 3; private collection; G. Groom, *Édouard Vuillard, Painter-Decorator* [New Haven and London, 1993], p. 21).

Both here and in his studies for the screen, Vuillard played the decorative effect of a striped dress against the dull, generalized color of the interior. A well-known later example of such a technique is *Woman Sweeping* of about 1899 (fig. 4; The Phillips Collection, Washington, D.C.). In all these instances, Vuillard, like Pierre Bonnard, was inspired by Japanese woodcuts. Even at this early date, he disregarded the established rules for the distribution of light and shadow (he had felt the rigidity of those rules when he attended Jean-Léon Gérôme's class at the École des Beaux-Arts for a short time). The dark spot at the top right corner cannot, strictly speaking, be called shadow; it is there only to emphasize the white dress, so that the stripes will be more pronounced. Neither the female figure nor the flowerpot on the bookcase cast any shadow. Chiaroscuro hardly concerned the artist, who spoke only the language of color and arabesque. Such an arabesque will become, for instance, the bookcase, which is just hinted at with a few quick brushstrokes.

A decorator with an extremely well-trained eye,

Vuillard knew from the beginning that a plain striped design takes on expressiveness in combination with large, solid color planes. There are two such planes in this painting: the grayish door and the floor. To show the floor, Vuillard did not even have to employ paints and brushes: he just left the cardboard as it was, unpainted (no less than one-third of the whole space of the composition)—a trick that the Nabis, as well as Lautrec, used.

Vuillard must have seen examples of prints by Bunchō, a Japanese artist who worked in the 1760s and 1770s. Bunchō specialized in portraying actors, young girls, and courtesans. A work of his dedicated to a famous beauty and hostess from Edo, *The Courtesan Osen in a Striped Kimono* of about 1770, most probably caught Vuillard's eye. The unusual position of the young woman may also betray the influence of Japanese woodcuts.

The decorative project of the Nabi group is reflected most vividly in this small but beautifully painted picture by Vuillard, first of all in the fact that the artist is much more interested in the dress than in the woman herself. Vuillard turned to the motif at one time explored extensively by the Dutch (he could have had in mind the Louvre paintings by Gabriel Metsu; in his early journals, one comes across the name of Gerard Dou), but this motif is totally transformed under the influence of the Japanese and discoveries of the Impressionists. A younger contemporary of Claude Monet and Edgar Degas, he relinquished the static interiors of the Old Masters without a second thought.

Due to the slight irregularity of the stripes on the dress, their somewhat shimmering look, one gets the impression of a woman moving. Her dress suddenly brings to life a new decorative combination. She is not the mistress of this interior, though, and there is no story behind her appearance, which we almost always feel when looking at Dutch paintings of the seventeenth century.

Almost a quarter of a century before Vuillard's *Young Woman in a Room*, Monet in such pictures as the *Woman in the Garden* (The State Hermitage Museum, St. Petersburg) was already attracted not by the character or even the image of the lady, but instead by the color spot of her dress. Another example of Impressionist painting worth remembering in this context is Edgar Degas's *Woman with Chrysanthemums* of 1865 (The Metropolitan Museum of Art, New York; Lemoisne no. 125), where the model is upstaged by a bouquet. It is quite probable that Vuillard had seen the picture, which was still in France at the time. Of course, Vuillard's bouquet in this painting is not as glamorous and occupies a more modest position, but without it the painting would lack counterpoint: the flowerpot and the dress, crushed by the empty gray plane of the door, create the color chord of the composition.

The woman is probably the artist's older sister, Marie. Vuillard loved her, calling her Mimi and constantly painting her portrait between 1891 and 1893, before her marriage to his closest friend, Ker-Xavier Roussel. Although we cannot see the face of the model, we sense the shy demeanor so characteristic of Marie; compare, for example, *Girl by a Door* of 1891 (private collection, New York; E. W. Easton, *The Intimate Interiors of Edouard Vuillard* [Houston and Washington, D.C., 1989], p. 31, no. 12), or *Mother and Sister of the Artist* of about 1893 (fig. 2; The Museum of Modern Art, New York).

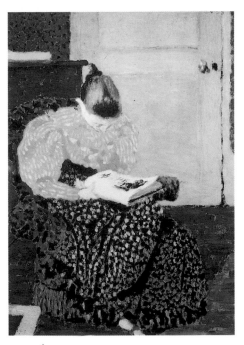

*Fig. 1. Édouard Vuillard.* Woman Reading. *1893. Private collection*

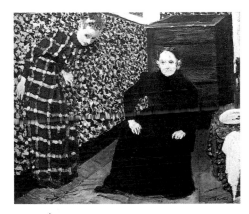

*Fig. 2. Édouard Vuillard.* Mother and Sister of the Artist. *c. 1893. The Museum of Modern Art, New York. Gift of Mrs. Saidie A. May*

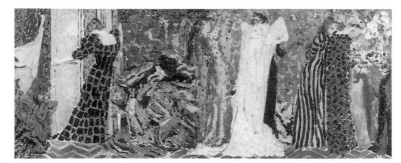

*Fig. 3. Édouard Vuillard.* The Dressmaking Studio, I. *c. 1892. Private collection*

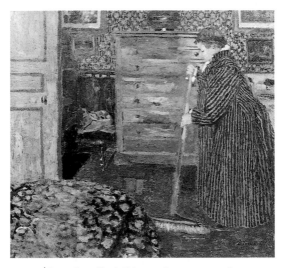

*Fig. 4. Édouard Vuillard.* Woman Sweeping. *c. 1899.*
*The Phillips Collection, Washington, D.C.*

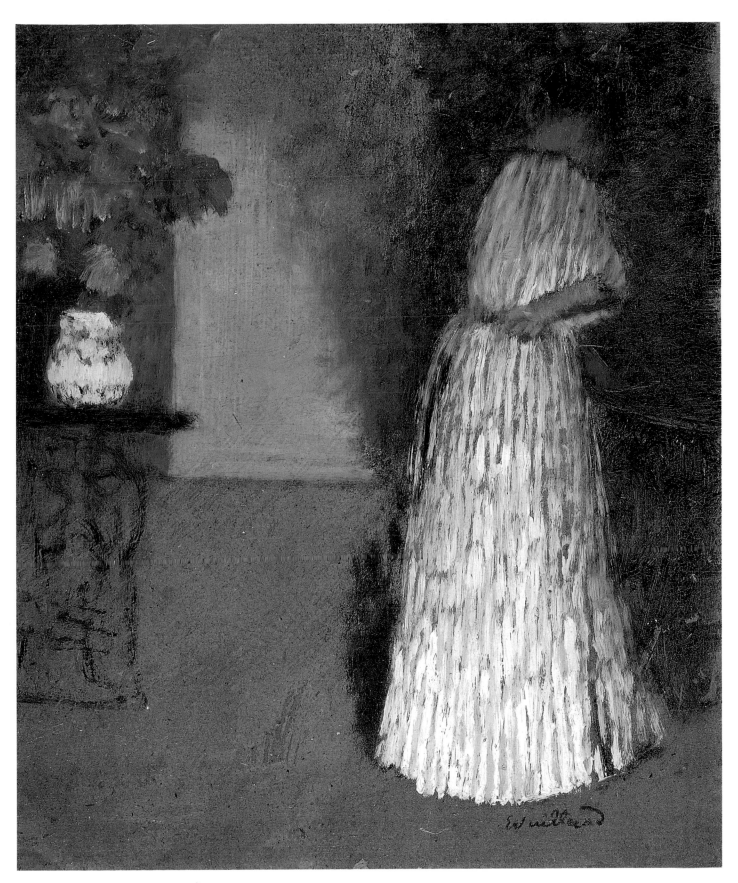

Èdouard Vuillard (1868, Cuiseaux, Saône-et-Loire–1940, La Baule)
## 64. YOUNG WOMAN IN A ROOM
*Jeune femme dans une chambre.* c. 1892–93
Oil on cardboard, 11⅝ × 9¼" (29.5 × 23.5 cm). Signed lower right: "E. Vuillard"
No. 3KP 539. Formerly collection Otto Krebs, Holzdorf

# ÉDOUARD VUILLARD

## OLD WOMAN IN AN INTERIOR

*Old Woman in an Interior* is an astonishing example of compositional mastery. At first glance, one might think that the artist has simply disregarded the principle of balance, filling the right side with details while leaving the left side practically empty. Nevertheless, Vuillard achieved a poised equilibrium in this painting comparable to the best interiors by masters such as Vermeer or Jean-Baptiste Chardin, whom he revered. Vuillard may have learned from the compositional scheme of such Vermeer paintings as *Girl Asleep at a Table* (The Metropolitan Museum of Art, New York), in which an intricately patterned carpet lies before the figure, while in the background various rectangles (pictures or a map on the wall, the door, and so on) create an almost mathematically calibrated structure. With Vuillard, a similar function is performed by the bookcase, the black frame, and the shelf on the wall. The patterned cloth tossed onto an armchair is as essential as the carpet is in the Vermeer picture. It softens the rigor of the rectangular construction and sets off the figure.

Vuillard's painting was created at the crossroads of different influences. The European tradition of the interior, in decline by the middle of the nineteenth century, here takes on new interest, in part because of the role played by Japanese prints. No doubt Vuillard knew the woodblock print by Ichiusai Kuniyoshi, *The Actor Nakamura Shikan* of 1834, which belonged to Maurice Denis. The pose of Vuillard's old woman, natural in itself, as if transcribed from reality, seems to demand another explanation after we study the Japanese master's depiction of the stooping actor.

The woman in the picture, though shown from the back (a technique characteristic of Vuillard), is easily recognizable: in the stylistically similar painting *Madame Vuillard by the Window* of 1893 (William Kelly Simpson collection, New York), the artist's mother wears the same dark gray robe. Vuillard was close to his mother, painted her more often than he did anyone else, and called her his muse. Marie-Justine-Alexandrine Michaud-Vuillard ran a dressmaking shop, and many of the artist's earlier works depict seamstresses. There are more indirect reminders of the craft in this picture: the woman is leaning down, perhaps about to pick up the cloth lying on top of the armchair; on the shelf are a basket and boxes of the kind that usually hold needle and thread. Here, as in many other instances, what Vuillard painted was not his mother's portrait but rather a scene of the everyday life around him, toward which he felt great affection. The woman is the mistress of this small, intimate world.

The picture on the wall is a reminder of another woman. As was usual with Vuillard, this detail serves several purposes. On the one hand, it breaks up the monotony of the wall and counterbalances the right side. On the other hand, it is a portrait of a particular person very dear to the artist. Despite the generality, even semi-abstractness of the image, a portrait can be deciphered. It is Vuillard's sister, Marie (see plate 64). The painting may have been done soon after she married and went to live separately from her mother and brother. At a later date, the artist and Madame Vuillard also moved. *Old Woman in an Interior* gives a sense of their new residence on the rue Saint-Honoré.

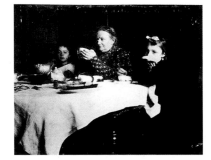

*Fig. 1. Photograph of Madame Vuillard with her grandchildren. 1897*

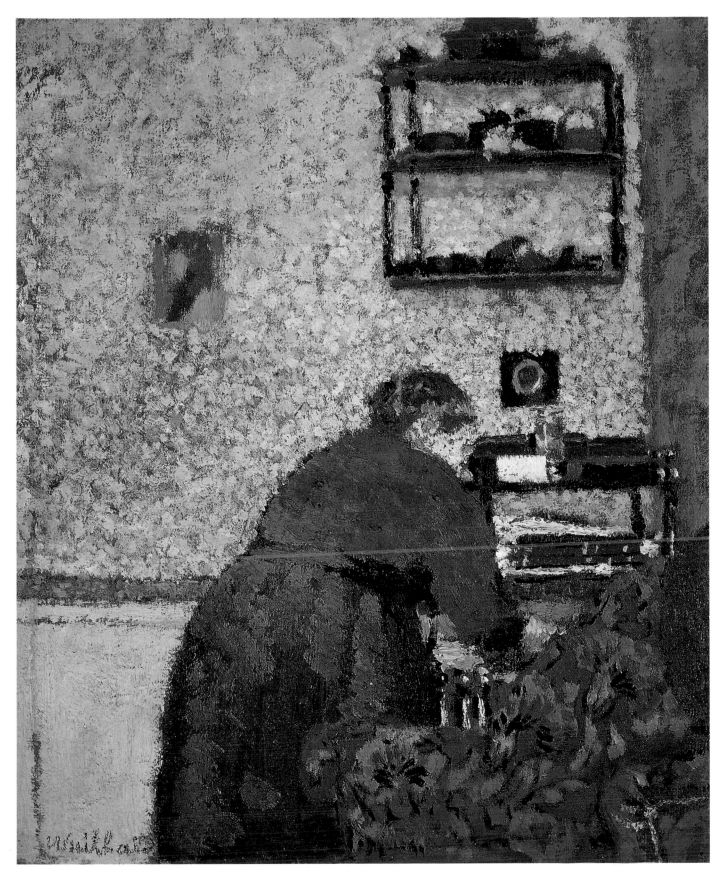

Édouard Vuillard
## 65. OLD WOMAN IN AN INTERIOR
*La Vieille femme dans un interieur.* c. 1893
Oil on cardboard, 10⅞ × 9" (27.5 × 22.8 cm). Signed lower left: "E. Vuillard"
No. 3KP 567. Formerly collection Otto Krebs, Holzdorf

# ÉDOUARD VUILLARD

## OLD WOMAN NEAR A MANTELPIECE

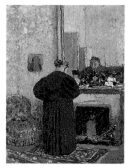

In his works of the early 1890s, Vuillard frequently painted his mother at home. Looking at these pictures, it is easy to think that the artist showed a new room each time; even when we see objects familiar from painting to painting, we cannot help but notice that they keep changing, and are always shown in a different setting. Despite such variations, Vuillard's interiors endlessly rehearse the same scenes. In this connection, it should be recalled that Vuillard loved the theater, as did the other Nabi artists. When his friend Aurélien Lugné-Poe founded the Théâtre de l'Oeuvre in 1893, he became very active in it, designing sets and programs. Moreover, like Pierre Bonnard or Roussel, he was histrionic in a more general sense as well, adopting a special attitude toward life and treating objects as theatrical props.

It may seem that the small interior reflects only the artist's home, but in fact, Vuillard is using its objects much as an ingenious stage designer does, to create settings for the actors to play in. To enliven these scenes, the objects are constantly varied: their proportions change, as well as their colors, ornamental patterns, and so on. It may seem that in such an interior the artist does not make anything up: after all, an armchair, a rug in front of the hearth, or a fireplace stoker much like those in this painting could be found in any middle-class home, and indeed, at the end of the nineteenth century no one could picture the everyday life of a Parisian family more accurately than could Vuillard. This authenticity is deceptive, however, for the surroundings have been created by the imagination, and not transcribed from life. We can see the way that Vuillard combined a sense of authenticity with imaginative variations by comparing *Old Woman near a Mantelpiece* with *Three Women in a Room with Rose-Colored Wallpaper* of 1895 (Josefowitz collection,

Lausanne; E. W. Easton, *The Intimate Interiors of Édouard Vuillard* [Washington, D.C., 1989], p. 54, no. 34), which also includes a three-panel screen, a red and green carpet, and an armchair. In the latter picture, each of these objects has been given a new coloring particular to the color scheme of a different composition. (Incidentally, the links to *Three Women in a Room* help corroborate the dating of the picture from the Krebs collection, to about 1895.)

The fireplace with a mirror plays an important part in this composition. It is almost identical to the one seen in the earlier picture *A Print Dress* of 1891 (Museu de Arte de São Paulo), where it is narrower, while the vertical ornaments of the mirror are wider. The main difference is that the fireplace is assigned only a decorative role in the earlier picture; it is part of the background. In the picture from the Krebs collection, the fireplace is much more prominent, supporting a mirror that is more important here than in other works of the same period. Pictorially, the mirror in *Old Woman near a Mantelpiece*, like the small picture on the left wall, repeats exactly the format of the painting as a whole. The rectangle of the mirror inside the rectangular composition opens another space, not unlike another picture, all the more so because it has a picture frame. This picture inside a picture offers another portrait of the old woman. The artist's playing with space and geometric forms in this way is seen throughout the painting: the tall background is inconsistent with the foreground, while further rectangles (the door, the screen) clash with the shape of the figure. The screen that you notice above—very common in nineties homes and something to which Vuillard, Bonnard, and Maurice Denis were obviously partial (the Nabis often designed screens)—in its utter geometric simplicity helps to define the composition.

Vuillard often used a mirror in his early days as an artist, in working on self-portraits. From the beginning, it was not just a mechanical tool that helped fix his features in a picture; it was a fascinating object in itself, almost magical, capable not only of reflecting but also of creating an image. In his self-portraits in 1888–91, Vuillard made it explicit that the image was created with the help of a mirror, introducing a part of the mirror into the composition, as in *Self-Portrait in a Mirror* of 1888–90 (Wasserman collection, Beverly Hills) and *Self-Portrait* of about 1891 (fig. 2; private collection, Switzerland).

On the wall to the left in the Krebs work is a small painting, which balances the mirror. The painting is so generalized as to seem more a spot of color than a picture. Nevertheless, the red beard allows us to identify it as a portrait of the artist. At a time when Vuillard was using a mirror to paint self-portraits, he placed a portrait of himself near the mirror in this picture, adding an element of play to the composition. The self-portrait is not without a touch of caricature: Vuillard's beard was actually shorter than this at the time. Moreover, a different turn of the head would be more characteristic of a conventional self-portrait. The painting of the son is arranged so that he is looking at the mother. At the same time, the mother is looking in the mirror; we, the viewers, can see her face in the reflection but try in vain to catch her eyes.

Not long before the picture was painted, Gustave Geffroy wrote that Vuillard was "an intimist with a delicious temperament, who knows how to combine the sad and the comical, doling them out with ease and making color shine and light magically flare up" (G. Geffroy, "Troisième Exposition d'un groupe de peintres impressionistes et symbolistes, chez le Barc de Boutteville," *La Vie artistique* [Paris, 1893]).

Unfortunately, part of the lower left corner of the painting is missing.

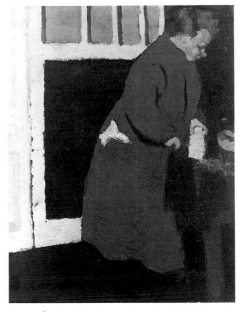

Fig. 1. *Édouard Vuillard.* Woman Cutting Bread. *1892. Private collection*

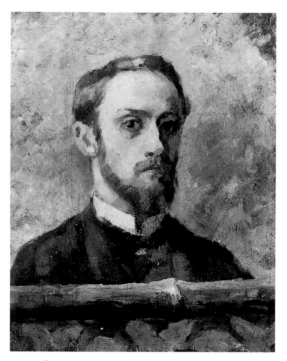

Fig. 2. *Édouard Vuillard. Self-Portrait. c. 1891. Private collection, Switzerland*

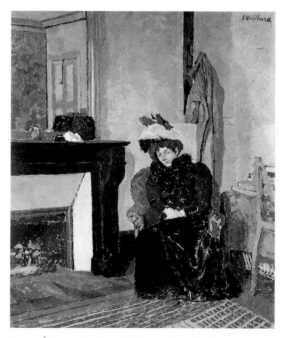

Fig. 3. *Édouard Vuillard.* Waiting (The Visit). *1900. Stiftung E. G. Bührle, Zurich*

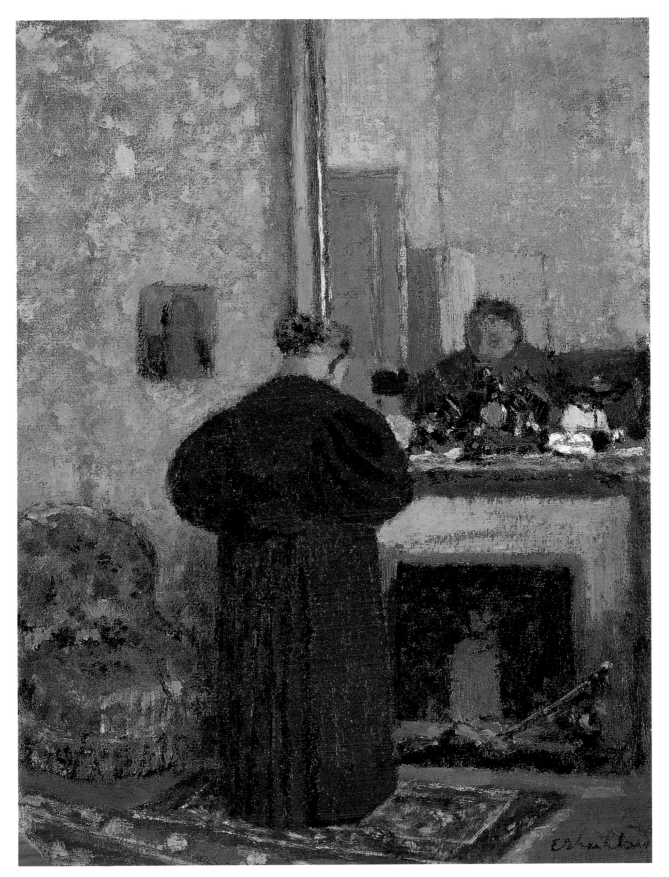

Édouard Vuillard
## 66. OLD WOMAN NEAR A MANTELPIECE
*La Vieille Femme près de la cheminée.* c. 1895
Oil on cardboard, 11⅝ × 9¼" (29.5 × 23.5 cm)
Signed lower right: "E. Vuillard." No. 3KP 540. Formerly collection Otto Krebs, Holzdorf

# PABLO PICASSO

## ABSINTHE (GIRL IN A CAFÉ)

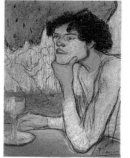

*Absinthe* is one of the best of the works that the young Picasso created on the border between painting and drawing. It is closely related to other pictures made in Paris in 1901, the most famous of which is *The Absinthe Drinker (L'Apéritif)* (fig. 1; The State Hermitage Museum, St. Petersburg).

The forerunners of the series were the sketches made by the young artist in a café in Barcelona in 1897–99. Even then, he may have known through reproductions the pictures by French painters showing café habitués. The works of Édouard Manet, Edgar Degas, and Henri de Toulouse-Lautrec were discussed often in the café Els Quatre Gats, where members of the Barcelona avant-garde gathered.

When Picasso arrived in Paris, the initial period of his work there showed acquaintance in particular with Lautrec, although one must not overestimate the influence. Lautrec, to a greater extent than Manet and Degas, focused not on the café itself but on the sole personage, by depicting a lone woman in *The Morning After* of 1889 (Fogg Art Museum, Cambridge, Massachusetts; pastel, Musée Toulouse-Lautrec, Albi).

Picasso's earliest composition in his Absinthe series (fig. 2; Jaffe collection, New York; Zervos I, no. 62) re-creates the situation of Lautrec's *The Morning After*. Like the earlier picture, it shows the profile of a woman at a table, but Picasso has added several narrative elements: the woman is sitting by a window, about to down a glass of the green liquid, while outside in the darkening evening, people are walking in slightly opalescent snow. Such details are consistent with the tenets of realist painting of the late nineteenth century, yet at the same time, the picture shows an expressive use of color that advances from the methods of Lautrec and takes the artist in a new direction of his own. The features of the crooked-nosed

woman are sharp and her bony fingers are drawn like the talons of a bird of prey, but her condition is perhaps most effectively conveyed by the intense colors of the picture: the red shawl and overly rouged lips are on fire. Even the window on the opposite side of the street is orange. The one soothing color—the green spot of absinthe—suggests only an illusory solace.

Picasso showed the Jaffe picture in his first exhibition at the Ambroise Vollard gallery in June and July 1901. Evidently, immediately afterward he started a new composition, *Absinthe (Girl in a Café)* from the Krebs collection. In the new work, he again divided the composition into two planes, but instead of a street outside he now showed dancing couples in an interior. Their indefinite forms in the yellow electric light may be no more than the lone woman's dream of the joys of life. At this time, the artist became fascinated by the theme of dance, sometimes as a sketch of a cabaret performance, and sometimes as a symbolic scene, such as *Little Girls Dancing* of 1901 (private collection, Paris; Daix/Boudaille no. V-15).

Dance is also the theme of one of Picasso's most unusual compositions of that time, *French Cancan* of 1901 (Barbey collection, Geneva; Daix/Boudaille no. V-55). Probably it was a variation of this picture that once appeared on the verso of the Hermitage *Absinthe Drinker* and was almost completely obliterated by the artist; just one of the dancers' heads remains. When comparing all these pictures, we can assume that *Absinthe* from the Krebs collection and *French Cancan* were made at the same time, perhaps one immediately after the other. It might not be accidental that the woman in the Krebs picture and the dancer in the front row of *French Cancan* look alike.

The agitation characteristic of the earlier work is

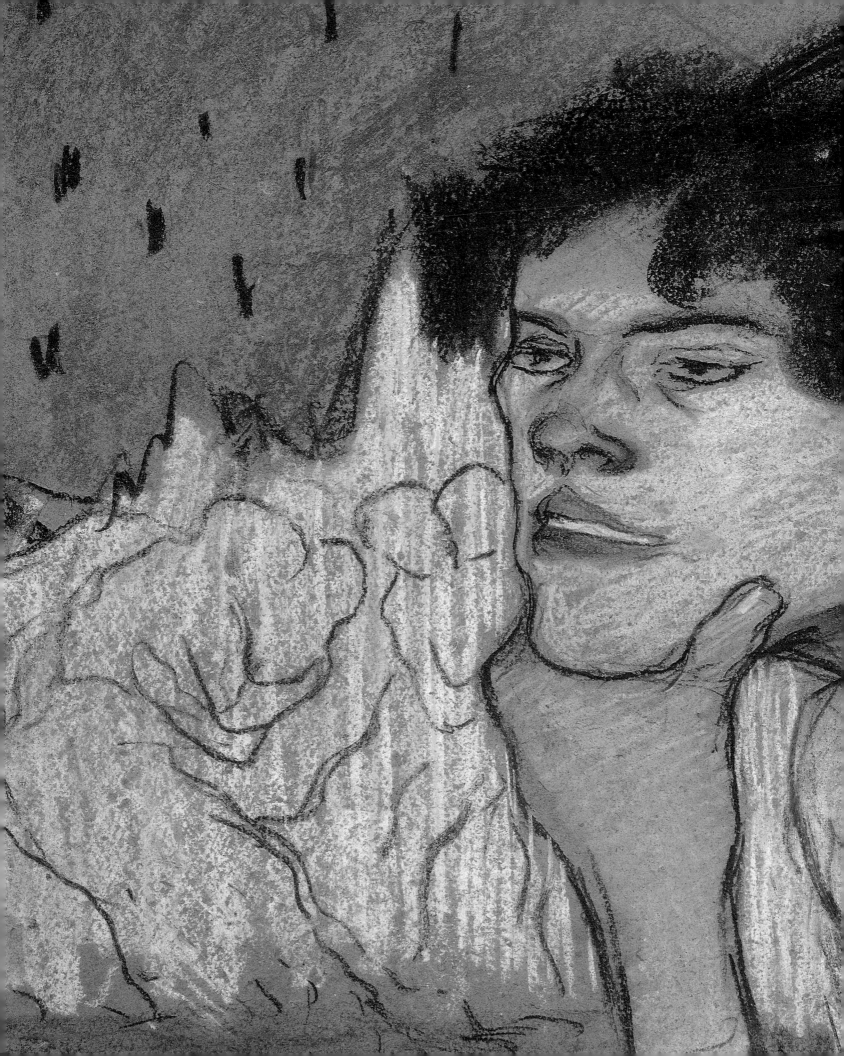

now gone. The principal feature has become not the nervous brushstroke but the smooth contour. And where earlier the key detail had been the hand over the glass of absinthe, now this hand is lying on the table. The other hand has also changed position: before, it was near the ear, as the woman perhaps tried to follow the words of a companion we cannot see; now, there is not even a hint at anyone else's presence. The woman in *Absinthe* is totally immersed in her thoughts, as suggested by the gesture of her fingers at her chin. Picasso did not discover this gesture at once; his revisions are there to be seen in the picture.

It is probable that the third picture, after the Krebs work, was the Hermitage *Absinthe Drinker*. Here, Picasso actively employs deformation: the fingers of the right hand of the drinker seem to grow before our eyes, clutching the shoulder. The isolation of the figure is emphasized: behind her is the wall, in front a table with alcohol—she is hemmed in on all sides, cornered, both literally and figuratively. The café itself appears cheaper, lower in class; there is no curtain, and no one is dancing. The dirty red of the walls establishes the atmosphere of a cheap drinking place and creates a joyless background, emphasizing the hopelessness of the woman's life.

The fourth Absinthe work, also called *Girl with Arms Crossed,* of 1901 (Charles Obersteg collection, Geneva; Zervos I, no. 100), preserves the background of *The Absinthe Drinker* from the Hermitage, as well as the looks of the woman. The principal change is in the new, somewhat defensive gesture.

Comparing all the variations, we can see that there are three types of women here, and knowing Picasso's ways of working, especially when he was young, it is easy to imagine that their prototypes were actual persons. However, no Picasso scholar has been able to offer concrete proof of this. The last absinthe drinker made a deeper impression on Picasso's work: we see her in *Woman with a Chignon* of 1901 (Fogg Art Museum, Harvard University, Cambridge, Massachusetts; Zervos I, no. 96) and in *Woman with a Cigarette* of 1901 (The Barnes Foundation, Merion, Pennsylvania; Zervos I, no. 99). Typically, she stoops and clutches one hand with the other.

Her predecessor in the picture from the Krebs collection (undoubtedly a portrait) remains a mystery. Picasso cast his models like actresses, auditioning first one, then another, then a third in a certain role. Each brings her own persona to the part and makes her own contribution to the image. All the auditions turned out well, but the last apparently satisfied the artist most.

LITERATURE: A. Cirici-Pellicer, *Picasso antes de Picasso* (Barcelona, 1946), no. 172; C. Zervos, *Pablo Picasso* (Paris, 1957), vol. 1, no. 81; A. Blunt and Ph. Pool, *Picasso: The Formative Years* (London, 1962), no. 19; P. Daix and G. Boudaille, *Picasso: The Blue and the Rose Periods—A Catalogue Raisonné of the Paintings, 1900–1906* (New York, 1967), no. V-73 (mistakenly indicated as Krenz collection); A. Kostenevich, *Western European Painting in the Hermitage: Nineteenth and Twentieth Centuries* (Leningrad, 1986), p. 350.

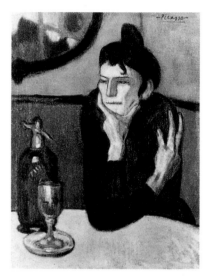

*Fig. 1. Pablo Picasso.* The Absinthe Drinker (L'Apéritif). *1901. The State Hermitage Museum, St. Petersburg*

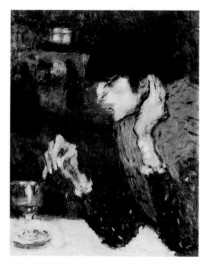

*Fig. 2. Pablo Picasso.* The Absinthe Drinker. *1901. Jaffe collection, New York*

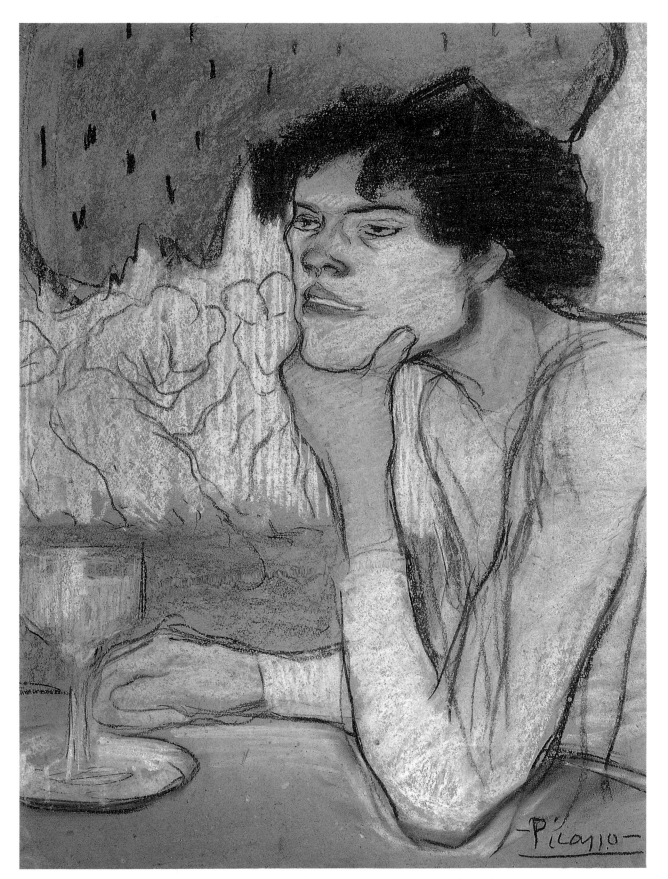

Pablo Picasso (1881, Málaga, Spain–1973, Mougins, France)
## 67. ABSINTHE (GIRL IN A CAFÉ)
*L'Absinthe.* 1901
Charcoal, colored chalk, gouache, and white chalk on paper, 25⅝ × 19½" (65.2 × 49.6 cm)
Signed lower right: "Picasso." No. GR 155–96. Formerly collection Otto Krebs, Holzdorf

# ALBERT MARQUET

## AVENUE IN THE LUXEMBOURG GARDENS

Albert Marquet worked in the Luxembourg Gardens as early as 1898, when he painted one of the garden avenues (F. Fosca, *Albert Marquet* [Paris, 1922], p. 16; see fig. 1). He went there most often in 1901–2, making the works called *The Luxembourg Gardens* of about 1902 now in the Musée des Beaux-Arts, Bordeaux (fig. 2), and the Von der Heydt-Museum, Wuppertal. In all the pictures painted there, his love of open space is manifest. The artist showed a wide square before the palace, a path running off.

His close friend Henri Matisse was working in the Luxembourg Gardens at the same time. If we compare Marquet's pictures with Matisse's *The Luxembourg Gardens* of about 1902 (The State Hermitage Museum, St. Petersburg), we can see that although the two started from similar positions, they grew further apart as their works developed. Matisse also depicts the avenue in the early morning light, but, responding to Paul Gauguin's work, he deals with large color areas already bespeaking his future bold simplifications. Marquet gives more attention to detail; it is remarkable how he discriminates among various shades of green in the foliage while the sun is only just rising over the horizon.

Marquet exhibited three pictures of the Luxembourg Gardens in the Salon des Indépendants in 1901. It is entirely possible that the landscape entitled *L'Allée du Luxembourg* in that exhibition's catalogue is in fact this painting, but one cannot say this with certainty since the catalogue does not indicate size or give other data on the work shown.

EXHIBITIONS: 1901, Paris, Salon des Indépendants, no. 645 (?).

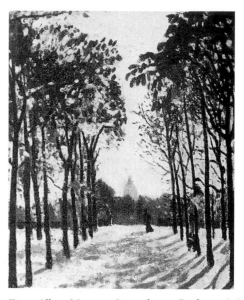

Fig. 1. *Albert Marquet. Luxembourg Gardens. 1898. Whereabouts unknown*

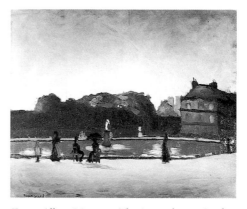

Fig. 2. *Albert Marquet. The Luxembourg Gardens. 1902. Musée des Beaux-Arts, Bordeaux*

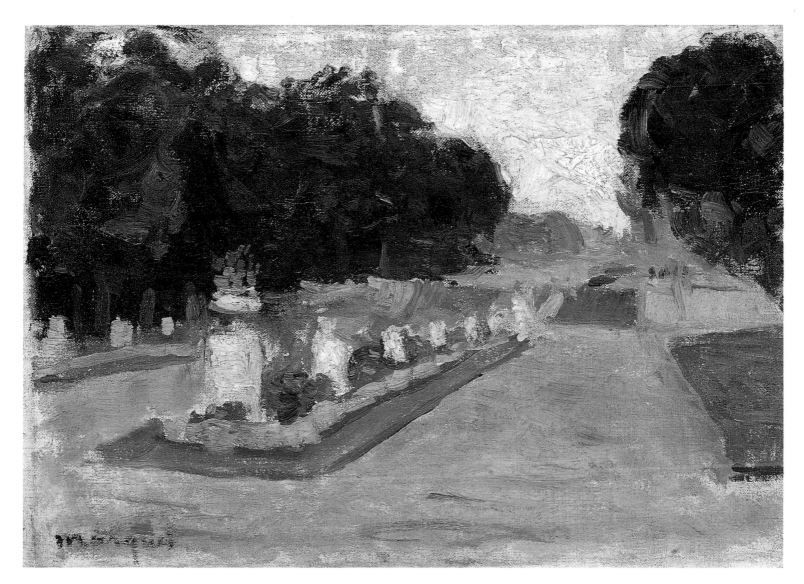

Albert Marquet (1875, Bordeaux–1947, Paris)
## 68. AVENUE IN THE LUXEMBOURG GARDENS
*L'Allée du Luxembourg.* 1901
Oil on canvas, 10 × 14" (25.5 × 35.5 cm)
Signed lower left: "a. marquet"
No. 3KP 541. Formerly collection Otto Krebs, Holzdorf

# ALBERT MARQUET

## QUAI DU LOUVRE, SUMMER

The quais along the Seine in the center of Paris are a favorite subject in Albert Marquet's work before and during the Fauvist years. Marquet's relationship with Fauvism never supposed absolute submission to its principles: like Henri Matisse and André Derain, he was for brightness of color and for simplification, but he remained more closely tied to nature than they. Similarly, while following in the steps of Camille Pissarro, Marquet dramatically revised the older artist's methods; comparing Pissarro's *Quai Malaquais, Sunny Afternoon* (plate 45) with the present work, Marquet's *Quai du Louvre, Summer,* painted not three years later, it is clear what he took from his predecessor and what he relinquished. Without the discoveries made by the Impressionists in depicting light, Marquet could not have painted his sunbathed landscape. At the same time, however, the dappled foliage, the shimmering atmosphere, and the sense of movement in the work of Pissarro, Claude Monet, and Alfred Sisley were foreign to this artist of the next generation. Neither the omnibus nor the pedestrians move in Marquet's picture: they are magically still. Nor does the diagonal of the quai have a dynamic function here, as it does with Pissarro; instead, it serves as the vehicle of a lucid calm.

Marquet's city is sparsely populated, though the Quai du Louvre was one of the busiest thoroughfares, even then. Like *Avenue in the Luxembourg Gardens* (plate 68), this picture reminds us that Marquet rose early and particularly valued early morning light. The long, greenish blue shadows of the Louvre and of the few pedestrians and the omnibus show that the sun had just risen. The shadows, the brilliant sidewalk, the rich green trees absorbing the warm light of a cloudless sky at the end of summer—this harmonious ensemble gives us the special poetry of Paris.

Marquet's first solo exhibition opened in February 1907 at the Galerie Druet. Most of the twenty-three pictures were of Paris. It is possible that *Quai du Louvre, Summer* from the Sachse collection was among them. Fosca recounts that Marquet was gaining popularity at this time and was known as "the one who paints the Seine from his balcony" (F. Fosca, *Albert Marquet* [Paris, 1922], p. 4). Unlike most of the views of the Seine actually painted from the window of his studio, first on the Quai de la Tournelle, then the Quai des Grands-Augustins, this one was done from a different viewpoint. The artist went to the opposite bank of the river, placing himself so that the mass of the Louvre would anchor the composition on the right, while a large chestnut tree in the foreground flanked the landscape on the left. He painted the row of the buildings on the Left Bank as a generalized, purplish gray line; it firmly defines a horizon enlivened by the silhouette of the Eiffel Tower and the dome of the Invalides. The glittering mass of the Seine in the center reflects the sky of Paris in all its astonishing transparency. Carefully balancing these elements in the picture, Marquet maintains a stable, solid composition even as he shows a sweeping expanse of space from an elevated vantage point.

PROVENANCE: Galerie Druet, Paris; Monica Sachse, Berlin.

EXHIBITIONS: 1907, Paris, "Albert Marquet," Galerie Druet (?).

LITERATURE: N. Lenyashina, *Albert Marquet* (Leningrad, 1975), no. 132.

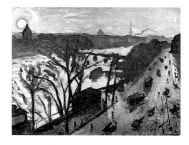

Fig. 1. Albert Marquet. Quai du Louvre. 1905. *Fridart Foundation, London*

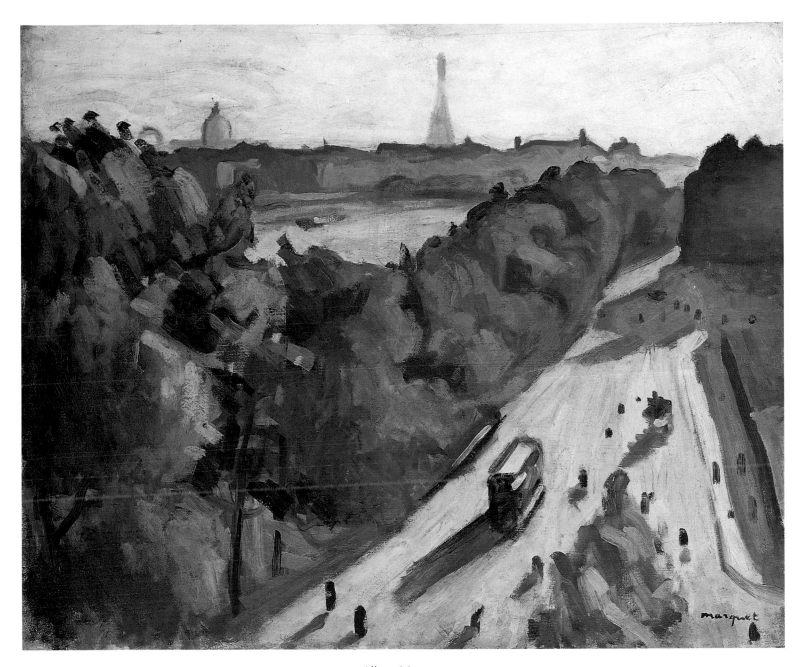

Albert Marquet

## 69. QUAI DU LOUVRE, SUMMER

*Quai du Louvre, été.* c. 1906

Oil on canvas, 19⅝ × 24" (50 × 61 cm)

Signed bottom right: "marquet"

No. 3K 1392. Formerly collection Monica Sachse, Berlin

# ALBERT MARQUET

## LANDSCAPE WITH A BRIDGE

Dating the picture is rather difficult. Stylistically, the canvas belongs with Marquet's work of the late 1910s.

Before, Marquet had painted either scenes of Paris or European seaports. The outbreak of World War I found him in Rotterdam. He came back to France in an attempt, together with Henri Matisse, to enlist in the army and turned for help to Marcel Sembat, their friend who became a government minister. However, Sembat advised them to "continue to paint; no one can replace you in that field" (see M. Marquet, *Marquet* [Paris, 1951]). Marquet went to the south, working in Collioure (1914), Marseilles and Nice (1915), and L'Estaque (1916–18). *Landscape with a Bridge* was not painted in the south, however, but in the Île de France. In this picture, the light particular to that region is conveyed with rare simplicity and expressiveness. In the summer, Marquet would return to Paris, but most of his paintings were landscapes done outside the city. Wrote his wife, Marcelle Marquet, "He spent the summer on the banks of the Marne or the Seine, in Poissy, Villene, Chennevière, La Varenne Sainte-Hilaire, Samois, Herblay, renting a small house or living in a hotel to be near the water" (Marquet, ibid.).

The subject of the present painting and its treatment of the trees and the sky link it to several landscapes titled *Samois* and executed there in 1917 (formerly Marcelle Marquet collection, Paris; private collection, Paris; Musée des Beaux-Arts, Bordeaux) as well as to the canvases painted two years later in and around Herblay, a small town not far from Paris, such as two works called *The Seine at Herblay* of 1919 (fig. 1, Musée des Beaux-Arts, Bordeaux; fig. 2, private collection).

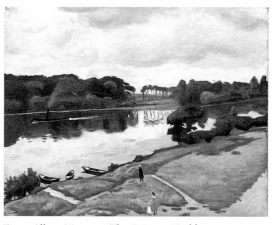

*Fig. 1. Albert Marquet. The Seine at Herblay. 1919. Musée des Beaux-Arts, Bordeaux*

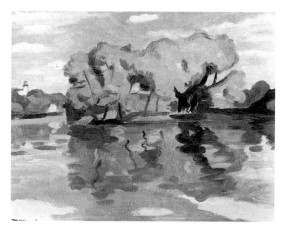

*Fig. 2. Albert Marquet. The Seine at Herblay. 1919. Private collection*

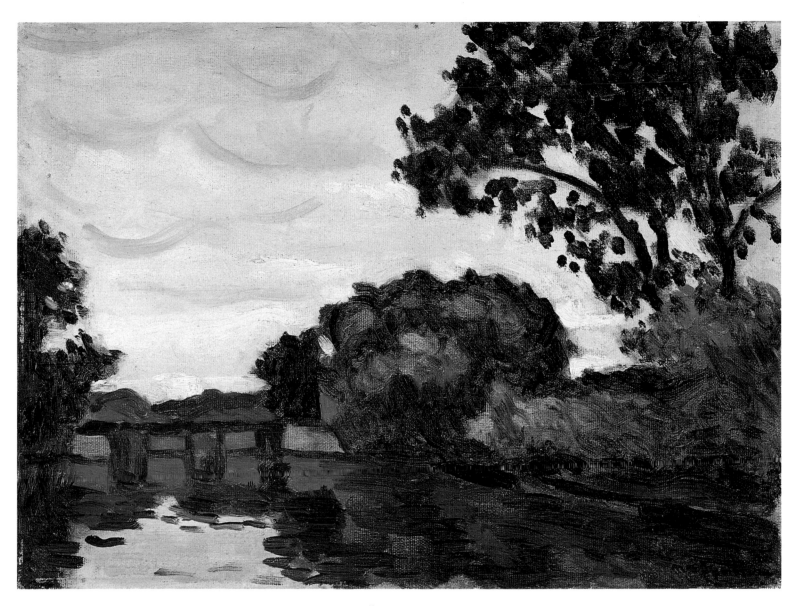

Albert Marquet
## 70. LANDSCAPE WITH A BRIDGE
*Paysage au pont.* c. 1917–19
Oil on canvas mounted on cardboard, 9⅜ × 12¾" (23.9 × 32.5 cm)
Signed lower right: "marquet." No. 3KP 543. Formerly collection Otto Krebs, Holzdorf

# GEORGES ROUAULT

## NUDE WITH RAISED ARM

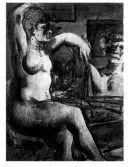

This work is from the series Filles. The first work in the series available to us, *Four Girls on a Beach (Prostitutes)* (Hahnloser collection, Winterthur), is dated 1903. Subsequently, over the course of several years, Rouault made dozens of compositions with prostitutes, such as the well-known one in the Hermitage (fig. 3).

In the winter of 1903, Rouault joined Albert Marquet and his other former classmates from Gustave Moreau's studio, who were now renting a studio on the boulevard de Clichy. From the window, Rouault could see prostitutes on the sidewalk, freezing in the cold, and had the idea of inviting them in to pose (the services of professional models were more expensive). The atmosphere of the studio is a part of the pictures he made: in one of the later watercolors, *Nude (Study)* of 1906 (Dorival/Rouault no. 182), we can see an artist at his easel in the background (said to be Marquet), while in several works there is a stove, a common studio accessory. Despite the studio trappings, however, Rouault was not one who in depicting these nudes could forget the true profession of the models. When he discovered this subject, which became one of the most important in his work, he quickly realized that the canons of the École des Beaux-Arts, where he had been one of the best students, no longer applied.

Édouard Manet and Henri de Toulouse-Lautrec were his principal predecessors in treating this subject. In the early twentieth century, forty years after the scandal of Manet's *Olympia*, paintings of prostitutes could still be expected to receive a cautious reception. As a counterpoint to Manet's *Olympia* and *Nana* and to the merciless bordello paintings and drawings made by Toulouse-Lautrec, a new, elegant way of showing women of ill repute was introduced; Léandre, Faivre, Truchet, and a few other successful painters produced risqué canvases of the Belle Époque. There is no doubt that the grotesque acuteness with which Rouault painted his *filles de joie* derived from his dislike for that kind of production, widely available in picture books and other printed media. Perhaps only Edgar Degas was as uncompromising as Rouault, in his monotypes devoted to whorehouses (see fig. 1). They were not exhibited in public in Degas's lifetime, however, and it is hardly possible that Rouault was aware of them. Nonetheless, the similarity between these works by Degas and Rouault's watercolors is striking.

When Rouault began to show his Filles at exhibitions, critics immediately compared him with Toulouse-Lautrec. Such parallels were for the most part superficial and never touched on the symbolic and pathetic aspects that the subject took on with Rouault. In this respect, the words of the artist himself in his letter to his friend André Suarès are of great interest:

*Things have taken a curious and unexpected turn concerning me. People I did not know say (though I never asked them to): "This is more powerful than Lautrec." Now I, who have never been a critic, will try to be one. There is no question about one being stronger or weaker; you know, I am just in another sphere. . . . Lautrec in his own element is stronger than me. With my clowns and circus girls I intrude upon the realm of poetry (have pride enough to claim it). He remains a very artful creator of posters and a realist painter but, I dare say, is not as original a pioneer in form and color as they claimed him to be, and he belongs to a certain era. He seems to be an extravagant realist; I a fantasizer of form and color.* (letter of September 30, 1917, in B. Dorival and I. Rouault, *Rouault: L'Oeuvre peint* [Monte Carlo, 1988], p. 111)

In essence, Lautrec was painting portraits, as in his

*Woman with an Umbrella* (plate 63), while Rouault was creating symbols. In this sense, Rouault's nudes are perhaps more truly comparable to the bathers painted by Paul Cézanne, a master whose work he admired. The difference, of course, is that Cézanne's bathers are plastic symbols in a severely constructed visual world. The artist from Aix sometimes seemed to treat his nudes as if they were apples or rocks or trees, as objects of prolonged observation. *Nude with Raised Arm,* like Rouault's other images, is full of portent. Incapable of movement, the body is ominously weighty. As with Cézanne's nudes, it can evoke the solidity of stones and rocks. Rouault chose to explore its reality, however harsh, to the depths. He conducted his unblinking observation not only with a sense of what may be repellent in human experience but also with a genuine sympathy that led him to find beauty in the most unlikely places. "Every moment I discover new beauty, and what unknown and wonderful beauty there is in the thick of the lowliest and most tragic things, transformed by genius" (*Georges Rouault, André Suarès: Correspondance* [Paris, 1960], p. 3). These words, which the artist wrote about Fyodor Dostoyevsky's novels, apply with no less accuracy to his own work.

Although themes related to prostitution have been common enough in art since ancient times, they left very little imprint on Rouault's work. Instead, literary sources had more to say to him: the Goncourt broth-ers, Guy de Maupassant, Joris-Karl Huysmans—Rouault read them intelligently and with great care. He did not try to illustrate their prose, but neither could he help comparing his heroines with the Goncourts' Elise or Huysmans's Marthe. Of course, he remembered Véronique from Léon Bloy's novel *Le Désesperé* only too well. Bloy, whom Rouault deeply admired in the early years of the twentieth century, was associated with Rouault's principal work exhibited at the famous Salon d'Automne of 1905, the triptych *Girls.* The central part presents Monsieur and Madame Poulot (inspired by Bloy's novel *The Poor Woman*), a former prostitute and her good-for-nothing husband. Madame Poulot could be a sister to the figure in *Nude with Raised Arm,* they are so much alike.

Rouault explored the motif of a nude in front of a mirror quite often in 1905–6—eight times. The largest and most significant of the pictures in this group are two watercolors: this one from the Krebs collection and one in the Musée National d'Art Moderne, Centre Georges Pompidou, Paris (fig. 2; Dorival/Rouault no. 189). In the Paris watercolor, the woman is also shown seated, in profile, and with arm raised, but she is looking in the opposite direction. She is wearing black stockings—a hint at her occupation, though the sheet is entitled simply *Girl at a Mirror,* while the Krebs watercolor has the even more general title *Nude with Raised Arm.* (Incidentally, in 1905 Rouault had painted

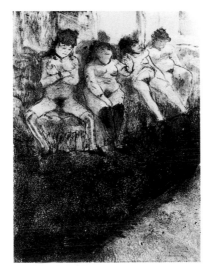

Fig. 1. Edgar Degas. Waiting. 1879.
Musée Picasso, Paris

the same figure, minus the mirror, in two watercolors bearing the title *Girl* [Dorival/Rouault nos. 219, 220]; the second of the two girls is particularly noteworthy, having the same face as the one in the Krebs picture.) In the Paris composition, the woman's posture is freer; she leans back, and behind her there is a sofa. In *Nude with Raised Arm,* the gap between the figure and the edge of the picture has been eliminated; the woman is sitting up straight, giving her a certain assertiveness.

Rouault's attitude toward these women was not simple, though rooted in deep and sincere Christian beliefs: the "fallen" woman portrayed as a victim of modern society was to him at the same time the living embodiment of Eve's fall. His complex, conflicted feelings found expression in oppressive shades of blue, a grotesque generality of forms, and a lack of "aesthetic distance" from the subject.

Originally, the sheet was a little larger. In mounting it on cardboard, the paper was folded over on all sides.

LITERATURE: P. Fierens, "Georges Rouault," in *Histoire de l'art contemporain: La Peinture—Publié sous la direction de R. Huygh et G. Bazin* (Paris, 1935), p. 137 (reprod.); P. Courthion, *Georges Rouault* (New York, 1962), no. 31, p. 410; B. Dorival and I. Rouault, *Rouault: L'Oeuvre peint* (Monte Carlo, 1988), no. 185.

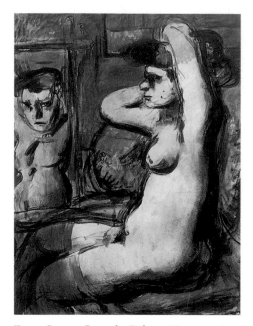

Fig. 2. *Georges Rouault. Girl at a Mirror. 1906. Musée National d'Art Moderne, Centre Georges Pompidou, Paris*

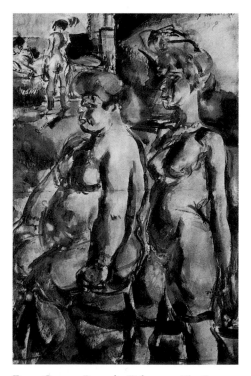

Fig. 3. *Georges Rouault. Girls. 1907. The State Hermitage Museum, St. Petersburg*

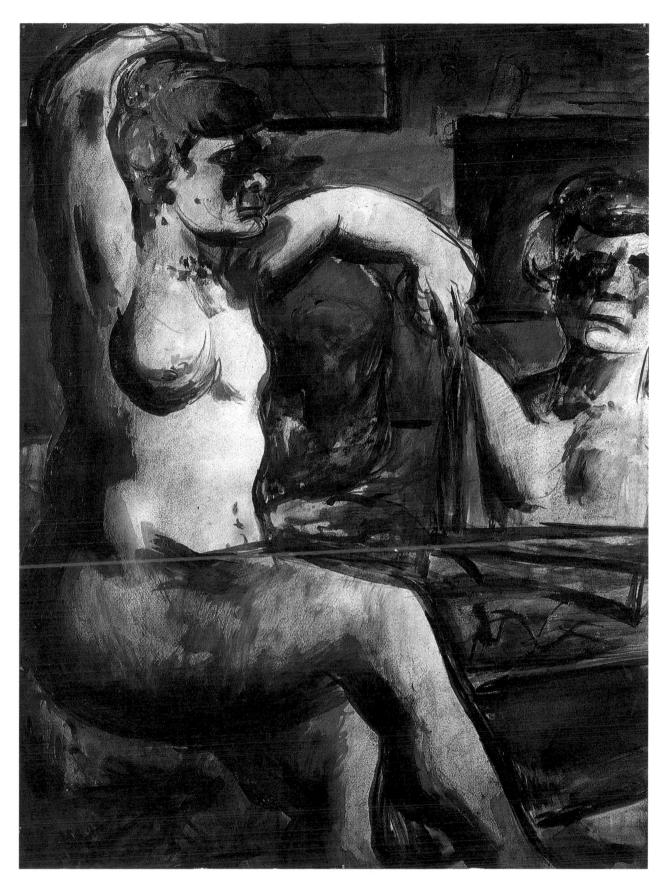

Georges Rouault (1871, Paris–1958, Paris)
## 71. NUDE WITH RAISED ARM
*Nue au bras levé.* 1906
Watercolor, gouache, whitewash, and colored chalk on paper mounted on cardboard,
27¾ × 20⅞" (70.4 × 53.2 cm) (slightly cut down after mounting on cardboard)
Signed and dated upper right: "GR 1906." No. GR 155–94. Formerly collection Otto Krebs, Holzdorf

# ANDRÉ DERAIN

## PATH IN A PARK WITH A FIGURE

The theme of a landscape with a path and a figure appears even in the years of André Derain's Fauvism, as in *Hyde Park* of 1906 (Musée Pierre Lévy, Troyes). Soon after this, under the influence of the Cubism of Pablo Picasso, Derain renounced brilliant colors in favor of earthen, almost monochromatic tones. Pictures made somewhat later, around 1911–13, reflect a new movement toward simplification, even naïveté. He learned about poetic naïveté from the paintings of Henri Rousseau, whom he was among the first to appreciate. Rousseau was known to paint garden avenues with figures, as in *The Luxembourg Gardens: The Chopin Monument* of 1909 (The State Hermitage Museum, St. Petersburg). Derain was interested not only in modern *primitifs* like Rousseau but also in historical examples from the Middle Ages and the early Renaissance. This is evident in his large picture *The Bagpiper* of about 1910–11 (The Minneapolis Institute of Arts), with its generalized primary volumes. Utterly simple, almost resembling children's drawings, the houses, the lone tree like a lollipop, and the winding road are all there.

The tiny *Path in a Park with a Figure*, similar in atmosphere, differs in style. Unlike *The Bagpiper*, with its monumental, locked-in forms, a cursory manner dominates this miniature; at first glance, it can easily be mistaken for a study from nature. However, Derain made such pictures not in the open air but in the studio. The drawn border added by the artist serves as a reminder of this.

When dating the picture, it is useful to compare it with *Hunter in Camiers* and *Landscape in Camiers*, both of 1911 (M. Kellermann, *André Derain* [Paris, 1992], nos. 201, 202, the latter in a private collection, Switzerland), which are stylistically close to *Path in a Park with a Figure*. One should also take into account some landscapes painted in 1912 in the valley of the

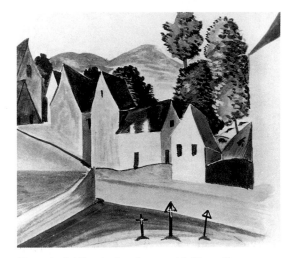

Fig. 1. André Derain. Landscape with Three Crosses. 1912. Private collection

Lot, near Cahors, such as *Le Lot* (formerly Flechtheim gallery, Berlin). Also to be noted is *Landscape with Three Crosses*, a gouache of 1912 (fig. 1; private collection) that once belonged to Guillaume Apollinaire.

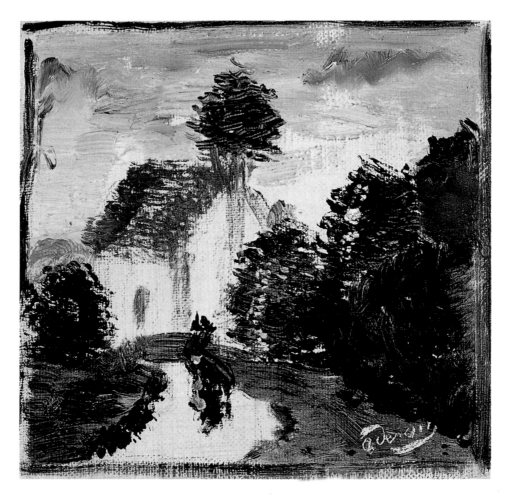

André Derain (1880, Chatou, Seine-et-Oise–1954, Garches, Seine-et-Oise)

## 72. PATH IN A PARK WITH A FIGURE

*La Route dans un parc avec un personnage.* c. 1911–13

Oil on canvas, 4⅞ × 4⅞" (12.5 × 12.5 cm)

Signed lower right: "a. derain"

No. 3KP 544. Formerly collection Otto Krebs, Holzdorf

# ANDRÉ DERAIN

## The Road to Castel Gandolfo

In 1921, Derain went to Rome to supervise the construction of the set he had designed for *La Boutique Fantasque*, for Sergei Diaghilev's Ballets Russes. Completely taken with Italy's charm, he remained longer than he had planned. Besides Rome, he also stayed in Castel Gandolfo, a picturesque little town and the Pope's summer residence, above Lake Albano, founded in the Middle Ages. Archaeologists discovered that it was the site of the legendary Alba Longa, the oldest city in ancient Latium, razed by Tullus Hostilius in 655 B.C.

When Derain found himself on the ancient road to Castel Gandolfo, lined by rocks and great, age-old trees, he could not help feeling at one with history. In this, the finest landscape of that period (which Otto Krebs acquired four years later), he conveyed the severe monumentality that he believed was the essence of Roman art. One does not immediately notice the lone female figure walking down the road, but it was absolutely necessary in order to establish a sense of proportion, making us aware of how small one person is in the face of the vast forces of History and Nature.

The transition to a more neoclassical style, discernible in Derain's work even before World War I, was hastened by his Italian trip. "You have to paint like Corot after you have gone through Poussin," said the artist. Remembering Camille Corot's Italian landscapes and enchanted by their poetry, he wanted to give his work greater majesty, and turned to Nicolas Poussin. It seemed to him that only in this way could he truly convey the spirit of the Roman Campagna, which attracted him much more than the countless churches of the Italian capital or the museums of the Vatican.

There and then, in 1921, Derain painted another, very similar landscape, *Environs of Castel Gandolfo* (formerly Galerie Simon, Paris; Carra, *Derain* [Paris, 1924], no catalogue or page number). He made another part of the road into a larger picture, like the present work also titled *The Road to Castel Gandolfo*, the same year (W. Raeber collection, Basel; Derain retrospective [Edinburgh, 1967], no. 66), but in a milder style.

PROVENANCE: 1924, G. K. collection, Paris; from 1925, Otto Krebs, Holzdorf.

LITERATURE: A. Salmon, *Derain* (Paris, 1924), p. 51 (as *Road to Albano* [*Route d'Albano*]); G. Hilaire, *Derain* (Neuchâtel, 1959), no. 31, p. 64.

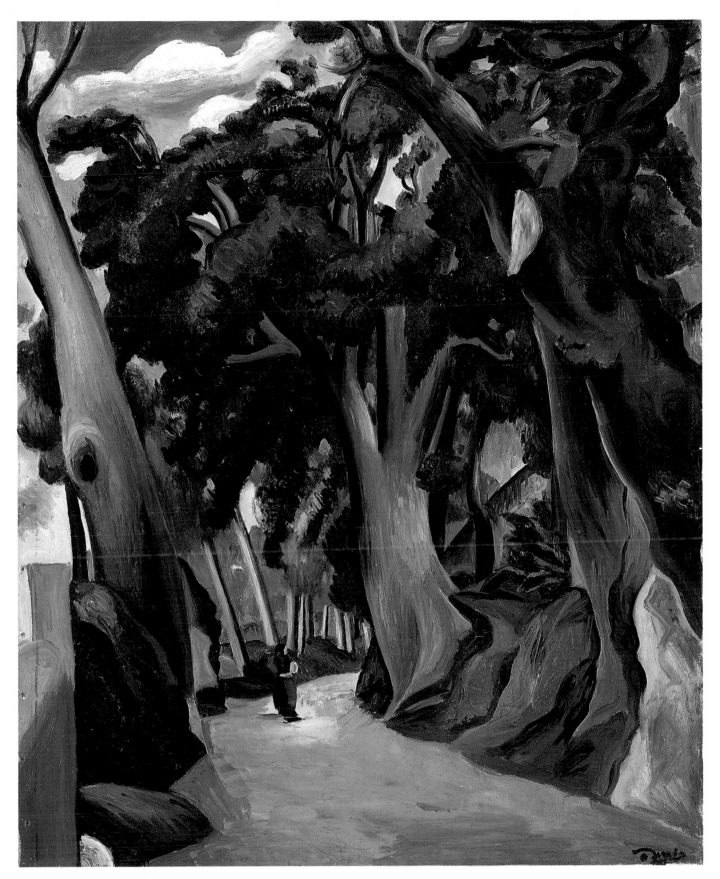

André Derain
## 73. THE ROAD TO CASTEL GANDOLFO
*La Route de Castel Gandolfo.* c. 1921
Oil on canvas, 24⅝ × 20" (62.5 × 50.8 cm). Signed lower right: "a. derain"
No. 3KP 519. Formerly collection Otto Krebs, Holzdorf

# HENRI MATISSE

## BALLERINA

In 1920, Matisse met a nineteen-year-old girl who for more than seven years would be his model and inform the spirit of many works of his Nice period. This beautiful young woman, Henriette Darricarrère, was studying ballet at the Studios de la Victorine, at times posing for a photographer. Matisse was no doubt drawn not only by Henriette's looks, her well-sculpted, strong form (it was not by chance that she also posed for Matisse's sculpture), but also by her artistry. She could transform herself into an *odalisque*, a Spanish lady, a violinist, or a pianist, as well as a dancer. Matisse encouraged her studying of dance, music, and even painting. Sometimes Henriette posed with the artist's daughter, Marguerite, her senior by four years.

The Darricarrère family lived in Nice, near the Place Charles-Félix, where Matisse had the studio in which he made the present painting. It was finished between January and May 1927. A photograph of the painting was taken for the Galerie Bernheim-Jeune the same May.

Matisse's interest in ballet increased following World War I, due to his contact with Sergei Diaghilev's Ballets Russes. In the fall of 1919, Matisse went to London to design costumes and sets for Léonide Massine's *Le Chant du rossignol* (to music by Igor Stravinsky). In Matisse's studio were ballet costumes of various colors, used as props in the twenties and later, though not many models tried them on. Few possessed Henriette's grace and professional skills.

*Ballerina* is remarkable for its simplicity of color scheme and compositional balance. The background is almost abstract: four horizontal bands of different colors accentuating the figure of the young dancer. One cannot even tell what Henriette was sitting on; Matisse did not bother to specify that detail. The wall and the straps of her costume are the same color, while the ballerina's stockings and the floor are also close in hue.

The picture from the Krebs collection is not the only one showing Henriette as a ballerina. The same year, Matisse painted her in *Ballerina (Harmony in Gray)* (fig. 1; private collection, Paris) in quieter, grayish pink tones. Another picture of Henriette in ballet costume, finished at about the same time, *Standing Dancer*, was until 1989 in the Galerie Schmit, Paris.

In 1928, Henriette married and the modeling sessions ended. By that time, the artist had begun losing interest in her.

PROVENANCE: 1928, Alex Reid & Lefevre Ltd., London; June 1928, Samuel Courtauld (1,600 pounds); July 1929, Alex Reid & Lefevre Ltd., London (as part of an exchange for Renoir's *The Skiff* [now National Gallery, London]); 1930, Reinhardt Galleries, New York; 1930 or 1931, Otto Krebs, Holzdorf.

EXHIBITIONS: 1927, Paris, Salon Tuileries.

LITERATURE: *Kunst und Künstler*, 1933, p. 169 (reprod.); House, *Impressionism for England: Samuel Courtauld as Patron and Collector* (London, 1994), pp. 24, 233.

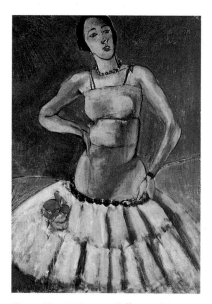

Fig. 1. *Henri Matisse*. Ballerina (Harmony in Gray). *1927. Private collection, Paris*

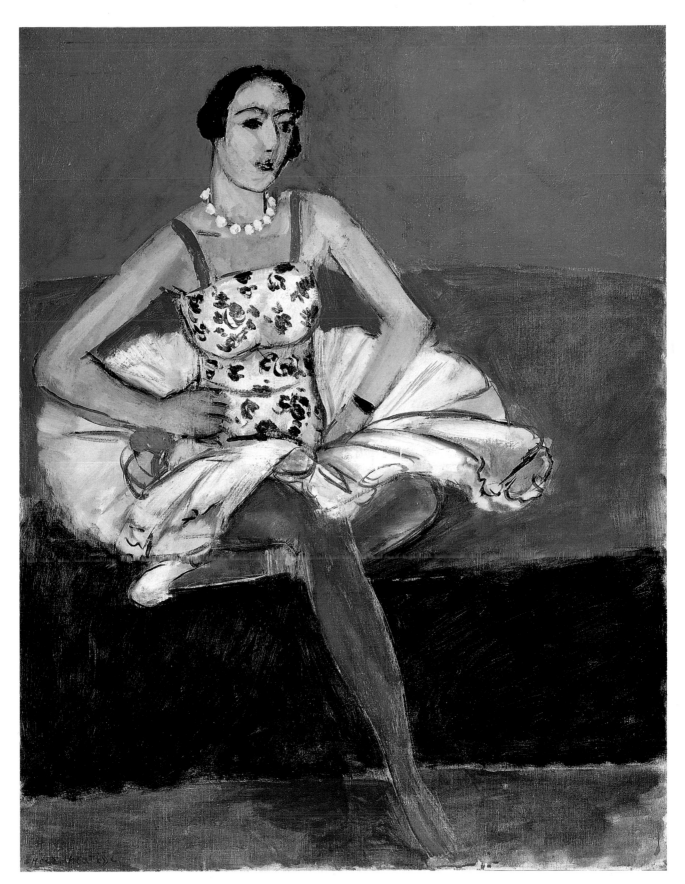

Henri Matisse (1869, Le Cateau-Cambrésis, Nord–1954, Nice-Cimiez, Alpes-Maritimes)

## 74. BALLERINA
*La Danseuse.* c. 1927
Oil on canvas, 25⅝ × 19⅝" (65 × 50 cm)
Signed lower left: "Henri-Matisse." Signed on back, on stretcher: "Henri-Matisse"
No. 3KP 514. Formerly collection Otto Krebs, Holzdorf

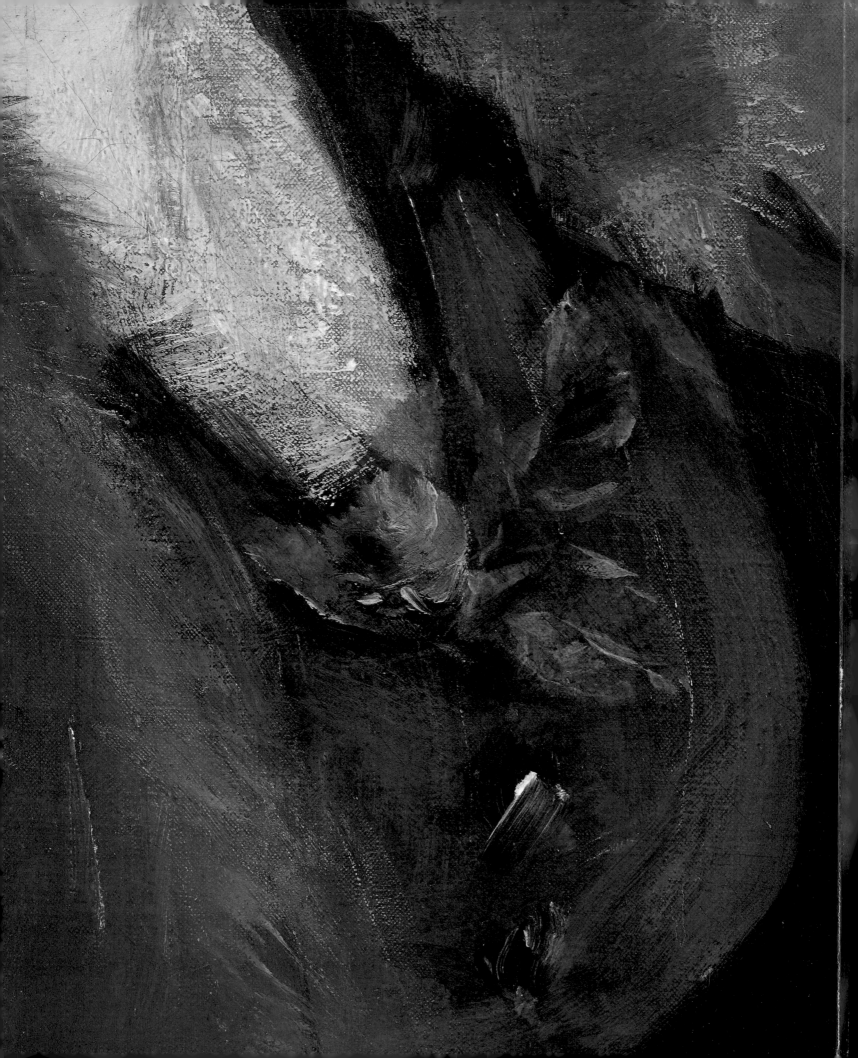